The

Personal Memoirs

of

Julia Dent Grant

(MRS. ULYSSES S. GRANT)

The Personal Memoirs of Julia Dent Grant

[MRS. ULYSSES S. GRANT]

Edited, with Notes and Foreword
by JOHN Y. SIMON

With Introduction by BRUCE CATTON

and
THE FIRST LADY AS AN AUTHOR
BY RALPH G. NEWMAN

Southern Illinois University Press
Carbondale and Edwardsville

91 90 89 88   4 3 2 1

Library of Congress Cataloging-in-Publication Data

Grant, Julia Dent, 1826–1902.
 The personal memoirs of Julia Dent Grant
(Mrs. Ulysses S. Grant)

  Reprint. Originally published: New York : Putnam, 1975.
  Bibliography: p.
  Includes index.
   1. Grant, Julia Dent, 1826–1902. 2. Grant, Ulysses S.
(Ulysses Simpson), 1822–1885 — Family. 3. Presidents —
United States — Wives — Biography. 4. Presidents —
United States — Biography. I. Simon, John Y.
II. Title.
E672.1.G73A3 1988   973.8'2'0924   87-20708
ISBN 0-8093-1442-8
ISBN 0-8093-1443-6 (pbk.)

ILLUSTRATIONS

BETWEEN PAGES 186 AND 187

Julia Grant in 1864, taken by Matthew Brady.
Second Lieutenant U. S. Grant in 1843. An engraving based on a
daguerrotype.
Nellie Grant in 1864, portraying "the Old Woman in the Shoe."
Ulysses S. Grant, Jr.
Frederick Dent Grant
Grant's headquarters cabin at City Point Virginia, winter of 1864–65.
The Grant Family in 1865.
Julia Grant in the White House years.
Nellie Grant and Jesse Grant, February, 1868.
Colonel Frederick Dent and Julia at Long Branch.
Nellie Grant in 1874.
The Grants on their front porch.
The Grants, with John W. Mackay, James G. Fair, and the Grants'
servant, Yanada, in Virginia City, Nevada.
Souvenir photograph made at San Francisco by John Russell Young
for Mrs. Grant.
Grant and Li Hung-chang.
The Grants, General and Mrs. Saigo, and Itō Hirobumi, at Nikko,
Japan.
Julia Grant in 1879, at San Francisco.
The Grants, 1879.

Introduction

STRANGEST of all careers open to American women is the one led by the wife of a famous man. She is likely to be both well known and obscure; a person whose name and face are familiar all across the land but who hardly ever comes out into full view as a person identifiable in her own right. She shines by reflected light, remembered because of the man she married.

This is especially true of the wives of Presidents. A very few, by force of personality or achievement (Dolley Madison, Eleanor Roosevelt) or by tragic circumstance (Mary Lincoln) are remembered clearly: We can see them, we know what they were like, they step out of the frame and become real. But most of them are names and not much more. If we recall them at all it is because of incidents—this one refused to let wine be served at White House banquets, that one was given to mild epileptic seizures which had an embarrassing way of developing at dinner parties—and, all in all, fame is somewhat freakish.

There was, for instance, Julia Dent Grant, whose repute was of a most singular kind. It was widely believed that her husband, especially during his career as a soldier, was much too fond of whiskey, and that the cure consisted in bringing Mrs. Grant to camp; in her presence, it was held, he instantly became a teetotaler. She kept the general on the rails and so, indirectly but effectively, helped bring Lee to Appomattox.

The fact that this contains hardly a wisp of truth makes no difference. That is the legend that has become attached to Julia Grant. It is a pity, because she was an interesting person in her own

[1]

right. In her old age she wrote her memoirs, which are as artless and ingratiating as anything you would care to see, and it is not possible to read them without concluding that she must have been a nice person to be with. What was she like? Well, as these memoirs show, she was *likable*. No longer is she just Mrs. Grant. Now she has three dimensions.

Julia Dent was the daughter of a Missouri planter, a man known as Colonel Dent, not because of military experience, but simply because a juleps-on-the-veranda farmer, in that time and place, was automatically dubbed a colonel. She grew up as the pampered daughter of this local magnate, she apparently was the belle of the neighborhood, and when she looked back on it long afterward it is clear that she saw it all as an idyll. She became the wife of a man who, all in all, had about as much to do with destroying slavery and humbling the planter class as anyone in America, but her viewpoint on the institution was strictly pre-1861. Her father's slaves were well treated and they were very happy. To be sure, the younger ones became "somewhat demoralized" at the beginning of the rebellion, when the plantation grapevine brought word that freedom for the black man was somehow coming down the wind, and she felt that as the war developed "all the comforts of slavery passed away forever"; but obviously she was looking back not so much on slavery as on her own girlhood, which had been a very happy time indeed.

She had wanted it to last. Typically, she remembers that when Grant proposed to her and began to talk about marriage she told him that she would very much like to be engaged to him but that she did not especially want to get married. There, of course, she was talking through her hat, and shortly after writing down that reminiscence she recorded her abiding conclusion: "General Grant was the very nicest and handsomest man I ever saw." They got married.

Apparently there were obstacles. Julia remembers that her father warned Grant that she was not the sort to be happy as a soldier's wife, and Grant replied that he had been offered a college professorship in Ohio and that he would resign from the Army and take it. Actually, Grant at the time was not at all sure that he himself was going to be happy in the Army, and for a long time he planned to become a teacher of mathematics in "some respectable college"; but the Mexican War came along, whatever academic opening he had seen evaporated, and in the end he married Julia and remained in the Army.

Army life had its ups and downs. The worst time came when Grant was transferred to a station on the Pacific Coast. Julia and the children had to remain behind, and she spent a good deal of time with

Grant's family. This she did not enjoy. Grant's father, Jesse, was a canny, hard-fisted leather merchant and livery stable keeper from the Ohio Valley, and his ways were not the ways of the Missouri planters. Julia recalls: "They considered me unpardonably extravagant, and I considered them inexcusably the other way," and things were somewhat difficult.

It is right at this point in the story that any biographer of General Grant feels obliged to explain that Grant drifted down to failure, disgrace, and misery. Lonely at an Army post in the far Northwest, he took to drink, had to resign from the Army, came home broke, ran a hard-scrabble farm in Missouri and failed at it, tried selling real estate and failed at that, wound up with a clerical job in old Jesse's harness shop at Galena, Illinois, barely managed to keep his head above water, and at last found himself and began to function again when the Civil War came along and pulled him back into the Army.

That is the story, and it seems fairly well documented . . . except that no reflection of it appears in Grant's own memoirs or in these written by Julia. Grant is on record as recalling the Missouri-Galena time as a time when he was happy, living with his family and making his own way, and Julia's only reference to the California difficulties is the statement that a supposed friend of Grant's defaulted on a $2,000 debt. For the rest: "The Captain"—*i.e.*, her husband, Captain Sam Grant as of the late 1850's—"was very kind to me when I was childish and unreasonable." If the difficult years left scars on these two people the scars never showed.

This may be because the Grants preserved a decent reticence about purely personal matters—an out-of-date attitude, of course, but still possible a century ago. But maybe the personal problems were not quite what modern writers think they were. For example: Central to the Grant myth is the idea that he drank far too much and that either Julia, General John A. Rawlins (his Chief of Staff), or the Almighty Himself intervened now and then to keep him sober.

Julia ran into this myth, head-on, in 1892, when the papers told how a letter from Rawlins to her husband had been read at a veterans' convention in Minnesota, the letter showing that Grant had been getting drunk during the Vicksburg campaign.

Now Julia was not at all dopey. She never bothered to affirm or deny this story, but promptly put her finger on the most interesting aspect of the whole business. She wrote:

"How could Rawlins have kept this letter? To me, it looks very like making a record for the future."

The business is worth a little consideration. Rawlins' letter was

[3]

dated June 6, 1863—just under a month before that Confederate stronghold surrendered, horse, foot, and guns. In the letter Rawlins remarked that "the great solicitude I feel for the safety of this army" leads him to broach "the subject of your drinking." Rawlins had heard various camp rumors, and that very evening "I find you where the wine bottle has just been emptied, in company with those who drink and urge you to do likewise": further, "the lack of your usual promptness and decision, and clearness in expressing yourself, in writing conduces to confirm my suspicion." He adds: "If my suspicions are unfounded, let my friendship for you and my zeal for my country be my excuse for this letter."

The letter was read in an address before the Minnesota Commandery, Military Order of the Loyal Legion of the United States, by Captain John M. Shaw, on December 8, 1891. Captain Shaw's copy of the letter contained an endorsement in Rawlins' hand:

"This is an exact copy of a letter given to the person to whom it is addressed at its date, about four miles from our headquarters in the rear of Vicksburg. Its admonitions were heeded and all went well."

So far, so good. Unfortunately, it is not easy to find out exactly what had happened to provoke the letter. The newspaperman Sylvanus Cadwallader, attached to Grant's headquarters, wrote in his own memoirs (which were not published until many years later) that Grant had gone on an enormous bender that evening and that he, Cadwallader, had at last got him into an ambulance and had personally taken him back to Army headquarters, pouring him out of it and delivering him into Rawlins' hands and giving Rawlins a play-by-play account of the evening's events. The trouble here is that Cadwallader's and Rawlins' accounts simply do not mesh. Cadwallader speaks of a wild, uproarious drunk about which Rawlins had firsthand knowledge; Rawlins, who was never mealymouthed, talks about finding Grant where the wine bottle had been emptied and admits that his suspicions may have been misfounded. The two men just cannot have been talking about the same thing, although the date is the same for both yarns.

Rawlins, be it remarked, was a lawyer, and also a headquarters bureaucrat, and in each capacity he knew the value of a written record. And as Julia remarked, the preservation of this letter looks very much as if this devoted defender of Grant's reputation had been trying to make a record.

There was more of the same, later. In the fall of 1863, at Chattanooga, Rawlins wrote Grant an impassioned letter begging him "in the name of a friend, an honest man and a lover of his country" to stop drinking, and asserting that "two more nights like the last will find you prostrated on a sick bed unfit for duty." This letter was never actually delivered. It stayed in Rawlins' files, bearing in Rawlins' hand the notation that "I talked to him on the subject to which it relates which had the desired effect." The catch to all of this is that this is one case in which it can be shown conclusively that Grant had not been drinking at all. The letter is dated, and on the night to which Rawlins refers, Grant had been attending a top-level conference on strategy, an affair of rigid and ponderous sobriety. A drunken party had in fact been going on, at a lower level of Army headquarters; Grant found out about it, angrily broke it up, and blistered the staff officer who gave the party so thoroughly that the man resigned and left the Army.

Rawlins must have known this; he could not have talked to Grant on the subject, as his note on the letter says he did, without finding out about it; and so why did he keep the letter in his files? Julia was right; he was building up a record. He was known as the keeper of Grant's conscience, and he did what he could to build up his own reputation. With a defender like Rawlins, Grant had no need of any enemies . . . and Julia was capable of detecting the fact.

What she was not capable of, apparently, was finding a suitable rationale for the general's life after his days in the White House ended. Being the wife of a famous man finally came to dazzle her. It was like the plantation girlhood in Missouri, something to be clung to retrospectively even after the conditions that brought it forth had vanished forever. The final third of her memoirs carries a slightly pathetic overtone. Both she and the general seem to be searching for something that is not there.

Which is to say that after they left the White House, the Grants in 1877 set off on a world tour, and Julia wrote a fulsome and lengthy account of it all. The tour followed no pattern whatever. It simply involved wandering from here to there as impulse directed. Everywhere, of course, there were formal receptions. Grant imagined that he was touring the world as a private citizen, but nobody else saw it that way. When he reached a foreign country—England, Germany, wherever—the official red carpet was rolled out. Kings and generals and cabinet members entertained him; there were reviews, parades, addresses of welcome, ceremonies without end, and the Grants moved from capital to capital with no apparent motive but to enjoy life.

What Grant himself made of it all is nowhere explicitly stated. Obviously it must have touched a responsive chord in his nature, for all the innate modesty that was one of his endearing characteristics. It

[5]

may just be that the reticence which never allowed him to complain about the hard, obscure days in California and on the poverty fringe in Missouri concealed something which could not quite get enough of public adulation and praise. Whatever life had done to him earlier, Grant was making up for it now . . . so he wandered, rather pointlessly, all around the world, never stepping off the red carpet.

It is all a little sad; pointing up the fact that the American way of life does not, unfortunately, offer a suitable career for a man who has lived eight years in the White House. Grant had been commanding general in a great and victorious war, and then he had been a two-term President . . . and he had no answer to the insistent question: What do you do for an encore?

Julia obviously enjoyed every minute of it, and she wrote this part of her memoirs with the air of a woman looking back on one of life's high points. Her account of that long tour, as a matter of fact, is highly interesting; she was having fun, and she conveys her feeling of pleasant excitement. But unconsciously she helps to underline one point: Grant's life was never quite in focus after the great day at Appomattox.

For the rest, Julia is capable of mildly poking fun at herself. She tells how she gave Grant advice on strategy, in front of Vicksburg, and writes as one who appreciates the absurdity of such an act. She recalls, too, how Grant once told her he was going to call her Xantippe because she gave him a wifely scolding for something or other. Toward the end of the war she talked Grant into pardoning a condemned deserter, after the man's wife had come to her with a sob story, and after signing the papers that saved the man from the executioner Grant dryly told her: "I've no doubt I have pardoned a bounty jumper who ought to have been hanged." When Grant's second term as President was coming to a close, he wrote and mailed a letter declaring that he would not run for a third term. Julia found out about it just too late, and asked him why he had not let her read the letter before he sent it, and Grant replied that if he had done so he knew the letter would never have been mailed. Julia liked having her husband on a pedestal.

Yet she was not really a glory-hunter. Apparently she enjoyed the fame Grant brought her, not as an end in itself, but as a quality which somehow was part of the love she and the general had for each other. At the very end she was able to write: ". . . and now, even though his beautiful life has gone out, it is as when some far-off planet disappears from the heavens; the light of his glorious fame still reaches out to me, falls upon me, and warms me."

[6]

One hardly ever thinks of this particular couple in that way, but the fact is that they shared one of the great, romantic, beautiful loves of all American history.

BRUCE CATTON

The First Lady
as an Author

THE TERM "First Lady" became a popular one after the production of a comedy, *The First Lady in the Land*, presented at the Gaiety Theatre in New York City, December 4, 1911. The play, by Charles Nirdlinger, had Dolley Madison as its central character. It is believed that the term was first used in referring to Lucy Ware Webb Hayes, the wife of President Rutherford B. Hayes, in a magazine article describing the Presidential inauguration of 1877.

Of our thirty-eight Presidents, only one, James Buchanan, was a bachelor. Grover Cleveland was a bachelor when he was elected the first time, but married in the White House during his second year in office. Four were widowers: Thomas Jefferson, Andrew Jackson, Martin Van Buren, and Chester A. Arthur. Rachel (Mrs. Andrew) Jackson died in the period between the election and the inaugural. Theodore Roosevelt had been a widower but had remarried before he became President. Benjamin Harrison became a widower in the White House and remarried after leaving the Presidency. Two others, John Tyler and Woodrow Wilson, lost their wives while in the White House and remarried while still in office.

Six Presidents, George Washington, Thomas Jefferson, James Madison, Millard Fillmore, Benjamin Harrison, and Woodrow Wilson, married widows. Andrew Jackson, Warren G. Harding, and Gerald R. Ford, Jr., married divorcees. Two widows of Presidents, Mrs. Grover Cleveland and Mrs. John F. Kennedy, remarried after the deaths of their husbands.

From Abigail (Mrs. John) Adams to Lady Bird (Mrs. Lyndon

Baines) Johnson, nine First Ladies have been authors, either by intent or posthumously through publication of their letters. Mention should also be made of a tenth First Lady author, Varina Howell Davis, whose husband, Jefferson Davis, was President of a part of the United States (then called the Confederate States of America) from 1861 to 1865.

The most prolific of author-First Ladies was (Anna) Eleanor Roosevelt. From 1932 until 1963 she was responsible, as author, for at least twenty titles, not to mention innumerable magazine articles, book introductions, and prefaces. While her style was not one to rival that of Mrs. Shelley or Barbara Tuchman, she did write easily, and in the main her subject matter was important. Her volumes of autobiography are very interesting, though revelations in the past few years about her domestic life and relationship with her husband indicate that there was much she did not reveal.

The first First Lady author became one posthumously when her letters were assembled and published by her grandson. Abigail Smith Adams, wife of John Adams, our second President, wrote well and frequently. Charles Francis Adams, her distinguished grandson, a member of Congress and Lincoln's minister to Great Britain, gathered these letters into two small volumes, which were first published in 1840. Most of the letters are addressed to her husband and demonstrate a fine style, as we can note when she writes soon after the Americans have evacuated Ticonderoga and Mount Independence:

> I dare say, before this time you have interpreted the Northern Storm. If the presages chilled your blood, how must you be frozen and stiffened at the disgrace brought up on our arms! unless some warmer passion seize you—and anger and resentment fire your breast.

On November 13, 1800, Abigail Adams wrote to her son, Thomas. It was a week after the Presidential election in which Thomas Jefferson defeated John Adams' bid for a second term:

> Well, my dear son, South Carolina has behaved as your father always said she would. The consequence to us, personally, is, that we retire from public life. For myself and family, I have few regrets.

The work was well received and a new, enlarged edition issued in 1841. In 1947 another collection of Mrs. Adams' letters was published. It was edited by Stewart Mitchell.

Dolley (Dorthea Dandridge Payne Todd) Madison also became an author posthumously when her letters, with a memoir by her grandniece, Lucia Beverly Cutts, were published in 1886. A modest volume, it nevertheless reveals Dolley Madison as an active partner of her husband in the politics of the day. Her letters are rich in historical and political references. One thrills at reading the letter she wrote to her sister, Anna Payne, from Washington on August 23, 1814, with the British just about to enter the city:

> My husband left me yesterday morning to join General Winder. He inquired anxiously whether I had courage or firmness to remain in the President's House until his return. . . . I have since received two dispatches from him. The last is alarming, because he desires I should be ready at a moment's warning to enter my carriage, and leave the city; that the enemy seemed stronger than had at first been reported, and it might happen that they would reach the city with the intention of destroying it. I am accordingly ready; I have pressed as many Cabinet papers into trunks as to fill one carriage. . . . Our kind friend, Mr. Carroll, has come to hasten my departure and in a very bad humor with me, because I insist on waiting until the large picture of General Washington is secured. . . .

In 1914, just a year after she and her husband left the White House, Helen Herron Taft's *Recollections of Full Years* was published. Though both she and President Taft were to enjoy many more useful years, he as Chief Justice (1921–1930), she does discuss many interesting aspects of their life when he was a judge, governor of the Philippine Islands, Secretary of War, and President. William Howard Taft was the first President to receive a salary of $75,000 a year. Mrs. Taft comments on her husband's inaugural:

> . . . since the ex-President was not going to ride back to the White House with his successor, I decided that I would. No President's wife had ever done it before, but as long as precedents were being disregarded I thought it might not be too great a risk to disregard this one. . . . There was nobody at the White House to bid us welcome except the official staff and some of their own guests. But it doesn't matter. There is never any ceremony about moving into the White House. You just drive up and walk in,—and there you are.

Mrs. Taft's good humor is present throughout her charming volume: "Fortunately we are a family that laughs."

Edith Kermit Carow (Mrs. Theodore) Roosevelt qualifies as an author because of her contribution to an anthology, *Cleared for Strange*

Ports, a collection of pieces by Mrs. Roosevelt, her daughter-in-law, Mrs. Kermit Roosevelt, Richard Derby, and Kermit Roosevelt, who edited the volume. Kermit Roosevelt, in his introduction, properly states that, "My mother after a number of years of unobtrusively continuous petition, at last, during the course of a long voyage to South America, wrote the 'Odyssey of a Grandmother.' It was expressly understood that it was written only for the perusal of the immediate family, and it took further cautious maneuvering to lift this embargo." Though not originally intended for publication, Mrs. Roosevelt's contribution demonstrates much warmth and not a little literary skill. Her ending is very touching:

> Now wanderings are done for the old nurseries are once again full of children, the fields and woods are the setting of their games. The Lilliputians have bound Gulliver, and the cords held in small hands are strong. The fire of life sinks for one generation, but its flames leap high for another.

Mary Todd Lincoln is one of the most misunderstood and vilified women in American history. It is only in recent years that we have come to have a fair appraisal of this unfortunate woman who had so much tragedy in her life. Just a few years ago, Justin G. Turner and his daughter-in-law, Linda Levitt Turner, compiled a scholarly and most readable collection of Mrs. Lincoln's letters. Her letters are never great literary efforts, but they do portray the many moods, trials, and sufferings of this First Lady who lost her husband in a terrible crime, saw three of her four sons die before they attained maturity, and wept while several of her brothers died in a war fighting against the cause championed by her husband. Though during the past years there have been a number of excellent books about Mary Lincoln, she speaks best for herself. In 1848, she writes to her husband, who is in Washington, serving his single term as a Congressman from Illinois:

> You know I am so fond of sightseeing, & I did not get to New York or Boston, or travel the lake route—But perhaps, dear husband . . . cannot do without his wife next winter, and must needs take her with him again—I expect you would cry aloud against it—How much, I wish instead of writing, we were together this evening, I feel very sad away from you. . . .

Almost thirty years later she writes to her sister, Elizabeth Todd Edwards, whose granddaughter, aged four, had recently died.

. . . sweet, affectionate little Florence, whom I loved so well. The information saddened me greatly & rendered me quite ill. I have drank so deeply of the cup of sorrow, in my desolate bereavements, that I am always prepared to sympathize, with all those who suffer, but when it comes so close to us, & when I remember that precocious, happy child, with its loving parents—what can I say? In grief, words are a poor consolation—silence & agonizing tears, are all, that is left the sufferer.

Edith Bolling Wilson was the First Lady whom many believed to be the acting President during the last year and a half of Woodrow Wilson's term of office. Her recollections were published under the title *My Memoir*, in 1939. President Wilson's first wife, Ellen Louise Axson Wilson, had died in 1914. In March, 1915, in the company of Helen Bones, the President's cousin and formerly the secretary to the late Mrs. Wilson, Edith Bolling met the President. Despite the problems of a country on the verge of war, he found time for a whirlwind courtship, and she became Mrs. Woodrow Wilson in December, 1915. Not at all modest, Mrs. Wilson nevertheless has significant history to relate. The account of her courtship, her experiences in Europe with President Wilson, and her trials during their last eighteen months in the White House, is absorbing and was, at the time of its publication, the first really intimate account written by a First Lady. Much has been said about Mrs. Wilson's role in the direction of the country during President Wilson's illness. Her own account begins:

> So began my stewardship. I studied every paper, sent from the different Secretaries or Senators, and tried to digest and present in tabloid form the things that, despite my vigilance, had to go to the President. I, myself, never made a single decision regarding the disposition of public affairs. The only decision that was mine was what was important and what was not, and the very important decision of when to present matters to my husband.

Perhaps the best-selling of all books by First Ladies, and the work most carefully planned, was Lady Bird (Claudia Alta Taylor) Johnson's *A White House Diary*. Mrs. Johnson began an audio diary a few days after Lyndon Baines Johnson became President in November, 1963. She spoke into a tape recorder whenever she could and wherever she might happen to be, whether in hotel rooms, at the LBJ Ranch, or in her combination dressing room and office on the second floor of the White House. It is a remarkable document, a great contribution to our literature about the Presidency, and was so

[13]

recognized by most of the book reviewers and press. Mrs. Johnson estimated that in all she spoke about 1,750,000 words in a little more than five years. She went over the transcribed text several times and finally distilled the work into a book of almost 800 pages. From the opening entry, dated Dallas, Friday, November 22, 1963:

> It all began so beautifully. After a drizzle in the morning, the sun came out bright and clear. We were driving into Dallas.

to the last entry made both in the White House and at the LBJ Ranch on Monday, January 20, 1969:

> A little past 9 I went to bed, with a line of poetry reeling through my mind. I think it's from *India's Love Lyrics*. "I seek, to celebrate my glad release, the Tents of Silence and the Camp of Peace." And yet it's not quite the right exit line for me because I have loved almost every day of these five years.

Legally, Varina Howell Davis does not belong on this list of First Lady authors, but she was, in fact, the wife of a man who was President of a part of the United States for four years. She wrote many articles and one book, *Jefferson Davis, Ex-President of the Confederate States of America: A Memoir by his Wife*. It was published in 1890, a year after her husband's death. It is a long work in two volumes. In her introduction Mrs. Davis states:

> I shall endeavor . . . to make the book an autobiography—to tell the story of my husband's life in his own words; to complete the task he left unfinished.

It is difficult to fathom whether Varina Howell Davis functions as her husband's biographer, ghostwriter, or attorney—she succeeds at none.

And now, out of the past, almost a century after it was written, comes the personal story of another First Lady. The last to be published, it is the first memoir to be written by a President's wife. Perhaps because it was such an innovative idea, it remained unpublished all of these years. In any event, here it is. Had it been published when written we would have had no previous works with which to compare it. Now, Julia Dent Grant, gone from this earth seventy-two years ago, has to compete and be compared with her successors. But remember, she had the idea first.

RALPH GEOFFREY NEWMAN

ADAMS, ABIGAIL SMITH, *Letters of Mrs. Adams, The Wife of John Adams. With an Introductory Memoir by her grandson, Charles Francis Adams*. Two (2) volumes. Boston: Charles C. Little and James Brown, 1840.

————, *New Letters of Abigail Adams, 1788–1801*. Edited with an Introduction by Stewart Mitchell. Boston: Houghton Mifflin Company, 1947.

DAVIS, VARINA HOWELL, *Jefferson Davis, Ex-President of the Confederate States of America: A Memoir by his Wife*. Two (2) volumes. New York: Belford Company, 1890.

JOHNSON, CLAUDIA ALTA TAYLOR (LADY BIRD), *A White House Diary*. New York: Holt, Rinehart and Winston, 1970.

LINCOLN, MARY TODD, *Mary Todd Lincoln: Her Life and Letters*. [Edited by] Justin G. Turner [and] Linda Levitt Turner. With an Introduction by Fawn M. Brodie. New York: Alfred A. Knopf, 1972.

MADISON, DORTHEA (DOLLEY) DANDRIDGE PAYNE TODD, *Memoirs and Letters of Dolley Madison, wife of James Madison, President of the United States, edited by her grand-niece* [Lucia Beverly Cutts]. Boston and New York: Houghton, Mifflin and Company, 1886.

ROOSEVELT, ANNA ELEANOR, *It's Up to the Women*. New York: Frederick A. Stokes Company, 1933.

————, *This Is My Story*. New York: Harper & Brothers, 1937.

————, *This Troubled World*. New York: H. C. Kinsey & Company, 1938.

————, *If You Ask Me*. New York: D. Appleton-Century Co., 1946.

————, *This I Remember*. New York: Harper & Brothers, 1949.

————, *Partners, The United Nations and Youth* (with Helen Ferris). Garden City: Doubleday & Company, 1950.

————, *UN: Today and Tomorrow* (with W. A. DeWitt). New York: Harper & Brothers, 1953.

————, *Ladies of Courage* (with L. A. Hickok). New York: G. P. Putnam's Sons, 1954.

———— *India and the Awakening East*. New York: Harper & Brothers, 1958.

————, *On My Own*. New York: Harper & Brothers, 1958.

————, *Your Teens and Mine* [autobiography] (with Helen Ferris). Garden City: Doubleday & Company, 1961.

————, *Book of Common Sense Etiquette*. New York: The Macmillan Company, 1962.

————, *The Autobiography of Eleanor Roosevelt*. New York: Harper & Row, 1963.

————, *Christmas Book*. New York: Dodd, Mead & Company, 1963.

————, *Tomorrow Is Now*. New York: Harper & Row, 1963.

————, *You Learn by Living*. Garden City: Doubleday & Company, 1963.

ROOSEVELT, EDITH KERMIT CAROW, *Cleared for Strange Ports*. By Mrs. Theodore Roosevelt, Sr., Mrs. Kermit Roosevelt, Richard Derby and Kermit Roosevelt. [Includes] "The Odyssey of a Grandmother," by Mrs. Theodore Roosevelt, Sr. New York: Charles Scribner's Sons, 1927.

TAFT, HELEN HERRON, *Recollections of Full Years*. New York: Dodd, Mead & Company, 1914.

WILSON, EDITH BOLLING, *My Memoir*. Indianapolis: The Bobbs-Merrill Company, 1939.

Foreword

———◆———

ULYSSES S. GRANT died on July 23, 1885, after a long and agonizing battle with cancer. The Grant family knew of the dread disease and its inevitable outcome in late 1884, and the public learned the facts a little later; in fact, doctors had not expected Grant to live as long as he did, and the whole nation marveled at the courage and determination with which he held off death to complete his memoirs, the only hope for restoring the finances of his family, which had been shattered by a Wall Street swindle. When Grant had accomplished all he could on the memoirs, he found release in death from the excruciating pain.

His widow wept uncontrollably for weeks. As she sat with her family in the parlor of the Mount McGregor cottage, she heard Methodist Bishop John P. Newman deliver a funeral sermon to a large crowd on the front lawn. A close friend of both Grants for many years, Newman paid tribute to the Grant marriage.

> As he was the typical American, should we be surprised to find that his was the typical American home? . . . Husband and wife the happy supplement of each other, . . . He the Doric column to sustain; she the Corinthian column to beautify. He the oak to support; she ivy to entwine. . . . She shared his trials and his triumphs, his sorrows and his joys, his toils and his rewards. . . . Side by side they shall sleep in the same tomb, and she shall share with him whatever homage future ages shall pay at his national shrine.[1]

Bishop Newman spoke appropriately; during their marriage, Julia Dent Grant's life had been intertwined with and overshadowed by that of her husband. As her memoirs show, she had a mind of her own, with the spirit and charm to accomplish her goals. At the same time, she had accepted the conventions of the day concerning the proper role of a woman as an adjunct to her husband. However innovative in military and political matters, Grant held many conventional social views, including a belief that women ought to devote themselves entirely to their families. Throughout their marriage Julia Grant generally accepted this role, believing herself amply recompensed by her husband's love and devotion. Writing later to a prospective Grant biographer, she cautioned him not to believe gloomy stories about Grant's financial hardship in St. Louis before the Civil War. Those days "were not dark but bright and charming, as it was always sunshine when he was near." [2] When he died, Bishop Newman offered nothing for the future save the promise of reunion in the tomb.

After the funeral at Mount McGregor, Grant's coffin was taken to New York City for a larger and more elaborate ceremony in which surviving U. S. Civil War generals joined an equal number of Confederate generals as honorary pallbearers. But Julia Grant was unable to leave Mount McGregor until the end of August.[3] At her home in New York City, she lived together with the family of her oldest son, Frederick Dent Grant, until he received an appointment as minister to Austria-Hungary early in 1889. Julia Grant accompanied the family to Vienna, finding much which brought back memories of the world tour with her husband. When she returned home at the end of the summer, she found herself truly alone for the first time in her life.

Probably about this time, she began to work in earnest on her memoirs.[4] The memoirs, however, originated some three years earlier. Asked by a journalist if he planned to publish anything about his father, Frederick Grant had replied:

Every day I devote an hour or more to taking down my mother's reminiscences of him. These mostly relate to incidents and events in my father's life during his tour around the world, and which were not embodied in Mr. John Russell Young's description of that journey. My father never related these incidents to any one, and my mother now tells them to me for the first time to anybody. They are, many of them, exceedingly interesting, being purely of a personal character, and full of what is called "spice." We have now nearly 1,500 foolscap pages filled with memorandums of these reminiscences of my mother.

She has also dictated to me a great many things in father's early life which are not known to the public, and has given me, too, several important documents never published as yet.[5]

Asked what he planned to do with this material, Grant replied that he did not know whether these "offhand reminiscences" would ever be published, but had collected them for his children. He pointed out that the Grant family had agreed with Charles L. Webster & Co., publisher of the *Personal Memoirs of U. S. Grant*, to publish nothing competitive elsewhere for three years, an agreement binding until May, 1889. "What I shall do when this date expires I cannot at present say." [6]

Mark Twain controlled the Webster firm, which was only nominally run by his nephew. Twain had long admired Grant, made a generous offer to publish his memoirs, and became a close friend to all the Grants during the harrowing battle to finish the manuscript. Even before publication of the second volume of the *Memoirs*, Frederick Grant proposed to write about his father's life after the Civil War, and Julia Grant discussed publication of the hundreds of letters written to her by her husband. Initially enthusiastic, Twain later cooled after Frederick Grant negotiated with Allen Thorndike Rice to print some anecdotes written by his father which had been removed from the manuscript of the *Memoirs* and also a diary kept by his father during his world tour. In addition, Julia Grant apparently tied her plans for publication of the letters to a position in the Webster company for her youngest son, Jesse.[7] Neither book appeared, and the collapse of the negotiations foreshadowed the fate of Mrs. Grant's memoirs.

When Frederick Grant first encouraged his mother to dictate her recollections, the trip around the world, two and one-half years of travel which immediately followed the Grant Presidency, provided an excellent place for her to begin, for this had been a time of unalloyed happiness. John Russell Young, the newspaper correspondent for the New York *Herald* who had accompanied the party for much of the time, had produced two thick quarto volumes chronicling the journey which told remarkably little about the Grants.[8] Young had known that the only way to gain access to material for his newspaper was to win the goodwill and confidence of the Grants; above all, the former President, traveling abroad to avoid publicity and controversy at home, wanted privacy. So Young created a discreet and graceful travelogue, especially pleasing to Julia Grant—to whom Young dedicated the volumes—as a record of where she had been and what she had seen. In preparing her own account, she added personal impressions, using Young's book as handy reference for names, dates, and other facts.

Near the end of her life, she reminisced about the origin of the memoirs.

> With the general's death, fifteen years ago, I thought my life had been lived, for we had been inseparable. I saw nothing that could brighten or make interesting the remaining years. For two years it was very dreary. Then I began the memoirs, reluctantly at first, and as a task, more to gratify the children's wishes than my own. Soon I became an inveterate scribbler. I preferred writing to eating or driving or seeing friends. The children said I had found a fad at last. But it wasn't a fad; it was a joy. I was living again, with the aid of my fancy and my pen, the life that had been so sweet to me.[9]

"I never anticipated writing a book," she told the interviewer, "but memoirs are different." Memoirs, she explained, were "a panacea for loneliness, a tonic for old age." [10] Beyond that, writing memoirs must have been an obvious thought since writing such an account dominated the last year of her husband's life, and the *Personal Memoirs of U. S. Grant* continued to mean much to the Grant family.

Grant's *Memoirs* had brilliantly fulfilled the author's intention of providing security for his family. The first royalty check for $200,000 was trumpeted as the largest such check ever drawn, and total royalties climbed toward an estimated $500,000.[11] Money was only part of Grant's last triumph; despite staggering physical obstacles, he had created a candid and perceptive book which greatly enhanced his reputation. Many volumes were sold to Americans who simply wanted to show their respect for the author, but others went to appreciative readers. Indeed, the *Memoirs* received instantaneous critical acclaim and achieved a literary reputation lasting to the present.

Because Grant wrote as his strength waned, early chapters contained far more personal observation than those written later. He first started to write for the public when approached by *Century Magazine* for a series of articles on his major campaigns; when the articles planted the seed for memoirs, Grant still stuck close to the military theme. In the published *Memoirs*, the Civil War occupies fifty-four of seventy chapters, the Mexican War more than half the remainder. Grant wrote with some charm of his courtship of Julia Dent, but she virtually disappears from the narrative after their wedding.

Thus the publication of the *Memoirs* meant that Grant had told his own story—but not all of it. By concentrating on his early years and his military career, he had written about that part of his life Julia Grant had not shared. He wrote little about nearly thirty-seven years of marriage and family life, nothing about eight years in the White House and eight as a former President. Conscious of treasured letters and memories, Julia Grant wanted to complete the Grant story.

Correcting as well as completing the Grant story appears to have motivated Julia Grant to compose memoirs. She began work about the time Adam Badeau finished *Grant in Peace*.[12] Badeau had joined Grant's staff in 1864 as aide-de-camp and military secretary, served on the staff through Reconstruction, then was sent by President Grant to the consulate in London in 1869. The first volume of his *Military History of Ulysses S. Grant* appeared in 1868, and this consular appointment probably was intended to provide an opportunity to complete another two volumes. Badeau, on the contrary, saw that the remaining volumes provided an opportunity to prolong his consular sinecure, and no more books appeared until 1881. Although many biographies of Grant had already been published, only Badeau had access to Grant's collection of military records and to Grant himself for critical readings of every chapter. His work, then, stood as an official biography, with its unreadably dense prose conferring the final seal of authenticity.

When Grant decided to write memoirs, he hired Badeau to assist him. Believing that the memoirs would hurt sales of Badeau's book, Grant agreed to pay him $5,000 of the first $20,000 in profits from the book, another $5,000 from the next $10,000. Badeau moved into the Grant house in New York City and began to work. In May, 1885, Badeau demanded a new agreement under which he would receive $1,000 each month and 10 percent of all profits. In a letter to Grant, Badeau claimed to have been connecting the "disjointed fragments" prepared by the author. Apparently resenting the aspersions on his writing even more than the demand for money, Grant refuted these claims by letter.[13] Badeau soon left the house and never saw Grant again. In later years, Badeau never lost his respect and affection for Grant, but blamed Frederick Grant, who had also assisted in the preparation of the memoirs, for influencing his father to reject the demands, and believed that the Grant family still owed him $10,000 under the original agreement.

When preparing her own story, Julia Grant remembered and resented Badeau's indiscreet but not wholly inaccurate stories of Mary Lincoln's rudeness and irrationality. She contradicted Badeau on the question of whether the Prince of Wales had treated the Grants with proper respect. What she resented most was a lawsuit filed against the

Grant family by Badeau in 1888, in which he embellished his claim for $10,000 with charges and innuendoes concerning the true authorship of the *Memoirs*.[14] The Grants settled the suit financially out of court; Julia Grant settled the matter of authorship in her memoirs by emphasizing her husband's composition of his report as lieutenant general, then dramatizing Grant's writing of his memoirs.

Badeau's stories appeared to weigh heavily on Julia Grant, but she had much more to correct. Her husband had dealt with persistent rumors of his drinking by ignoring them in his *Memoirs*; Mrs. Grant, especially outraged by the disclosure of a warning letter to Grant from John A. Rawlins, chose to meet the issue with direct denial. In addition, she sought to clear her husband of any involvement with scandals which blackened the White House.

At many points in her memoirs Julia Grant corrected or struck back at those who had offended her or her husband, but this is only a minor part of the work. Her happy days vastly outnumbered those that were clouded; the number of people who admired and respected her husband vastly outnumbered his enemies and detractors; and both Grants had found satisfaction in their lives. Julia Grant had often entertained and diverted her husband with amusing anecdotes and unusual observations. As she composed memoirs, her talents as storyteller again emerged, and she took obvious delight in preparing accounts of past pleasures. The trip around the world occupied disproportionate space not because she thought it more important than the Civil War or the Presidency, but because this had been such a happy time for both Grants.

When Julia Grant began to gather her recollections, her ultimate intentions about readership may have been vague, but she definitely planned publication of the finished work. In 1890, she wrote a brief article containing several anecdotes also incorporated in her memoirs.[15] Once the manuscript was complete, the large profits from her husband's *Memoirs* were on her mind as she wrote that she felt "much anxiety" about what she would "realize from its sale." [16] Little more than a year later, her hopes were crushed.

But now I am going to open my heart to you, and tell you of my disappointment and *sorrow*[.] My book, my book, on which I have worked so hard for the last three long years, my book, in which I took so much pride and so much pleasure[,] my book, on which I have built so many castles, is by the critics pronounced *too* near, *too* close to the private life of the Genl for the public, and I thought this was just what was wanted[.] You can well imagine my great disappointment and sorrow[.] My publishers made me liberal terms, but I am advised by critics not to publish,—So that Ignes fatuus fortune has fleed again from me. I had hoped to realize a nice little fortune from my work and what castles I built.[17]

The next year she confided to the wealthy Mrs. Leland Stanford that she had written a letter asking her to buy the manuscript, planning to use the proceeds to buy the Stanford house in Washington, but had not mailed the letter and would not, since the manuscript was under consideration by a publisher.[18] Disillusion followed quickly.

I was greatly disappointed when this morning the man who had my book under consideration and who had written me such a flattering letter (after its perusal) telling me of its great value as a historical reminiscence and saying everything that was pretty about it advises me to let him publish it as a subscription book, as The Generals was. No publishing house he says, could at this time of financial stress place the amount I ask[.] He assures me I will surely get more by making it a subscription book. I therefore have not made the arrangement I had hoped to, so that I cannot even think now of the house I wrote you about[.] [19]

There seems to be no simple explanation for the fact that the memoirs were not published. Julia Grant lived quietly in Washington after 1894, seeing few people outside her family and a circle of friends from earlier days. Apprehensive about criticism and controversy which might follow publication, she negotiated cautiously with publishers. A granddaughter recalled that she said, "I don't want all this published for several generations. Some one might get mad, because I'm telling how they really felt and acted." [20] In addition, the great profits from her husband's book created an unrealistic view of the value of her own. Accordingly, she rejected the offer to sell her book by subscription, refused another offer which carried a $25,000 advance, and wrote of her expectation of receiving $100,000 for her book.[21] Ambivalence about publication probably influenced the price set on her book. But she had no pressing need for money; in addition to income from Grant's *Memoirs*, Congress had voted her a $5,000 annual pension.[22]

In the last years of her life, the memoirs remained on her mind. In 1898 she supervised a typewritten version, presumably so that carbon copies could be distributed to her children.[23] The next year, an enterprising journalist, Mrs. John A. Logan, widow of the Civil War general and U. S. Senator, urged her to sell an extract from the manuscript to a newspaper. Julia Grant characteristically resisted these "most tempting pecuniary offers" with the hope of selling the manuscript outright to Mrs. Stanford.[24] Meeting no response, in 1901 she offered the manuscript to financier Andrew Carnegie for $125,000, stating that she could not "undergo the anxiety and care of publishers' exactions." [25]

At the time of her death in late 1902, no plans existed for either sale or publication of the memoirs. An obituary spoke of the memoirs as intended for her grandchildren, "but it may be that in after years the General's descendents may be persuaded to give at least some portions of it to the public in the interest of history." [26] For many years, the manuscript stayed with the family, with most scholars unaware of its existence. Major General Ulysses S. Grant 3rd, eldest grandson of President Grant, permitted Ishbel Ross to read the manuscript, "not to draw from it in any way, but to give me fuller understanding of her character and personality." [27] Bruce Catton later read the manuscript and used information from it without direct quotation, as did the editor of *The Papers of Ulysses S. Grant*.[28] General Grant 3rd himself quoted from the memoirs in his posthumously published biography of his grandfather.[29] Later, his daughters graciously consented to the publication of the entire manuscript.

Preparing a manuscript for publication composed some eighty years earlier has presented some special problems. Had it been published in Mrs. Grant's lifetime, editors of the day would undoubtedly have tightened some of the prose, eliminated repetition, and regularized punctuation, spelling, and capitalization. The manuscript would have undergone the "publishers' exactions" Mrs. Grant dreaded, but with her final approval of the edited text as a document which would tell her story as she agreed to have it told. With the passage of time, what might once have been treated like other book manuscripts became something else—a historical document, deserving authentic presentation.

Julia Grant began her memoirs by dictating to her son Frederick and later apparently dictated more to her secretary. The conversational tone of the narrative indicates composition by dictation, as does the final manuscript version—the only one available—which contains many pages written by Mary Coffey, her longtime secretary, some written by others, and a few in Mrs. Grant's hand. As a young girl, Julia Dent had poor eyesight; as she grew older, her eyes weakened. During the decade she prepared her memoirs, advancing age forced her to dictate some personal correspondence. Essentially, then, the words are those of Mrs. Grant, the form in which they appear in both the manuscript and the typescript is the work of others.

Since Julia Grant personally commissioned the typescript and even made a few handwritten emendations, this was assumed to represent her final intention. The final manuscript, checked word-for-word against the typescript, revealed only a few discrepancies, most of them representing misreadings by the typist, which could then be incorporated to restore the original intent. The text of this book, then, follows the text of the typescript, only rarely emended by the manuscript. Editorial insertions are bracketed. Punctuation, capitalization, spelling, paragraphing, and related niceties of slight concern to Mrs. Grant have been regularized as a convenience to the modern reader. In general, such matters were handled in accordance with current practice, though some nineteenth-century stylistic conventions followed consistently in the typescript remain. Foreign place names were verified in a turn-of-the-century gazetteer to avoid anachronism. Those quotations from printed material which could be tracked down have been altered when necessary to conform to the original source. With the exception of a few minor grammatical corrections and removal of superfluous words, no alterations in wording have been permitted to come between Mrs. Grant and the readers she hoped to have.

In accordance with a convention of her day, Mrs. Grant often referred to persons of whom she wrote by the first initial of the last name. By doing so, she could avoid both the appearance of gossip and offense to persons still living or to their descendants. The passage of time and the value of her account as a historical source nullified the need for this device, and the editor attempted to fill in as many names as possible. A reference to "Mrs. F., wife of the Secretary of State," and other usages of this sort presented no difficulty. Others did, and a few remained ambiguous or so obscure that they still appear as initials alone.

All notes were prepared by the editor to explicate, amplify, and, if necessary, correct the text. In the belief that notes are interruptions, they have been held to a bare minimum. Factual matters which could be verified from other sources were checked, and discrepancies became the subject of notes; to avoid burdensome annotation, accurate reminiscence went unremarked. To be fair, however, I should state at least once that these memoirs are, indeed, remarkably accurate, particularly considering their preparation after so many of the events involved had already faded into the past, while the author apparently used no diaries or memoranda to refresh her memory, no research assistant to verify names, dates, or facts. Indeed, Julia Grant's accurate memory of the life she shared with her husband represents a last witness of their love.

Julia Grant concluded her memoirs with the death of her husband. In the years since, she had watched and sometimes fostered the careers of her three sons, taken great pleasure in her grandchildren, and kept in touch with a dwindling number of old friends. Her rare contacts with the public came at ceremonies honoring her husband, such as the unveiling of the Grant statue in Chicago or the dedication of his tomb. In assembling recollections, her primary purpose was to share with posterity her pride in her husband. These memoirs, an important contribution to a full understanding of the Civil War period of American history, also belatedly introduce a woman of charm and wit who deserves to be better remembered.

A decade ago, General Grant 3rd permitted the Ulysses S. Grant Association to film his grandmother's memoirs for research purposes. We owe much to his generosity in sharing with us both manuscripts and personal memories of his grandparents. His daughters, Mrs. John S. Dietz, Mrs. David W. Griffiths, and Mrs. Paul E. Ruestow, have consented to the publication of this book and made available family photographs for illustrations. Mrs. Griffiths has the manuscript of Julia Grant's memoirs; the contemporary typescript is in the Grant Family Papers at Southern Illinois University.

This book has been prepared as a project of the Grant Association, and two of its officers, Ralph G. Newman and Bruce Catton, gave special assistance. Harriet Furst Simon served ably as editorial assistant, David L. Wilson as research assistant. We are also indebted to M. Elaine Cook of the Grant Association, Sara Dunlap Jackson of the National Historical Publications Commission, Frances H. Stadler of the Missouri Historical Society, and Karl L. Trever of Arlington, Virginia.

JOHN Y. SIMON

NOTES

1. James P. Boyd, *Military and Civil Life of Gen. Ulysses S. Grant* . . . (Philadelphia and Chicago, 1885), pp. 706–7.
2. To Hamlin Garland, December 26, 1896, Garland Papers, University of Southern California, Los Angeles.
3. Thomas M. Pitkin, *The Captain Departs: Ulysses S. Grant's Last Campaign* (Carbondale and Edwardsville, Illinois, 1973), p. 113.
4. In 1892, she stated that she had worked three years on her book. To Mrs. Leland Stanford, April 30, [1892], University Archives, Stanford University.
5. Undated newspaper clipping placed among others dated January–February, 1887, Grant scrapbooks, Mark Twain Papers, University of California, Berkeley.
6. *Ibid.*
7. Samuel Charles Webster, *Mark Twain, Business Man* (Boston, 1946), pp. 334–57; Hamlin Hill, ed., *Mark Twain's Letters to his Publishers 1867–1894* (Berkeley and Los Angeles, 1967), pp. 191–97. Twain blocked publication of the diary; the anecdotes appeared in Allen Thorndike Rice, ed., *Reminiscences of Abraham Lincoln by Distinguished Men of his Time* (New York, 1886), pp. 1–4.
8. John Russell Young, *Around the World with General Grant* . . . (New York, 1879).
9. Undated newspaper clipping of an interview with Julia Dent Grant reprinted from the New York *World*, 1900, Grant family scrapbooks, Ulysses S. Grant Association, Southern Illinois University, Carbondale.
10. *Ibid.*
11. New York *Times*, October 14, 1886; Bernard DeVoto, ed., *Mark Twain in Eruption: Hitherto Unpublished Pages about Men and Events* (New York and London, 1940), pp. 186–87.
12. Adam Badeau, *Grant in Peace from Appomattox to Mount McGregor: A Personal Memoir* (Hartford, 1887).
13. Bruce Catton, "U. S. Grant: Man of Letters," *American Heritage*, XIX (June, 1968), 97–100.
14. The suit received much newspaper coverage, reflected in scrapbook 14, series 7, Grant Papers, Library of Congress.
15. Penelope Grant, "The Married Life of General U. S. Grant," *The Home-Maker*, V (October, 1890), 3–5. Another anecdote appeared in the brief introduction she wrote for Annie Wittenmyer, *Under the Guns: A Woman's Reminiscences of the Civil War* (Boston, 1895).
16. To Mrs. Leland Stanford, March 1, 1891, University Archives, Stanford University.
17. To Mrs. Stanford, April 30, [1892], *ibid.*
18. August 8, 1893, *ibid.*
19. August 11, 1893, *ibid.*
20. Princess Cantacuzène, Countess Speransky, née Grant, *My Life Here and There* (New York, 1921), p. 165.
21. Julia Grant to Mrs. Stanford, September 18, 1894, University Archives, Stanford University; Ishbel Ross, *The General's Wife: The Life of Mrs. Ulysses S. Grant* (New York, 1959), p. 330.
22. File WC-219-162, Civil War and Later Pension Application Files, Record Group 15, National Archives.

23. Julia Grant to Mrs. Stanford, July 19, 1898, University Archives, Stanford University.
24. May 29, 1899, *ibid.*
25. Ross, *The General's Wife*, p. 330.
26. New York *Times*, December 15, 1902.
27. Ross, *The General's Wife*, p. v.
28. Bruce Catton, *Grant Moves South* (Boston and Toronto, 1960); Catton, *Grant Takes Command* (Boston and Toronto, 1969); John Y. Simon, ed., *The Papers of Ulysses S. Grant* (Carbondale and Edwardsville, Illinois, 1967–).
29. Ulysses S. Grant 3rd, *Ulysses S. Grant, Warrior and Statesman* (New York, 1969).

Genealogy

GRANT FAMILY

Jesse Root Grant (1794–1873)
  married (1821) Hannah Simpson (1798–1883)—6 children
    Ulysses S. Grant (1822–1885)
      married (1848) Julia Boggs Dent (1826–1902)—4 children
        Frederick Dent Grant (1850–1912)
          married (1874) Ida Marie Honoré (1854–1930)—2 children
          Julia Grant (1876–   )
            married (1899) Michael Cantacuzène (1875–1955)—3 children
          Ulysses S. Grant 3rd (1881–1968)
            married (1907) Edith Root (1879–1962)—3 children
        Ulysses S. Grant, Jr. (1852–1929)
          married (1880) Fannie Josephine Chaffee (1857–1909)—5 children
          married (1913) America Workman Will (1882–1942)
        Ellen (Nellie) Wrenshall Grant (1855–1922)
          married (1874) Algernon Charles Sartoris (1851–1893)—4 children
          married (1912) Frank Hatch Jones
          Algernon Edward Sartoris (1877–ca. 1907)
            married (1904) Cecilie Houfflard—1 child
        Jesse Root Grant, Jr. (1858–1934)
          married (1880) Elizabeth Chapman (1858–1945)—2 children
          married (1918) Lillian Burns Wilkins (1864–1924)
    Samuel Simpson Grant (1825–1861)
    Clara Rachel Grant (1828–1865)
    Virginia Paine Grant (Jennie) (1832–1881)
      married (1869) Abel Rathbone Corbin (1808–1881)—1 child
    Orvil[le] Lynch Grant (1835–1881)
      married (1857) Mary Medary (1835–1894)—4 children
    Mary Frances Grant (1839–1905)
      married (1863) Michael John Cramer (1835–1898)—2 children

DENT FAMILY

George Dent (1765–181?)
   married (1785) Susannah Dawson Cromwell—6 children
     Frederick Fayette Dent (1786–1873)
       married (1814) Ellen Bray Wrenshall (179?–1857)—8 children
       John Cromwell Dent (1816–1889)
         married Ellen Dean—1 child
         married Anna Amanda Shurlds
       George Wrenshall Dent (1819–1899)
         married (1841) Mary Isabella Shurlds—3 children
       Frederick Tracy Dent (1820–1892)
         married (1852) Helen Louise Lynde—3 children
       Lewis (Louis) Dent (1823–1874)
         married Anna Elizabeth Baine (1839–?)—4 children
           Baine Carruthers Dent (1856–1916)
             married Lulu Green
       Julia Boggs Dent (1826–1902)
         married (1848) Ulysses S. Grant (1822–1885)—4 children
       Ellen (Nellie) Wrenshall Dent (1828–1904)
         married Alexander Sharp (1824–1904)—10 children
       Mary Dent (died in infancy)
       Emily (Emma) Marbury Dent (1836–?) married
         (1861) James Finnie Casey (1830–1888)—6 children

The

Personal Memoirs

of

Julia Dent Grant

(MRS. ULYSSES S. GRANT)

Chapter 1

MY FIRST recollections in life reach back a long way, more than three-score years and ten now. We, my gentle mother and two little brothers, were on the south end of the front piazza at our old home, White Haven. We had just arrived. Dear papa, coming out with seeming great pleasure, caught me up and held me high in the air, telling me to look, the very trees were welcoming me, and, sure enough, the tall locust trees were tossing their white-plumed branches gleefully. I watched too the white clouds flying across the blue sky. All this I distinctly remember. It must have been early in May, for the locust trees which surrounded our home were in bloom. The following June, 1828, my little sister next to me, Nellie, came. Life seemed one long summer of sunshine, flowers, and smiles to me and to all at that happy home.

My father and mother were great favorites in St. Louis, where they had resided for ten or twelve years, and ten miles over a very bad road was not considered too great an effort for friends to make for a day spent with Frederick Dent and family. Our home was then really the showplace of the county, having very fine orchards of peaches, apples, apricots, nectarines, plums, cherries, grapes, and all of the then rare small fruits. Our flower garden was the admiration of the county. Papa kept an excellent gardener, old Sturdee, who later challenged my father's vote during the Rebellion, thereby questioning his loyalty. Dear father was very, very indignant at this, as he considered it a downright insult, and told the patriotic old foreigner to be d—d, swore a blue streak at him, refused to vote, and threatened the poll guard with a caning.

During my childhood, I remember very pleasant interchanging of visits with friends in St. Louis and at Jefferson Barracks, and of many friends coming from Pittsburgh: the Nevilles, O'Haras, Wilkinses, Robinsons, Dennys, Ogdens, etc.[1] Our friends from Jefferson Barracks were many and changing. Louisville and Cincinnati also furnished us many who did not think the road too long from St. Louis to White Haven, our home, to prevent them visiting their old friends. Governors Clark and McNair[2] were frequent visitors at my father's house while they occupied the gubernatorial chair. When they were visiting us, mamma and papa would ask them to make some diplomatic visits to some of our neighbors and would kindly send a courier to inform the families that they might expect a visit the next day from the governor, his wife, and themselves; whereupon the houses were put in order, all the homespun linen, linsey-woolsey, knitted socks and stockings, quilts and blankets were brought out and put on exhibition, the little ones looking their best; and of course these most hospitable of neighbors brought out the best they had, felt much pleased with their governor, and more pleased with their neighbors, Mr. and Mrs. Dent.

I have often heard my mother say she always felt her unworthiness and incompetency as a western pioneer's wife when she was making these visits and saw their wealth of handiwork, none of which she had to show. How should she know anything of all these matters, educated as she was in a large eastern city. Mamma was a generous housekeeper. She trusted her servants. There was no help for that, for she was delicate and often unable to attend personally to such matters. Frequently, Kitty, one of mamma's devoted maids, received her orders and carried them out perfectly. Mamma, like my father, was a great reader, fond of poetry and music. She was beautiful, kind, and gentle. She spent much time in reading aloud to us her favorite authors, calling our attention to some passage that pleased or touched her. She loved to hear us sing her favorite old ballads to Emmie's guitar as we sat on the piazza in the summer moonlight. Happy days those.

Most of our old colored people were from Virginia and Maryland, and papa used to buy for them great barrels of fish—herring from that part of the country. Molasses, tobacco, and some whiskey (on cold, raw days) were issued regularly to them from the storehouse, and then they had everything the farm produced, such as all vegetables, bacon, beef, and, of course, poultry. I think our people were very happy. At least they were in mamma's time, though the young ones became somewhat demoralized about the beginning of the Rebellion, when all the comforts of slavery passed away forever. My father was most kind and indulgent to his people, too much so perhaps, as later in life, as the old Kentucky song says, "By'n by Hard Times comes a knocking at the door," and how hard this was for him who had been so independent, helping by endorsement (and invariably meeting the notes himself when they came due) many of the small farmers to secure their homesteads, and not a few impecunious relations who wanted to turn over a new leaf and begin again; and so it came about that late in life this dear, chivalric, generous old gentleman heard hard times knocking at his door.

My four dear brothers, John, George, Fred, and Louis, were brave fellows, and to my mind and also to papa's and mamma's were heroes. Such eloquence, when they began to learn their speeches, I have never heard surpassed, and they were wonderful athletes too—such leaps, handsprings, pitching of quoits, as papa, mamma, Nell, and I used to witness from the front piazza! They were usually performed on the lawn in front of the house; in the trees above were small houses for the swallows and martins; when the boys would begin their sports, these feathery habitants would really join in. Fred said it was "fight in them," and that they meant to protest against such intrusion into their leafy homes.

Coming as I did to the family after the fourth great boy, I was necessarily something of a pet. I cannot remember ever having been coerced into doing anything. It was always, "Will little daughter like to do this?" "No!" Then little daughter did not do it. But I think I was a good little girl, not the least spoiled by this unprecedented indulgence; on the contrary, I remember doing many little kindnesses for the menservants, uncles Charles, Bob, Willis, William, and Jim, who invariably came to me when they wanted a little tobacco, whiskey, or money. Any of these men would say, "Won't little Mistress tell Master I would like to go home tonight," or, "Our tobacco's gitten mighty low," or, "Won't little Mistress tell Master the cold's mighty penetratin' this mornin'," or, "Little Mistress, won't you tell Master I's going to see my old wife this evenin' and would like to take her some sugar for her coffee." In I would go and thrust my hand into papa's pocket up to my elbow until my hand caught a half dollar or a quarter. When my dear papa would say, "What are you doing, you little rascal?" I would draw out my hand in triumph, showing a coin or two, saying, "Uncle Willis or Uncle Charles is going home tonight and wants to buy something for his wife." And these dear old black uncles always brought to me pet rabbits, squirrels, and all the prettiest birds' eggs they found. The first ripe strawberries, the reddest apples, and their first melons were brought to "Miss Julia."

During the next four or five years, my time and sister Nellie's was passed mostly out-of-doors. I had my nurse, dear old black Kitty, and Nell had Rose, a pretty mulatto. Besides, we always had a dusky train of from eight to ten little colored girls of all hues, and these little colored girls were allowed to accompany us if they were very neat. We would wander by the brookside, catch minnows with pin-hooks—or try to. I, being of a provident nature, required these little maids to each carry a bucket to bring home my captives. Sometimes I would catch a minnow, sometimes two or three. Oh! what happiness to see that nibble, to feel the pull, and to see the plunge of the cork; then the little quivering, shining creature was landed high on the bank. The whole cavalcade rushed to take the minnow off the hook, which I could not do. I would then have one of those numerous buckets filled with clear water and plunge my little captive happily in its depths. I remember when we went to gather wild strawberries I required abundant preparation to be made for the quantities we *expected* to gather but which were never realized, usually finding that a few oak leaves fastened together were sufficient to carry the store we had gathered to bring home to dear mamma. We were so very much out-of-doors that I attribute our good health to this fact. Our playhouses were first under the Judas trees; we played under their brilliant boughs until their blossoms were scattered on the ground; then the sweet dogwood was our home, later the apple and wild cherry in turn.

Once, when I was about nine years old, I, with my dusky train, had wandered far up the brook and deeper than usual into the woods when we came upon a beautiful, shadowy, moss-covered nook. My little maids exclaimed: "Oh! Miss Julia! Have this for your playhouse, and we will mark it out with all the pretty stones we can find." Hastening to the brook, they gathered all the "petrified honeycomb" and round boulders they could find, placing these so as to mark the supposed walls of my mansion. Anne (my special maid) and Susanna disappeared for about a half hour, and, to my astonishment, when they returned, I found they had been to the house, had gone into the sitting room, had filled their aprons with mamma's beautiful shells (she had many of these treasures of the sea), and had brought them to me for decorations for my sylvan bower. I told them they ought not to have done this, but the shells were so very, very pretty that I let them remain for a long time. One of my brothers while out hunting about three weeks afterwards found them still in our pretty haunt. These little maids of mine were full of fairy lore. I had read to them all of the pretty stories of the times, and when they built this bower for me they declared the fairies would be sure to come there to dance that night, would be so pleased with all we had done for them, and be glad to know such a pretty, nice, white lady had come to live during the day in their pretty bower.

My school days are only pleasant memories. I was very young and small when I first attended school, and was often carried most of the way by my brothers George and Fred. Louis was too small to assist them in making a chair for me by clasping hands, thus forming a firm, safe seat; and then dear Kitty would carry me sometimes, and occasionally I would ride mamma's pony led by Kitty.

Imagine what a pet I was with my three, brave, handsome brothers. The young girls attending this school, I assure you, fully appreciated my attractions. The larger girls always included me in their games and made me prominent in them, much to the chagrin of the other little girls. The first, ripest, mellowest of apples, peaches, and pears were mine, as also the brightest of flowers, all of which I owed to my brothers.

The old schoolhouse was a picture. This temple of ours was built of logs hewn from the adjacent forest and was, I should think, about twenty-five feet square. We entered its only door from the east. To the right, as we entered, sat the teacher, always kind to me. The north end of the cabin was occupied by a large fireplace, which was filled with green branches and bright flowers in summer and a glowing fire in winter. On the west side was a long, narrow window: the girls sat on this side; on the south was a high, wide window: the young men sat on that side. The little fellows sat in front of the large boys, or between them and the teacher. Only think, there were no backs to any of the seats. Mamma sent a nice little armchair for my use.

From the large south window you looked out upon the most delightful of playgrounds, green as emerald, except in the spots selected by the boys for their sports, such as shinney, quoits, and ball. The girls used to jump the rope, play "open the gate as high as the sky and let King George and his men pass by," and "ring around a rosey," but our favorite pastime was telling and listening to fairy tales. This was always my great delight, and I can listen now to "The Culprit Fay" with unabated pleasure. The three great oaks that shaded and sheltered our playground, reaching out and lifting up their branches so high, I thought then, must reach quite nearly to the sky; but I must not forget the lovely brook that "chattered, chattered" as it flowed to join the brimming river, nor the spring gushing out over a broad, flat rock at the foot of the hill across the brook. When school was called, we would all fly to this spring for a last taste of its cooling waters "so sparkling and bright." It was always sweetest from a cup formed of oak leaves and handed to us by the hero of the play or of the sham Indian fight of the day. We had our heroes even at Gravois School.

We often changed teachers. I remember Merrill Parks as one, and Mr. Tabor, and Mr. Whithy; both of these latter gentlemen were excellent teachers and were graduates of some New England college. Mr. J. F. Long[3] of St. Louis was my last teacher at this sylvan temple of learning. He was so kind to all, *too* kind to me. I remember on one occasion he gave to our class some of those dreadful roman numerals to learn for Monday morning, saying that if we did not know the task set he really would punish us and with the rod. Well, I spent all of my Saturday holiday conning this, to me, most unpleasant task and, thinking I had mastered it, went proudly to school. Mr. Long called up his little sister Ella to recite. She did not know her lesson—he kept his word. I was the next one called up, and lo! not a number did I know. I could not tell whether the I's came before or after the V's and X's. I turned pale and trembled, when kind Mr. Long stooped down (he was over six feet, four inches in height) and said in a low tone, "You don't know it, do you, little one?" I replied: "I thought I did when I came, but I don't now." He said kindly: "Never mind, don't trouble your little head about it any more now, you will learn it in good time." I never did, however, as through life I have always had to ask the General or one of my children.

When I was ten years and about eight months old, I was sent to St. Louis to the Misses Mauros'[4] boarding school, where I remained for about seven years, studying about what I liked. After the first year, the young ladies undertook to discipline me. I, feeling that they had been a little, or very, unreasonable, did just as I pleased, declining to recite again in English grammar and absolutely refusing to look at the multiplication table, spending this most valuable time in reading *Rienzi, Paul Clifford, The Bandit's Bride, Elizabeth of Siberia, Ivanhoe, Peveril of the Peak,* and all other books I could lay my hands on; but the kind young ladies had no fault to find with me when I came to recite in philosophy, mythology, or history. In every other branch I was below the standard, and, worse still, my indifference was very exasperating.

I remember one Sunday afternoon the girls were all lying on the grass on the lawn reading their Sunday school books, of which they soon tired. I was reading a book (not a Sunday school one) called *The Dashing Lieutenant,* when one of the young ladies yawned as if tired of her book and said: "Girls, let us say what we would like to have as the occupations of our husbands when we get them, as we all expect to sometime." So we began: one wanted a lawyer, another a banker, one a judge, another a merchant, two or three wanted farmers, and when it came to my turn I declared emphatically a *soldier,* a gallant, brave, dashing soldier—and I got him, did I not? Then came Sarah Dunlap's turn to say. She said: "a statesman." She had evidently met Stephen A. Douglas. She lived at Jacksonville, Ill., and had just returned from her vacation, when, I think, she had met Mr. Douglas. She married General McClernand.[5] Meeting him early in the late war, I mentioned this school day episode. He replied at once, "Yes, but Sarah married both a *statesman and a soldier.*"

I do not wonder now that men get so excited and troubled over elections. I remember very vividly that when our May Queen was elected by ballot there was a great hubbub made by one of the young ladies declaring in the most solemn manner that she had seen another young lady place *three* tickets in the ballot box. The ballots were all counted, as were the voters, and they tallied. The informer did, however, see one young lady put three tickets in the box, but the two extra ones belonged to two young ladies in the infirmary who had asked her to place their votes in the box. The informer, dear girl, was expelled from our school for making this disgraceful accusation, after being confined to her room for several days. Oh, how I begged of her to escape from her prison, as I termed it, entreated on my knees that she should fly. I volunteered to arrange everything for her, but no! She was too wise to do anything so wild and improper. She was restored to her place in school very soon after, as the whole school petitioned earnestly for her restoration, and she really did see three ballots cast.

At this school, as at the one in the country, I was very happy and had the privilege of inviting one of my kind teachers, and one or two of my schoolmates, to go home with me every other Friday afternoon to remain until the following Monday. Our carriage was large and roomy but curious as I remember it now: the coachman was perched high up in front on a small square seat, which was hung round with a curtain of drab cloth, the coachman's coat and the carriage lining corresponding in color. At the back was a platform for the footman, who of necessity had to accompany us, as there were great heavy steps to let down before we could descend to terra firma. Our rides through the ten miles of shady woodland roads were always delightful, and on our arrival the welcome we received—well! How can I tell you of its kindliness, or express to you the pleasure it seemed to give my beloved parents to welcome me and my friends?

How well I remember those homecomings: my gentle, beautiful mother and noble father, of both of whom I was always *so* proud; sisters Nell and Emma in their snowy muslins and silken curls; and the background of smiling faces of those who used to form my dusky train, who were now much grown, having attained the dignity of white aprons (not pinafores) and with gay bandannas bound around their heads making picturesque and becoming turbans; then the tea, or, more properly, the supper table of broad mahogany, covered with the sweetest and finest of linen, the heavy cut glass (we had no other in those days), china of the daintiest and most delicate white and gold. The silver was solid and plain and always bright, and our table, well, mammy, black Mary, was an artist. Such loaves of beautiful snowy cake, such plates full of delicious Maryland biscuit, such exquisite custards and puddings, such omelettes, gumbo soup, and fritters— these were mammy's specialty. She sometimes made them of straw-berries and again of pineapple. She even became so esthetic as to make these dainty little delicious morsels of flowers from our acacia, rose-tree, and from the locust flowers, telling Nell and me that such dainty, delicate young ladies should live on such food. I must not forget to mention the great bowls of cut glass filled with delicious strawberries, raspberries, and peaches and cream, and the two beautiful cut glass pitchers filled with such milk that used to decorate the corners of the table. Papa and mamma were married in 1814 at Pittsburgh, and the mahogany, cut glass, silver, and fine linen were the same they began housekeeping with.

My parents were both of English descent. My father's people came to this country in 1643, three brothers settling in Maryland: one on the Potomac at Acquia Creek, one at the mouth of the eastern branch opposite Washington, where he had a large estate and called it Giesborough, and another, I have heard papa say, at Georgetown Heights or Blue Plains. My grandfather, George Dent, had no brother and was a resident of Bladensburg. After his marriage with Susanna Marbury, he lived in Cumberland, Maryland.[6] Miss Marbury was also of English descent. Papa always said she was a great beauty, and, by the way, I have a very pretty sketch of Marbury Hall, Cheshire, England, the homestead of the ancestors of grandmamma. Mamma has told me that the only time she ever saw Grandpa Dent he wore knee breeches, a chapeau, a queue tied with black ribbon, buckles on his shoes, ruffles on his shirtfront, and that he was a very handsome and distinguished looking man. Mamma always said brother Louis was very like him.

My mother, Ellen Bray Wrenshall, was English-born and came to America when she was quite a little girl. Grandpa Wrenshall came to this country as a merchant and belonged to the firm of Wrenshall, Peacock, and Pillon. Mamma told me they had their own ships and exported to China an article the natives were fond of called ginseng—a root, I believe. Grandpa Wrenshall was a Methodist of the Wesleyan school, very strict and uncompromising. He considered it a sin to dance or to enjoy yourself in any way.[7]

Mamma has told me of riding on horseback all the way from Pittsburgh to Philadelphia, where she was sent to school, and of once meeting Aaron Burr and his army in the Allegheny Mountains encamped around the little tavern which contained one room and a kitchen. This one room was, of course, occupied by the officers. Mamma, though much fatigued, was very loath to lie on the settle, or bench, before them all to rest until they pressed around and made for her a bed and a pillow of their cloaks and begged her to rest, telling her she would be just as safe there as in her mother's arms. Lying down at last, they covered her with another martial cloak, and she slept as soundly as the princess in the fairy tale.

There is another little incident I must tell. Soon after she went to Philadelphia, mamma was invited to dine at a fashionable house, the Vanrixtens, the daughter of this house being her particular friend, and although accustomed to living in puritanical simplicity at home, she was much surprised to find only soup served. Finding this very excellent, however, she requested a second plate and discovered too late that she had made a great mistake as she was unable to taste the delicious and elaborate dinner which followed. Many Philadelphia names are familiar to me through my mother.

About two years after the marriage of my father and mother, they removed to St. Louis, Missouri (then called Upper Louisiana). Their mode of traveling was quite magnificent for the times. They had a flotilla of three rafts made of huge logs fastened together with chains; on each of these rafts were erected snug little frame cabins of two or more rooms, one occupied by my father, mother, baby John, and a friend, Mr. Edward Tracy.[8] The cooking was done on one of the other rafts, which conveyed servants, household furniture, carriages, horses, etc. The party consisted of papa, mamma, baby John, Mr. Edward Tracy, a friend of father's, also two indentured slaves, Hester and Bob, with men for handling the rafts, etc. Nearly all Pittsburgh assembled on the river bank to wish pretty Ellen Wrenshall and her brave young husband Godspeed. As the little crafts were cut loose and swung out into the current, great shouts and some sobs went up for them, for it was thought then a great undertaking for these two young people to start on their perilous journey to the wilderness beyond the Mississippi. They went as far as Shawneetown in the boats and thence across the country (the prairies of Illinois) in their own private carriage. This ride, mamma said, was sublime, through one great sea of waving grass and flowers. Papa was a merchant of the firm of Dent and Lindell.[9] Mr. Lindell left a vast fortune at his death, reaching two millions of dollars, I believe. I am quite sure papa's life was the happier of the two, living, as he did, very comfortably, and leaving a large and, I think, most worthy family to lament him.

My parents remained in St. Louis about eight or ten years, but their family was getting large and they thought it best to have a place in the country for the summer months, and they purchased the old homestead with about a thousand acres of land lying ten miles south of St. Louis on the Gravois Creek. They named it White Haven in memory of some English place. I think papa's family came from White Haven, England. Papa found this place and the life so delightful that he gradually gave up all occupation and passed his time in the summer months sitting in an easy chair reading an interesting book, and in the winter, in the chimney corner beside a blazing hickory fire, occupied in the same way.

Do not understand this as a reflection on my beloved and honored father, for he was one of the most devoted of husbands, the most indulgent and generous of fathers, and the kindest of masters to his slaves, who all adored him. I call back the memory of those Christmas holidays and Whitsuntide festivals, the weddings of those poor people (they often got married without getting divorces), the fine suppers the master and mistress always gave them on these occasions; then the corn shuckings of which they also made a feast; they would pile the freshly gathered corn in a rick ten or twelve feet high and, it seemed to me, a hundred long. They would invite all of the colored people from far and near, and, after greetings had passed and they had something to drink, they would gather around, sometimes two or three hundred strong, and word, song, and chorus would begin, and as I see the fire lighting up the weird company and hear the wild, plaintive, and, to me, pathetic music, it brings up a most pleasant memory.

Dear old Bob, who sometimes was either frightened or more likely had his dear old tender heart touched by some special kindness, would "get religion," as his companions said. He would go away down in the meadow by the big walnut trees nearly half a mile off and pray and sing so we could hear him distinctly on our piazza. He would give out the hymn, two lines at a time, and then sing it all by himself. How pathetic it all was. I think old Bob went to Heaven.

It was Bob's business to build the fires for the house, and as this was long before matches came in use, he often, when he was careless and let his fires go out, had to ignite his fires with a flint and a piece of punk, something taken from decayed wood, or else he would have to walk a mile to some neighbors and bring home a brand of fire from their backlog. I well remember the first matches I ever saw. Brother John brought a box out from the city where he had gone to learn to be a merchant. They made a blue blaze and had a very bad odor. They were called lucifer matches, and we were rather afraid of them.

My mother hated the country and this place especially, feeling that all the sacrifices of society and friendship (I will not say love, for that she always had) she had made on leaving her eastern home were lost. Papa enjoyed farming; he was progressive, and while a merchant he purchased one of the first steamboats, while they were yet experiments, to bring his coffee, sugar, etc., from New Orleans. He did not like the mercantile business after he had once enjoyed the repose of a country life. He once said to me when I asked why he did not remain in business in the city: "My daughter, the Yankees that have come west have reduced business to a system. Do you know now if a man wants a loan of a few thousand dollars for a few days—God bless you!—they want a note and interest. This was not so in my time. Old Rector, Hempstead, Chenie,[10] and I used to do business differently. No! no! if we did any business now we would simply bind ourselves to a treadmill." He had all the first and best improvements in farm machinery such as the first thresher; people came from far and near to see it working. He had one of the first reapers, fine-blooded horses, short-horned Durhams, Berkshire and Chinese hogs, imported fowls: in fact, everything that could be obtained. I remember a fine Maltese jack which he always kept locked up; once in a while he would escape and give much trouble. A young nephew of mamma was visiting us and was sleeping in a room on the first floor. The head of his bed rested near the window. It was summer, and the window open. The jack, getting out, wandered up to the house, thrust his head in the window, and, raising his voice, gave a series of prolonged, terrific brays. You can imagine Cousin Jim was awakened by this terrific bellowing, with the animal's head about one foot from his. I don't know what he thought; he might have imagined it another *Midsummer Night's Dream*. He said he thought it was the Devil.

John, having refused to attend school longer and spending his time playing truant, hunting, fishing—in fact, at anything but school—was sent off to St. Louis to learn to be a merchant. George soon after was sent to Augusta College, Kentucky. Fred and Louis went with me to our little country school for about two years longer. St. Charles College, Missouri, was started, and my uncle, John Fielding,[11] was called from Augusta, Ky., to become its first president. When this fine institution was started, all four of my brothers attended. John usually passed his time indulging in wild freaks, generally being the ring-leader. At one time he was put "in bounds" and not allowed to leave the college grounds. When all the young ladies of the town joined in a petition to the faculty to have Mr. John Dent released from bounds because society was broken up and life was insupportable without his presence, he was released. Another time, an old friend told us he met John in the interior of the state dressed in a brilliant cavalry uniform. John, coming suddenly face to face with him, said in a most independent manner: "Good day, Father Monroe,[12] I am here on recruiting service for the navy." "I see! I see!" replied our old pastor, "but, Captain, take my advice and return to college," which he did.

I remember the homecomings of those early college days. They always brought two or three friends home to spend the holidays. I was a great pet with these fellows, often accompanying them on their fishing excursions, and even hunting with them. One early morning, I joined Fred and a friend on their morning hunt for pheasant. As we passed down the creek and around the meadow which was white with the dew, and the sky rosy with the coming sun, Fred stopped and, with a wave of his arm, exclaimed:

Aurora, now fair daughter of the dawn
Sprinkling with rosy light, the dewy lawn[13]

I thought then that this fine effusion was original with Fred. How vividly this little incident returned to me the early morning I went on deck to have Mount Olympus pointed out by my son Jesse and half a dozen young navy officers; the sun was not yet up, the sky was gloriously rosy, the sea danced and sparkled in this rosy light, and proud Olympus reared high his shaggy head. We tarried there to get a *firman* to enable us to proceed to Constantinople.

Louis was next older than I and was much more of a companion than the other brothers. He used to gallantly bait my hook for me, saying, "Little sister must not do a thing so cruel." He and Cousin Charley Page[14] used to capture the heavy-laden bumblebee wending his way home and strip from his fat sides the full bags of golden honey for me, then toss him high in air to go and gather more. Those golden drops were very sweet to me. On one of his vacations, Louis complained that he had not had a bit of corn bread since his return home. Mamma said: "I am sure you have had some kind of corn bread at every meal." "No," he said, "I want those cakes old Aunt Eadie makes." (Old Eadie cooked for the farmhands.) An order was

[44]

sent to Eadie, and at the next repast a plate was upon the corner of the table upon which rested three golden corn "dodgers" (a cake familiar to every southern and western home). Just as mother, Nell, Louis, and I were sitting down, Louis exclaimed, "Mamma, may I say grace?" Mamma bowed assent, feeling much pleased and surprised at the request, when Louis, in the most solemn manner, said:

> Three corn dodgers for four of us,
> Thank the Lord there are no more of us.

Mamma only looked her reproof. Nell and I enjoyed it and thought Louis very clever indeed.

Louis rather lorded it over poor little me after he had been at college for a term or two. On one occasion, I was helping him make and fly a kite (such beautiful ones he made too) when he shut his knife in a very manly way and thrust it deep in his pocket and, pointing upwards, said: "Little sister, see yonder white clouds piled in masses along the sky." "Yes," I said, expectantly looking at him. He said: "Well, that shows the gods have washed their shirts and hung them out to dry." I did not quite like this and thought Louis was poking fun at me. Soon after this, I went to St. Louis to school where I too began to study mythology and was soon as familiar with the ways of the gods as was Louis. And how much I owe this dear, princely brother of mine, who used to read so many, many delightful books to me. How we enjoyed Byron's "Corsair" and "Siege of Corinth," and all the rest of it. And Shakespeare, how we all enjoyed his readings of *The Tempest*, *Romeo and Juliet*; in fact, all of this best of educator's works. Ah, Louis! What pleasant, pleasant memories of long summers at our old home come back to me as I write.

I must not fail to tell of the wealth of our forests in game at this time. It was no unusual sight to see from two to five wild deer bounding across the fields near our house. Foxes also were numerous, to the consternation of the farmers' wives, and, as I remember, the gentlemen all enjoyed the sport of hunting them down. My father and his three eldest sons were very fond of field sports. Rabbits and squirrels with all other small game abounded; wild turkeys were plentiful, as were also the wild geese, ducks, white and blue cranes, pheasants, grouse—or, as we called them, prairie chickens—quail, woodcock, plover, and wild doves. The pigeons used to fly in myriads in their flight to the south so that there was no sport in shooting them, but our colored people made a pleasant frolic in taking wagons and going to the bottom lands or valleys, where these little migrators

[45]

roosted, and from the heavily-laden boughs of their resting places gathered thousands and brought them home in barrels and bags, feasting on these delicious morsels for days, generously supplying their master's table with all we could use. Brother Fred (General Dent) was our huntsman, or, as mamma used to call him, "our Nimrod," and how handsome he was in his hunting jacket of dark green velveteen and drab knickerbockers of the same material, and how pretty his paraphernalia of game bag, powder horn, and shot pouch were, his cap decorated with a fox's brush, or a quill from the wing of an eagle, or some other wild bird. Dear Fred was something of a dude, but that is not what we called it; it was dandy then.

Mamma was very handsome. The colored maids said to us when they saw us more becomingly dressed than usual, "Oh, young Missus, you are looking very pretty, but you never will come up to old Missus in looks."

Papa used to be handsome in ruffles and white necktie and white fur hat. I can remember the first black hat he wore. As he stood before my mother expecting approval, mamma said: "How did you come to get a black hat?" He replied: "To tell you the truth, a white hat has become the insignia of a gambler." Mamma said: "Indeed, is that so?" "Yes," papa said, "when you see a white hat, you may know that man is a blackleg." And I, poor little girl who heard everything and never forgot anything, whenever I saw a gentleman wearing a white hat, thought, poor gentleman, he has black legs. I thought it a great misfortune. At the same time my father gave up his white hat for a black one, he also gave up the white cambric neckerchief and the ruffles on his shirt bosom.

Once Nell and I went with mamma to visit St. Charles College (where my brothers were at school) and our friends there. While there, we attended church where faith was the theme and strongly commented upon by the preacher. He said: "If ye have faith even as a grain of mustard seed, ye may move mountains and walk on the waters." This he repeated over and over so earnestly that I was entirely convinced, as everyone else seemed to be. Soon after our return home, Nell and I were wandering along the Gravois chasing butterflies and gathering flowers and did not notice that the brook was so much swollen until we came to the usual crossing; what to do, we did not know. We never once thought of turning back, for our intention was to get a branch of wild clematis that grew a quarter of a mile on the opposite side. There we stood confounded, watching the waters fairly laughing at us as they leaped and rushed over our steppingstones. We stood looking on until all at once the bright thought of faith and all the minister had said came to me, and I informed Nell of my determination to make the crossing on the deepest and smoothest place, reminding her of what the preacher said about faith. She was much alarmed and timidly asked: "What is faith, sister?" In great superiority, I replied: "Little goose, believe that you can and you can." She then proposed that I start a little way up the bank in a run so that I might pass quickly over the brook and not give my feet time to sink, in case I had not faith enough. This good advice I ignored with some feeling of pity for Nell. I stepped out on the water and plunged in up to my armpits. I was surprised and looked back at Nell with a frightened smile. I went on, however, to the other side and scrambled up the bank—crushed flowers, dead butterflies, and wet little girl. Nell chose the rough place where the waters were broken and took a smart run, but met the same fate, only she stopped in the middle of the stream and began to cry. I went in and helped her out. We both sat on the bank until our clothes were dry and the brook fell.

I left Miss Mauro's school in the month of June, 1843, the year my brother Fred graduated from West Point. My summer was passed most pleasantly at the farm, meeting many friends and acquaintances from St. Louis and Jefferson Barracks, where some of my schoolmates dwelt. We really depended more on Jefferson Barracks for society than on St. Louis, as it was only half the distance, less than five miles away. I met all of the officers stationed there and their families, and the young officers many times. They often came out to visit brother Fred.

Fred was ordered to Fort Towson [Indian Territory], and I went up to St. Louis to spend the winter with friends of my parents, Colonel and Mrs. O'Fallon,[15] who lived in more elegance than any other family in St. Louis. The daughter of this house was an heiress and beautiful and, of course, had many suitors. I was the shyest of little girls, and if I had any admirers, I am sure I did not know it. Carrie's friends saw that I had partners at the dance and were not chary of their attentions to me.

My first party was the wedding of my schoolmate, the daughter of Mrs. General Ashley (who afterwards married J. J. Crittenden, a distinguished senator of Kentucky), who married Andrew McKinley.[16] How brilliant this wedding was! Then followed many routs, balls, and dinners. I remember a gay ball at Colonel Taylor's which lasted all night, given to Fannie Wash, their niece.[17] Many parties were given her that winter. She always came in late after everyone had been surveyed. She would dash in like a very meteor in her fresh, gauzy draperies, her only ornaments natural flowers. How radiant she was! a very queen among us all. Colonel William Preston was at this ball, and Josephine Harris of Newport, Ky., so handsome and so queenly in her bearing.

There is another party I must mention, this same winter of 43–44. On February 22, Colonel R. Lee gave a party for his daughter Mary's debut.[18] I had left the O'Fallons and was spending a few days on my way home at Mr. J. Brady Smith's[19] (the most charming and refined family I ever visited). Mr. Brady Smith was my escort, and after paying our respects to our host and hostess and the young debutante and strolling around the large and handsomely decorated rooms a few times, I modestly suggested to my escort that I would relieve him of the care of me and would take a stand near the folding doors, where he might find me when he and his daughter, Miss Julia, wished to return. He remonstrated, but at length let me have my own way, and as each newly-arrived lady took her stand near my place I was soon absolutely against the wall, when a bevy of young officers arrived looking so handsome in their brilliant uniforms with epaulettes and aiguillettes, and chapeaux in their hands. There was handsome Longstreet, Baker, Sid Smith, Hoskins, Sykes, Garnett,[20] and many others, all of whom I knew. How delighted I was when Hoskins, glancing over the room to take observations, recognized me and with an expression of suppressed surprise asked me what I was doing there and said: "Do you not want me to come to your rescue?" I answered, "yes," and he did most gallantly. I knew all of these young officers, and how very pleasant they made this evening for me.

I left the city a few days after this and was glad to return to that best of homes—dear, noble, kind papa and gentle mamma, so pretty, so gentle, and so kind. She never, even once in all of my life, chided me, nor did papa.

I had been home from school about eight months, had spent a winter in society in St. Louis, and returned home heart-whole. About three days after my return, Lieutenant Grant called to pay his usual weekly visit to our house. After that first visit he became a daily visitor. Such delightful rides we all used to take! The Lieutenant rode a bonny little brown steed with flowing wavy mane and tail. He called him Fashion. My horse was a beauty, a chestnut brown, and as glossy as satin, and such pretty ears and great eyes. She was part Arabian, and I named her Psyche. Such rides! in the early spring, the tender young foliage scarcely throwing a shadow. Well, I cannot tell of those two winged months. He was always by my side, walking or riding. We often had many visitors from the city and from the Barracks, young people of both sexes, and Lieutenant Grant was greatly liked, but he always most kindly escorted me. I remember he was kind enough to make a nice little coffin for my canary bird and he painted it yellow. About eight officers attended the funeral of my little pet.

Towards the end of April, Lieutenant Grant obtained a leave of absence to visit his home in Ohio. He came out to bid us goodbye and spent the whole day with us. As we sat on the piazza alone, he took his class ring from his finger and asked me if I would not wear it. He had told me previously that whenever he gave that ring to a lady, he would give it as an engagement ring. I declined, saying, "Oh, no, mamma would not approve of my accepting a gift from a gentleman." He seemed rather put out at this and soon after took his leave, lingering near me and asking me if I would think of him in his absence. I, child that I was, never for a moment thought of him as a lover. I was very happy when he was near, but that was all. Oh! how lonely it was without him.

Within a day or two after Mr. Grant left, orders came for the regiment to go to Louisiana. All of our young friends rode out to make their adieux, and more than one ring was pressed upon us and declined as was Lieutenant Grant's. Lieutenant Hazlitt [21] assured us that if Mr. Grant were not out to see us within a week from the following Saturday week, we must understand that he had gone on down the Mississippi and would not be at the Barracks again.

Saturday came and no Lieutenant. I felt very restless and, ordering my horse, rode alone towards the Barracks, not feeling afraid. I halted my horse and waited and listened, but he did not come. The beating of my own heart was all the sound I heard. So I rode slowly and sadly home, where I found two young ladies and two gentlemen had arrived to remain over Sunday.

And now I must relate a very odd dream I had. My room had just been newly furnished. The bedstead had been set up that morning. There is an old superstition that whatever you dream the first night in your new bed will surely come true. When we young ladies retired, Josephine S. and I slept in my new bed and, according to custom, named the bedposts, and of course my absent friend was not forgotten. I did dream of Mr. Grant. I thought he came at Monday noon and was dressed in civilian's clothes. He came in, greeted us all most cordially, and seated himself near me; when I asked him how long he would remain, he said: "I am going to try to stay a week." When I told my dream, my friends all exclaimed: "That dream will not come true, Julia. Mr. Grant is now calmly sailing down the Mississippi, far below the mouth of the Ohio," and so thought I. Monday morning my young friends had departed, and I was about to retire for an afternoon siesta, when my colored maid came and, looking up towards the front gate, said: "Law, Miss Julia, if there isn't Mars John and, I declare, Mr. Grant, and he has on citizen's clothes and how odd he looks in them too."

Sure enough, there he was. As soon as I could arrange my toilet, I repaired to the sitting room and, to my surprise, found Lieutenant Grant in the dining room, not far from my door. He seemed to be expecting me. I was, of course, pleased at his return and told him so, saying, as we seated ourselves with the family in the drawing room, "How long do you expect to remain, Mr. Grant?" He replied: "I am going to try to stay a week." Then my sister exclaimed, "You have said the very words sister dreamed you did." I had not thought of my dream all of this time. He turned to me and asked if I had been dreaming of him. I replied that I had named one of my new bedstead posts for him, and all of my dream had come true: he had returned at noontide, replied to my question as to how long he would remain, and was dressed in citizen's clothes. On inquiring how he happened to be dressed so, he told me he was wearing borrowed plumage; that he had plunged into Gravois Creek and was nearly drowned; was of course very wet and had to borrow dry clothing from brother John, who lived some two miles from us.

Lieutenant Grant remained just a week in Missouri. Nearly all of the time was spent at our house. He went with me to St. Louis, where I was to stand as bridesmaid for a schoolmate. On this ride, he declared his love and told me that without me life would be insupportable.[22] I was surprised at his telling me this, for although I was just eighteen, I was very young for my age and very shy indeed. When he spoke of marriage, I simply told him I thought it would be charming to be engaged, but to be married—no! I would rather be engaged. I do not think he liked this arrangement, but as he was going away and could not have taken me with him, even if I had thought it as pleasant to be married as engaged, he let the matter rest.

I remember that at this wedding party several young gentlemen, citizens, were very devoted to me. They seemed determined to monopolize all of my time to the exclusion of the Lieutenant. I do not think I half liked their attentions, as I thought I would greatly prefer a little of Mr. Grant's company, but he was near me all evening and I was, in a measure, happy. After we returned home, the balance of the week was most agreeably passed in long rides and walks. The day of parting came too soon. I begged him not to say anything to papa about our engagement, and he consented to this simply on account of shyness, he acknowledged to me. When he asked me now to wear his class ring I took it and wore it until he replaced it by the little band of gold I have worn so long.

Lieutenant Grant went direct to Camp Salubrity, La., where he remained until the next spring. I was still at White Haven, occasionally going to Jefferson Barracks and to St. Louis to attend parties and weddings. I was constantly receiving letters and books from Mr. Grant. In the spring of '45, my father decided to go to Maryland to settle some old business matters and offered to take me with him, but it seemed such an undertaking that I concluded not to go. Papa really had his will made before he left. He engaged a young man of the neighborhood to accompany him in case of illness or accident. The neighbors came in from all directions to say goodbye. It was then thought to be such a journey. Sunday afternoon, the day before papa's departure (he took an early start Monday morning), the piazza was full of our kind neighbors who had come to say farewell, when who should dash up to the front gate, mounted on a superb dapple gray, but Lieutenant Grant! He walked hurriedly up to the house. I was sitting near the steps and arose to greet him, as did all the others, but he scarcely touched my hand but passed on to greet the company, many of whom he knew. Later, when he learned that papa would go east in the morning, he told me quietly he would go up to the city with him, see him off, and also ask that, to us, most important question. Mr. Grant went up to the city and asked papa for an interview. Papa (Mr. Grant told me) said he did not think the roving life I would have to lead as a soldier's wife would suit me at all, when Mr. Grant immediately said he had been offered a professorship in a college in Ohio;[23] so, if that was the only objection, he would resign.

My father thought it best for him to stick to his profession, and to convince him that he had no objection to him personally, said: "Now, if it were Nellie, I would make no objection, but my Julia is so entirely unfitted for such a life," but the Lieutenant was not eager to avail himself of this Laban-like suggestion and, I am sure, convinced papa that if the life did not suit me, he would make me happy. At all events, permission was obtained for us to correspond. If we who were so young should not change our minds in a year or two, he would then make no objection. This was satisfactory to both of us, and we considered the matter settled. The General often used to tell Sister Nellie (to tease her) that papa had offered her to him, but he had declined. This was told her when she was inclined to put on more airs than the General thought she was entitled to. They were always good friends, however.

Mr. Grant passed the next ten or twelve days at White Haven, and such a two weeks! It was May, and the country was beautiful. The days were passed in reading, walking, and riding, and full of such pleasant, pleasant memories to me. The locust trees were more heavily laden than usual with their white plumes. The forests were more tenderly green, and our seat on the piazza was one bower of eglantine and white jessamine. I remember most pleasantly the hum of the bees in that bower of ours and how near the swallows would come as they whirled past us making music with the fluttering of their wings. For

There is music in the forest leaves
When summer winds are there

And to finish this couplet, I ought to say

And in the laugh of forest girls
That braid their sunny hair

only I had ceased braiding my hair two years ago and really wore it coiled up in a very womanly manner. Nell wore hers in a mass of golden curls and was called by her young gentlemen friends "Maid of Athens." All things have an end; so with these pleasant days.

Mr. Grant bade us farewell and joined his regiment at Salubrity; soon after, the regiment was ordered to New Orleans. I did not meet him again until 1848, when the army returned from Mexico. In the meantime, I received by every mail long letters from him, many written on the field, after he went to Mexico. Twice he wrote me that they were written on the head of a captured drum; these letters I especially prized and I have them yet.[24]

When my father returned from this journey, he was looking so well and brought us all such beautiful presents. I remember too he brought home a telegraph message, all in little dots and lines stamped on a long narrow strip of paper. This was among one of the first messages sent over the wires between Washington and Baltimore. It was in the summer of 1845. I think this must have been the first telegraph line erected in the United States.[25] My father was in Washington and sent the message to Baltimore, making some inquiry, and received an answer within an hour. He said it savored of magic.

My sister was now home from school. She found it rather dull in the winter, and papa found it a great deal of trouble to send us to all of the parties we, or Nell, wanted to attend, so after a great deal of persuasion on Nell's part, he consented to our having a little house in the city so we might more conveniently enjoy the gay society of St. Louis, and I am sure no two country lassies ever had a gayer or more delightful three winters than Nell and I did. It was customary fifty years ago in St. Louis for the sterner sex to make sweet music at the midnight hour beneath the windows of their dulcineas, and dear old

Mr. C., Mr. K., Mr. M., and Judge S. used to tell us that it was impossible for them to get rest enough as our serenades were so continuous. They used to say, "We thought this would not last long. We were willing for all of the young beaux to have a chance to serenade Julia and Ellen two or three times a week, then matters will settle down, but 'mon Dieu' young ladies, it grows worse and worse. We cannot sleep, and that makes us cross, and our families must suffer. We will have to complain of you or of your serenaders." We would ask these gentlemen what we could do, we cannot help it, and besides it is so pleasant to have a half-dozen nice, handsome, manly young fellows beneath one's window pouring out their very souls in song, and hear

> Thou art fair as any flower,
> Lady mine, Lady mine,
> Thou art silver to the sheen,
> Thou art moonlight to the beam

or again

> When stars are in the quiet skies[26]

and

> Good night, good night, good night, my dearest

accompanied by two or more lutes or guitars. What could we do? One of the elderly gentlemen said: "Tell Ellen not to throw any more odd gloves out of the window nor any more flowers. We hear them scrambling for these favors, and of course the disappointed ones come again and again, and we cannot sleep; we will report to your father when he comes up to town, and he will veto this whole proceeding."

It was customary fifty years ago to be at home Sunday afternoon, and we had many calls. We used to have our tea served a trifle earlier on that day and we called it "high tea." It consisted of some cold chipped beef, or ham, or chicken, delicious little Maryland biscuit or home biscuits, cake, fruit, tea, and coffee. Nell and I enjoyed our callers greatly. Mamma remonstrated, saying she did not think it was quite right for quiet Methodists to have such a gay company on the Sabbath day. Nell argued that it was pleasant for us and a real kindness to the gentlemen to receive on Sunday. Nell was always kindly disposed in that direction and was also always a very great favorite. Our winter was passed in a round of gaiety and happiness. Nell said more than once: "I hear people speak of simple country girls—simple indeed! If I stay in the city for two or three winters, I shall have no sense at all, for I have not had time to read a book since I came up to town." Our gaiety reached its climax just before Lent, when Nell and I had to divide: I accompanying mamma to all the quieter parties where there was no dancing; Nell, being claimed by some of our gay old French friends, went to the great balls with them.

A great many of our friends used to go to New Orleans to be present at the Mardi Gras festival. Nell and I wanted to go, but it was not convenient for papa to allow us. I must tell of a very strange dream I had about this time. I had been reading George Sand's *Consuelo* and was much wrought up over the reception in Venice so vividly described, and I dreamed that I arrived at New Orleans amidst hurrahs, salutes of cannon, a great display of flags and flowers, and there were bright carpets spread for me to walk upon, or rather for the party I was with. I told this to my young friends, telling them that when I went there all this would happen. When I did visit New Orleans for the first time it was with my beloved, my hero husband, on his return from Mexico in 1880 where we had been on an extended and delightful journey. A train loaded with the nicest people of New Orleans came to meet General Grant and to escort him to the city. As we approached the landing opposite, a salute of twenty-one guns was fired, and a shout of applause went up as we landed. This city of flowers was literally bedecked with flags, banners, and garlands. The people were dressed in holiday attire and smiles. Bright carpets were spread for us to walk upon.

I am afraid you will pronounce me superstitious, but I must tell you of another dream I had. I had not received a letter from Lieutenant Grant for a month, and I suppose felt troubled about this, as he never missed sending me a letter by each mail out of Mexico. I dreamed the Monday morning paper was handed me and there the second name in the D's in the list of advertised letters was Julia Dent-2. I was leaning out of the window when the paper was handed to Sister Nell, who had just gone to the front door. I called down to her not to open the paper until I told her my dream, that she must look at the second name in the D's in the list of advertised letters and see if it was Julia Dent-2; and sure enough, there it was, and I lost no time in sending for those two very nice letters.

Of course, I was enchanted when the war with Mexico was over and I was expecting Lieutenant Grant home. He came within a week or ten days after the arrival of his regiment at Pascagoula, Miss. He remained at the Planters' House, St. Louis, for ten days, visiting me daily and all day long. My father's family did not go out to the farm that summer. I do not know why, but I know we young ladies did not care to go, as we always found it more pleasant in the city. Mr. Grant came late in July and urged that an early day be appointed for our wedding. He had to go home, he said, "and would be back by the 15th or 20th of August." So the 22nd was the day appointed for our marriage.

I had had four years in which to prepare for this event and therefore required only a week or so to make the few last arrangements. I decided, as it was midsummer, to wear an India mull muslin such as was worn by my mother on her wedding day some thirty years before. Just as we had arrived at this decision, who should appear but my good angel and kind friend, Mrs. O'Fallon, with her footman, Charles, bearing in his arms a large white box, which he placed on the drawing room table. My friend met mamma, Nell, and me, asking, "Am I too late? Have you your wedding dress yet?" and being answered in the negative, she said: "I am so glad, for I have brought you a beautiful one, and I hope you will accept it with as much pleasure as I have in bringing it to you, Julia." [27]

This was a beautiful present, a magnificent, rich, soft, white, watered silk. It was so lovely! The veil also this kind old friend of ours brought me. It was white tulle with lovely wide fringe. This floated around my head and enveloped me in its fleecy folds. My dear old friend, Mrs. Judge Shurlds,[28] brought me, in a moss-lined basket, a lovely corsage bouquet of white cape jessamines, also a number to fasten my veil with. I was quite satisfied with this simple but rich dress; as a whole, it could not, I think, have been improved. Mrs. Shurlds told me she had been nursing the jessamines for two weeks for me and was so fortunate in having a sufficient number bloom in time to serve for my wedding dress.

My wedding was necessarily a simple one. The season was unfavorable for a large gathering, and our temporary home in St. Louis was small. We were married about eight o'clock, and received during the evening all of our *old* friends in the city. It is not necessary to say who these friends were. A table was set at the end of the back parlor upon which were served ices, fruits, and all that papa's hospitality and good taste could suggest for the occasion. My wedding cake, I was assured, was a marvel of beauty. We had music, and I think two of my gay bridesmaids took a turn around the room, saying they could not resist waltzing just a round or two. I am sure that the miraculous accounts written of my wedding in some of the papers many years afterwards were obtained from persons who were not guests. My bridesmaids were my sister Nellie Dent, Sarah Walker,[29] and my cousin Julia [Boggs]. Lieutenant Grant's groomsmen were Lieutenant Cadmus Wilcox, Bernard Pratte of St. Louis, and Sid Smith.[30] The first two surrendered to General Grant at Appomattox; the latter (Sidney Smith) was an Adonis and was almost idolized by the society young ladies at that time.

The day following our wedding, Mr. Grant and I started on a visit to his friends in Ohio. This was my first visit away from St. Louis and my first trip on a boat. How I marveled at this great creature, as I felt it to be, gliding so swiftly along and obeying the slightest motion of the hand in the pilothouse. It seemed to me almost human in its breathing, panting, and obedience to man's will. I was really greatly impressed with the power of man when I realized what he had accomplished in this great boat; and then the canal and locks around the rapids at Louisville were wonderful to me. Then I enjoyed sitting alone with Ulys. This was very, very pleasant. He asked me to sing to him, something low and sweet, and I did as he requested. I do not remember any of the passengers on that trip. It was like a dream to me and always pleasant.

At Louisville we visited cousins of Lieutenant Grant, Mr. Solomon Grant[31] and his charming family—Cousin Lizzie I remember very pleasantly. She accompanied us to Ohio and made a visit to father Grant's. We also visited another cousin of Mr. Grant's, Mr. Hewitt's family.[32] They lived a few miles in the country at a beautiful countryseat. They entertained us very handsomely; they lived a few miles up the Ohio River from Louisville. The approach to their beautiful residence was through broad meadows until we reached the hills covered with a fine old forest. Winding through this forest and up the hills, we reached their lovely villa, where we were most kindly received.

This house was filled with everything beautiful, suited to the wealth and cultivated tastes of our host and hostess. I remember too that my dear husband intimated very modestly that if he saw any chance for a business opening he would be glad to resign, and although these gentlemen had large business connections at New Orleans, New York, Liverpool, and, I think, Paris, not one of them offered even to introduce him to any businessman. I always remembered this, and did not forget it when my Lieutenant was General-in-Chief nor when he was President of the United States. How these same friends petitioned for favors, and how I chafed at being *compelled* to accept the hospitality of a member of the family at New Orleans on our return from Mexico. It made me ill. I spent nearly all of the time in bed while there.

We had a lovely sail up the Ohio, leaving Louisville about eleven A.M. and reaching Cincinnati the next morning. When I came out into the cabin of our steamer, there stood my dear husband's little brother Orvil with his flaxen curls and blue eyes—as pretty a boy as I ever saw. He had come all the way down to meet us, saying he could not wait for us. I think we took the stage up to Bethel, Ohio. I remember the nice dinner or luncheon we had on the road.

At last we arrived at my husband's home. As we approached the house, I must confess I was beginning to feel nervous, or rather anxious, but their cordial welcome soon calmed me, and I felt quite happy with this truly interesting family, which I so hoped would like me and take me to their hearts. Grandmama Simpson, the Captain's grandmother,[33] was of the party, having come up purposely from the country to meet Ulysses and his bride. She was quite tall and robust, quite my ideal of a Revolutionary mother. She was dressed in a rich, dark-brown, Irish poplin, a snowy muslin kerchief about her shoulders, and a soft white muslin cap with wide, white, muslin ties forming a soft bow under her chin. This old lady was sweet and lovely to me then and always. The Captain's father met me cordially, I might say affectionately, and his voice was low and pleasant. He was much taller than his son. Mrs. Grant, the Captain's mother, was then a handsome woman, a little below medium height, with soft brown eyes, glossy brown hair, and her cheek was like a rose in the snow. She too gave me an affectionate welcome, and I must say right here she was the most self-sacrificing, the sweetest, kindest woman I ever met, except my own dear mother. Clara, the Captain's eldest sister, was pleasant and kind also. Next came Jennie, the Captain's favorite sister, with her golden hair and dark dove-like eyes. Her complexion was exquisitely fair with just a tinge of pink, and this sweet girl was as good as she was beautiful. I say everything when I say that she was like her mother. Orvil was a handsome boy of about eleven years old, with blue eyes and light curly hair. I saw him but seldom except at table, when he was quiet and shy. Mary, the youngest child, was about eight or nine, and gave promise of great beauty. She had gray eyes and a brilliant complexion. Her vocabulary was even then a marvel to me. She never by any chance used any but the most elegant words to express her childlike thoughts. Altogether, I was well satisfied with my dear husband's family.

I enjoyed greatly riding about and visiting Captain Grant's family and relatives on both his father's and mother's side. We spent three months on this trip and visited friends of my husband in Cincinnati, Georgetown, Maysville, and Bethel. We saw these places through magic glasses, and it would require the pen of a poet to describe them

[57]

as I remember them. The rides were charming over those great forest-clad hills and through the valleys so cool and shadowy. Ulys always preferred to take me in a buggy with a fleet little steed to draw us. We let his sisters go in the diligence.[34] Some of the homes we visited were humble, some were not. All were charmingly hospitable and pleasant. Mr. Grant was much pleased that I liked his family and his Ohio friends.

We returned home about the middle of October, when my struggle at parting with my father began. My heart was well-nigh broken when the time approached to say farewell. This parting, I felt, was to sever my bonds with home. My first journey with Ulys was only a short one of two or three months and I knew I was to return again, but now I was to leave my dear home and make one among strangers— and then parting with papa! I could not, could not, think of it without bursting into a flood of tears and weeping and sobbing as if my heart would break. This disturbed my husband greatly, as he did not know what to do for me and was very unhappy seeing my distress. The week before we were to leave, papa came into the sitting room where Ulys and I were. Ulys was telling me how troubled he was, and that for four years he had been anticipating how pleasant it would be for us to spend our days together, and here at the end of the first two months I was relenting. My father said: "Grant, I can arrange it all for you. You join your regiment and leave Julia with us. You can get a leave of absence once or twice a year and run on here and spend a week or two with us. I always knew she could not live in the army."

Ulys's arm was around me, and he bent his head and whispered: "Would you like this, Julia? Would you like to remain with your father and let me go alone?" "No, no, no, Ulys. I could not, would not, think of that for a moment." "Then," he said, "dry your tears and do not weep again. It makes me unhappy."

There was never again a word said about my staying at home. Papa broke the link that bound me by this unparalleled proposition for my husband to leave me and come occasionally to see me. But my home, my dear home, was sweet to me. I have never met with one like it, so bright, so kind, always, always. Home! dear home! Truly, "There is no place like home."

We left St. Louis late in November to join the Fourth Infantry stationed along the lakes. Our station being Detroit, Michigan, we went by Cincinnati and took advantage of our proximity to Bethel to again visit our friends there. The ride up was delightful; it was moonlight, cool and fresh, and as our fleet steed went flying over the hills and dales, striking stars at every fall of his steel-clad hoofs, how merry we were, I gaily singing as everyone had long since gone to dreamland and I knew my only listener was a partial critic. After a very pleasant visit to our friends in Bethel, and having prevailed upon the Lieutenant's sister Miss Clara to come with us to Detroit for the winter, we left home again and traveled all the way from Cincinnati on the railroad. This to me was more wonderful even than the magic boat. I was rather frightened though at the mob of porters that met us at the stopping places and, I must say, felt considerable anxiety for my baggage. The arrangements were not so perfect then as now. Indeed, nowhere on the globe can one travel as comfortably and as free from care as right here at home.

When we arrived at Detroit at the expiration of my husband's leave of absence, we found, greatly to our indignation and chagrin, that our kind old Colonel had been prevailed upon to retain Lieutenant [Henry D.] Wallen at headquarters and to order Lieutenant Grant to Sackets Harbor. My husband remonstrated, telling the Colonel that he (Lieutenant Grant) was regimental quartermaster and his station was at headquarters. The Colonel said, "Yes, yes, I know, I know. I will send you your orders to proceed to Sackets Harbor at your earliest convenience." Lieutenant Grant replied, "I will, of course, obey your orders, Colonel [William] Whistler, but you must know I will make a remonstrance at once to Washington."

We had a long, fatiguing, and expensive trip to Sackets Harbor, as navigation was closed and we had to hire any conveyance we could to reach this far-off and out-of-the-way place. Lieutenant Grant made a most emphatic remonstrance, and just as we had concluded that it would be very pleasant at Sackets Harbor for the winter, we received orders from Washington to return to Detroit.[35] As navigation was now closed entirely, Lieutenant Grant asked permission to remain where we were until the opening of navigation. This permission was readily granted at Washington.[36] We had a lovely winter, made many friends, and when we left for Detroit by the first boat in the spring, I really shed tears at parting with them.

Our first dinner after we went to housekeeping at Madison Barracks [Sackets Harbor] was on Sunday, and just as we returned from church Ulys said: "When will dinner be ready? I have asked two or three officers in to dine with us." Imagine my consternation! "Why, Ulys, how could you ask them? How do we know that our cook can cook?" He looked surprised and said: "All cooks know how to cook, don't they?" "Why, no indeed! and what shall we do?" I asked him to go over and tell them not to come until we had tried our cook, and he did so. He told me afterwards that the gentlemen invited had no dinner that day. Our dinner was a success, and I regretted I had not allowed them to come, as it had the charm of being our first dinner in addition to its quality. All of these young gentlemen were invited for the next day and took much pleasure in teasing me. They knocked timidly at the door, opened it just a little, and asked if everything was all right and if they could really come.

Ulys always liked company and I enjoyed it with him. I have always had the reputation of being an extra good housekeeper and am sorry to confess that I nearly bankrupted my dear husband the first few years of our married life by my experiments in this direction. We had such fine old servants at home that I was under the impression that the house kept itself. We had a good supply of servants. One made the preserves, pickles, and jellies. One cooked dinner, and another supper and breakfast. And I do not think mamma was very thorough either. She required everything to be scrupulously neat, and beyond that I do not believe she cared. She used to go to the kitchen, when she was well enough, at about eleven o'clock to inspect. She would then go to the larder and give out all necessary for the day. When I first took the responsibility of a house on my then small shoulders, I tried to direct the making of many dishes we had at home, but they did not look like those at home, and I gradually allowed the cook to have her own way. I did know how to make a delicious cake and made one once a week at Madison Barracks, and it was always the occasion of a little party. I made some nice currant and quince jelly while at the farm in Missouri long after this. I remember how embarrassed I was at the Executive Mansion. Just before the Centennial Exposition some ladies wanted to get up a cookbook and wrote to me for an original recipe. I did not know what to do. The cake I had obtained from a cookbook and the jelly I had considerable help with, and I was forced to ask the advice of a friend, who advised me to tell these ladies that I did not have an original recipe, did not know much about these matters, and had always depended on my cook. I did send them a recipe for making chicken gumbo given me by my friend, Mrs. General B[eale?], whose table had always the very best of everything, but I never saw it in the book. In fact, I do not think I ever saw the book. If it is there, the honor belongs to my friend.

Soon after we were settled in our house at Madison Barracks, I requested my husband to give me a regular allowance—just what he thought he could afford to give me for housekeeping expenses, feeling that this plan would be the most satisfactory in the future. It would save me the trouble of reminding him, or of asking for it, and give me the privilege of using our *little* to the best advantage. Besides, I had a horror of bills, which in those days were only sent in every three or six months—when, of course, all bills necessarily seemed enormous. I had more than once seen a really loving, good, and devoted wife with her cheeks crimsoned with distress and shame and her eyes full of tears when the bills came in, her usually most generous and kind husband declaring the bills were *too* large and feeling quite injured at the extravagance of his very careful wife. I did not intend to have any such scenes in our dovecote. No, indeed! The Captain readily agreed to this commonsense plan, made me a most liberal allowance for his limited means, and always brought it to me with seeming great pleasure. I never once had to ask for this. I felt now that I had assumed a very great responsibility and at once procured a small blank book in which to keep my accounts. This was an undertaking for me, for, to tell the truth, my little book never, no never, added up quite right. I never was very good at arithmetic, and there was *such* a variety of little items. It was quite impossible for such a novice as I to make it come out right. Sometimes I had too great a balance and sometimes not enough. I sometimes appealed to my husband for help, but he would only offer to make up the deficit, which I would not at all accept. He would say with a smile, "I cannot make out your mathematical conundrums. Do not bother any more. Come and let us have a ride." To this day I keep my account book and with the same result: it hardly ever comes right. I suppose I forget to note everything, but it is a satisfaction to me.

I must say just a word as to my pretty table appointments. I had some very pretty silver given me both by the Captain's family and my own, and a very pretty set of china decorated with gay flowers. (I have some of the same now, Dresden.) These were my especial joy, and my table was simply delightful with the beautiful china and the handsome tea and coffee set of Sheffield plate. Our pretty silver spoons and forks and all were so bright and new. The carpets were bright and beautiful, soft and warm, and their selection was the occasion of more than one happy, gay ride up to Watertown behind the Captain's fleet steed. The curtains for my two or three rooms I brought from my home. They were a dark, rich crimson of some soft woolen material and *very* pretty over ivory-tinted embroidered muslin, and with the pretty little trinkets and souvenirs I brought from my dear home made our rooms look very pleasant indeed.

We were very happy at Madison Barracks. The officers all seemed to think a great deal of Captain Grant and when they visited us would say, as they looked around our pretty quarters: "Grant, you look so happy, so comfortable here, that we are all almost tempted to get married ourselves." These gentlemen were always so very attentive and kind to me, any one of them *ready* and *willing* to escort me if the Captain happened to be officer of the day. I remember once Captain [Thomas R.] McConnell bringing me a jar of preserved limes all the way from his home in Georgia. The jar was like the ones mamma used to get her preserved ginger in, with a basket frame and handles. He told me he carried this in his hand all the way as one would a pet bird. He said that I ought to prize these preserves very highly, for not only he but *everybody* in the stage had *helped* to care for that jar of limes on the whole route from Georgia to Madison Barracks, Sackets Harbor in New York.

NOTES

1. Prominent residents of Pittsburgh at the time Frederick Dent lived there included Presley Neville, a wealthy landowner and merchant, who had served as aide to General Lafayette in the American Revolution; James O'Hara, quartermaster of the U.S. Army during the Whiskey Rebellion, who prospered in salt manufacturing and by establishing a glassworks; William Wilkins, prominent attorney and bank president, later U.S. Senator and Secretary of War; William Robinson, a leading merchant and later a railroad president; and Ebenezer Denny, first mayor of Pittsburgh.

2. William Clark, of the Lewis and Clark expedition, Governor of Missouri Territory 1813–20, lived in St. Louis until his death in 1838. In 1820, as candidate for first Governor of the state of Missouri, Clark was defeated by Alexander McNair, register of the St. Louis land office.

3. John F. Long, who began to teach at Gravois school in 1836, later a farmer and neighbor of the Dents, eventually became a close friend to both Grants. A reminiscent interview with Long appeared in the *Missouri Republican*, July 24, 1885.

4. P. Mauro and his daughters, the Misses Mauro, operated an Academy for Young Ladies at Fifth and Market streets, St. Louis. The course of study was advertised *ibid.*, July 2, 1838.

5. John A. McClernand, Illinois Democratic politician and Civil War general, Grant's rival for command of the expedition against Vicksburg, married Sarah Dunlap of Jacksonville on November 7, 1843.

6. On April 28, 1785, George Dent married Susannah Dawson Cromwell, widow of Joseph Cromwell, then settled in Cumberland, Maryland. Harry Wright Newman, *The Maryland Dents* (Richmond, 1963), p. 70. Perhaps the Dents had ties to the prominent Marbury family of Maryland, since Frederick Dent named his youngest daughter Emily Marbury. At any rate, the genealogy cited above contradicts many details given by Julia Grant of her family background. A privately printed genealogy, based partly on family tradition, states that George Dent "married Susan Dawson, and afterwards a Marbury (Cromwell)." [Gustave Anjou], *The Dent Family* (n.p., n.d. [ca. 1906]), p. 26.

7. For amplification of Julia Grant's maternal background, see Josiah H. Shinn, "John Wrenshall, Julia Dent and Ulysses S. Grant," *New York Genealogical and Biographical Record*, 34 (April, 1903), 97–98; Kenneth Dann Magruder, "Methodism's Struggle for a Permanent Foothold in Pittsburgh," *Western Pennsylvania Historical Magazine*, 23 (September, 1940), 156–62.

8. Edward Tracy of New York, a merchant, began business in St. Louis in association with the firm of Dent & Rearick.

9. St. Louis histories mention Frederick Dent's partnership with George W. Rearick, but record no connection with the prosperous merchant Peter Lindell, whose partners were his brothers, John and Jesse G. Lindell.

10. Colonel Elias Rector, postmaster of St. Louis; Captain Stephen Hempstead, Sr., father of a large family active in St. Louis affairs including the first Missouri delegate to the U.S. Congress, Edward Hempstead; and Antoine Chenie, a prominent merchant and proprietor of the first bakery in St. Louis.

11. John Fielding, a Methodist minister formerly at Madison College, Uniontown, Pennsylvania, and Augusta College, Augusta, Kentucky, was married to Julia Dent's aunt, Sarah Wrenshall.

12. Probably Andrew Monroe, a prominent Methodist minister.

13. Homer, *The Odyssey*, 3. 621–22.

14. Charles A. Page of Louisville, Kentucky, son of Samuel K. Page and Julia Dent's aunt, Emily Wrenshall Page.

15. John O'Fallon, born near Louisville, Kentucky, in 1791, served in the U.S. Army during the War of 1812, holding no rank higher than captain, but was commonly called "colonel" in St. Louis. A wealthy St. Louis businessman and civic leader, his second wife was a cousin of Frederick Dent. Caroline O'Fallon, their daughter, became a close friend of Julia Dent.

16. The last wife of General William H. Ashley, who had married three times, was the widow of Dr. Wilcox. Widowed again, she married Senator John J. Crittenden of Kentucky. Her daughter, Miss Wilcox, married Andrew McKinley, son of U.S. Supreme Court Justice John McKinley.

17. Frances Wash, daughter of Robert Wash, justice of the supreme court of Missouri. After the death of his first wife, the mother of Frances, Wash married Eliza L. Taylor, daughter of Colonel Nathaniel P. Taylor.

18. Probably Major Richard Bland Lee, Jr. (first cousin of Robert E. Lee), then commissary officer at St. Louis.

19. John Brady Smith, born in Kentucky in 1798, president of the Bank of Missouri (1837–42).

20. James Longstreet, later a Confederate general, was a cousin of Julia Dent. The other young officers included Charles T. Baker, Sidney Smith, Charles Hoskins, George Sykes, and Richard B. Garnett. Smith and Hoskins were killed in the Mexican War; Sykes served as a general in the U.S. Army during the Civil War; Garnett died at Gettysburg as a Confederate general.

21. Robert Hazlitt of Ohio, Grant's close friend, was killed in the Mexican War.

22. Julia Grant gave a more detailed account of the marriage proposal to a journalist in 1890. Foster Coates, "The Courtship of General Grant," *Ladies' Home Journal*, VII (October, 1890), 4.

23. In a letter of October, 1845, Grant wrote to Julia Dent that he had an offer of a professorship in mathematics at a college in Hillsboro, Ohio. John Y. Simon, ed.,

The Papers of Ulysses S. Grant (Carbondale and Edwardsville, Illinois, 1967–), 1, 59.

24. See *ibid.*, p. 84.
25. The telegraph connection between Washington and Baltimore, the first in the country, had been completed in May, 1844.
26. Title and first line of a poem by Edward Robert Bulwer-Lytton.
27. In 1898, when Caroline O'Fallon died, Julia Grant wrote to John J. O'Fallon, Jr. "Your mother, Caroline O'Fallon, was the beautiful angel of my childhood; so many acts of kindness, so many kind words of hers fill my heart's memory. Do you know your dear mother brought me my beautiful wedding gown? and with such sweet, kind words—they still linger with me." *Missouri Historical Society Bulletin*, XXVIII (July, 1972), 285.
28. Jane Shurlds was married to Henry Shurlds, a prominent attorney, former Missouri secretary of state and public auditor, then cashier of the state bank. Her daughter, Mary Isabella, had married George Wrenshall Dent, brother of Julia Dent. Another daughter, Anna Amanda, later married John Dent, brother of Julia Dent.
29. In letters from Mexico, Grant twice mentioned Julia Dent's friend Sarah Walker. Grant, *Papers*, 1, 82, 118.
30. Second Lieutenant Cadmus M. Wilcox, later a prominent Confederate general, was a close friend of Grant. Bernard Pratte III was the son of a former mayor of St. Louis. Julia Grant is in error concerning Sidney Smith, who had been killed in the Mexican War. James Longstreet may have been the third groomsman. Ishbel Ross, *The General's Wife: The Life of Mrs. Ulysses S. Grant* (New York, 1959), p. 48.
31. Solomon K. Grant, nephew of Jesse Root Grant, married Elizabeth Thornton in 1837.
32. Clarice Grant, sister of Solomon Grant, married James Hewitt, who was a business partner of her father, Peter Grant, Jesse Root Grant's wealthy half-brother. At least two of the Hewitt sons later served in the Confederate Army, and Julia Grant discusses one of them in Chapter 4.
33. Sarah Hare Simpson Grant's grandmother, the second wife of John Simpson, was the stepmother of Hannah Grant, whose mother died before the family left Pennsylvania.
34. A public stagecoach.
35. Two letters from Grant of February, 1849, protesting his assignment to Sackets Harbor, New York, are in Grant, *Papers*, 1, 173–77.
36. See *ibid.*, p. 181.

Chapter 2

W E RETURNED in the early spring to Detroit, I going on home to St. Louis for a short visit. Ulys, during my absence, secured a sweet, pretty house which had been occupied by Quartermaster [Ebenezer S.] Sibley for several years, a man both of wealth and good taste, and who knew how to enjoy both comfort and elegance. It is true, as a late chronicler says, our pretty house was of wood. But at that time there was no other kind of house in Detroit. Senator [Lewis] Cass and, in fact, everyone we knew lived in wooden houses. I can recall but a few exceptions: Mr. Z[achariah] Chandler, then a merchant and afterwards U. S. Senator, lived in a pretty little brick house—also General [Hugh] Brady and Colonel Whistler. I was not long at home until my husband came on for me. We returned by way of the Illinois River and crossed from La Salle, Ill., to Detroit by canalboat. This was another novel experience for me and very delightful. We sat on the deck in comfortable chairs and looked out all day long on the broad, beautiful prairies, decked in bright flowers. I remember that Colonel and Mrs. [William] Turnbull of Washington, D. C., and Captain [Robert E.] Clary, with his wife and two charming daughters, made this same trip with us. It was a pleasure to meet these same people long afterwards at the capital.

When we arrived at our house, everything was in readiness. Some friend had secured a nice house girl for us, and we had the boy (Gregorio) Ulys had brought from Mexico as a valet to attend the table and door. Gregorio did not remain with us quite a year, some meddlesome person prevailing upon him that he could do better for himself. He was a nice, cheerful boy until this was put in his head, and then he became sullen. So the Captain told him he was at liberty to go. The boy did say he was willing to stay until the Captain was satisfied for his passage from Mexico and for his clothes and schooling. The Captain said he was entirely satisfied and that he should go.

Our house was very snug and convenient: two sitting rooms, dining room, bedroom, and kitchen all on the first floor. This last was so convenient for me to make my culinary experiments. The grounds were quite large, extending around the house on all sides, and at the back was a nice carriage house and stable for Nellie Bly, the Captain's pretty, fleet, little mare of which he was so fond and so proud. I must not forget the arbor of delicious grapes extending from the front door quite around and down past the dining room windows. We not only had grapes enough for ourselves, but plenty for all our army friends.

We made many friends, or acquaintances rather, in our new home. Let me see: there was dear old General Brady, Mr. and Mrs. Backus (the General's daughter), Preston Brady, the Casses, the Norvells, the Kerchevals, and the Wilkinses (who were old friends of my parents from Pittsburgh). Senator Lewis Cass was also an old friend of my father when at Chillicothe, Ohio, as was Mr. Norvell, and he and I had many mutual friends. The Trowbridges, the Stewarts, pretty Mrs. Brush, the Campaus, and a hundred others I remember as being so kind and polite to us.[1]

Our station at Detroit is one pleasant memory: the pleasant people we met, the gay parties and dinners, the fêtes champêtres, the delightful boat rides on the gallant Captain Willoughby's magnificent lake steamer. And then Ulys used to go fishing, and what sport for him, and how we enjoyed the result of his day's sport. I made many experiments in the culinary art now. We often had company in an informal way. Our stay at Detroit was most pleasant in the spring and summer, but I was not very well, and Dr. [Charles S.] Tripler thought I had better go to St. Louis. The day before I left, all the friends I knew called to say goodbye. I was quite worn out with this company, and as I bade one of the young officers adieu, quite late in the afternoon, he said: "You must not stay long, Mrs. Grant, we will miss you." I was very tired and nervous and broke into a flood of tears, almost sobs, when the young gentleman said: "Oh! Madam, I will see you on the boat." When I told the Captain this he was amused and, I think, a little annoyed, and said: "He is vain enough to think it was his adieux that caused the tears."

I arrived safely at St. Louis, at my dear home, and how glad they all were to see me. For some time past I had been making preparation for a very welcome addition to our small family. Such dainty, soft, pretty, and fairy-like little articles were made with a loving heart by my deft fingers. I am sure no loving wife ever made prettier than those made for our boy Fred, who was born at St. Louis, Mo., May 30, 1850. And no one, we thought, ever had such a fine, great boy. How often we wondered what the baby was thinking about as he would open his great eyes and look around in such wonder and surprise, and all the time so serious. We were very fond of this baby and proud of him too.

He was called for my father, Frederick Dent, who was very proud of his little grandson and namesake, and during the presence of some Kentucky friends he did not hesitate to predict, one day when the baby was brought out on exhibition, that some day that boy would be a great general, and Colonel Scott exclaimed: "I predict he will one day be President of the United States; he looks grand enough." All the time this was being said, my baby boy was looking wonderingly around from one to another, clasping and unclasping his pretty, dimpled hands, until at length, seeing me, he broke into a smile and stretched out his little arms to his mamma. Ulys came to St. Louis for his family and took us back to Detroit, where we remained until next May.

That winter we messed with Major [John H.] Gore. This arrangement was much more economical as there was but one house and one set of servants to be kept instead of two. Of course, each gentleman kept his own horse and carriage, and we ladies each our own nurse. Otherwise the expenses were divided, and we lived very happily together. The Captain and Major Gore both were members of several clubs, and each member had to give a dinner or supper to each club during the winter. Several had already been enjoyed when Mrs. Gore and I playfully protested, saying, "You gentlemen are having more than your share of pleasure." They at once proposed that we ladies give a ball. We were delighted, and they told us to write out a form of invitation, make a list of the guests we wished invited (and send to the barracks), and that they would have the invitations written and sent out for us. Just before they were sent up to the barracks, Mrs. Gore said to me: "Do you not think it would be charming to have a fancy dress ball?" Of course I was delighted with the idea, and without any reflection ("Fancy Dress") was added to our pretty little invitations. If one could only imagine the excitement these little billets created in Detroit. Everyone began to study costumes, ladies and gentlemen alike.

Shopping was the occupation of the day. Dressmakers became more important than the Colonel himself. Of course, Mrs. Gore and I were

[67]

very much interested as to what we should wear—so much so that on the morning of the ball Major Gore asked where we would have our refreshments set. Then we were reminded that we had not thought about refreshments, but had only sent out our invitation cards; what should we do? The Major and Ulys went to a hotel and ordered a handsome supper sent down and served for us.

Another incident that marred our happiness occurred the Sabbath before the ball. The ministers of the Catholic and Presbyterian churches spoke of the frivolity and sin of such an entertainment and requested their members not to attend. This was entirely unlooked for. We only wished to give pleasure and did not for a moment think of any impropriety and could not see that there would be any. At St. Louis, our Catholic friends were our gayest ones. Our friends who attended those churches did not come to the ball, but many of them assembled on the piazza, which we had covered in and lighted so as to increase our accommodations on this occasion. Of course, I was greatly distressed to find that our kindest intentions were looked upon as radically wrong.

Well, how well, I remember that gay night: the Sultana of Turkey (Mrs. Gore), the veiled prophet of Khorassan (Captain McConnell of Georgia). The Captain wore a turban of white gauze, a crescent made from a small mirror, and a veil of silver gauze. He borrowed from Bishop McC. a large round cushion, upon which he (the prophet) sat cross-legged. Pretty Mrs. Brush was a flower girl. She wore a black lace hat with field flowers, and how very handsome Mrs. Campau looked as a peasant girl. Pretty Miss Farnsworth was Red Riding Hood. There were one or two fortunetellers and a Scotch peasant. We had kings, knights, troubadours, and every other character pretty and gay. Gallant, handsome Dave Stewart was a troubadour. Ulys would not put on a costume but wore his uniform. Major Gore wore a handsome suit of velvet with slashed sleeves and a long, wavy, drooping plume in his hat, which I loaned him from my winter bonnet.

I, after much consideration, decided upon the costume of the ideal tambourine girl. I needed the warm, bright colors of such a costume. The dress was pretty, bright, and becoming. Ulys called me "Tambourina" for a long time afterwards. He was much pleased with my dress and selected the tambourine for me himself. I remember that after the guests were gone and the lights were nearly all out, Ulys, Major and Mrs. Gore, and I sat talking it all over, when I exclaimed: "I wish, I wish—" Ulys said: "What do you wish, little Tambourina?" "I wish the ball was for tomorrow night." The good, wise men were not far wrong; the bad effects were being felt already. Our ball was a great success. It gave much pleasure and was much talked about.

The winter was nearly over and the officers were expecting orders to move somewhere, so they concluded to take rooms at the new hotel, the Biddle House. The first of May, when we had to give up our houses, found the Biddle House not yet open. We and the Gores were invited to mess with Colonel [John B.] Grayson, who had a large house and his term of rental had not expired. When I say we messed together I mean we occupied the same house, shared the same table, and, of course, shared the expenses. A week after this pleasant arrangement was made, an order came from Washington scattering our little society far along the Great Lakes.

Colonel Whistler selected Sackets Harbor for headquarters. This was pleasant for Ulys and me, as we had not a few friends there. I went home from Detroit just to show how our boy had grown and to see my loved ones again. The Colonel and staff left for Madison Barracks a few days after I started for St. Louis.

I had a very happy summer at dear old White Haven. In September, Ulys wrote that I must come; that he was anxious to see his little son and, I *think* he said, *me* also.[2] He wrote me to telegraph him the day I left St. Louis and he would meet me at Detroit and we would stay over for a few days.[3] I telegraphed and on arriving at Detroit, let my nurse go at once to visit her family.

When I learned that Ulys had not arrived, I concluded at once to go on to Buffalo, where I surely would meet him; but no! he was not there. I was getting a little nervous and frightened and not a little fatigued, having had the entire care of my great boy, who had to be amused, dressed, and led by his mamma now, and she had been so thoughtless as to leave her nurse at Detroit. I determined to go on by rail to the end of my journey, and a friend escorted me to the train. That same night, at nine o'clock, my boy nestled on the seat beside me (we had no sleeping cars in those days), I felt very contented with the speed with which we were flying to meet the Captain, when all at once a very large man sprang up in his seat and yelled out in a wild manner. Imagine my terror on learning that this man was a maniac en route to an asylum. Of course, I stopped over at the next stopping place, which was Canandaigua. I remained over Sunday, and on Monday began anew my now wearisome journey.

I arrived at Watertown at about eight o'clock, took supper, ordered a carriage, and proceeded to Madison Barracks. To my great disappointment, I found the sally port closed. I called out, "Guard, Guard, Guard." The sentinel replied, "Who comes there?" I answered, "an officer's wife, Mrs. Grant." "Oh! Madam," and he at once opened the great gates, while another member of the guard ran off to inform the Captain, who came running out to meet us. The telegram arrived the next day by mail, and this caused me all of my anxiety and fatigue.

The Captain had our quarters all prettily fitted up. I remember a fine center table and two large fine chairs that were so high that when I sat in them my feet were quite a foot from the floor. This mistake was overcome by his having two pretty little stools made for my feet to rest upon when I sat in those chairs of state.

Our baby was soon a great boy, and being the only baby in garrison, he was, of course, a great pet, all his acts of prowess being heralded and canvassed throughout the garrison. He was often taken to the soldiers' mess room by the Captain's servant man and to the band room, and was permitted to look into the great brass trumpets. Soon, he took his turn at feats of agility with the young officers, such as jumping from the piazza. They all took great interest in measuring Fred's leaps and found he jumped his length every time (he could not well do less, he being then about two feet tall). How very pleasant to me is the memory of that winter in Madison Barracks. Our principal exercise was in rolling tenpins, at which I believe I was quite adept.

We used to take long rides over the frozen lake. We thought nothing of driving ten or twelve miles in our sleighs to a party at Brownsville or Watertown, where dwelt the charming families of Colonel Kirby, Major Brown, and the Bradleys. We would dance and play whist and, after a splendid supper, drive home with great glee.

Then we had our own parties. Once, when I went with Lieutenant R. in his cutter for a ride on the lake—his horse was a beautiful one with long flowing mane and tail—as we went flying along over the frozen lake surface and his mane floated out on the wind, I said: "I feel as though we were flying," and remarked that I had never seen such speed. As we dashed into the sally port and our horse stopped, panting at our door, Lieutenant R. told me that he had been unable to do anything but try to bring him around again to the barracks as he had been running away at full speed ever since we started. When I reproached him for not telling me, he said: "Well, I really thought you were enjoying the mad ride."

A visit to a maple sugar camp was a novel treat. We took our luncheon and all enjoyed it. Another pleasant reminiscence is a ride to Watertown in a mammoth sleigh, muffled to the eyes in buffalo robes, and drawn by six horses, all with bells. At length the ice on Lake Ontario broke, which was a matter of rejoicing to our little garrison.

The season progresses rapidly in this northern latitude, and we were soon sailing in our boats where we had so lately sped with horse and cutter. We were planning and anticipating a visit to the Thousand Islands, where we expected to camp out. The gentlemen expected great sport fishing and hunting; when lo! a knell, in the shape of an official order from Washington, came ordering the entire regiment to rendezvous at or near New York preparatory to sailing for California.

This order was unexpected and, I think, unwelcome to nearly all, but soon I began to think it would be most pleasant. I, in imagination, even drew vivid pictures of our course through the Caribbean Sea, parting its slashing, phosphorescent waves and sailing under the Southern Cross, seeing the bright and beautiful tropical foliage; and all this time, I was the only one of the party destined not to make the voyage. When we were almost ready to ship, my dear husband quietly and calmly told me that he had been all of this time thinking it over and he had come to the conclusion that it would be impossible for me to go with him in my condition (our second son, Ulysses, was born on the 22nd of July following). Of course, I was indignant at this and said I would go, I would, I would; for him to hush; that I should not listen to him; that he knew nothing whatever about the matter; and that I would go, etc., etc. And, of course, I shed tears. This he could not stand and begged me not to grieve about it, as the doctor and all advised that I should not go now. He said: "You know how loath I am to leave you, but crossing Panama is an undertaking for one in robust health; and then my salary is so small, how could you and my little boy have even the common necessaries of life out there; and there are two nice homes awaiting you; and when this crisis is over, if we have not sailed from New York, I will hasten to Ohio for you."

Ulys asked me to think it all over, and if on the morrow I felt as I then did, I should go with him anyway, as he could not bear to see my distress; that he thought it would be running a great risk, both of my life and that of our boy, but that he would not insist on my remaining at home if I still continued opposed to it. So I slept well and did conclude that it would be a great deal better to remain with our friends until this, the greatest of woman's ordeals, was over, but I expected, hoped, to yet accompany my dear husband to California. In this I was disappointed. He sailed July 5; my second son, Ulysses, was not born until July 22. My dear husband made every provision for my comfort and independence (this he always thought of), sending me more than I needed always. His letters were full of encouragement and affection for his loved ones.

I cannot refrain from making mention just here of a person who behaved in a most craven manner. It is rather strange, too, for the mother and sisters of this person were unusually refined and cultivated. It was really for their sake that the officers stationed at Madison Barracks elected him post storekeeper, and again induced Captain Grant and [Lewis C.] Hunt to commute their servant's transportation to California, to which they were entitled, to give it to this young man, thus not only securing transportation all the way to California (then a most expensive journey), but securing for him a first-class cabin passage with themselves. On arriving in San Francisco, this young man proposed starting at once in some business, a sort of general store (that is, every sort of thing). He asked Captain Grant to join him in this and help with any means he might have. The Captain gladly joined him, handing to him all of his pay that had accumulated since he left New York, and for a month or so everyone thought and was told that this fellow was coining a fortune, when suddenly the man said he was losing money in place of making any, though all this time there was no decrease of custom. This complaining went on until he one day told the Captain that he would feel better if he had the business all to himself; that he would not like to be the cause of any harm coming to the Captain. The Captain told him that if it would make him (the merchant) any happier, he would take what money he had put in (fifteen hundred dollars) and retire from the business entirely. So it was arranged, the man giving the Captain three notes of five hundred dollars each; he even after this prevailed upon the Captain to destroy these three notes before his own eyes, saying he could not sleep at nights about these notes for fear the Captain would come on him for the money when he did not have it to give him. How I chided Ulys when he told me this, telling him that the Vicar of Wakefield's Moses[4] was a financier beside him. He should have given him something to *make* him sleep: the poker. When I chided him thus, he said: "I believe you are right, for when I resigned and arrived in New York with but little means, I thought of this debtor who had returned to Sackets Harbor and I borrowed sufficient from a friend, Major Simon B. Buckner[5] (afterwards general and governor), to pay my expenses there, having notified C. of my coming and for what I was coming (the amount of his debt to me). On arriving at Sackets Harbor, to my dismay I found the fellow had gone on his yacht (he kept a yacht now) the day before, and no one knew when he would return." Ulys turned to me and said: "You know I had to wait in New York until I heard from you."[6]

I think just here is a good place for me to reply to an article I read in some western paper which relates most circumstantially the facts of

Captain U. S. Grant procuring through the quartermaster ([Robert] Allen, I think) transportation from California to New York.[7] General Grant has told me and more than once of how he had deposited about two thousand dollars with an acquaintance who was on leave of absence (or maybe temporarily suspended from his ship) and, trying like everyone else out there to turn an honest penny, had started a small banking business. The Captain told me of his depositing his little all with this man, *declining* the two per cent a month the bank offered, saying, "I wish this as a *special* deposit for *safekeeping until* I *want* it."

So when the Captain resigned and was on his way home, he called on S. for his money and was both surprised and disappointed when the banker told him that just then he could not pay it, but if the Captain could wait over for the next steamer, he would surely have it for him. And it was with much inconvenience the Captain did wait. He had to, as he had little other means, and besides wishing to bring his money home with him. He then went on a visit to my brother's at Knight's Ferry[8] for the two weeks between steamers. Returning to San Francisco the day before the steamer sailed, he again called on S. and was told the banker was out of the city; and so, I suppose, this is how it happened that Captain Grant had to depend on the quartermaster for transportation to New York.[9]

Upon making inquiry in regard to this statement, I learn that it was customary *then* for the steamship company, which was doing a great deal of carrying for the army, to give *all* officers on leave for home complimentary passes, the officers only paying for their meals en route and, perhaps, for passage across the Isthmus. *Surely* Captain Grant then was entitled to this privilege. The fact of the publishing of this incident just now, when General Grant's superb tomb is being dedicated [1897], grieves me deeply. And this same banker it was who, on the score of old friendship, was most persistent later in his demands for preferment.

Fred, baby Ulysses, and I remained at Bethel, Ohio, until the baby was about six weeks old, when I went with them to St. Louis, accompanied by Miss Jennie, my husband's sister. It was this summer my brother Fred was married and brought his really beautiful bride[10] home for a brief visit. We were greatly pleased with her. One morning, as Kitty, an old and favorite servant, and very handsome (a black Juno, I would call her, since I have seen the statuary of Europe), came in to bring water for their room, Fred (Captain Dent) inquired: "Well, Kitty, how do you like my little wife?" "Oh! Mars Frederick, she is lovely; she is a real white dove, and then too she seems to *similate* with my young ladies more than any other young lady I ever saw; and

I want now to wish you every happiness," and, with a curtsy, left the room, feeling much pleased with having had the privilege of expressing her approval in her best style and taking much pride in her selection of words.

It was a pleasant summer. A number of parties and receptions were given and attended by us with Captain Dent and his lovely bride. I must not forget to mention the pretty sylvan temple reared and dedicated to Terpsichore, where all the lads and lassies in our neighborhood (White Haven) assembled once a week to pay court to this happy goddess. How pretty the lassies were! Pretty Susie L., her flaxen hair and eyes of blue, gaily leading the Virginia Reel, followed by charming Kate and Eliza McK., and my sisters Emma and Nell. How pretty they were in their soft white muslins and wide straw hats decked with field flowers. They also danced these happy hours away.

I received letters by every returning mail from my dear husband. He was greatly pleased to learn that my trials were over, that our babe was a boy, and that I had given him his father's name, Ulysses, although my sisters insisted that he should be called Telemachus, facetiously telling me that I would yet have to call on this little Telemachus to find and bring back to me my wandering Ulysses. Friends calling would ask: "Where was the baby born—in Ohio?" When he was brought out, they would say: "He is a beauty if he *is* a buckeye." And others would ask to see my little buckeye boy until the family children gradually began to call my baby, who bore the classic and poetic name of Ulysses, "Buckie," and, as he grew older, "Buck." I call him by his name and try even now to correct others, but it is of no avail.

As Fred would soon be three years old, I felt anxious to see him in pantaloons and therefore arranged to change his entire costume. He was very proud, and we all were, of our little man. A gentleman bringing letters from Captain Grant was invited to dine with us, and he requested that Master Fred be allowed to dine with him. Fred was, of course, dressed in his trousers. He looked very pretty with his dimpled knees and shoulders—the children's arms and legs were bare in those days. He was seated between the gentleman from the Pacific Coast and myself. He took no notice of this gentleman, but gazed with a look of suprise at a young officer opposite to him, who happened to be dining with us that evening. He suddenly exclaimed: "Mamma, is that ugly man my papa?" Of course this caused some merriment at the officer's expense. Fred was quite pacified when told that it was his papa's friend he was to dine with, not his papa. Soon after he put on trousers, he put his little pudgy hands in his pockets and, stretching himself up as high as possible, said: "Mamma, do you think my papa is as large as I am?" Another time my little Ulysses, opening out his arms so as to make a great circle, exclaimed: "Mamma, I love you this much." Whereupon Fred, glancing up from his top which he was winding, said: "Mamma, I love you as much as the sky out in the country."

I used to give these dear boys lessons every day, asking them where they supposed the carpets, window glass, and the different articles of furniture came from; and they were much amazed to learn that the dark old wardrobe was once a towering walnut tree growing near the creek, that the old bookcase and escritoire were once great trees growing in the forests of Central America, that the clear glass in the windows and on the table was made from sand just like grandpa had Jim bring four miles for them to play in, and that their trousers, flannels, the warm blankets, and the soft carpets were all made from the fleece of the pretty white sheep and lambs. The little fellows learned with great pleasure all about these matters and pushed their questions sometimes beyond my patience and capacity too.

After an absence of over two years, Captain Grant, to my great delight, resigned his commission in the U. S. Army and returned to me, his loving little wife. How very happy this reunion was! one great boy by his knee, one curly-headed, blue-eyed Cupid on his lap, and his happy, proud wife nestled by his side. We cared for no other happiness.

I have been both indignant and grieved over the statement of pretended personal acquaintances of Captain Grant at this time to the effect that he was dejected, low-spirited, badly dressed, and even slovenly. Well, I am quite sure they did not know *my* Captain Grant, for he was always perfection, both in manner and person, a cheerful, self-reliant, earnest gentleman. His beautiful eyes, windows of his great soul; his mouth so tender, yet so firm. One must not deem me partial if I say General Grant was the very nicest and handsomest man I ever saw, and I have seen his great army of one million men, all brave, all handsome, gallant soldiers. May I confess right here and tell of how my loving heart swelled with pride and gratitude to know that my own beloved General was commander of this grand, victorious army?

Ulys always wished to farm, and as my father gave me about one hundred acres, he decided to become a farmer. Our home for the first two years was at Wish-ton-wish, a pretty villa erected by my brother Louis on a hill about one and a half miles south of White Haven in a magnificent forest of oaks. The Captain's farm lay about a mile north of our old home. This place, as well as Louis Dent's, was a part of the old farm. How happy I was at having my beloved one near me again, to have him hold my hand in his and feel his warm breath on my cheek.

We remained at my father's in Missouri for a few weeks, and after urgent and repeated invitations from the Captain's family in Kentucky, we left home to visit them. As we stepped from the boat onto the Kentucky shore, the sun (which had shone most gloriously all morning) was at that instant overcast, and a dark cloud overshadowed us as we stepped ashore. I remarked to Ulys: "I hope this is not ominous of our visit." He said: "Oh no! do not think so." There are no pleasant memories of that visit. After we had been there a few weeks, the Captain's father proposed that he, the Captain, should join his brother, S. Simpson Grant, in Galena and learn the business. My husband was much pleased with the proposition; but when it was suggested and made a necessary part of the agreement that I and my two little boys should remain in Kentucky with them, so as to have the benefit of their school of economy, or go to my father in Missouri, Captain Grant positively and indignantly refused his father's offer.

We returned immediately to St. Louis, where we had a pleasant winter. In the spring, we went up to Wish-ton-wish, which belonged to my brother Louis (Judge Louis Dent), but, as he was called back to California, he was delighted to have us occupy it. My daughter Nellie was born there on July 4, 1855. Mamma, papa, and my sisters called during the day to congratulate me and to bless my little pet. And all of the servants, young and old (through the kindness of black Mammy), sought a glimpse of the little fairy before she was a week old, the older ones saying, "Really, Miss Julia, we all think she is going to look like old Mistress" (meaning my mother), which they thought would make me very happy, paying this compliment to my little darling. The younger ones said, "We have all been calling on the good fairies to give her everything good—beauty, health, and wealth—and, Miss Julia, we ask she may be gentle and kind and beautiful like Mistress, her grandma."

The Captain insisted on naming the baby Julia. I always wanted her to be called after my mother, Ellen. The servants all addressed her as "Old Mistress," but when she was eighteen months old we had the three children christened, and Ulys voluntarily suggested that her name be changed to Ellen. My mother was very ill and died within a month of this. I regret now that I did not keep the name Julia for her. It is a soft, pretty name, and it was her father's choice. How selfish in me to eagerly seize his consent to the change in place of feeling gratified that he wished our little one called for me.

Ulys was really very successful at farming. His crops yielded well—that is, much better than papa's, but not as much as he anticipated from his calculations on paper—and I was a splendid farmer's wife. Ulys brought me all the new breeds of chickens: the Shanghais, the Brahmas, and the pretty little Bantams. The two little boys and I used to greatly enjoy throwing handfuls of wheat and other grain to this beautiful feathery portion of our family. Of course, each of these distinguished foreigners had appropriate names: for instance, my large, beautiful silver-gray, with her proud, haughty step, I called "Celeste" (from the Celestial Empire), and her lord, "The Great Mogul," and I remember how a magnificent domestic cock with gorgeous plumage used to lord it over these clumsy foreigners, with only size to boast of. I noticed the same little tricks of gallantry in these foreign birds that could be noticed in ours. For instance, they would pretend to find some choice tidbit and would call loudly for the poor, innocent hens to come and share it, and every time these lords of the barnyard were fooling them and would quickly eat it up themselves.

I must tell you of one instance which made me believe that chickens really understand the English language. Once after a heavy snow-storm, one of my women came in and asked if Jeff had not better put the chickens which were out in the chickenhouse, "as dem Chinese chickens did not know how to take care of themselves." Very soon, I was informed that one of my pullets could not stand on her feet. I at once went out to the hennery to examine for myself. After giving the necessary directions for the poor thing's relief, I told Phyllis to bring out a bowl of cornmeal mixed with water. She had hardly started when the old cocks on the roosts aloft passed the word by a softly murmured cackle to their numerous families, and at once they all descended and surrounded me, looking wistfully and expectantly up at me. Of course, they were sent to bed well fed and were never again neglected in stormy weather.

My chickens were marvelous in their yield. I never had the least trouble. As I would miss one after another and ask about them, my woman would say: "I reckon they are setting, Miss Julia." And sure enough, in proper time, all of these truants came strutting proudly up, with wings spread and a noisy cluck (expecting a hearty greeting and plenty of food, both of which they got), surrounded by a chirping downy brood of from fourteen to eighteen little chicks.

I churned once and but once. Having discharged the servant who attended to this, and Phyllis having reported that there was churning to be done that day, and as the person I had dismissed had made great trouble about churning, I felt rather startled at the announcement and

[77]

inquired of Phyllis if she understood churning. She replied: "No, ma'am, but anyone can churn butter." Sending her for the cookbook, I found explicit directions there, and seeing that my little maid followed exactly these directions, I took hold of the dasher (an old-fashioned up and down one), and bade her bring from the spring a bucket of cold water to cool the butter in. She, smiling, left me, saying, "I will not be gone ten minutes, Miss Julia, but you will be tired before I get back." She had not been gone her ten minutes when I saw her returning, bringing in her slender hands the bucket overflowing with its sparkling contents. All at once I felt the dasher grow heavy as lead. As the cookery book said you must on no account stop after having begun or all would be spoiled, I dared not stop, but called to Phyllis to come and see what was the matter; she came and lifting the lid from the churn, exclaimed: "Miss Julia, only see, surely! surely! the fairies have been here and helped you. I never, never saw anything so lovely. Why, the churn is full, yes, *full* of golden butter. I have not been gone ten minutes and the butter is here." I rested here on my laurels. This was my first and only trial at such work (my dear husband on all occasions furnishing me with the necessary *help* to do my work), and after this little incident I never could be persuaded that churning was a great labor.

Speaking of "fairies' visits," I have had more than one in my life. You will say I am superstitious, but once, soon after we had moved up to the new log house on the Captain's farm, I was feeling quite blue (which was rare with me), when a feeling of the deepest despondency like a black cloud fell around me, and I exclaimed (aloud, I think): "Is this my destiny? Is this my destiny? These crude, not to say rough, surroundings; to eat, to sleep, to wake again and again to the same—oh, sad is me!" All at once the dark shadow passed away and a silvery light came hovering over me, and something seemed to say, "No, no, *this* is not your destiny. Cheer up, be happy now, make the best of this. Up and be doing for your dear ones." That was my last dark visitor. I have never since lost my courage, not even in the dark day of that (what shall I call him?) [Ferdinand] Ward.[11] I knew that my dear ones were pure and true. I had no fear and did not lose my courage.

I must say a word of this, our cabin. I cannot imagine why the Captain ever built it, as we were then occupying Wish-ton-wish, a beautiful English villa belonging to my brother Louis Dent, and situated in a primeval forest of magnificent oaks. This house suited me in every way, but I suppose the Captain was tired of going so far to his farm and decided to build. He thought of a frame house, but my father most aggravatingly urged a log house, saying it would be warmer. So the great trees were felled and lay stripped of their boughs; then came the hewing which required much time and labor; then came the house-raising and a great luncheon. A neat frame house, I am sure, could have been put up in half the time and at less expense. We went to this house before it was finished and lived in it scarcely three months. It was so crude and so homely I did not like it at all, but I did not say so. I got out all my pretty covers, baskets, books, etc., and tried to make it look home-like and comfortable, but this was hard to do. The little house looked so unattractive that we facetiously decided to call it Hardscrabble.

My dear father used to often ride up to see me here. I remember one morning my cook met me in the hallway with a waiter filled with glasses of quince jelly, clear as amber. I took one up and, while holding it up to the light to better admire it, my father rode up and called out: "What is my Queen Bee doing today?" I held the glass higher and answered, "See, your Queen Bee is gathering honey for her little hive this winter." He informed me that the queen bee never gathered honey, so I felt that he did not intend to compliment me after all.

Speaking of a bee reminds me of another little incident which occurred about this time. One of our neighbors, who had a house full of little ones and who had lost his wife, invited all of his lady friends to come and spend the day and help his young people make up their pretty things. In fact, we were invited to a "bee" at this most hospitable gentleman's home. After waiting until half past ten A.M. for my two sisters, who had promised to call for me, I armed myself with my little gold thimble, the only one *then* in the neighborhood, and after a brisk walk of over a mile, much exhilarated and a little out of breath, made my apology for being so late, asked for something to do, and was much pleased when a sleeve for a flannel night-slip was handed me. After about an hour, my tongue having been as busy as my needle, and feeling quite sociable, supposing I had greeted everyone in the room, I handed my sleeve back and asked for the other, saying, with some pride, "I think I can make the entire slip today." Then a dear old lady, of whom I was very fond and had not seen on entering, spoke out and said: "Give me another pair of pantaloons; these are finished." Imagine my astonishment! Turning to her, I said: "My dear Mrs. M., are you here? When did you come? I have not seen you nor heard a word from you." She replied, with some stiffness: "I came at eight o'clock and 'tis true you have not heard me talking. I came here to sew, and I am one who can do but one thing at once and do it well." This was intended as a rebuke for me, whose tongue had been as busy as my needle, but I smiled and said: "If you admit that, my dear Mrs. M., we will be calling you an old fogy." The dear old lady never forgave this little speech. I think she thought *fogy* was a very bad word.

We were but three months in the log house, as we had moved from Wish-ton-wish late in September, and, as my mother died in the following January, father insisted that we should come to him at White Haven, as he was so lonely. My husband conducted his own farm and father's as well. Father was getting quite old and missed dear mamma deeply. We had been about a year and a half at White Haven when Captain Grant's father came to visit us. He then proposed that the Captain join him in his business, and *urged* it upon him. The Captain was then suffering from malaria and had chills and fever every other day, and our two older children were getting large enough to begin going to school. Hence he reluctantly consented to give up farming and go to Kentucky. I was bitterly opposed to this arrangement and felt no chagrin when, through the interference of Captain Grant's sisters, the plan was not carried out.

In anticipation of this move, we had sold our farm, horses, farming implements, and crops. The four slaves we kept. Captain Grant soon made arrangements to enter into partnership with Mr. [Harry] Boggs, a cousin of mine, who bought and sold real estate, negotiated loans, etc. I cannot imagine how my dear husband ever thought of going into such a business, as he never could collect a penny that was owed to him if his debtors, and he had several, only expressed regret and said: "Grant, I regret, more than you do, my inability to pay you." He always felt sorry for them and never pressed them again, saying: "I am sure they will send to me, knowing now, as they do, how much I need it, all they owe me as soon as they possibly can." We never heard from these *fine* debtors. On the contrary, they were persistent in their demands for favors later.

We went up to St. Louis early in April. The Captain went in March and secured a neat little house for us which was simply but comfortably furnished. I was joyous at the thought of not going to Kentucky, for the Captain's family, with the exception of his mother, did not like me, which may, perhaps, have been my own fault; but I always respected them and could have been fond of them, but we were brought up in different schools. They considered me unpardonably extravagant, and I considered them inexcusably the other way and may, unintentionally, have shown my feelings. Our little household was conducted on a simple scale. We had brought into the city with us the four servants my father had given me, but these were young, ranging from eighteen to twelve years of age. They were born at the old farm and were excellent, though so young.

A very amusing incident occurred soon after we went to the city (on the occasion of a visit from my father), when my two little boys began making inquiries about their house pets. Leo, a Newfoundland dog, who was claimed by Ulysses, was especially inquired for. Grandpa said: "Now that you are living in the city, what do you think of selling Leo to me?" At first the little fellow was grieved, but upon being told how much happier Leo would be in the country and that he could play with him just the same, Ulysses reluctantly consented. Father then asked him how much he would take for his dog, and the boy said, "ten dollars." "Oh! ask something in reason, young man," exclaimed grandpa. Ulysses then said "two dollars and a half," which grandpa counted out at once.

On the following morning, not having seen my two small boys since breakfast, and Johnny not calling as usual for his orders, I went out to inquire for them. What should I behold but at least seven dogs tied to the back fence, all howling and pulling back and barking in a most dismal manner. In answer to my question as to what in the world all these dogs were doing there, my little boys exclaimed with great glee: "Mamma, Johnny has caught every one of these dogs since breakfast, and we are going to sell them all to grandpa for two dollars and a half apiece." Of course, the unhappy captives were at once released, and the boys were not reproved for cutting up my laundress's new clothesline.

Within a week or two, we were comfortably settled in our very simple little home. My boys were attending the district school, but it was not long before I noticed that my dear husband was not as hopeful as at first, and after some three or four months he said to me: "I am sure your opinion of Mr. Boggs is correct. As you said, 'He makes his patrons' business a subject of conversation,' which, as you said, 'is improper.' There is also a sudden falling off of business generally. We have nothing to do and, as Boggs is not at all congenial to me, I have dissolved my business connections with him." I am sure there was no regret on my part at hearing this.

The Captain told me at this time that his name had been suggested for the appointment as city surveyor or engineer.[12] I did not feel hopeful even about this—though I did not tell him so—for then he told me he had met Bernard Farrar, an old and intimate friend of our family, and that when he mentioned this subject to him, Farrar only said: "We have to make a very decided stand against the opposition party." Captain Grant had voted, with all my family, the Democratic ticket at the last presidential election and this young man was a "Wide-Awake" or "Know-Nothing." [13] I drew my own conclusions and knew that if he intended to give his support to the Captain, he would have said so at once. This same person during the war remained in safety in St. Louis as provost marshal, persecuting defenseless women whose husbands had gone to fight for their cause. He even had the impudence to say to me that General Grant had surrendered to General Lee on such terms as those made at Appomattox. I will not repeat my reply to this would-be "American Robespierre."

The Democrats then appointed two more county judges who had the confirmation of these appointments, but the "Wide-Awakes" got ahead of the Democrats again. The Democrats, who had but one of the three judges at first, now appointed two more, one of them being a German from the lower part of the county. The "Wide-Awakes" at once took for their candidate, in opposition to the Captain, a German who could not speak our language and who had been in the country but a few months. Of course, the new German judge at once voted for his countryman, thus giving him three out of five votes in the county court.[14] I went out to meet the Captain as he returned from uptown and asked if he had any news. "Yes," he replied, "I am defeated." "Oh!" I said, "I expected that after our friends nominated a German; he, of course, would vote for his countryman. The *Germans* are loyal to each other."

That evening, Captain Grant sat reading in our little drawing room while our children were happily playing in the garden under a pink cloud of peach and apple blossoms, all unconscious of the anxiety that filled the hearts of their parents. Suddenly it occurred to me that the Captain ought to go to Kentucky to see his father, and I called to him from my room, telling him so. He replied: "I do not see that I can very well. It will cost something, and we have nothing to spare." I urged him, telling him his father had always been not only willing but anxious to serve him (in his own way, to be sure); besides, it would be pleasant for him to have a trip home, and I felt sure it would be best for him to go. After a little hesitation at leaving me with the children and servants, he decided to start the next day.

In less than a week, I received long and cheerful letters from my husband telling me how glad all at home were to see him and that his father was very anxious for him to go to Galena. So in two or three weeks we were packing our household effects for a journey north.[15]

We rented our pretty little home and hired out our four servants to persons whom we knew and who promised to be kind to them. Papa was not willing they should go with me to Galena, saying the place might not suit us after all, and if I took them they would, of course, be free, "and you know, sister, you cannot do without servants." There is not one word of truth in the statement made by a late chronicler of General Grant that he ever offered to sell one of these dear family servants of mine, nor in the statement that one of these girls was left with, or given to, Mr. Long for debt. Captain Grant did not owe Mr. Long or anyone else in Missouri anything when we left there or at any other time.[16] Eliza, Dan, Julia, and John belonged to me up to the time of President Lincoln's Emancipation Proclamation.[17] When I visited the General during the war, I nearly always had Julia with me as nurse. She came near being captured at Holly Springs.

Again in reference to Captain Grant's indebtedness, I remember whilst at the hotel in St. Louis, just after the war, a man—a blacksmith who lived on the road to the old farm—called, and the General, supposing he called to pay his respects, went to the parlor door to meet him, when the man presented a bill for (I think) about fourteen dollars. The General glanced at the bill, then sharply at the man (who became greatly embarrassed), and said: "Why, I paid you my bill when I left here." The man said: "No, General." The General replied: "I am sure I did, but I will give you the benefit of the doubt and pay you again."

Again, another time, this same man had the impudence to come with the same bill, and the General paid it, saying: "You have run this about long enough." But the General lost all patience when he came the third time, and said: "I have once paid this bill and twice I have given you the money because I thought you needed it, but this is impertinence. Now be off with you and do not let me see you again."

And when I was last in St. Louis, this same man brought a horrid old wagon up to where I was staying, sending me word that he had brought General Grant's old wagon for me to see, but I sent word that I did not think the wagon the General had used was in existence, and that he must excuse me.

It was hard for me to leave my dear father, and I bade him farewell with a swelling heart, but hoping we should soon meet again. We took passage by steamer for Galena. After a journey of four or five days, we arrived at Galena, a charming, bustling town nestled in the rich ore-laden hills of northern Illinois. The atmosphere was so cool and dry, the sun shone so brightly, that it gave us the impression of a smiling welcome, and Galena, I must say, has always thus welcomed General Grant and his family. She has greeted us with open arms. I have only pleasant, kindly memories of this home.

We were quartered with Captain Grant's brothers for two or three days. The Captain had already secured a nice little brick house of seven rooms, which was nestled high up on the hill on the west side of the town in the best neighborhood and with a lovely view. The assistant, secured for me by my sister-in-law, was pretty and willing but inexperienced. I kindly volunteered to show her how to make Maryland biscuit, but, to my sorrow, I found I did not know exactly myself. The biscuits were utter failures. Each one had a soggy, black spot in the middle. They were not at all like home biscuits. I told the Captain it was because the flour was not good, and then he asked me rather severely (thinking, I presume, that the cook would have done better) if I had ever prepared any before. I really had not. I had only cut out small cakes with my thimble from the dough prepared by black Mammy. During the day, Miss Jennie arrived, and for tea and breakfast we had delicious bread. The Captain, turning to me, said facetiously: "I see, Julia, you have come to a good stratum in the flour." "Yes, I think so," I said.

The Captain was very kind to me when I was childish and unreasonable. The Captain remained at the house with me to help arrange and place the furniture. On opening a box, we found an old mirror, that had been in my father's house for more than fifty years, broken to pieces. I cried and sobbed like a child when I saw this. The Captain, in place of being impatient with me, tried to soothe me, saying, "It is broken, and tears will not mend it now." I sobbed out: "It has always been at home, and then it is such a bad sign. It is a sign someone will die in the house before the year is over." He proposed having two or three small mirrors made from the pieces and asked me very earnestly if I thought the fact of the breaking caused the misfortune to come. I told him, "No, not at all, it only foretold the misfortune." He assured me then that since this did not bring the misery, I had no cause for grief. His sympathy and my tears did me much good. I cheered up and soon set my little household in order. Jennie was a great help to me. She was cheerful, practical, and always good company.

The Captain's father, mother, and sisters visited us and, I think, were much astonished at my executive ability. My little house was always in exquisite order; our cuisine most excellent. In fact, I was surprised myself at the ease with which my housekeeping moved on. I never interfered with my one maid's routine. I read, sewed, and called, or received calls. This one girl did all of our work. Once when I thought she had too much to do, I offered to wipe the china and glass used at breakfast. She exclaimed: "Oh, please! no, Madam, do not interfere with me or my work." And I never did again. She used to bring me my bonnet and wrap, and if it were damp, my overshoes, and put them on, and when I returned, would come and take my things and take them away.

The Captain always remained at home after coming to dinner. I never failed in my attention to my little ones, their toilets always being made fresh for this evening meal and the half hour spent with their papa; nor did I ever forget my own simple toilet. The appointments of our table were unexceptionable. This half hour was spent usually listening to Fred's stories of his prowess and sometimes of his defeats, the latter always accompanied with the express determination (as the boys say) of getting even yet.

I insisted upon our second son, Ulysses, wearing his beautiful curls, which reached quite to his waist, until he was eight years old, when, being no longer able to resist his importunings (all his manly instincts rising in rebellion against this girlish adornment), I consented to the shearing of my lamb. He announced this to his schoolmates, who appeared in force Saturday morning, petitioning for some of "Deliciouses' " curls, which, of course, they got. Ulysses had a protégé at this time, little Johnny S., who, he told me, had no mother, only a big sister, and she did not know how to take care of him. Ulysses took great pleasure in the permission given him to bring Johnny home on cold days and to give him his dinner in the kitchen. He often did such acts of kindness and protection to small boys, courteous and gallant—I could fill a volume with his pretty doings and sayings.

Nellie, being the only girl, was forced to participate in amusements more suited to boys: marbles, "mumble peg," etc. Fred used to protest, but all the same Nell had her turn at all these games. She was a great pet at school, as she was at home, and so gentle and pretty. She was her father's favorite, who always called her "my little daughter."

Jesse was a most important member of our household. He was first waited on at table. His smallest word was listened to by all of us, and, if there was the least hint of a jest, he had an appreciative audience. At two years old, he aspired to wearing his father's boots. Awakening from his noonday nap one day, he espied a pair of his papa's boots lying near, and with much difficulty inserted each little leg in a boot and started downstairs. The result was dreadful. His neck was not broken, but his four front teeth were broken squarely off, and he lay quivering and fainting in my arms. I wished then I had never come to Illinois, nor left my faithful nurse.

Jess would challenge his father to a wrestling match. His father would say, "I do not feel like fighting, Jess, but I can't stand being hectored in this manner by a man of your size." Whereupon, being struck on the knees by his opponent's little fists, he would roll on the floor with Jess in his arms and, after a few struggles, place the little fellow firmly on his breast, saying, "It is not fair to strike when a man's down." The Captain would take twenty or more punches from the dimpled fists, and so it went on until he thought Jess had had fun enough, when he would cry for quarter, saying, "I give up. I give up." Then Jess would proudly step off and help his father to arise.

After this, the good-night kiss was given, and I led them off to bed, teaching each one his prayers and tucking them all snugly in bed. The trouble now was that each one desired to have the last kiss from mamma; Fred, the little tease, always claiming to have had the last and best. After the little ones had retired, our evening was spent by the Captain reading aloud the papers which were teeming with interest just then, after which he read aloud some interesting book until eleven o'clock, and I was happily employed in sewing for my little ones and listening to that dear voice doing so much to amuse and entertain me.

We had many pleasant acquaintances. Our little ones, I think, attracted the attention of our neighbors, who soon called. The Captain's family had been living in Galena several years and, of course, had many friends whom we also met. Then I remembered the names of several old friends of my own family, and I sent them my card, with my maiden name written upon it also. They all called and were most cordial in their welcome. I soon felt quite at home in this picturesque town and among these most charming people in whom I always take intense interest. We were most pleasantly situated, although the Captain was occupying rather a humble position (I think), being only a clerk in his father's business house and necessarily having but a small salary. But it was enough, and we were happy.

During the autumn, there was great excitement in all political discussions. As I was a Democrat at that time (because my father was), I felt called upon to, and did, defend my party and its leaders whenever I heard them assailed. On one occasion, a person speaking of Sam Medary of Ohio,[18] said: "He is a blackguard." Of course, I expressed indignation at this and said: "You astonish me. I have been under the impression that he was not only a man of high character and dignity, but also of rare talent." "Oh," he replied, "he is a Democrat and, therefore, a blackguard." I quickly answered: "Excuse me, sir, but taking you as a criterion, I am happy to see that all the blackguards do not belong to my party." He only laughed at this.

It was with a heavy heart I sat with my little ones in a secluded nook high up on the bluffs overlooking the town and watched the long torchlight procession wend its way to the courthouse. It reminded me of a great, fiery serpent, and I thought that, as Laocoön and his sons were crushed, this serpent would crush in its folds the beloved party of my father, of Jefferson, of General Jackson, of Douglas, and of Thomas Benton.

Oh! how intensely interesting the papers were that winter! My dear husband Ulys read aloud to me every speech for and against secession. I was very much disturbed in my political sentiments, feeling that the states had a right to go out of the Union if they wished to, and yet thought it the duty of the national government to prevent a dismemberment of the Union, even if coercion should be necessary. Ulys was much amused at my enthusiasm and said I was a little inconsistent when I talked of states' rights, but I was all right on the duties of the national government.

I remember now with astonishment the feeling that took possession of me in the spring of '61. When reading patriotic speeches, my blood seemed to course more rapidly through my veins, and I remember how enthusiastic I was when Governor Jackson called for 20,000 troops to protect my native state, and also my indignation when General Harney was relieved from duty by an order from the national government.[19] Harney was our western hero. He was a grand old soldier and an old friend of my family.

NOTES

1. Among those mentioned are Brevet Major General Hugh Brady, longtime commander of the northwest frontier, and his son, Preston Brady; Lewis Cass, military hero of the War of 1812, Governor of Michigan Territory, Secretary of War, Minister to France, and 1848 Democratic candidate for President, who had been at Chillicothe, Ohio, in the early nineteenth century as a member of the Ohio legislature; John Norvell, once a Philadelphia journalist, later U. S. Senator from Michigan; Benjamin B. Kercheval, early Detroit merchant; Ross Wilkins, formerly of Pittsburgh, U. S. district judge at Detroit; Charles C. Trowbridge, Detroit banker, railroad promoter, and mayor.

2. Letters written by Grant in the summer of 1851, May–August, in which he speaks of missing his wife as well as his son, are in Grant, *Papers*, 1, 200–27.

3. Early in the summer, Grant had written about meeting Julia Grant in Detroit, but on August 17, 1851, wrote to her that she should travel from Detroit to Sackets Harbor on Captain Willoughby's steamship *Ocean. Ibid.*, pp. 202, 227. No letter written in September, 1851, is known.

4. Moses Primrose, second son of the Vicar of Wakefield in Oliver Goldsmith's novel, had been "designed for business," but was easily swindled.

5. For an account of the assistance given to Grant by Captain Simon Bolivar

Buckner in New York City based on family tradition, see Arndt M. Stickles, *Simon Bolivar Buckner: Borderland Knight* (Chapel Hill, 1940), pp. 33–34.

6. For details on Grant's business deal with Elijah Camp, see Grant, *Papers*, 1, 268, 301, 305, 339–40. Grant claimed that Camp left owing him $800.

7. For Captain Robert Allen's account of his assistance to Grant in returning to New York City, see Hamlin Garland, *Ulysses S. Grant: His Life and Character* (New York, 1898), pp. 128–29. For variations, see Lloyd Lewis, *Captain Sam Grant* (Boston, 1950), pp. 336–38.

8. John C. Dent then operated several enterprises at Knight's Ferry, California, which Grant had described after a visit in August, 1852. Grant, *Papers*, 1, 259.

9. In 1863, Julia Grant wrote to Commander Thomas H. Stevens asking for payment of $1,750 owed since 1854. *Ibid.*, pp. 420–21.

10. Helen Louise Lynde, daughter of Major Isaac Lynde.

11. See Chapter 12.

12. On August 15, 1859, Grant applied to the commissioners of St. Louis County for the office of county engineer. Grant, *Papers*, 1, 348.

13. In the confused politics of the day the opponents of the Democrats in Missouri were sometimes called Free Democrats, Free-Soilers, or Wide-Awakes. Not until later did the title Republican acquire acceptability. The Know-Nothings or Americans, however, the anti-foreign party of the mid-fifties, represented a different brand of politics.

14. The former county court had been replaced by a commission, and one of the commissioners, Dr. William Taussig, later wrote that the vote had followed party lines; the two Democrats among the five commissioners voted for Grant. Taussig, the only German-born commissioner, did vote for Charles E. Salomon, but Taussig was an enthusiastic Republican and also hostile to the Dent family. "Personal Recollections of General Grant," *Missouri Historical Society Publications*, 2 (1903), 4–7. Resenting the commissioners' choice of a German, Grant joined a Know-Nothing lodge. *Personal Memoirs of U. S. Grant* (New York, 1885–86), I, 212–13.

15. Grant applied for the office of county engineer in August, 1859, and knew about his rejection the following month. Julia Grant appears to have condensed chronology here. In February, 1860, Grant reapplied for the office of county engineer, and the following month wrote from his father's home. Apparently the second rejection led him to go to his father. Grant, *Papers*, 1, 354–56. In the meantime he had been employed in the customhouse. In early spring, 1860, the Grants moved to Galena.

16. In a letter to Charles W. Ford of St. Louis, December 10, 1860, Grant refers vaguely to some debts he still owed. Grant Papers, Library of Congress.

17. Since Missouri was exempt from the Emancipation Proclamation, Julia Grant's slaves probably remained her property until the ratification of the Thirteenth Amendment in 1865.

18. Samuel Medary, Ohio Democratic politician and newspaperman, temporary chairman of the Democratic Convention of 1856, served as Governor of Kansas Territory 1858–60 while national attention focused on the slavery struggle there.

19. When the Civil War began, Governor Claiborne F. Jackson of Missouri refused to furnish troops to the federal government; instead he called out the state militia. Brigadier General William S. Harney, then commanding the Department of the West, attempted to follow a conciliatory policy, and this led to his removal.

Chapter 3

—◈—

GALENA was throbbing with patriotism. The men were holding meetings and calling for volunteers. The boys were playing at war, wearing military caps, beating small drums, guarding the crossings, and demanding countersigns. The ladies held meetings and were determined to do their part in the great national struggle. I attended some of these meetings and once, at a strawberry festival, timidly approached one of the busy managers and asked if there was anything I could do to help her. She quietly gave me a quart bowl of strawberries to hull. After finishing this bit of work, another lady and myself spent our time in draping the portrait of Stephen A. Douglas, our late leader,[1] which we noticed had been overlooked.

At another meeting for sewing, feeling that I ought to do something as well as the others, I again went and offered my services. The lady to whom I spoke had already distributed her sewing but asked me if I could knit. I rather shyly answered, "yes, a little." As I had made more than one pair of reins for my boys, I felt I could truthfully say this. Imagine my embarrassment when she handed me needles and yarn enough to make a pair of socks, saying, "Try and get them in by our next meeting, in a week." I had to confess to her that I did not even know how to begin them and that I feared the war would be over before I could possibly finish them. She then gave me the sleeve of a double gown which I did finish, but I never attended the sewing meetings again. As my husband had already offered his sword and his services to his country, I felt it to be my duty to give all my care to his little ones, which I faithfully did.

When Galena's first company was raised and equipped, all Galena escorted it to the depot. Captain Grant was greatly interested in giving them the benefit of his West Point education and accompanied them to Springfield, where he remained for a week or two. When the next company left, everyone, as usual, went to the depot to see them off. The captain of this company was a Democrat and enthusiastically loyal. I do not think his wife was in sympathy with him. I was standing with my children in the station house, near the south window, and, turning, saw Captain Howard stride in and stop within a few feet of his wife and two little boys and her mother, all of whom were standing near the middle of the room. Folding his arms, he gazed sorrowfully at her. She returned his look but did not move. The mother said in a low voice, "Speak, Helen, meet him," but she did not move. The two little boys running up to him, he stooped and, clasping them in his arms, said: "God bless and keep you, my darlings," and, turning, he strode out to his company, already seated in the cars, and rolled away. Within a week, there was great mourning in Galena. Captain Howard, with ten or twelve of his men, was borne back dead, the train that carried them having been precipitated from a bridge, killing all these brave fellows.[2]

Four years later when the General and I returned to Galena, there was a tremendous and enthusiastic outpouring of the people to welcome him. The town was decorated with flowers and bunting. Many arches were built, and at one, whose motto was "Welcome to Galena, General Grant," a dozen or more young ladies sang songs and scattered flowers on their hero. After a glorious triumphal ride around the hills and valleys, so brilliant with smiles and flowers, we were conducted to a lovely villa exquisitely furnished with everything good taste could desire (and which, we were told, was to be our own) from Galena. I wept over this devotion to my dear husband, and that night thought of poor little Helen, who had lost her dear *all*. I asked Ulys if he had seen her. He had not, nor had I. We then arranged to see her soon. In a day or two, we found her nestled high up on the hills in a simple little house on the west side of the river. The General told her that as soon as her sons were old enough he would send one to Annapolis and one to West Point, and, leaving a substantial evidence of our friendship, we bade her adieu. Whenever we revisited Galena our call was repeated. The General fulfilled his promise in regard to the two sons. They both graduated high at the national academies and have proved excellent officers.[3]

I must not forget to tell a dream I had in the spring of '61. The Captain had gone on a visit to Kentucky to see his family and to see

[George B.] McClellan. On leaving, he told me to open his letters and, if any were important, to forward them to him. One night I dreamed at three separate and distinct times the following dream, viz.: I received through the mail a peculiar package from which, upon opening, an old and familiar ring of my mother's (which I had always considered mine, but which was claimed by my sister at my mother's death) tumbled out, wrapped up in tissue paper, and, as I loosened the paper, the little ring flashed out bright stars on the surrounding paper. Of course, I put my interpretation on this singular dream so oft repeated and wrote to my sister Emma, saying, "I will surely receive the ring before the week is over. Nell will remember it was mine and send it to me." Now comes the strange part of this dream. About the middle of the week (I had the dream Saturday night and wrote to Emma Sunday), I did receive an unusual looking letter addressed to "Colonel U. S. Grant. Official Business." The difference in rank in the address I did not notice, but on opening it, I found it contained a sheet of vellum, the face of which was entirely covered with tissue paper, and as I raised my hand to draw down the tissue covering, I exposed to view the great seal of the State of Illinois, which is spangled over with stars; just as in my dream, the little ring flashed out its starry light. A prophecy of mamma's, made long ago, now came vividly to my mind. This then was the meaning of my dream. Mamma had sent her little diamond ring as a reminder, and so I interpreted it. The letter contained the commission of U. S. Grant as colonel of the 21st Illinois Volunteer Infantry.[4]

During the summer of '56 or '57, when the western territories were suing for admittance as states, there was great anxiety as to whether any should be admitted as slave states. Two gentlemen from Leavenworth were on a visit to my brother at my home, White Haven. After dinner, my father, brother, Dr. Sharp,[5] Captain Grant, and the two visitors went to the piazza to smoke. Mamma remained for a while and, of course, heard them discussing the all-absorbing subject of slavery or no slavery. Nellie and I were already resting in our loose wrappers. Mamma came in half an hour later and was also lying down resting. She raised up and, pointing her finger on which was this same diamond ring towards us, said: "My daughters, listen to me. I want to make a prophecy this Sunday afternoon. Remember what I say. That little man will fill the highest place in this government. His light is now hid under a bushel, but circumstances will occur, and at no distant day, when his worth and wisdom will be shown and appreciated. He is a philosopher. He is a great statesman. You will all live to see it, but I will not." Sister Nell looked up and said: "Mamma, do you mean my husband?" "No," mamma answered, with a slight show of impatience, "no, I mean Captain Grant. I have been sitting on the piazza for the last half hour listening to those men talking without the least enlightenment on this important subject, until Captain Grant, in a few sentences, made the subject so clear and our duty so plain that I pronounce him a statesman and a philosopher."

Victor (this was a favorite pet name for the Captain, after he had read to me the triumphs of Victor Emmanuel) [6] returned home in a few days after the commission as colonel of the 21st Illinois was received and was soon ready to join his regiment.[7] Strange to say, I felt no regret at his going and even suggested that our eldest son, just then eleven years old, should accompany him. I think it was a tender thought for my beloved husband that prompted this suggestion, as well as a desire to gratify the importunings and pleadings of our boy Fred. You must not forget, though, that these regiments were only called out for three months,[8] and I considered it a pleasant summer outing for both of them. I did not think Captain Grant's occupation in Galena entirely congenial to him, and was willing, therefore, that he should go out on this expedition as he wished to, no matter how lonely I might be without him. The Colonel and Fred bade us adieu. Many friends assembled to say goodbye. Colonel Grant's regiment was at Springfield, I think.

I received letters from him almost daily. His mother and his brother, who was greatly out of health, spent several weeks with me that summer. Mr. S. S. Grant died at St. Paul and was brought to my house and buried from it.[9] This sad event brought Colonel Grant's father and sisters also to Galena, and I had the pleasure of entertaining them.

When Colonel Grant was ordered to Missouri, he wrote me he would send Fred home from Quincy, Ill., saying, "We may have some fighting to do, and he is too young to have the exposure of camp life." I instantly wrote to him, "Do not send him home; Alexander was not older when he accompanied Philip. Do keep him with you." But I was too late. Fred had started. Colonel Grant was rather amused at my letter.[10] The dear boy demonstrated, however, that I was right, for he walked the whole distance from Dubuque to Galena, seventeen miles, and carried his own knapsack, not a light one by any means. The cars had started when he arrived, and imbued with his father's future tactics, no doubt, he pushed ahead and was quite exhausted when he arrived.

Our house was now the center of attraction in Galena. The Colonel moved over to Missouri and wrote me very interesting letters. He was sent to southern Missouri and afterwards to Cairo, Illinois. He wrote me many times, urging me to visit him there, which I, at length, with much timidity, decided to do. He desired the children to accompany me. This wish it was that deterred me in the first place, I thinking it such an undertaking to go with four children.

The day I started about the middle of the afternoon I felt nervous and unable to go on with my preparations, and, asking a friend who was assisting me to excuse me, I went into my room to rest for a few moments, when I distinctly saw Ulys a few rods from me. I only saw his head and shoulders, about as high as if he were on horseback. He looked at me so earnestly and, I thought, so reproachfully that I started up and said "Ulys!" My friend in the next room said: "Did you call?" and when I told her, she said I was only a little nervous thinking of him and would soon meet him. I started that evening with my little ones. We heard of the battle of Belmont, however, before we left. Ulys met me almost before the train stopped. I told him of my seeing him on the day of the battle. He asked at what hour, and when I told him, he said: "That is singular. Just about that time I was on horseback and in great peril,[11] and I thought of you and the children, and what would become of you if I were lost. I was thinking of you, my dear Julia, and very earnestly too." I told him I thought the look was almost reproachful. I told him I thought he was displeased with me for not coming sooner. He said, "I ought to have been but know you had good reason for not coming."

The General, the children, and I had rooms at headquarters, as did also Colonel Hillyer's family.[12] Our mess was kept by a colored man, who also did the cooking. He supplied attendance on the dining room; our nurses did the chamber work for our families. Several of the staff messed at this mess. This is the only time during the war that I remember the General having a comfortable mess. The General supplied the steward with means to run it, and when we were breaking up for the army to move on Donelson, the General assumed two-thirds of the expenses (he often having to entertain visitors at headquarters), leaving one-third to be divided amongst the staff. One of the gentlemen offered to make this division. I was very indignant when one of these officers, the doctor,[13] sent me a little roll of bills (thirty-five dollars), with a bit of paper wound around it, with this written on it: "To Mrs. General U. S. Grant, $35, for five weeks board." I thought he meant to be insolent. Perhaps I was wrong.

I remember how high and angry the river was and how desolate Cairo seemed. The children and I managed to be comfortable in the great barracks our house resembled. That was all. But I made many pleasant acquaintances, among whom were Commodore Foote, a patriotic Christian gentleman, Major McPherson, Colonel Erwin,[14] and many others. It was my great delight to go accompanied by Mrs. Hillyer and our little ones to see the reviews which I noticed generally preceded a movement by our troops.

How proud I was sitting there in our ambulance with my friend Mrs. Hillyer and our little ones witnessing the reviews and hearing the bands play "Hail to the Chief" as *my* General rode down the columns inspecting! And when the last regiment was passed, old Jack, a beautiful light sorrel, with sweeping white mane and tail, would come dashing up to the flagstaff near which our ambulance was placed and, turning around, would proudly stand for the regiments to pass him in review.

When all was over, those gallant brave heroes would crowd around our ambulance to pay their respects with a bow or a smile, asking how we were pleased with the review. I always answered, with the greatest enthusiasm, that nothing could be more interesting, more thrilling, than to see these columns of brave men in motion. There was poetry in every move. No pageant since has ever thrilled me or given me such intense interest as did those at Cairo and Bird's Point.[15] We were always escorted back to headquarters by half a dozen or more of these gallant, brave men.

Once at a review at Cairo, when accompanied by some friends from Galena who had come to see the army, a gentleman with us kept putting his head out of the carriage window, much to his inconvenience and greatly obstructing the view of the rest of the party. As he drew in his head for the twentieth time, a malicious puff of wind took off his hat, with it *his wig*, leaving the poor horror-stricken man's head as bare as a billiard ball. I shall never forget the consternation depicted on that kindly old face as he anxiously watched the pursuit, which was long, and the final capture of that hat and its treasure. My regard for this Galena friend kept me from shouting with laughter. I simply remarked as the hat was handed to him, "Oh! Mr. H——, you cannot now lay all the vanities at the door of the ladies. If you do, I will tell on you." This little sally seemed a great relief to the nice old man, and he did not put his head out the carriage window again.

I went down the river two or three times on a flag of truce boat, Mrs. Hillyer and the children accompanying me for change of air, and, I must say, hoping to see or hear something from the front, but I can remember nothing of importance. We went once on a trip to Paducah, which had so recently capitulated to General Grant. I remember how the patriotic songs of the —— brothers[16] thrilled me.

They stood on the forward deck of the vessel, singing as I went on board, and so they sang at every landing or stopping place. How their soul-stirring patriotic songs thrilled the crowds that gathered to listen to them and brought many recruits. The government owes much to these gentlemen, and to music, and I think ought in gratitude to establish and maintain a musical conservatory at the capital.

On our return trip, a number of persons who had been detained at Paducah at the time of the surrender, and who lived down the river, obtained permission from the boat's captain to go to their homes. Some three or four of these were of the gentler sex. I remember one of them who most industriously, I really thought spitefully, knitted all of the way. Her knitting needles clashed like lances and, dear me, how she snapped me up when in reply to something she said, I remarked, "It is dreadful; why, this mania for secession seems to be epidemic throughout the South." "Mania! Mania! Madam! Epidemic! Madam! Why the whole South has gone *ravin'* mad!" After this outburst, I was very quiet indeed and did not venture an opinion again on political matters in public.

On our return from one of these trips, I found Ulysses, my second son, who had declined to go, very ill with inflammatory rheumatism. Everything skill could suggest was done for him without avail, until at last Dr. Kittoe[17] told me of a medicine which could be procured only at a French chemist's in St. Louis. He had used this, he told me, with marvelous success, and again without the least effect, but if I wished, he would yet have time to telegraph General Grant, who had gone to St. Louis (to see General Halleck),[18] to bring with him this valuable medicine, and Ulysses could have it by seven o'clock the next day. When the General arrived at seven A.M., Ulysses was delirious with pain and fever. The doctor began at once to administer the medicine, and at the same hour the next day the little fellow was sitting up in his chair eating his breakfast.

At this time, the General was very busy arranging for his attack on Donelson and Fort Henry. He was compelled to bring his office materials and maps to my sitting room, as he was so often interrupted by a man appointed by the President to take command of the merchant boats used by the Army. The captains of these boats came in a body to General Grant and positively refused to obey the orders or serve under this man. The General said to the captains: "The boats I must have. Captain Kountz is appointed by the government and must be obeyed. There is no time to discuss whether it is agreeable or not, and I hope, gentlemen, you will see this as I do." These fine fellows talked together for a few moments and then said: "General, we have decided, at your request, to submit." [19] It was after this the General moved his writing material to my room.

Captain Kountz was earnestly desirous to do his duty and kept interrupting the General to talk over his plans. The General wished the Captain to look after his own affairs and was impatient at these frequent interruptions. General Rawlins was more than impatient. He told Captain Kountz that by his importunities he had driven General Grant out of his office. The Captain was indignant at this charge and attempted vindication. Then Rawlins made a rush at him, ordered him out of the office, and enforced the order.

Of course, Captain Kountz was very angry and at once proclaimed broadcast that General Grant and his staff were all drunk. Colonel Hillyer of the staff, hearing this, at once placed Captain Kountz in arrest and placed him under guard in the guardhouse. At the dinner table that day Hillyer was all excitement, telling what he had done, and I think he said he had ordered the scoundrel to be gagged. As soon as General Grant heard of this, he ordered Kountz released, saying, "We must bear with this man. He is overzealous in doing his duty, that is all." [20] But General Grant did not know Kountz. He was always malignant, afterwards interrupting telegrams between General Grant and General Halleck, thereby causing much serious trouble. I know this to be true, for Colonel Hillyer, who came down from Fort Donelson to see General Grant's family and his own off for their homes, told me he had discovered that General Grant's telegrams to Halleck and Halleck's to Grant had all been stopped in the office at Cairo by order of Captain Kountz. Colonel Hillyer straightened it all out. It had to be done at personal expense. He said his pay was small. I immediately handed him my purse. He took twenty dollars, saying he thought that would suffice.[21]

I thought the preparation for the departure of the troops was unusually great, and the day before General Grant left he came into my room. I thought he wanted to say something special and asked him what he wanted to tell me. He replied, "Nothing, only I expect to leave here tomorrow morning and I was thinking that you and the children had better return to Galena or go to Kentucky to my family, and I think it rather better for you to go to Kentucky, as you will be nearer me, and then you will be with friends. If I want you to visit me—and I am sure you will want to come, will you not?—you can leave the children with my people and can come to me without anxiety." We agreed to this arrangement. He handed me a roll of money, six or eight hundred dollars, and when I asked him what I should do with such a large amount, he said: "Take care of it; you will need it. It may be some time before I can give you any more, as I expect to be on active duty from this on."

We were much interested in the marshaling and departure of the troops. How pretty the steamers looked as they swung out into the stream laden with troops and bright with flags! My enthusiasm almost amounted to a delirium. I never once expected to hear bad news from my General. I do not know why. I knew—I felt—he would be victorious and—well, did not the little ballad I used to sing to him declare "the faithful soldier to be God's special care," and how true it was.

As the young officers were hurrying to and fro, many called to bid me adieu, one saying he was going to win his spurs, another "a strawberry leaf"; one aspired to "an eagle," and another said, "Really, I expect to have a bright star on my shoulder," [22] and "We are all coming to you to place them there, and we are sure of having your kind wishes," and, I added, "my prayers."

The days immediately after their departure were full of anxiety. We listened pale and anxious all day and late into the night at the eastern windows to the booming of cannon and the bursting of shells.[23] Our anxiety reached a climax when three of the vessels which had so lately, and so proudly, rounded out into the river returned, bringing with them the news of victory to Grant and his army. How my heart swelled with gratitude to Almighty God. Kneeling, I asked and pled for his favor for my nation and my beloved husband.

On one of the boats, Colonel Erwin lay dead. He was brought to headquarters and placed in one of the lower rooms with his martial cloak around him and, over all, a bright new flag. They told me how calm and pale Mrs. Erwin was, that not a sob escaped her. How well I know this calm, deep grief when one seems to be turned to stone!

I was greatly disappointed that Ulys did not return with these troops. He wrote me a letter by every bearer of dispatches, however, telling me of his progress. I have many of these now, written at the siege and after the fall of Donelson.[24]

The country simply went wild over the success of the General, and he became the recipient of many enthusiastic attentions. Fred accompanied one of the staff officers up to Fort Henry and brought back some "war trophies" consisting of some grapeshot, two empty cigar boxes, and a pipe or two, which he generously divided with the other children, becoming, as on all similar occasions, a genuine hero in their eyes. Jess, who was only four, was, of course, given one of the best of these treasures, a small cannonball, and while rolling it tenderly on the windowsill, it fell on his poor little foot, causing him to give a loud cry of pain. Fred, seeing the situation, exclaimed: "A soldier never cries, Jess." Whereupon the dear little fellow grasped his wounded foot in both hands and sank quivering and pale on the floor, but no sob escaped him. After that, he too was a hero. Fred called him a little Spartan.

Shortly after this, the General wrote me, asking me to visit his family for a week or two and, if I found it agreeable to all, to make arrangements to remain there for the present. After leaving Cairo and my husband, I was very lonely and, after retiring for the night, I wept like a deserted child; so overcome was I with my desolation that my sobs brought a kind lady passenger to my side. She asked if she could do anything for me. I could hardly say to her that I was only homesick. Only once again in my life—when I left the White House—did this feeling of desolation come over me.

Mr. and Mrs. Grant were very kind to the children and became very fond of them, but I was not at all happy there after there had been such a change in the tone of the Cincinnati newspapers, which, up to this time, had been filled with praises of General Grant. They did tell, though, of the gallant charge led by the General at Shiloh, which decided the fate of those two hard, cruel days.

General Grant says in his *Memoirs* of this:

This [second] day everything was favorable to the Union side. We had now become the attacking party. The enemy was driven back all day, as we had been the day before, until finally he beat a precipitate retreat. The last point held by him was near the road leading from the landing to Corinth, on the left of Sherman and right of McClernand. About three o'clock, being near that point and seeing that the enemy was giving way everywhere else, I gathered up a couple of regiments, or parts of regiments, from troops near by, formed them in line of battle and marched them forward, going in front myself to prevent premature or long-range firing. At this point there was a clearing between us and the enemy favorable for charging, although exposed. I knew the enemy were ready to break and only wanted a little encouragement from us to go quickly and join their friends who had started earlier. After marching to within musket-range I stopped and let the troops pass. The command, *Charge*, was given, and was executed with loud cheers and with a run; when the last of the enemy broke.[25]

I remember with what enthusiasm General Rawlins (General Grant's chief of staff) told me of this action. When General Grant rode up, he realized the situation as if by inspiration and called out, "Now, men, join me, and we will drive them and hold the field." At once nearly two regiments of brave men fell into line; then Grant with sword held high in air rode rapidly forward, shouting the order "charge," and the field was carried and held.

I must tell of a prediction I made about this time. Hearing loud shouting in the street, I went to the window and found the houses as far as I could see draped with bunting and flags. I inquired the meaning of this. One of the General's sisters exclaimed: "Have you not heard the great news? Richmond has fallen." "No," I declared, "that is not, cannot, be true. Richmond will fall only before *Grant* and *his* army." And *so I felt always.*

One day, following soon after the most enthusiastic and thrilling encomiums that filled the Cincinnati newspapers over the surrender of Fort Donelson to Grant and his army, I sat shocked and almost stunned at an article (many of them) in ribald abuse of my husband just after the battle of Shiloh, where in the first part of the first day's battle some of the new troops behaved badly, taking shelter, as they did, under the river bluff, and were only moved by turning on them one of the fieldpieces that ought to have been doing different service. But I must say that when these men did return to the field they did brave and gallant work; they were only panic-stricken, which sometimes happens to the bravest men, I have heard. Of course, the report of all this must be forestalled, and report went out that General Grant was not in the field, that he was at some dance house. The idea! dear Ulys! so earnest and serious; he never went to a party of any kind, except to take me.

As I sat reading this article from the papers (I felt too deeply wounded to weep; I felt hard and revengeful), a tall, handsome woman, clad in deepest mourning, entered the little parlor in the house of Mr. Grant, my husband's father, in Covington, Kentucky. Coming directly up to me, she said: "Mrs. Grant, I am an entire stranger to you, and I have come a long day's journey out of my way to tell you this." She paused a moment, choking down a sob, and continued: "I am the widow of Colonel Canfield.[26] I have just lost my husband at Shiloh. I must tell you of your husband's kindness to me. Notwithstanding orders had been published that no women should be allowed to come up the river, I felt so impelled to go that I went. When I arrived, it was the evening of the first day of that dreadful two days' fight. I was told on my arrival at Shiloh—as I felt all the time it was so—that my husband, Colonel Canfield, was among the wounded and was then lying in a hospital I had passed a few miles down the river. I was in despair when I learned that I could not go to him, that it was impossible. Just then a cavalcade rode up, and I saw it was General Grant and his staff. As I stood there in my despair, I saw General Grant was unable to dismount. He was helped off his horse and almost carried into his dispatch boat. I was told that I could not enter. The General was ill. I hesitated, but at last my intense anxiety to go to my husband overcame all else, and I boldly entered the boat. The orderly on guard said, 'You cannot enter,' but I passed on and entered. As I approached, I saw the doctors cutting the General's boot off his foot, which they told me he had injured the night before while on a reconnaissance. His horse had stepped on a rolling stone and had fallen upon it. He said he had not felt it all day until he went to dismount and was astonished to find his leg quite swollen and numb. I told him of my anxiety to reach my husband, knowing that he needed me, 'and, General, he has been wounded, and they tell me I cannot go to him. Do, for God's sake, allow me to proceed.' He replied, 'I will write my report at once, and you may go on the dispatch boat that carries my report in about an hour.' Paper and ink were brought, and the General sat rapidly writing, not once stopping until his report was finished; then folding and addressing and sealing it, he rapidly wrote an order to pass me on the dispatch boat, and that I should be permitted to visit the hospital in which my husband was, kindly bidding me goodbye with the hope that I would soon meet Colonel Canfield. All this so kindly, so gently, so full of sympathy; and to think of the horrid things one sees in the papers of this great, good man."

I asked: "Did you reach your husband in time, Mrs. Canfield?" "Oh, no," she sobbed: "I was too late, too late. I was conducted down the aisle between the cots in the hospital, and my escort paused and pointed to a cot, the blanket drawn up so as to cover the face. I knelt beside it and drew the covering down. He was dead—my husband, my beloved, my noble husband. I thrust my hand into his bosom. It was still warm, but his great heart had ceased beating. The blood was clotted on his beard and breast. I think he might have lived if I had been near," she sobbed. "I have determined to devote my time to the wounded soldiers during the war. My husband only needed the services of a kind nurse."

And this gentle, lovely woman did go, and for three long, weary years devoted her entire time to the hospitals, nursing and caring for our wounded and sick soldiers. How well I remember her as I saw her that morning, so fair, so tall, draped in her robes of mourning, and then again I saw her when the war was over and our victorious armies passed in triumphant review before the President, the Senate and Congress—in fact, before the whole grateful country—down Pennsylvania Avenue. Grant was there; so were Sherman, Sheridan, Meade, Thomas, Logan, Hancock. All these grand soldiers excepting General Grant, who was, of course, the reviewing officer and remained on the stand during the whole two days of review (and I sat near him), came upon the stand as their armies passed and paid their respects personally to the reviewing party. How magnificent the marching! What shouts rent the air! Ah! glorious memories to me. Ah! I was saying, I saw Mrs. Canfield, the soldier's widow, the soldiers' nurse, when all this was passing. She, yes, she had grown older in these three long, weary years, for her dark hair showed threads of silver, her fair face and brow were furrowed and browned by care and exposure, her mourning robes looked worn and faded, as did the flag of her husband's old regiment as it passed on that glorious day up Pennsylvania Avenue.

We remained at Covington until towards the end of June, when the General sent for us to come to him at Memphis. Nellie was delighted with the salvos of artillery fired on the Fourth of July, saying, "Mamma, who told them this was my birthday? Why, really this is very kind of the rebels. I do not think papa ought to wish to fight them." Fred had told her it was all in her honor, and now Ulysses, our little grandson, is enjoying the same happy delusion, as the Fourth is his birthday also.

As we wended our way to Memphis, I learned that General Pope had taken Island No. 10 with many prisoners; the number was greatly exaggerated, however. When we arrived at Memphis, I learned with some chagrin that Pope had been called East to command the Army of the Potomac.[27] Afterwards on the piazza with General Grant and a number of his staff, I began to protest upon the gross impropriety of this exaggerated report of prisoners going to the President. They all laughed immoderately, the General as well as the rest, at my great interest in the affair, and when I seemed annoyed, Rawlins exclaimed in a conciliatory tone, "Never mind, Mrs. Grant, they will find out how many prisoners were captured when they come to draw their rations."

We remained with the General until September when we returned to the North, leaving the three older children with their grandfather Grant. I went to Louisville and boarded with my aunt.[28] From there, I took my cousin, a charming girl,[29] Jesse, and my colored nurse Julia on a two week visit among the General's relatives and old schoolmates in Ohio, who were most kind and hospitable.

I had perfect ovations in Georgetown and Bethel. One evening, while at a party in Georgetown, I was requested to enter an adjoining room, where about a dozen gentlemen were assembled. On entering, they all arose and one of them said: "Mrs. Grant, we, as friends of your husband, wish to learn from you if General Grant stands by his Paducah platform." This was deep water for poor me, as I had not the slightest idea what they meant. And looking inquiringly at them, I repeated: "Paducah platform?" "Yes, his Paducah proclamation is a sound and profound state paper, earnest and patriotic. We want no better platform than that." I at once comprehended: "Oh, the General's proclamation to the people of Paducah! [30] Yes, he meant that. He is very earnest. He greatly regrets the secession and would be glad to have them back peacefully if possible. He feels deeply our country's troubles and has expressed to me his gravest apprehensions as to the fate of the South. He tells me they have plunged into this and now they feel they cannot come out with honor until they are utterly destroyed, and he feels for them the greatest sympathy."

I stopped at Cincinnati on my return from this pleasant visit to do some necessary shopping, selecting with great care a quiet hat for the autumn, a nut-brown uncut velvet, the ornament in the front being a knot of red and white velvet. After the first promenade with my cousin, I said to her: "I am afraid my bonnet is a little conspicuous after all. Yet I selected it as the quietest the milliner had. Did you notice nearly everyone glance at my bonnet as I passed, or did I imagine it?" "Notice it? Of course I did. I would not dare wear that bonnet in the streets of Louisville. No, indeed. I am sure I would be arrested." "What do you mean?" I exclaimed. "Why, Cousin Julia, don't you see your bonnet is butternut brown and your ornament is nothing else but our Confederate flag: red, white, and red. Do you wonder that you attracted attention?" "Why did you not tell me before I purchased it and wore it?" "I thought you knew our colors," she replied. She was an outrageous little rebel and was immensely amused at my dilemma, which forced me to buy another bonnet.

I think it was about this time General Grant sent for me to visit him at Corinth, Tenn.[31] When we arrived at Corinth the first time, we found the General's ambulance awaiting us at the depot. The General and two or three of his staff officers accompanied us on horseback to headquarters. The General was so glad to see us and rode close beside the ambulance, stooping near and asking me if I was as glad to see him as he was to see me. He reached out and took my hand and gave it another and another warm pressure. Dear fellow! how kind he always was to me!

As we entered the encampment, which extended from near the depot to far beyond the headquarters, the campfires were lighted, and

I do not think I exaggerate when I say they numbered thousands. So it seemed to me. The men were singing "John Brown." It seemed as though a hundred or so sang the words and the whole army joined in the chorus. Oh, how grand it was! And now when I hear "John Brown" sung, that weird night with its campfires and glorious anthem and my escort all come back to me. The General's headquarters were in a handsome and very comfortable country house, situated in a magnificent oak grove of great extent. The house was a frame one, surrounded by wide piazzas, sheltered by some sweet odor-giving vine—Madeira vine, I think. On the grounds were plantain, mimosa, and magnolia trees. A wide walk extended around the house. It was like a garden walk without sand or pebbles on it, only the mold or earth. It was kept in fine order, as it was sprinkled and raked morning and evening. It was the delight of Nellie and Jess to make footprints with their little rosy feet in this freshly-raked earth. Each day, as they were being bathed and dressed for the evening, the same petition came. "Mamma, please let us make footprints. It is so cool and pleasant. Do, mamma; it is such clean dirt. Let us, please." The General would answer, "Yes, you can. Come, why do you not ask me? I would always let you. It will not hurt you at all." The staff officers joined in the petition, so the little ones made the footprints and enjoyed it too. Sometimes I had to appeal to the General when the children were inclined to be a little insubordinate, and he would say, looking quizzically at me, "Come, children, you must not quarrel with mamma. You must always mind what she tells you. Remember that always."

I think the General must have had some important news, as he sent us suddenly home to St. Louis, and soon after my arrival there we heard of the dreadful battle of Corinth.[32] Just a day or two before I left there, I received a letter from an old acquaintance of mine, and in the letter the following was found: "I was so glad to hear you had cut that horrid Yankee woman, the minister's wife in Memphis, when she called on you." I was indignant at this, read it aloud to the General, and said: "Did you ever hear of such an untrue report? There is not the slightest foundation for the story. On the contrary, I should have treated her with the greatest consideration if I had known her husband was loyal." As I made this remark, I happened to look up and saw a young man standing near the door. He started and looked surprised. I did not recognize him, and the thought flashed across my mind, "What is he doing here? He must be a spy." I at once wrote on the margin of my letter, "Who is this strange young man? He is much interested in what is going on here. I am sure he is a spy." The

General wrote, "You are right; he is in our employ." And would you believe it? It was found afterwards that he was a spy for both sides. He asked many questions: how each room was occupied and by whom. Soon after this came the fierce battle of Corinth.

Again the General sent for me to join him at Jackson, Tennessee. His headquarters was a straggling old country house, part log, part frame, with a long, low piazza fronting south. As usual, many of the general officers with their staffs called to pay their respects to me. McPherson, Hurlbut, and, I think, Marsh,[33] with one or two more, remained after the others left. General Rawlins having just entered, McPherson said to me: "Mrs. Grant, we are very glad to have you with us again for more reasons than one. We want to reach the General's ear through you. In justice to General Grant—in fact, in justice to ourselves—General Rosecrans ought to be relieved." I said: "General Rawlins mentioned this to me this morning, and I have already spoken to the General about it." He expressed great regret, saying, "Rosecrans's action was all wrong," but that it was his (Grant's) right to find fault, and that he had not done so, knowing Rosecrans "to be a brave and loyal soldier with the best of military training, and of this kind we have none to spare at present. Besides, 'Rosy' is a fine fellow. He is a bit excited now but he will soon come around all right. Do not trouble yourself about me, my dear little wife," and smiling, said: "I can take care of myself." This he said to me, but, of course, I did not repeat it all to these officers, not more than the first sentence: "Rosecrans's action was all wrong."

The General had returned to his office at the east end of the piazza before this conversation. When he returned to me, I repeated it to him, including what they told me about an address Rosecrans had published to his men which had given these officers great dissatisfaction. The General replied, "Yes, I know. I cannot understand Rosecrans. I feel reluctant to part with him and hope that he will yet come out right." We sat in silence for a while, both thinking of our late conversation. I liked Rosecrans too. He was handsome and brave, and I liked him also because the General did. So it was with regret I heard of his disaffection, but I could not sympathize with General Grant in his disbelief of this disloyalty to him, which General Rosecrans has since so glaringly proven.

The General rose silently and again went to his office. After an absence of fifteen or twenty minutes, he came back looking so happy, and smilingly holding up a slip of paper, he said: "There is good news, good news. Rosecrans is promoted and ordered to take command of the Army of the Cumberland. I feel so happy. It is a great compliment, and he leaves us feeling friendly in place of the other way, which I fear would have come, as he was going wrong and I would have had to relieve him. His promotion is a real pleasure to me. I could not bear to relieve him." [34]

From Jackson, I went with General Grant on a visit to McPherson's headquarters near Bolivar. We spent only a day with McPherson, who brought in to me his first general's shoulder straps and, kneeling on one knee before me, asked me to fasten them on his shoulder. I did so with pleasure, and having my little gold thimble in my satchel (the same I used at the sewing bee in Missouri), I firmly fastened McPherson's first stars for him on his brave, broad, handsome shoulders.

I think the army now moved to La Grange.[35] The General went ahead and sent Colonel Hillyer for Mrs. Hillyer and me. The headquarters occupied on this occasion was also in the suburbs, but a little more pretentious than the one at Jackson. I remember we had a stationary washstand there, and as I sat on the floor one morning, near the bright wood fire which an old black mammy had fanned into a flame with a turkey wing, I fell to thinking how strange it was that I should be in someone else's house, and I wondered where the former occupants of this room were, and if they were as comfortable as I. I was sorry for them. I looked up, and seeing General Grant observing me, I exclaimed: "Ulys, I don't like stationary washstands, do you?" "Yes, I do; why don't you?" I replied, "Well, I don't know." He said: "I'll tell you why. You have to go to the stand. It cannot be brought to you."

In passing through La Grange everything was so familiar—the old Negro quarters, the colored people warming themselves in the sun, the broken windows filled with old clothes—all seemed so familiar that, as I had never been there before, I must have seen them in my dreams.

From La Grange, we went to Holly Springs. As Colonel Hillyer was too ill to accompany us when we were sent for, I missed the General, who had been obliged to move on two days before I arrived at Holly Springs. He left a kind letter, however, telling me how much he regretted not meeting me, and as soon as the road was finished through to Oxford he would have me come to him.

Jesse was with me and Jule, my nurse and maid, a slave born and brought up at my old Missouri home. Colonel [Theodore S.] Bowers of the General's staff had secured very nice quarters for us in a fine house belonging to Mr. Walker, who, I think, had formerly been a cabinet officer at Washington.[36] It was occupied by the wife of a Confederate officer. Her husband, son, and brother-in-law were with the Southern army. She was a fine, noble woman, as so many of these Southern women were. The ladies sat up late to receive me, which was very kind, and after being refreshed by a light supper, I was conducted to my apartment by Madam ———. Before bidding me goodnight, she said: "Breakfast will be about nine o'clock" and that she would have it announced to me. At breakfast I felt happy. I did not realize for a moment that I was actually in the enemy's camp until, arising from the table with the family, we entered the hall, and I naturally, or thoughtlessly, turned towards the door of the drawing room where I had been received the night before; when suddenly the hostess stepped forward, and placing her fair hand on the doorknob, said: "Excuse me, Mrs. Grant, but I have set aside a drawing room for your use." Only imagine my chagrin and mortification. I realized instantly my mistake, and feeling that I had turned very pale, I said "thank you" and waited for her to indicate the room. It was a large, front drawing room on our right.

I never after entered their apartments except by special and very pressing invitation. Once, when these ladies were calling on me, they learned that I had never heard any of their rebel war songs, so they begged me to come in and hear some of them, and I went. They sang grandly, with power, pathos, and enthusiasm. The young ladies asked me how I liked their national songs, saying I must come in again and listen to them. I answered, "no, never again. I would be a traitor to listen again to such songs." Another time, wishing to have something done to a dress, I asked one of them to recommend a dressmaker. She did, and offered to go with me. The following day, I found not less than ten or a dozen ladies at the dressmaker's, who were at once presented to me. We were soon chatting pleasantly, when one said: "You are Southern, are you not?" "No," I replied, "I am from the West. Missouri is my native state." "Yes, we know, but Missouri is a Southern state. Surely, you are Southern in feeling and principle." "No, indeed," I declared. "I am the most loyal of the loyal."

Then they talked of the Constitution, telling me the action of the government was unconstitutional. Well, I did not know a thing about this dreadful Constitution and told them so. They seemed much astonished and asked: "Why, surely you have studied it?" "No, I have not; I would not know where to look for it even if I wished to read it, and, besides, the Northern people think and say it is unconstitutional for any of the states to secede." I really was much grieved at my ignorance of these matters, but since then I have learned that even the chief justice is sometimes puzzled over the interpretation of this same Constitution.

My hostess had a dear little boy and he soon made friends with Jesse. They played amiably together as warm friends.

It was at this time the General was annoyed by many persons importuning him for permits to pass the lines and to buy cotton, coming armed, many of them, with permits from the Treasury Department at Washington. It was then General Grant wrote that obnoxious order expelling the Jews from his lines for which he was so severely reprimanded by the federal Congress—the General said deservedly so, as he had no right to make an order against any special sect. General Grant was always grateful to Mr. Washburne for his able and timely defense of him at this critical time.[37]

The General soon sent me word that the road was finished and to come. Of course, I was delighted, and, inviting Mrs. Hillyer to accompany me, we started in the afternoon of the same day I received the notice, taking Jesse and my maid with me. We had a long, fatiguing ride, and I was surprised that the General did not, as usual, meet me at the depot. As we drove up to his headquarters, he came hurriedly out, saying, "You have arrived a little sooner than I expected, but I could not have met you, as I am fully occupied. I have only time to kiss you; and Jess, you little rascal, are you glad to see me? I must go back now to my office." I asked if there was important news, and he said: "Yes, I'll tell you when I come in, if I can come at all. I am very busy and am glad you are here and safe."

When he came, he told me Colonel [T. Lyle] Dickey had come in from a scout only a half hour before my arrival and reported that he had passed at a distance a column of troops said to be [Earl] Van Dorn's, and that Van Dorn was striking for the railroad over which I had just passed. The General had been busy all evening telegraphing orders to be on the lookout and to give Van Dorn a warm reception. The next morning, before we were fairly awake, a knock at our door announced important telegrams. Holly Springs with 2,000 of our troops had surrendered; hospital, and hospital and commissary stores burned; my carriage burned and horses captured. Van Dorn paroled the prisoners, thus rendering them useless for the present, and then dashed on to do further mischief.

Before leaving Holly Springs, I was told, some of Van Dorn's staff officers rode up to the house of which I had lately been an inmate and asked for me. My hostess assured them I was not there, that I had gone the previous evening to visit General Grant. They demanded my baggage, and this also the kind and noble lady protected by her earnest and personal requests. The loss of this baggage, little as there was of it, would have entailed endless annoyance.

[107]

Our troops came on in hot haste, exasperated beyond measure and rightly so. Colonel Murphy, commanding officer at Holly Springs, had received General Grant's telegrams and, quietly putting them in his pocket, went to dine with a citizen of the town, so that our troops were surprised.[38] They indignantly said: "If we had had the slightest idea Van Dorn was coming, he never would have taken us. Why, d—n it all, when he dashed in upon us, some were just waking up, some were making their toilets, and others cooking coffee and bacon. We were captured and paroled before we knew it." When they learned that Colonel Murphy had received ample information—well, Colonel Murphy left very shortly.

To show that General Van Dorn was not bent on conquest but was only raiding to cut the roads, the following incident was recounted: General Morgan of our army was stationed at some old mills with a small detachment, but, having been notified by General Grant of Van Dorn's proximity, was ready for him, and when that dashing officer rode up at the head of his column and demanded Morgan's surrender, he replied, "Come and take me." Van Dorn rode on to larger and easier conquests.[39]

General Grant sent Colonel [John K.] Mizner to the relief of Holly Springs, but, growing impatient, concluded to return himself with all the troops. I was with the General during this retrograde movement, which was in no sense a retreat. He retired to Holly Springs as he would be better situated for observing the field of action. At the request of Colonel [William H.] Coxe of this place, General Grant occupied his residence, a beautiful Italian villa.

While here I frequently saw the young ladies of the Walker house. On some feast day—Christmas, I think—they sent me a fine turkey and some other poultry, which I was loath to accept, knowing how very valuable they must be, and I wished I could return the compliment with some delicacies from the North, but our mess was always indifferent at best. All the nice things I had brought with me were long since gone.

One morning, a lady said to me rather triumphantly, "Oh, Mrs. Grant, you Yankees have at last come to a stopping place. You cannot go any further (smiling). You have reached an impassable barrier, the Yalobusha swamp," I think she said, or maybe it was the "Yalobusha River." I said: "You know we have portable bridges which are carried with the troops. I think they call them pontoons. They are boats' fastened together and are very light. With these, they can cross anything." She exclaimed: "Oh, these Yankees, these Yankees! Will nothing stop them?"

When General Grant evacuated Holly Springs and went to Memphis, as we were leaving the house, I asked my maid if she had put Master Jesse's silver cup in the satchel. She replied, "No, ma'am, I forgot and left it in the trunk." And the trunks had already gone. I said to her: "You are careless. What am I to do?" Colonel Coxe overheard this, stepped back to his dining room, and returned with a beautiful, slender-stemmed wineglass, saying, "Will this answer, Mrs. Grant?" To my demur, not wishing to break his set of glass, he replied, "Ah, no! Keep it as a souvenir of the house. I only wish I could add to it a bottle of rich, old wine, but mine is all gone." And that slender, little pink glass was the only souvenir I ever brought from the South.

While at Colonel Coxe's residence, I was again made mediator between General Grant and his impatient generals. I was informed that General Grant had *let* Sherman have command of the expedition on Vicksburg and he (Grant) was here to hold the Rebs in check by threatening Grenada. It was General Grant's right to command the expedition, for if Sherman were successful, he would get all the credit, but if he failed, Grant would get all the blame. "Besides this, Mrs. Grant, we are looking after our own laurels as well, and we all chafe under this. We want you to tell the General he is too unselfish, but if there is a chance, we young men would like to add a few leaves to our wreaths. You see how it is, do you not?" Of course I did, and appealed to the General at once, and what do you suppose he said, smiling at my anxiety for his fame? "We will hope that Sherman will be successful and, in that case, he will be entitled to the credit." "Yes," said I, "but suppose the contrary happens—what then?" "Ah," said the General, "we will not suppose. We must hope for the best." And so we were there for a few weeks longer. I suppose the expedition was not a success, as the General found it necessary to go on to Memphis.

While at La Grange, on the road to Memphis—I think it was there—two ladies were calling on me, and one said in an undertone, but with ill-suppressed glee, "Did you hear the news? The road between here and Memphis has been cut and a bridge burned." "Yes," I said, "I am so sorry." "Have you read General Grant's orders since the reception of this news?" "No, what is it?" Then, taking up the slip of paper from my table, I read the order. It said: If hereafter the military roads are interfered with, the country will be cleared for ten miles each side, the country devastated, and the people driven back.[40] "The road, you know, must go through, or our soldiers must live on the country. Of course, the invading army is not going to be hungry in the midst of plenty."

As General Sherman's expedition was not a success, another was proposed, and General Grant went in person, taking Fred along, who was on a visit to us in Memphis. I was left at Memphis with my children and my friend, Mrs. Hillyer.

He moved down the Mississippi towards Vicksburg. I remained at Memphis for several weeks, having Ulysses, Nellie, and Jesse with me. Mrs. Hillyer and her little ones were also there. I remember nothing of interest now except there was great restlessness and anxiety and some murmuring at the army's seeming inactivity. General Grant was at Lake Providence and Milliken's Bend on the Mississippi, waiting for the waters to subside that he might move on Vicksburg.

Once, when the General came up from Milliken's Bend, we were seated in our parlor at the Gayoso House, the General looking over his mail and I sitting near him, when two cards were brought in to me. I handed them to the General to read, as even then I was unable to read a card except in a very strong light. The General, glancing at them, said: "Bishop O—— and Miss G——." The General remarked to me, "I know what they come for. It is to have Captain Govan put on his parole again." I inquired what he meant, saying, "I thought he was already on parole." "Yes," the General said, "but Jeff Davis has published a very severe order and, in retaliation, an order has come from Washington to place every man on parole under strict surveillance." He said to me, "Go in and see the Bishop and Miss G——, but do not make promises, for I am sure they wish to see you on this subject." And so I found their petition was to have Captain Jack Govan again placed on parole. I had become much interested in this family while I was at Holly Springs, especially in Captain Jack, who was in very poor health. In reply to them I only told them how much I regretted to hear this, that I would tell the General what they said, and hoped he could grant their request. When I returned to the General, I rapidly related what they had said to me and said, "Ulys, of course you will continue Captain Govan's parole." He said: "No, I will not. I cannot." I said: "Oh! Ulys, you can, you will. Captain Govan is a very sick man, as ill as your brother was, who died in Galena this past summer. It will kill him if he is confined in a dungeon. He is too ill to do any harm to anyone." The General said: "I cannot help it. The order is imperative." I said: "Ulys, I ask it as a personal favor." To this he replied: "You have no right to ask a personal favor in this matter." I said: "You refuse to grant this to me?" He said: "Yes." At this, I turned to the window and shed tears of bitter disappointment. I seated myself at some distance from the General and occupied myself with a book, never looking towards him. People were coming in and going out for two hours. At last, when a card was brought in to the General of a Mr. Hiller, saying it was for Mrs. Grant, the General glanced at it, arose, brought it to me, and said in a low tone, "If he comes in behalf of Captain Jack Govan, I will place him on parole." Of course, I was delighted, and when Mr. Hiller entered and approached me, after bowing to the General, I said in some haste, "Do you come in behalf of Captain Jack Govan?" He said: "I do." I said, smiling delightedly, "The General has just now told me he will place him on parole." He did not linger, but hastened with the glad news to Captain Govan's friends and took the parole with him.

General Lorenzo Thomas passed through Memphis, and we were told he came as the mouthpiece of President Lincoln and could make and unmake men, and I must not be surprised if General Grant were removed; that the country was tired of the inactivity of the army. I not only assured this person, Mr. [James E.] Yeatman of Cincinnati, of my astonishment, but of my most just indignation. It was with great delight I received that same day a letter from the General telling me to come down on the first boat and to bring the children for a short visit. Starting at once, we were with him in a few days and how glad we were to see him again.

I had hardly said "how do you do" before I began to make suggestions, asking the General, "Why do you not move on Vicksburg at once? Do stop digging at this old canal. You know you will never use it. Besides, that is what McClellan has been doing.[41] Move upon Vicksburg and you will take it." The General was greatly amused and inquired if I too had a plan of action to propose. Of course I had. "Mass your troops in a solid phalanx at a point north of the fortress, rush upon it, and they will be obliged to surrender." He said, smiling, "I am afraid your plan would involve great loss of life and not insure success. Therefore I cannot adopt it. But it is true I will not use the canal. I never expected to, but started it to give the army occupation and to amuse the country until the waters should subside sufficiently to give me a foothold and then, Mrs. Grant, I will move upon Vicksburg and will take it, too. You need give yourself no further trouble. This will all come out right in good time, and you must not forget that each and every one of my soldiers has a mother, wife, or sweetheart, whose lives are as dear to them as mine is to you. But Vicksburg I will take in good time."

"But," I exclaimed, "Old Thomas has come down here to relieve you." This he explained, saying, "The President has sent General Thomas here to arrange some plan for taking care of the freed slaves, who are in a sad condition. I have already had a most interesting conversation with General Thomas on this subject, and he and I are in sympathy." And I think he said, "I suggested this to the President." The General said: "I am glad you arrived in time to witness the running of the blockade. I have ordered three transports to be prepared, and tonight after dark they are to drop silently down the river as far as possible and then put on all steam and go flying past Vicksburg and its batteries to where I want to use them. [David D.] Porter, who is a gallant fellow, insists on taking two or more gunboats as escort and to return the rebel fire. He says it would not look well to run past and not return their broadside."

The steamer from which we witnessed the running of the blockade was the *Henry von Phul.* We dined on board with many officers and two or three ladies, and when quite dark we silently dropped down the river. All was going well when a red glare flashed up from the Vicksburg shore and the flotilla of gunboats and transports and our own boats were made plainly visible. Indeed, it was a grand sight: the long stretch of river at the end of which was the blazing house illuminating it. How vividly that picture is photographed on my mind; the grand roar of the cannon rests in my memory. The batteries of Vicksburg poured shot and shell upon the heads of the devoted little fleet, but Porter was there—thank Heaven!—to return broadside for broadside. The air was full of sulphurous smoke. The batteries were passed, and we rested here awaiting the report of casualties and were happy to learn that there had been no loss of life, although some few were wounded—poor fellows! The smoke cleared away, the stars looked down tenderly upon Union and Rebel alike, and the katydids and the frogs began again their summer songs.

Running the blockade was, I think, satisfactory to General Grant, as he repeated the action on the 22nd of April, this time sending six more transports loaded with supplies and a number of barges. I remember the General was much disturbed by the inefficiency of the officer who was ordered to make ready these boats. He was relieved, however, and two of the staff officers performed this duty of getting the boats ready.[42] The relieved officer went north on the same steamer I went on, and he predicted with great confidence the failure of the expedition.

The ladies I alluded to as having accompanied me on the *Henry von Phul* the night of the running of the blockade were Mrs. General McClernand of Illinois, who was also on a short visit to her husband, and Mrs. Major Belle Reynolds,[43] wife of Lieutenant Reynolds of McClernand's staff, a second Florence Nightingale, who so often cared for and cheered the sick and wounded of the regiment that when

Governor Yates of Illinois visited the army he conferred on her (in jest, of course) the title of major, thus making her outrank her husband, who now no longer had the right to officially order her back from the front. We called her *our* Nightingale.

The following morning, the army moved about eleven o'clock. I left Fred to go with the General and in about an hour after their departure I left with the three younger children for St. Louis on the *Henry von Phul*, the same steamer from which I witnessed the running of the blockade. On arriving at St. Louis, we at once went to my father, who was occupying our home at Wish-ton-wish. The General had purchased this pretty villa from my brother for me.

My summer was not a happy one. Our neighbors were all Southern in sentiment and could not believe that I was not; no matter how earnestly I denied it, they would exclaim: "It is right for you to say you are Union, Julia, but we know better, my child; it is not in human nature for you to be anything but Southern." They would imprudently speak of mails going to the South from various places, and when I remonstrated with them, saying, "I might feel it my duty to repeat these things to the authorities," they would smile and say, "We know you will not. We know how you have been brought up and an oath would not be more binding than the sanctity of your roof."

We enjoyed the country greatly: the lofty trees, the singing birds, and my dear father's society. He argued and argued with me constantly upon the constitutionality of secession. I was dreadfully puzzled about the horrid old Constitution anyway, and once, when quite worn out with listening, said: "Papa, why don't they make a new Constitution since this is such an enigma—one to suit the times, you know. It is so different now. We have steamers, railroads, telegraphs, etc." He looked aghast and left me, saying with a groan, "Good Heavens! If Old Jackson had been in the White House, this never would have happened. He would have hanged a score or two of them, and the country would have been at peace. I knew we would have trouble when I voted for a man north of Mason and Dixon's line."

One afternoon early in July, as we were sitting in an upper room chatting, we were interrupted by a perfect salvo of artillery. I started up much excited and called down from my window to papa, who sat on the piazza reading the papers, asking what he supposed the matter was; if he thought Vicksburg had surrendered. "Yes, I should not wonder if both Vicksburg and Richmond had fallen from the infernal noise they are making." But dear papa was always pleased at any success of my husband and was immensely proud of him, notwithstanding his great sympathy with the South. Soon a courier arrived with the news of the surrender and with an invitation for myself and family to go to St. Louis to witness the grand parade in honor of the great victory of Grant, but I did not go. Almost directly, a rumor was afloat that the news was not true; that Admiral Porter had anticipated the fact and had sent a dispatch boat up with the news, and it was simply one of Porter's canards. In a few days, however, one of General Grant's staff officers, Major [William M.] Dunn, arrived at Cairo, and, after telegraphing the glorious news to the Secretary of War, was privately directed to come to St. Louis and to escort the children and me to Vicksburg to visit General Grant.

I see from this morning's papers (1892) that *a Judge Peck* has been out lecturing, and that he has been *indelicate* and *unjust* enough to read before a large audience a letter purporting to have been written by General Rawlins to General Grant whilst before Vicksburg (and marked *"strictly confidential"*) beseeching him to be temperate. *If* such a letter was *ever sent*, General Grant *must* have felt that *devotion alone prompted such a letter*, but how could Rawlins have kept this letter? To me, it looks very like making a record for the future.[44]

This story is incomplete without relating also the one told of President Lincoln, who, on being importuned to relieve General Grant for his intemperance, anxiously inquired, "Do you know what brand of whiskey Grant drinks? I would like to get barrels of it and send to my other generals." [45]

NOTES

1. U.S. Senator Stephen A. Douglas died on June 3, 1861.
2. Captain Bushrod B. Howard of Galena, 19th Illinois, was killed on September 17, 1861, along with many soldiers of his regiment, when a train fell through a bridge in Indiana. Howard had served as first lieutenant in the Mexican War, as a Democratic member of the Illinois House of Representatives (1851–52), and as postmaster of Galena.
3. Thomas B. Howard graduated from the U.S. Naval Academy in 1873; Douglas A. Howard graduated from the U.S. Military Academy in 1878.
4. On June 15, 1861, Governor Richard Yates of Illinois appointed Grant to command the 7th Congressional District Regiment. Although Grant called his command the 21st Illinois on June 19, the name did not officially change until the regiment was mustered into U.S. service on June 28. Grant, *Papers*, 2, 42–46. Yates appointed Grant by executive order originally; he did not issue a commission until October 23. Lawrence A. Frost, *U. S. Grant Album* (Seattle, 1966), p. 62. Chronology thus contradicts Julia Grant's account of learning of her husband's appointment through the delivery of the commission.

5. Dr. Alexander Sharp of Lincoln County, Missouri, husband of Ellen (Nellie) Dent.

6. Victor Emmanuel II (1820-78) added Lombardy to his kingdom of Sardinia through war with Austria in 1859; then in 1861, having annexed central and southern Italy, was proclaimed King of Italy.

7. Grant returned from Cincinnati to Springfield, took command of his regiment on June 18, then left on June 21 for a quick trip to Galena, returning accompanied by his son on June 24. Grant, *Papers*, 2, 42-51.

8. Early in the war, Illinois had raised six regiments for three months service; Grant's regiment, however, enlisted for three years.

9. Samuel Simpson Grant died on September 13, 1861, near St. Paul, Minnesota.

10. Grant mentioned this letter in *Personal Memoirs of U. S. Grant* (New York, 1885-86), I, 248. In August, 1861, he referred to a letter from Julia Grant "in which you gave me fits for sending Fred. home by himself." Grant, *Papers*, 2, 83.

11. In his *Memoirs*, I, 277-79, Grant described his narrow escape from enemy bullets while supervising the departure of his troops after the battle of Belmont on November 7, 1861.

12. While Grant was in partnership with Harry Boggs in St. Louis in 1859, the firm rented office space in the law offices of McClellan, Hillyer and Moody. William S. Hillyer, a native Kentuckian who had served a term in the Indiana legislature before moving to St. Louis, accepted the position of aide-de-camp with the rank of captain on Grant's staff in August, 1861. Albert D. Richardson, *A Personal History of Ulysses S. Grant* (Hartford, 1868), pp. 189-90. His wife, Anna Rankin Hillyer, the mother of three young children—Willie, Jimmie, and Mamie—became a close friend of Julia Grant.

13. Probably Surgeon James Simons, medical director on Grant's staff.

14. Captain Andrew H. Foote, who took command of U.S. Navy forces on the western rivers on September 7, 1861; Lieutenant Colonel James B. McPherson, chief engineer on the staff of Major General Henry W. Halleck, assigned by him to the same position on Grant's staff for the Fort Henry campaign; Lieutenant Colonel William Erwin, 20th Illinois, who had served as first lieutenant, 1st Illinois, in the Mexican War.

15. Part of Grant's command at Cairo was stationed directly across the Mississippi River at Bird's Point, Missouri.

16. Probably Frank and Julius Lumbard of Chicago, popular singers of patriotic songs, who later performed for the troops besieging Vicksburg. Benjamin P. Thomas, ed., *Three Years with Grant as Recalled by War Correspondent Sylvanus Cadwallader* (New York, 1955), pp. 96-97.

17. Dr. Edward D. Kittoe of Galena, then surgeon of the 45th Illinois, later a member of Grant's staff.

18. After he assumed command of the Department of the Missouri on November 19, 1861, Major General Henry W. Halleck was Grant's immediate superior. In late January, 1862, Grant went to St. Louis to ask Halleck for permission to move against Fort Henry.

19. A petition of Cairo boatmen declaring Captain William J. Kountz "obnoxious" is in Grant, *Papers*, 4, 111.

20. On January 14, 1862, Grant wrote that he had ordered the arrest of Kountz, who had been troublesome and disobedient. *Ibid.*, pp. 53-54. Hillyer acted under

Grant's orders in arresting Kountz, who remained in arrest until he resigned in April. Grant prepared no formal charges against Kountz, but Kountz brought serious charges of drunkenness against Grant. *Ibid.,* pp. 110–16.

21. On March 4, 1862, Halleck removed Grant from command of the Tennessee River expedition for disobeying orders by not reporting his strength. By this time, however, Julia Grant had left Cairo and Hillyer had rejoined Grant. If intercepted telegrams were involved in Halleck's quarrel with Grant, they were a minor part, and Kountz, while under arrest, could not have intercepted them. *Ibid.,* pp. 317–21.

22. Leaves were the insignia of lieutenant colonels; eagles those of colonels; single stars those of brigadier generals.

23. Since the bombardment of Fort Henry took place some seventy-five miles from Cairo, and Fort Donelson was farther away, no sounds of battle reached Cairo.

24. See *ibid.,* 203–4, 211–12, 229–30.

25. *Memoirs,* I, 350–51.

26. Lieutenant Colonel Herman Canfield, 72nd Ohio, killed at Shiloh. His widow, Mrs. S. A. Martha Canfield, organized a "colored orphans' asylum" at Memphis. *History of Medina County and Ohio* (Chicago, 1881), p. 336. During the Grant administration, she was employed as a clerk by the U.S. Bureau of Education.

27. Since Major General John Pope's assignment to command the Army of Virginia was announced on June 26, 1862, and Julia Grant arrived in Memphis on July 1, she may well have learned the news on her arrival. But Island No. 10 in the Mississippi River with some seven thousand prisoners fell to Pope on April 7, and this could hardly have been unknown to Julia Grant. She may have intended to state that on the way to Memphis she read exaggerated accounts of the number of prisoners captured by Pope.

28. Emily Wrenshall Page, Mrs. Samuel K. Page, younger sister of Julia Grant's mother, Ellen Wrenshall Dent.

29. Ellen Page, twenty-three-year-old daughter of Samuel and Emily Page.

30. For Grant's proclamation of September 6, 1861, to the citizens of Paducah, see Grant, *Papers,* 2, 194–95.

31. Soon after Julia Grant joined her husband in Memphis in July, 1862, Grant moved his headquarters to Corinth, Mississippi, and there the family remained together for about a month before Julia Grant left for a visit to her father in St. Louis.

32. Julia Grant left Corinth in August, 1862; the battle of Corinth occurred on October 3–4.

33. Major General Stephen A. Hurlbut then commanded the District of Jackson in Grant's command. Colonel C. Carroll Marsh, 20th Illinois, though recommended by Grant for appointment as brigadier general and accordingly nominated by Lincoln, was not confirmed by the Senate.

34. On October 23, 1862, Grant received orders to send Major General William S. Rosecrans to Cincinnati for further orders. *The War of the Rebellion: A Compilation of the Official Records of the Union and Confederate Armies* (Washington, 1880–1901), series I, vol. xvii, part 2, 290. Hereafter *O.R.* Relations between Grant and Rosecrans had steadily deteriorated following a disagreement about the pursuit of the enemy after the battle of Corinth and had reached a highly unpleasant stage just before the transfer. *Ibid.,* pp. 283, 286–87. Julia Grant's account of what Grant said is

inaccurate on at least two minor points: Rosecrans had been promoted earlier, and Grant did not then know that Rosecrans would command the Department of the Cumberland.

35. Grant occupied La Grange, Tennessee, on November 4, 1862, as the first stage of his campaign into Mississippi along the line of the Mississippi Central Railroad.

36. Robert J. Walker, U.S. Senator from Mississippi (1836-45) and U.S. Secretary of the Treasury (1845-49). One authority, however, states that Julia Grant occupied the house of Harvey W. Walter in Holly Springs. J. G. Deupree, "The Capture of Holly Springs, Mississippi, December 20, 1862," *Publications of the Mississippi Historical Society*, IV (1901), 58. According to an undated newspaper clipping owned by the Grant Association describing the Walter Mansion at Holly Springs, Walter left Holly Springs early in the war, entrusting care of his home to Mrs. Pugh Govan, wife of a Confederate soldier. Later in her memoirs, Julia Grant described her special efforts to obtain the release of Jack Govan. In 1874, Cato Govan, formerly a slave of the family, described how Mrs. Govan had protected two trunks belonging to Mrs. Grant during the Confederate raid on Holly Springs. Claim No. 3394, Marshall County, Mississippi, Southern Claims Commission, Record Group 217, National Archives.

37. Grant's General Orders No. 11, December 17, 1862, expelling Jews from the Department of the Tennessee, notorious and controversial from its issuance to the present, receives extensive discussion in Bertram Wallace Korn, *American Jewry and the Civil War* (Philadelphia, 1951) and in a forthcoming volume of Grant, *Papers*. Both houses of Congress eventually rejected resolutions of condemnation, and U.S. Representative Elihu B. Washburne defended Grant vigorously. See John Y. Simon, "From Galena to Appomattox: Grant and Washburne," *Journal of the Illinois State Historical Society*, LVIII (Summer, 1965), 176-77.

38. On December 25, 1862, Grant wrote a report of the capture of Holly Springs on December 20 which blamed Colonel Robert C. Murphy, 8th Wisconsin, for failing to prepare his command. *O.R.*, I, xvii, part 1, 477-78. On January 10, 1863, Murphy was dismissed from the service. *Ibid.*, p. 516.

39. Colonel William H. Morgan, 25th Indiana, defended Davis' Mill, Mississippi, on December 21, 1862. See *ibid.*, pp. 521-23.

40. On January 3, 1863, Grant telegraphed to Brigadier General Isaac F. Quinby that "if necessary to secure the railroad" all persons and property nearby would be removed. *Ibid.*, part 2, 524.

41. Major General George B. McClellan had been removed from command of the Army of the Potomac on November 7, 1862, because of dissatisfaction with his unaggressive tactics. Because Julia Grant's conversation with her husband dates from the following April, she may have referred to McClellan but would not have used the present tense.

42. Dissatisfied with "delay and neglect" in preparing barges to run the batteries, Grant relieved his quartermaster, Lieutenant Colonel Charles A. Reynolds, and placed in charge of the fleet George W. Graham, who was a civilian employee of the quartermaster's department, and staff officer Clark B. Lagow. *Ibid.*, I, xxiv, part 3, 194, 216-17, 227.

43. For Belle Reynolds, wife of Second Lieutenant William S. Reynolds, 17th Illinois, see Frank Moore, *Women of the War: Their Heroism and Self-Sacrifice* (Hartford, 1866), pp. 254-77. Her commission as honorary major, not issued in jest, recognized her services in caring for the wounded.

44. The letter of June 6, 1863, from Major John A. Rawlins to Grant is printed in James Harrison Wilson, *The Life of John A. Rawlins* (New York, 1916), pp. 128–29, and has been discussed perceptively in Bruce Catton, *Grant Moves South* (Boston and Toronto, 1960), pp. 463–64. Although Rawlins wrote of Grant's drinking, he also stated that his suspicions might be unfounded; for that reason, the occasion of the letter remains obscure.

45. This popular story was apparently disclaimed by Lincoln. David Homer Bates, *Lincoln in the Telegraph Office* (New York, 1907), p. 197.

Chapter 4

BEFORE LEAVING for Vicksburg, I called to say farewell to Mrs. B——, the wife of our family physician, and to my surprise found a number of our neighbors assembled there. They were apparently in high glee and said: "So, Mrs. Grant, you are going to join the General, we learn." "Yes," I replied, "I came to bid adieu to Mrs. B——, as I intend leaving in the morning." At this, they glanced at each other in amazement. In answer to their usual inquiry as to when I should join the General, I would say, "as soon as Vicksburg is ours." They would say, "not till then? Do you know that Vicksburg is as strong as the Rock of Gibraltar; how can it ever fall?" "I do not know how it will be taken," I replied, "but I do know that General Grant will never leave there until it has surrendered, and as soon as Vicksburg is ours, the same messenger who brings the news of victory to be sent to Washington will be my escort back to the General. For I know he will send for me as soon as he can have me." So when I said I would leave the next day, I gave them their first *authentic* information of the fall of Vicksburg.

Just before I left home, my son Fred arrived. He was not at all well, but I did not realize how ill he was or I should not have left him. Ulysses begged to remain with his brother, to which I consented, and left the two little fellows with their grandfather.

We had a pleasant sail down the Mississippi. On arriving at Vicksburg, General Grant met us with his ambulance. He and some of his staff accompanied us on horseback to headquarters, which were located on the heights of Vicksburg in a large, white, colonial house, not unlike the Executive Mansion in Washington. The offices and our sleeping and living apartments were on the first floor; the family of Mr. Lum, the owner, occupied the second and third floors. We never occupied a house unless it was vacant. Otherwise, we boarded as at Nashville, or were invited as at Holly Springs by Colonel Coxe. But the morning after the surrender, as General Grant's escort company was riding out looking for a suitable place for headquarters, a belligerent young woman (a visitor, the family told me afterwards) stood with other members of the household near the entrance gate of the Lum residence and imprudently made ugly faces at our handsome captain, who was at once attracted by the spacious grounds and buildings and said, "This will suit us," and took possession. The ladies were greatly alarmed and fled like a flock of partridges before the company as it marched in.

These ladies were amiable, gentle, and grateful to our army for its real kindnesses. One day, the old lady said to me: "Only think, we have been sacrificing everything to keep you Yankees out, have reduced ourselves to poverty and lived on half rations; and now that you are here, in place of harming us, as soon as he heard we were eating mule flesh, General Grant gave orders for rations to be issued and gave us flour, coffee, sugar, tea, bacon, and everything we needed." [1]

A Miss [Mary Emma] Hurlbut from Connecticut was with this family as governess. She was very pretty and was often made the medium for obtaining privileges for the family. They would often ask for a pair of horses to be attached to their carriage, their own having been long before contributed to the Confederacy. Of course, a pair of horses necessitated a driver, and the young officers—particularly one—were most happy to serve the ladies. The Chief of Staff at length grew tired of this and in very emphatic terms declared to the General one morning when I happened to be in the office that he did not think it just the thing for a United States soldier wearing the United States uniform to be acting as coachman for a lot of rebel women. The General smiled and asked, "What is it all about? Who is doing it, Rawlins, and why do you permit it? You are chief of staff." "Well, you see, General, these women ask a favor, not a very great one, I admit, and the fellows are glad to make their positions as comfortable as possible, but I for one do not believe it is just the thing." The General replied: "Nor do I. That is not what they are here for, surely." Rawlins arose to depart, and I looked rather reproachfully at him, when he, smiling at me, said: "This is war, Mrs. Grant, war in earnest, and we must not forget it."

I do not know whether the young ladies enjoyed any more rides or not, as soon after this I returned to St. Louis to place my children in school. General Grant and staff accompanied me as far as Memphis. After placing the children at school and making a brief visit home, I returned to Vicksburg, taking only my youngest child, then nearly five years old. Before starting, I learned that General Grant had been injured at the review in New Orleans, but not seriously, by his horse rearing and falling back on him. This hastened my departure.

On my arrival, I found the General in bed, but in a few days he was up, using a crutch, however. During the afternoon of my arrival, Dr. [Henry S.] Hewit came in to see the General. During his call, he remarked to me, "Do you see any changes about headquarters?" "No," I said, looking around, "what is it?" "What? no change in anyone?" "Oh," I exclaimed, "why, yes. I think General Rawlins is looking splendidly. Has he consented to let you take him in hand?" The Doctor was delighted and said: "I knew your woman's wit would see it at a glance. Oh, you know how it was when you left. Those ladies upstairs were 'rebel women.' Rawlins could not stand to see Uncle Sam's soldiers and uniforms degraded, but Lord bless you, my dear lady, all that is changed. Soldiers, uniforms, and chiefs of staff even are sacrificed!" "What does it all mean and how did it happen?" I inquired. "Well," he exclaimed, laughing heartily, "you know how Miss Hurlbut made her petition for any favor always so modestly, with burning cheeks and downcast eyes. One morning she came down wearing a little blue apron, the same she has on this morning, with her pretty hands thrust in the pockets; well, to make a long story short, the pockets in that apron were too much for Rawlins. He simply surrendered unconditionally, and since then we and they all ride as much as we like and so does the Chief of Staff." General Rawlins and Miss Hurlbut were afterwards married.

On one occasion, as I sat at the side of General Grant's couch, a beautiful woman, tall and majestic as Juno, was shown in. Her business was in connection with her plantation. Her slaves and provisions were all gone, she explained; they had been taken by one side or the other. "What am I to do?" she said, "I, who never gave a thought as to any expenditure for luxuries, am now wondering where I am to get food for my old slaves, who are too decrepit to leave me or be taken from me." The General replied: "I am sorry I cannot do anything for you at present, Mrs. Bass. I suppose these matters will be partially rectified in the future by being brought before a commission, and if there has been any injustice, it will be righted." I said to her, "You go to Washington and plead your own cause. I am sure you will be successful." When I went to Washington, I found she had taken my advice and had been successful, and had, in the meantime, married the Italian minister, and was the handsomest and most admired woman in Washington.[2] A diplomatic stroke on my part, was it not, to remove this fair petitioner from my husband's vicinity?

One morning, Mrs. Lum, whose house we were occupying, and one of the young ladies met me, saying in much distress, "Oh, Mrs. Grant, is it not dreadful? Old Mr. Porterfield is ordered outside the lines and at once." "For what?" I asked. They did not know. The daughter of this gentleman came to see me and told me her father had been imprudent enough to say to Surgeon [John] Moore after dinner, who was an inmate of his house, that he was sure that "yellow jack" (meaning yellow fever) would drive the Yankees out if shot and shell did not. So this with some other little indiscreet speeches was reported to our provost marshal, who at once issued an order that the old gentleman must leave within twenty-four hours or he would be sent to a Northern prison. The poor young girl wept as she related this, and I said: "You must tell this to General Grant." "Oh," she said, "the order is very explicit and says we must not appeal to General Grant." I at once arose, entered General Grant's office where he was alone, and related the story, ending with "it is a shame," and called to Miss Porterfield to enter. She only sobbed out, "Oh, General, this will kill papa if he must go." The General wrote on a bit of paper and, handing it to Miss Porterfield, said: "Tell your father to be more careful of his speech in the future." The ending of this gave me much pleasure, as Madam Porterfield, who was a relative of Jefferson Davis, had sent me more than one lovely bouquet.[3]

Another afternoon, as I sat reading in my little drawing room, I heard the rustle of silk and, looking up, beheld a perfect vision of loveliness. A tall, fair young woman clad in a robe of shimmering azure silk, with filmy lace about her throat, a Gainsborough hat of garnet velvet which was decorated with a superb white ostrich plume, stood before me. As I looked up, she smiled brightly and came forward, saying, "I wanted so much to meet you, Mrs. Grant. I could not wait any longer. My father has met the General, and we have heard of you from our friends, so I have come to see you. You are surprised at my costume, I know, but really all of my plainer clothing is gone; this gorgeous dress is one of my few precious relics, and I wear it in your honor, Madam." Bursting into a merry laugh, she exclaimed: "I wish you could see my equipage—it is too absurd—an old, white-covered wagon, a split hickory chair for a seat, and drawn by one old mule and a bony horse. Can you imagine anything worse?

If I had waited for a better one, I could not have gotten here at all." This gay butterfly fluttered her bright wings for a brief season and enjoyed the havoc she made among our young officers. They all admired her, and one in particular was very constant in his visits to Magnolia Hall, the home of our fair Psyche.

One morning, when I had returned from a longer ride than usual, I found the snowy tents that filled the grounds around headquarters all lying on the ground and considerable commotion at headquarters. In fact, everyone was hurrying but the General, who calmly told me we would leave Vicksburg for the north at exactly four P.M. It was now fifteen minutes of two. The young Colonel, our "young Lochinvar" we called him, hearing the General say this, came to me at once to remonstrate, saying, "Why, you can't be ready before sundown, Mrs. Grant." "No," I answered, "I cannot be ready before then. Go and make your adieux at Magnolia Hall," and he went. The headquarters moved at sundown precisely. Young Lochinvar returned in time, but seemed to be a trifle impatient and out of sorts. I wonder why?

The pilots of the boats refused to travel at night, claiming that for the past three years they had never traveled at night as they considered it dangerous, and proposed tying up for the night at or near the bluffs of the Mississippi, where *our* boats in passing this locality were almost always shelled by the Rebels, and it was considered necessary by the Federals to have the escort of a gunboat when passing. General Grant was amused when he heard of the precaution of the pilots, who were Southern, and replied to their earnest suggestion that he had perfect confidence in their skill in carrying us safely through; that we would not tie up for the night but move on. And we did.

Arriving at Cairo, we found a special train awaiting us and went to Indianapolis, where the General met Secretary [Edwin M.] Stanton. After this, we went to Louisville, where we were detained an hour waiting for a ferryboat. I was greatly troubled that someone of the staff had not telegraphed for a boat to be in readiness, as the weather was bad, with rain and sleet, and Mr. Stanton was suffering from a severe cold. But I afterwards learned that this seeming neglect was intentional, as it was not considered safe to telegraph in the portion of the country through which we passed the presence of the Secretary and the General.

The Secretary and the General held a long conference at the Galt House the night we arrived, and I think the General went to relieve Rosecrans,[4] whose troops were now reported to be in a forlorn condition in or near Chattanooga.

I remained until the General left, and then went at once to my aunt, with whom I boarded until the General sent for me to join him at Nashville. While at my aunt's, the news of the two great victories[5] achieved by this gallant army soon after General Grant took command was received. We were reading all about them and telling my little boy Jess. He anxiously inquired, "Who whipped?" The answer was "Grant," and Jess called out joyfully, "Hurrah! Hurrah! Bully for Grant!"

We remained in Louisville until December, when General Grant wrote for us to join him at Nashville. I went to the Galt House for the night so as to get an early start in the morning. That evening, the Quartermaster General ([Robert] Allen, I think, was his name) called, who, by the way, was a fellow townsman of my husband.[6] He informed me he would place a special car at my disposal and would send his ambulance to take me to the train. I invited Mr. Dox, member of Congress from Alabama[7] (Huntsville), and his wife, an old friend of mine, to accompany me on the special car, they going to Nashville to visit an invalid sister. On arriving at the train, I found an orderly standing guard over the best seats, saying, "These are for the General's lady." Not wishing to proclaim myself the lady named, I quietly took a seat on the sunny side, expecting to be reseated as soon as it was discovered I was in the car. Imagine my astonishment when a large man and a lady walked in and took the reserved seats. It was General [William Farrar] Smith, usually called "Baldy." I did not mind it, as there was really not much choice, and then too, the Quartermaster had asked if I had any objection to General Smith and his wife going in my car. We hardly exchanged a sentence during the long day's journey. The General did converse some with Mr. Dox. General Smith seemed weighed down with care and responsibility. He was very quiet and thoughtful.

As we approached Nashville, he came to me and said: "Mrs. Grant, my ambulance will be at the station and I will be glad to drive you and your little son wherever you want to go." I thanked him and said: "General Grant will meet us, General." He remarked, "Ah, that is not likely. General Grant has too weighty matters on his mind to think of these little things. You must not expect him." I replied: "He will not fail to meet me." "Well," he said, "if he does not, I will be glad to give you a seat in my ambulance." I bowed my thanks, and as the cars slowed up, I heard: "Is Mrs. Grant aboard?" and saw dear Ulys coming forward on the train greeting each one kindly as he came to meet us. Giving me his arm, he led me out to a handsome ambulance. As we turned from the depot, I saw General Smith gazing after us with, I thought, some chagrin. I then thought of his invitation and asked whose ambulance we were in. The General said it was his. It belonged to headquarters, and he used it at his pleasure. I told him what General Smith had said, and General Grant said: "He has no claim on this. I suppose he has one of his own."

The General had taken rooms for me at the house of Mrs. ——. General [William] Sooy Smith and wife also had rooms at the same house. About two days after we arrived, Longstreet began giving trouble near Knoxville. General Grant was anxious and did much telegraphing. At length, about midnight Christmas Eve, he said: "I will have to start for Knoxville at early dawn. I am sorry to leave you and at Christmas, too." I inquired why he must leave. He replied: "Oh, those fellows are giving trouble. I have been trying to manage it by telegraph, but I must go myself and go early." In four or five days he returned and went or returned through Lexington, Ky. He told me of his visit there and of the many pretty young ladies he met. I think he enjoyed that visit very much.

On his return, I told him of the rumor going around to the effect that as soon as Mrs. Grant heard the General's headquarters were moved to Nashville, she had posted down, losing no time, and the General was so annoyed with her for coming he had taken his staff and left the city. He said: "What did you say to all this?" "That you had sent for me." And he said: "You might have added that I moved my headquarters to Nashville for the sole reason that I might have you near me."

The weather was intensely cold just then, and the soldiers suffered very much, and many became ill. I went to visit the hospitals on several occasions and saw many sad sights. I returned each time laden with petitions for discharges. At last, the General positively prohibited me going any more, saying, "I hear of these all day long and I sent for you to come that I might have a rest from all this sad part. I do not want you to know about these things. I want you to tell me of the children and yourself. I want and need a little rest and sunshine." It was time to stop my going. I became so absorbed in these poor fellows, the wounded, the sick, and the dying, I could think of nothing else.

I remember one little fellow, not over thirteen, a German, was lying ill with typhoid fever in one of the wards. He was in a heavy stupor and very ill. The hospital nurse who was with me tried to arouse him. Every effort failed until she exclaimed, "Come, my soldier boy, we are going to fight *mit* Sigel." He looked up and smiled, shook his poor, aching head approvingly, and fell off again into a deep slumber.

About this time, telegrams came from St. Louis saying our son Fred was very ill and advising me to go to him. I went on, taking Jesse with me. At Louisville, my nurse (a girl raised at my home) left me, as I suppose she feared losing her freedom if she returned to Missouri. I regretted this as she was a favorite with me. However, she married soon afterwards. Major Dunn escorted me to St. Louis, and I fear I must have tried him very much, for on arriving at East St. Louis we found the river frozen over, and the passengers were carried across in omnibuses. I absolutely refused to go in one of these huge vehicles, fearing they might break through, and so I had to walk at midnight over the frozen road nearly a mile, leading Jesse by the hand, and the young Major walked beside me.

I found Fred very ill with camp dysentery and typhoid fever. He did not improve until the attending physician was called away and sent his partner, who, upon examining Fred, told me he was very ill, and that he must change his medicine. He gave him nox vomica. Well, this medicine acted like a charm and cured him, and the General, who had been sent for later, returned to Nashville, taking Fred and myself with him.

While in St. Louis, an old acquaintance called to see the General to get a pass through the lines so she could join her husband's friends in Georgia. Poor thing! She had lost her husband at Vicksburg, fighting on the Confederate side. I was very sorry for her, and, although she had not asked for me, I told the servant when she called again I wished to see her. When she came, I went down, taking with me a roll of Confederate bills captured at Vicksburg and given me as a souvenir, amounting to something over $4,000 and, handing her the permit wrapped around these bills, I said: "Dear Mary, I hope the enclosure may be of use to you. They were given me simply as souvenirs." My conscience troubled me after she left. I feared I had aided the cause of secession and confessed the whole to my husband, who only smiled at my fears and said I had done a service to the Union in doing just as I had; that the more of that kind of money there was in circulation, the better it would be for us.

I remember another occurrence of that visit. I had often been urged in my girlhood by Dr. [Charles A.] Pope, the most distinguished surgeon in the country at that time, to permit him to make a very simple operation upon my eyes. I had never had the courage to consent, but now that my husband had become so famous I really thought it behooved me to try to look as well as possible. So I consulted the Doctor on this, to me, most delicate subject, but alas! he told me it was too late, too late. I told the General and expressed my regret. He replied: "What in the world put such a thought in your head, Julia?" I said: "Why, you are getting to be such a great man, and I am such a plain little wife. I thought if my eyes were as others are I might not be so very, very plain, Ulys; who knows?" He drew me to him and said: "Did I not see you and fall in love with you with these same eyes? I like them just as they are, and now, remember, you are not to interfere with them. They are mine, and let me tell you, Mrs. Grant, you had better not make any experiments, as I might not like you half so well with any other eyes." And I never did, my knight, my Lancelot!

On my return to Nashville, Mrs. Dox called and told me that Dr. [W. A.] Cheatham, the most distinguished physician in the city and at the head of the insane asylum, whose wife had been confined to her bed for several years, had received an order from one of General Grant's staff officers, General William F. Smith, to vacate his house at once, as he wished it for himself and wife. When I told General Grant, he said: "Oh, no! There is some mistake. Smith (the same who came in the cars with me) would not do such a thing when he knows that I, his commanding officer, have taken two rooms only and am boarding with a family so as not to incommode anyone. He would hardly move anyone out of his home. You are misinformed; Smith is a gentleman and would not be guilty of such an act."

When my friend called again, I told her what the General had said, but she replied: "There is no mistake. They are now preparing to move and are looking for quarters for themselves, and Mrs. Cheatham is very ill in consequence." I said: "Send the Doctor to see General Grant, and then he will believe." So Dr. Cheatham called and told General Grant, but the General could scarcely credit it even then, saying, "I cannot understand it. It is so unlike what I thought of Smith. Could there be any personal reason?" "No," Dr. Cheatham said, "unless it is because I happen to be the brother-in-law of John Morgan, who has been on a raid through Ohio and Indiana." [8] The General gave him a safeguard which amply protected his home, and Smith went east soon afterwards. [9]

Fred grew well rapidly and accompanied his father to Washington when he was called there to receive his commission as lieutenant general conferred by Congress. When I expressed my delight at this honor, the General said he had but one regret at receiving it. In answer to my astonished "regret?" he said: "Yes, regret, for this means my station henceforth will be in Washington, and I had hoped when the war was over I might have a choice of stations," blushing slightly at acknowledging before me that he had hoped for choice of stations. He said: "My choice is the Pacific slope, but (with a sigh) this breaks that all up."

He went to Washington, and what glorious accounts came back of his enthusiastic reception there. The papers said that when General Grant was announced at one of the President's levees, the guests became wildly excited, mounting on sofas, chairs, and even tables, to get a look at Grant. When Ulys told me of this afterwards, he said: "Really, it was very embarrassing. I heartily wished myself back in camp." The President and cabinet decided while General Grant was at the capital that the Lieutenant General must come at once to the East.

Before we left Nashville, a magnificent sword was presented to my husband from Jo Daviess County, Illinois. It was brought to him by two faithful and devoted friends, Mr. L. S. Felt of Galena and dear Mr. Charles Rogers of New York, formerly a resident of Galena.[10] The sword was a gem. The top of the hilt was encircled by a band of flashing brilliants. The guard was of gold, richly and appropriately carved. The lines of the blade were graceful and perfect, the etching upon the same exquisite, setting forth the history of why and to whom it was given. The scabbard, which I admired most, was decorated on one side with Moorish designs, upon which were written the names of the many victorious battles in Mexico in which the General participated. On the reverse, a ribbon floated down its length on each fold of which was written the name of one of his victories: Donelson, Chattanooga, Vicksburg, Shiloh, Henry, etc.[11] This much-prized heirloom of our children, with the magnificent gold medal presented to General Grant when Vicksburg surrendered by our most gracious Congress, with the jeweled sword voted to him by the city of New York, and many other mementos of his prowess, loyalty, and honor, now lie in the cabinets of the Capitol at Washington, presented through the princely generosity of one of New York's citizens, Mr. W. H. Vanderbilt.[12]

On his return from Washington, General Grant arranged for his immediate departure for the East to take command of all the armies. He said to me: "Now I can order your brother Colonel Dent to report to me for duty on my staff. For some reason I have not been able to secure his services, though I have made requests to Halleck for him more than once."

En route to Washington, General Sherman joined us. Perhaps he went with us from Nashville. He and General Grant had long conversations, I think in reference to Sherman's subsequent march to the sea.[13] After that subject had been discussed, General Grant said: "Sherman, it may be necessary to change some of the men east. If so, I will send them out to you, and you must take care of them. They are all soldiers and good ones, and we must not let them go under if we can help them in any way." Sherman responded cheerfully and cordially to this suggestion and said: "I'm glad you feel so, Grant. They are fine fellows, all of them, and I entirely sympathize with you in this. Send them out and I'll see they are provided for." McClellan, Sykes, and Newton were mentioned.[14]

As this was my first visit to Washington, and knowing that General Sherman had often been there, I asked his advice as to etiquette, saying, "General, tell me what I must do when we reach Washington." He stopped suddenly, looked a trifle annoyed—I think I interrupted his thinking on some great war problem—and, repeating the question, he said: "What shall you do in Washington? Why, return all of your calls, every one of them, and promptly too, and you will be all right."

The journey to Washington was fatiguing, and I was glad when we stopped for a day at Philadelphia, as my wardrobe, necessarily always simple, was now quite depleted, and the few additions I was enabled to make at Philadelphia gave me both comfort and peace of mind.

We arrived in Washington at night, and at breakfast next morning I experienced my first shock. My *vis-à-vis* at table, a stout but not an old lady, with a bunch of hard, black curls on each side of her forehead, great heavy black eyebrows, and a very white face, deliberately raised her glasses and stared me out of countenance. So annoyed was I that I asked the General to take me to my room. After this, I hardly ever went to table d'hôte.

Well, as General Sherman said, I had all I could do if I returned my calls, which I never did. After many trials, I succeeded in arranging a tolerably fair list, so that in a few weeks I might have done so, if an order had not come to the young staff officer, who had kindly volunteered his services as escort to me, to report at once to headquarters. This broke up all my plans, and the one valuable maxim given me by General Sherman was never carried out.

The President and Mrs. Lincoln invited General Grant and me to their reception. The General had already gone to the front, but I had a sufficient escort in Admiral [David G.] Farragut, who was just then being tremendously lionized by society, and two of General Grant's staff officers, who had not yet joined their chief. After entering the Red Room, we soon reached the President. He at once recognized the Admiral, who presented me. Mr. Lincoln repeated: "Mrs. General Grant?" greeted me in the most cordial manner, taking both my hands in his, expressed great pleasure at meeting me, and asked, "But where is the General?" I said: "I begged the General to remain and accompany me, but he said he must go to the front and he was sure the President and Mrs. Lincoln would excuse him."

The President was delighted with this reply, and presented me to his wife, who, after a few pleasant words of welcome, asked me to stand near her and see the company pass, but feeling a little shy, I did not accept, and, the crowd pressing a little, we moved on. I looked up for the first time and saw the crowd of beautiful women and brave men who filled the Blue Room behind President and Mrs. Lincoln. Every eye was turned on the gallant Admiral. He said: "Mrs. Grant, there is not standing room here. Shall we pass to the Green Room?" He added in low tones: "The 'commonality' go there; will you venture?" I replied gaily: "I think I may venture anywhere on the arm of Admiral Farragut." He blushed, smiled, bowed, and we passed on to the Green Room. Hardly had we taken position there when the guests in the Blue Room, cabinet ministers, senators, foreign ministers, judges of Supreme Court, army and navy officers, with a hundred or more of the belles and beaux of Washington, passed before Admiral Farragut and the wife of General Grant, smiling a pleasant welcome and greeting me with a cordial grasp of the hand. When this was over, I was escorted by half a dozen distinguished old gentlemen, amongst whom were Frank P. Blair, Sr., and several others, to the East Room, and through the corridors to the conservatory, all showing me every consideration for the General's sake. I attended receptions at each secretary's, also at the Chief Justice's, Mr. [Salmon P.] Chase, and never once thought of the calls I must at last return.

The General came up for a day and told me I had better go to St. Louis, where the three children were at school, and that I might return by way of New York, where I could visit Colonel and Mrs. Hillyer. The Colonel was then in Washington and would escort me to his house and also secure me a suitable escort to St. Louis.

During my stay in New York, Mr. Stanton kindly sent me all telegraphic reports from the seat of war. Many distinguished people called on me, and I made some friends then whom I still greatly prize. During this visit, I attended the great Sanitary Fair. A magnificent jewel-hilted sword was being voted for, to be given to the favorite general. As we made the rounds of the dazzling hall, we came to the table where the sword was. Colonel Hillyer said: "Mrs. Grant, here is the famous sword. Wouldn't you like to cast a vote?" "Of course I would," and paying my fee, one dollar, I quietly wrote my name under that of General McClellan. Colonel Hillyer exclaimed: "What, voting for McClellan? How is this? I am astonished!" I replied, "Of course, I wish my husband to get the sword, but, Colonel, it would not be in good taste for me to vote for my husband, would it? You see this is a very nice question. I never voted, save at school for our May Queen, and I am sure the etiquette on such occasions should be that the rival queens vote for each other. Any other course there would have been looked on as selfish and dishonorable, and, Colonel, I voted upon that precedent." The next day, the papers were full of praise of this little act. Public opinion said it was right and savored of the days of knighthood.[15]

I remained much longer in New York than I intended, waiting for an escort, which at length was secured for me. I arrived at St. Louis, finding my darlings, Fred, Ulysses, and Nellie, happy and well. I had left them boarding with and in the care of a friend there.[16]

The children were much excited with their attendance at the great Sanitary Fair, which had just been held at St. Louis. Nellie had been representing the old woman in the shoe who had so many children she didn't know what to do. Nellie was delighted with her metamorphosis, seated as she was in a mammoth black pasteboard shoe filled with beautiful dolls of all sizes. Nellie wore over her pretty curls a wide, ruffled cap and a pair of huge spectacles across her pretty, rosy, dimpled face. She was delighted with the selling of dolls and her photos, telling me the ladies gave her a half dollar for every doll and every picture. She gave one of these to me with much pride. My darling boys, too, filled my lap with all the pretty things they had secured by purchase and raffle on this occasion, some of which I have yet.

I was happy to be at home again, busied myself putting my house in order, and hoped soon to have the pleasure of a visit from my husband. Our colored people had all left, but their places were readily filled by German and French men and women, who were most excellent substitutes. How lovely our little villa was, with its cool new India matting and muslin curtains, and how happy we all were on our rose-covered piazza, dear papa so entertained by all I had to tell him. The trees and grounds around our home were large and handsome. We had a great deal of company, and then it was we missed the old family servants. That was the first time we felt that there was trouble in entertaining, much as we enjoyed it.

When the summer was over, the General sent for me to join him in the East, and, in accordance with his instructions, I proceeded with my four children to Philadelphia, where my brother General Dent met me. We stopped at the Continental Hotel until we could find a suitable house to rent. As the General had formed a very high opinion of the morale of Philadelphia, he wished me to remain there and send the children to school.

Failing to find a house or to make suitable terms at the hotel, I sent my brother General Dent to Burlington, N.J., hearing excellent reports of the schools there from my friend, Mrs. General Stephen Kearny. My brother secured a nice cottage pleasantly situated, and I immediately took possession. I would have saved myself much trouble and expense if I had gone to the hotel and sent the children to boarding school, which those schools proved to be—no day scholars were allowed. But the considerate Mr. Gibson made an exception in my favor when he learned that all my arrangements had been made with the intention of having my two boys attend his school as day scholars.

Burlington proved a delightful place of residence. The people were kind and hospitable to us, and I remember with pleasure our stay there. I made the acquaintance of several charming Quaker ladies there and spent many pleasant hours at their quiet homes. The children were also happy with their many little friends, though Fred had to give battle more than once to establish his western prowess. After a chiding once for fighting on the Sabbath, he said: "I had to thrash the fellow or he would have thrashed me. He made the attack. I simply defended myself. Was there any harm in that on Sunday?"

The General visited us three or four times while in Burlington. On one occasion, we looked for him home to dinner, but something detained him, and at half past ten he had not arrived. So I told the children we would retire and hope that papa would come tomorrow. After they were in bed, Nellie called to me: "Mamma, papa will be sure to come tonight, for I asked God in my prayers to please let him come." She was chagrined when Jess asked in a wrathful tone, "Nellie, did you say your prayers in bed?" Nellie, looking very guilty, said, "yes, Jess." "Then," he said, "papa won't come for your prayer, you bad girl. If he does come, it will be purely accidental." This was a big word for little Jess, but he brought it out correctly, syllable by syllable. The children had hardly ceased speaking when the bell rang and the General arrived. He said it was because he knew Nellie wanted to see him.

These visits were not very satisfactory after all, as the General was necessarily hurried and we had throngs of visitors, but he used to send for me to visit him and that was pleasant. He always sent a ship or boat to meet me and allowed me to invite friends to accompany me. He would come down the James River in his own boat and meet us at Fortress Monroe, and taking the party on his boat, we would arrive at City Point the next morning. On one occasion, as I came out of my stateroom where the General was still asleep—he always slept late and went late to bed—an excited young woman approached me carrying a rosy baby in her arms, saying, "I want to see General Grant." I replied: "He is not awake. You cannot see him." She exclaimed wildly, "I must see him! I must see him! I will!" and, bursting into tears, cried, "Oh, Madam, let me see him. My husband is sentenced to be shot." "When?" I asked. She exclaimed, "this day, at twelve o'clock, and it was all my fault. You see, the baby here was over seven months old, and he had never seen it, and, sure, I thought they could never miss him from out all these thousands of men. So I wrote and begged him to come just to see the baby, you know. He did come, and now they have caught him and say he is a deserter, and, sure, Madam, it is all my fault, as sure as I stand here, before my God! Oh, let me see General Grant!"

I went to the stateroom and hurriedly repeated the woman's statement. The General replied: "I cannot interfere. She must go to General [Marsena R.] Patrick." "But," I exclaimed, "it is today the man is to be shot, at twelve o'clock, and it is nearly nine now." He still said: "I cannot interfere." So I threw open the door and said to the woman: "You may enter and tell the General yourself." The baby was amusing itself by reaching up and pulling down its mother's veil, whose face was bathed in tears. I told her to sit down and tell her own story. The General soon called to me to send him paper and ink. And the woman shortly came out, looking almost transfigured, saying, "God bless you, Madam, and God bless the General." When I went in to thank the General, he replied: "I'm sure I did wrong. I've no doubt I have pardoned a bounty jumper who ought to have been hanged."

My visit on this occasion was delightful, as were all of my visits to camp. I met the staff officers, the corps commanders, and the many distinguished visitors at headquarters, and that made it very pleasant. There were many ladies, too. They generally asked for a button from the General's coat, which troubled me some, for it was both inconvenient and troublesome to replace them. These loyal and devoted ladies did not consider how the General would appear minus a half-dozen buttons or so. And I fear there was also a dash of jealousy in my feelings. He was mine, and I did not wish another to have even one of his buttons. I told him I thought it was very silly for them to be cutting buttons off of his coat. After that, he referred them to me when they wanted any, and I was obliged to consent, for it was too trifling a thing to refuse.

On our return from this visit, the General accompanied us to Fortress Monroe. He suggested that Jess should remain in camp with him. Barnes,[17] his servant, would take entire care of him. I objected, and the General did not like it. He said: "Jess would like it immensely if you would consent." We called the little fellow and made known his father's wish. Jess said yes, he would like to stay if mamma was willing. The General was delighted and told Barnes to get out Jesse's baggage, as we were nearing the packet steamer. I felt a trifle hurt that Jess had decided to remain, and the General said, more than once, "I knew he would stay with me, only he was afraid you would not like it." When the parting came, it was too much. As our steamer swung out into the bay, dear little Jess climbed onto a large chair and, throwing himself violently to the floor, cried out: "I am hurt, very much hurt, and must go with them." Our steamer was hove to until Jess could arrive on the dispatch tug from his father's steamer, and, in the meantime, I gave emphatic orders to Fred, Ulysses, and Nell not to say anything to Jess about his change of plan. They must only express great pleasure at his coming. I am sorry to say this was very hard on Fred, who really felt it was hard on him that he (Fred) was not permitted to remain in the field, having gone through the Vicksburg campaign.

As we returned from one of these visits to the front, I with my party passed through Washington and, of course, tarried there for a few days to see the Capitol and all the other beautiful buildings. Mr. [John B.] Steele, a member of Congress from New York, was our escort, as we, Mrs. General Dent and I, with my little son Jesse (then about six years old), ascended the steps of the Patent Office. Jesse stopped in amazement at the magnitude of the pillars that surrounded this beautiful edifice, stopping halfway up the steps and calling out in great excitement, "Mamma, are these the same kind of pillars Samson pulled down and killed three thousand people? Say, mamma, are they?" I told him to run on and ask Mr. Steele, and he did. Mr. Steele asked the child what he knew about Samson. Jesse only replied: "Tell me, are these the same kind of pillars?" Mr. Steele thought they were. Jesse stood and looked for a while and then said: "Well, he *must* have been a strong man!" The party passed on into the building where there was a showroom. In one of the glass cases in this room was a suit of military uniform, either of Washington or Andrew Jackson. The little fellow lingered near these, seemed thoughtful, and at length asked me, "Mamma, is there any of Caesar's clothes here?" "No, Jess." "Is there any of Alexander the Great's clothes here?" "Oh, no," I said, "the moths have eaten those long ago." "Then, mamma, is there any of my papa's clothes here?" The little fellow had already associated his papa with all these great men. "Not yet, Jess dear." He stood for a while longer in deep study, when, coming up to me, he said: "Mamma, now I know why Alexander cried that there were no more worlds to conquer." "Yes, why, Jess?" He answered brightly, "Because America was not yet discovered. Is that not so, mamma?"

"Yes, Jess, you are right." Of course, this historic lore was gathered from his brothers Fred and Ulysses, who no doubt told him all these stories, for little Jess had not yet attended school.

Fred demanded and secured permission to spend his Christmas holidays with his father, then in camp at City Point on the James River, Va. Whilst there, Fred went off in great glee duck shooting. He wore the uniform of his school at Burlington, N.J., gray trimmed with black. He took a colored servant of his father to row his boat and was anticipating great sport, when, lo! in passing one of the many gunboats then in the James River he was fired on and ordered to. I think he said heave to. Fred was a captive and had some trouble in convincing his captors that he was not an enemy though he wore the gray, but the son of their General Grant.

I remained in Burlington until after New Year's, when a delightful and most unexpected event occurred. A deed of gift to General Grant of a house and furniture on Chestnut Street, Philadelphia, was sent me: a home, a lovely home, given to my dear, brave husband by a number of strange gentlemen of Philadelphia! In the West and South we looked upon all people east of the Alleghenies as Yankees, and to think of Yankees showing this magnificent generosity! I at once sent the deed to the General, and he returned it to me for safekeeping.

I prevailed on my sister-in-law, Mrs. General Dent, to remain with my children, while I went, at General Grant's request, to make him a prolonged visit, as he was now domiciled in the cabin which now stands in Fairmount Park, Philadelphia. The Quartermaster [Rufus] Ingalls built this for the General so I could be with him he said. They all flattered me by saying that I must stay with him and that at headquarters they missed me. And so for the rest of this eventful winter, I was domiciled in this little cabin, enjoying not only the society of the Commanding General but of all the distinguished men and generals that visited headquarters that winter.

How many came that winter! I remember General Sherman coming from the South and holding a conference with General Grant in his cabin. I was there writing letters. General Grant looked up at me and remarked: "Sherman, do you think it is safe to let Mrs. Grant hear us?" Sherman turned and said: "Well, I don't know. Let me see. Mrs. Grant, can you tell me where the Tombigbee River is?" I answered wide of the mark, of course. Then he inquired, looking much puzzled himself, if I could tell him where the Chattahoochee River was? That was what he wanted, not the Tombigbee. I had forgotten where that was also. Then, turning to the General, he said: "Oh, yes, Grant, I think we may trust her."

I was throwing dust in Sherman's eyes all the time. And now I am going to tell all that I remember. After a long talk of troops and movements, Sherman said: "Grant, if you want me to help you, I can come up. Yes, I can manage it, I am sure." But General Grant replied: "No, I can manage everything myself. You hold Joe Johnston just where he is. I do not want him around here."

[Major General Edward O. C.] Ord came daily. His visits were social, I think. Perhaps it was to report upon the condition of the Army of the James. He was always most welcome. Then General Meade was often there also. He was feeling great anxiety about his confirmation by the Senate and came more than once for letters from General Grant. I remember how exasperated he was when the enemy broke his lines the only night he was away from his headquarters. His family had been to visit him, and he came up to City Point to see them off and remained all night. When he heard of the disaster, he rushed from General Grant's headquarters to his office so, so impatiently declaring it was his infernal luck as usual.[18]

One afternoon, soon after Sherman's visit to City Point, not long before the last eventful and successful movement on Richmond, General Grant and I were alone in his cabin office when I said to him: "Ulys, why do you not tell me something of your plans?" I felt much injured that I had not been informed before. The General said: "Would you like to know of my plans?" "Of course I would." Then he turned to a map which lay on his office table and said: "I will show you with pleasure. There (sweeping his hand over the Southern states) is the entire field. Here to the right rest the Army of the Potomac and the Army of the James. There (pointing towards West Virginia and Tennessee) I have placed [Major General George] Stoneman with a large body of cavalry to guard the passes of the mountains, be on the alert, and keep me informed of everything. There (placing his hand on the Gulf states) I have placed [Major] General [Edward R. S.] Canby, and here (becoming at once much pleased and interested as his finger rested on a point on the eastern coast of Georgia) is Sherman. Now you have the position of all the armies. You observe it is a perfect cordon from sea to sea again." "Yes," I said, "what next?" "Do you want to know more?" "Yes, of course; everything I ought to." "Well," he said, "I am going to tighten that cordon until the rebellion is crushed or strangled." So I knew it all now, felt sorrowful, and said so to the General. "Yes," he replied, "war is always sorrowful, but only think how dreadful it would be if a cordon like that I have just pointed out to you encircled our Union."

The James River was full to overflowing. General Ingalls seemed both disappointed and disturbed that the enemy made no demonstration. He came in regularly, morning and night, and said to General Grant: "General, what do you suppose those fellows mean by not coming down? I do not understand them. By all rights, they ought to have been down here three days ago." "They are coming, Ingalls. You keep a sharp lookout and be prepared for them."

The last night this was talked over, we sat quite late and had at length retired, when a sharp, quick, nervous rap was heard at our cabin door. The General at once called: "Hello! Enter." Captain Dunn entered the office door and said hurriedly: "General, the rebel rams are coming down the river and have passed the obstructions."

The General at once arose, drew on his long boots and his coat over his pajamas. He lighted a cigar and seated himself, writing one dispatch after another. All this time, the only expression of excitement was the rapid and sharp puffs of his cigar. I remember it was like a little steam engine. I quickly dressed, entered the office room, and asked: "Will the ram shell the bluff?" "Yes, of course." "Then what shall I do?" The General looked up and for the first time thought of me. He simply said: "You have no business to be here." And he had sent for me, mind you! Captain Dunn laughingly proposed, if the General would consent, that he should take me back far out of danger in an ambulance.

The General now asked my volunteer escort if the gunboat he had sent him for had arrived. "No, General, it will be up in about two hours." The General said: "Take a tugboat and bring her up at once." "Yes, General," and he went. The rebel ram did pass the obstruction, but was so crippled in doing so that it lay utterly helpless just beyond them and could not move another rod, so that there was no anxiety to know if by "the rockets' red glare, the bombs bursting in air, . . . our flag was still there." No roar of cannon, no bursting of shell, no great military pageant for me! Our flag, our bright, beautiful flag, was fluttering to the balmy breezes, and all was quiet on the James.

The next morning I was there when the peace commissioners came, and our President, Mr. Lincoln, came to meet them.[19] I often saw Mr. [Alexander H.] Stephens and Mr. [John A.] Campbell. On one occasion towards the end of the conference, Mr. Lincoln came into our cabin (the General was at his office), and, being anxious, I at once became inquisitive and asked Mr. Lincoln if any conclusions in the interests of peace had yet been reached. He hesitatingly replied, "well, no." He had evidently come to have a talk with the General and perhaps thought my questions premature, as they undoubtedly were. I exclaimed: "No! Why, Mr. President, are you not going to make terms with them? They are our own people, you know." Then he answered, "Yes, I do not forget that," and quietly taking from his pocket a large paper, he carefully unfolded it and read aloud the terms he proposed to them, which were most liberal, I thought. After finishing, he looked up, and I said: "Did they not accept those?" He smiled wearily and said, "no." Whereupon I wrathfully exclaimed: "Why, what do they want? That paper is most liberal." He smiled and said: "I thought when you understood the matter you would agree with us."

I had quite an interview with the commissioners, telling them they held a brother of mine as a prisoner and that he was a thorough rebel if there ever was one. I knew this to be so as I had had many a battle royal with him on this subject. These gentlemen asked if General Grant could not exchange him. "Why, of course not," I explained, "my brother is not a soldier." He was on a visit to a friend in Louisiana when he was captured. I had already approached General Grant on the subject, and he had asked me if I thought it would be just for him to give a war prisoner in exchange for my brother, when we had so many brave men languishing in prison who had fought for the Union. It was hard, but I knew he was right. He consoled me by saying, "It will not hurt John to have a good, wholesome lesson, and I hope and trust the war will soon be over, and then John will come home with the crowd, and I will do all I can for him then." So dear brother did not get back until the general exchange of prisoners took place at the close of the war.

There was another war prisoner, young Hewitt, a cousin of the General, who was confined for months at Johnson's Island in Lake Erie.[20] His mother and family, who were living in Paris for security, often wrote to General Grant, making earnest appeals for his release. Of course, the General could only follow the routine and wait until it should be Mr. Hewitt's turn to be exchanged. So when this young man arrived at the depot where the prisoners were exchanged, General Grant telegraphed: "When Mr. Hewitt's exchange is accomplished, have him report to my headquarters." The telegram was read to Mr. Hewitt, who, with evident disappointment, repaired to the Commanding General. The General greeted him kindly and said: "I have some letters here from your mother," and, handing him the package, continued, "If you wish to avail yourself of this opportunity, I will be most happy to give you safe conduct, and if you need money, that also. You must read these letters and decide." The young soldier read the letters and sat thinking. Then he arose, thanked the General, and said: "For me to accept this now, at the very gates of Richmond, would savor of desertion. The cause, our cause, needs every man at his post, and I must go on to Richmond." The General said: "I can't but admire your decision, but I think it most unwise." The young gentleman proceeded to Richmond, and about a fortnight afterwards we heard of his death.

Following the first visit of the President came the Secretary of War, Mr. Stanton, accompanied by Mrs. Stanton and their eldest son, Edwin, and a young lady from Columbus, Ohio. The troops were all marshaled and review followed review. I am sure the Secretary must have been thrilled with enthusiasm when these magnificent pageants filed past him. I was.

We had all returned from a review of the Army of the James, and I was ready for luncheon. Our party had assembled in the saloon of our boat—I think, the *Mary Martin*. I went to Mrs. Stanton's stateroom, where I found Mrs. Stanton still with her wrap and bonnet on. I said: "Luncheon is about ready." She replied: "Yes, I know, but I feel so discouraged with Mr. Stanton. He is so unreasonable." Of course, I only looked my surprise and sympathy and only inquired, "indeed?" "Yes," Mrs. Stanton said, "when Edwin was in Columbus at school,[21] the family of this young lady who is with me was very kind to Eddie. Edwin had often mentioned their kindness to him, and now that one of the family is in Washington, I felt it not only a pleasure but a duty to do what I could to make it pleasant for her, and I invited her to accompany us on this visit to the James River. Mr. Stanton has an idea that Edwin is in love with the young lady and says I am doing everything to bring about a match."

This was all most interesting to me. Only think, a delightful romance right beside me, involving all the requisites: two young lovers, a wronged mother, and a tyrant of unusual power. Oh delightful! delightful! I could see it all now. Why did I not see it before? I certainly would have arranged for the young people to be near each other. I remembered that the Secretary was rather, well, impatient and thought he chafed at being in the ambulance when all the officers were on horseback. I said to him I thought he ought to have a horse. But he said: "Oh, no, that would be impossible for me. I am not well enough." And so I thought.

Mrs. Stanton promised to soon be ready, and I joined the party already assembled in the boat's saloon. The young lady (Mrs. Stanton's friend) was seated opposite me and near her was a vacant chair. We were all in gay good humor with our morning's pageant and delightful ride and were chatting gaily together when a tall, handsome, young officer came up the boat's passageway nearest me or

[139]

where I was sitting. He greeted us all and, after a moment, bowed and walked down the passage again. I supposed he had gone, when one of General Grant's staff officers, General [Orville E.] Babcock, whispered to me, "I am going to take the chair near Miss A——. I want you to watch General P—— and see how he will blush when he comes up and finds me seated in the chair he has gone all the way round to secure beside Miss A——, to whom he is engaged to be married. It serves him right, too. He ought to have better tactics. He, a soldier and nearly four years in the field." Well, he came, blushed *so* red, stammered something, turned, and walked rapidly off to the other end of the boat. The young lady at once missed her handkerchief—when is a woman unequal to such an emergency?—and hastened to her stateroom or to the other end of the boat to find it. Well, as I held in my hand both ends of this silken thread, I lost no time and walked, not very leisurely, to the shore end of our boat, and there stood our fair young guest, looking wistfully out, hoping to get one, only one, glance from that brave, gallant, but shy, young soldier. But he had gone, and near her stood young Stanton. Just then, I saw I was quite near Mr. Stanton, whom I at once addressed, asking him how he had enjoyed the review given in his honor that morning. His reply was most ungracious: "Enjoy? I did not enjoy it at all. I wish I had not come down here." "Why, Mr. Stanton, I am astonished." He hastily exclaimed: "Look there! That boy of mine thinks he is in love and wants to take a wife. He could not pay for his own bread and butter, let alone take care of a wife."

I gently asked: "Whom does he wish to marry, Mr. Stanton?" "Why, that girl (pointing towards them) and Ellen, my wife, is doing everything in her power to bring it about and encouraging them in every way. The girl is good enough for anyone, but Edwin is too poor and too young to marry, and I shall put a stop to it *at once*." I said: "My dear Mr. Stanton, do not give yourself the least trouble on that score. The young lady is, I know, already engaged to General P——, the handsome young officer who has only just now left the boat." He roughly demanded: "How do you know this?" I simply replied: "Why, I know it. Everyone does. It is a fact well known." Well, the transformation in Mr. Stanton was something wonderful. He was simply angelic during the rest of his visit and liked reviews. The young lady was married to the gallant young General when the cruel war was over.

Late one afternoon, about four o'clock, not long before the last move toward Richmond, I entered from my bedroom General Grant's office, where I found General Grant in conversation with General

Ord. General Grant said to me: "See here, Mrs. Grant, what do you think of this? Ord has been across the lines on a flag of truce and brings a suggestion that terms of peace may be reached through you, and a suggestion of an interchange of social visits between you and Mrs. Longstreet and others when the subject of peace may be discussed, and you ladies may become the mediums of peace." At once, I exclaimed: "Oh! How enchanting, how thrilling! Oh, Ulys, I may go, may I not?" He only smiled at my enthusiasm and said: "No, I think not." I then approached him, saying, "Yes, I must. Do say yes. I so much wish to go. Do let me go." But he still said: "No, that would never do." Besides, he did not feel sure that he could trust me; with the desire I always had shown for having a voice in great affairs, he was afraid I might urge some policy that the President would not sanction. I replied to this: "Oh, nonsense. Do not talk so, but let me go. I should be so enchanted to have a voice in this great matter. I must go. I will. Do say I may go." But General Grant grew very earnest now and said: "No, you must not. It is simply absurd. The men have fought this war and the men will finish it."

I urged no more, knowing this was final, and I was silent, indignant, and disappointed. Then I turned to General Ord and inquired how such an idea could have been suggested. He told me he had gone over on a flag of truce, saying our men and the rebs were exchanging papers, tobacco, even running races, and on good terms apparently, and he thought it was high time this was stopped. After settling this little matter, Ord said: "I said to Longstreet, 'Why do you fellows hold out any longer? You know you cannot succeed. Why prolong this unholy struggle? Every day you hold out you are worsting your-selves.' " I think General Ord said he had proposed the ladies as a medium of peace—he was always kind—but this I do know: such a proposition never emanated from General Grant. Strange to say, since writing this little scrap of history as I know it to be, I find after many months this version of the same incident. But what I write are the simple facts. Such a proposition never emanated from General Grant.[22]

While I was at headquarters in March, 1865, the papers daily announced the exhausted appearance of the President. On more than one occasion, I petitioned the General with hospitable intent to invite Mr. and Mrs. Lincoln down to visit the army; so many people were coming, and the weather was simply delightful. The General would always reply to my request: "If President Lincoln wishes to come down, he will not wait to be asked. It is not my place to invite him." "Yes," I urged, "it is. You know all that has been said about his interference with army movements, and he will never come for fear of appearing to meddle with army affairs." But the General did not invite them. One day, Captain Robert Lincoln, in reply to my inquiries about his father's health and my asking why his father and mother did not come down on a visit, said: "I suppose they would, if they were sure they would not be intruding."

General Grant at once telegraphed them an invitation to visit the army and said he was sure a sail down the river would be beneficial and restful to both of them. Before bedtime a reply came saying the President and family would leave Washington at twelve o'clock the following day on the steamer *River Queen*.[23] They arrived in due time. Captain Robert Lincoln, a noble, handsome, young fellow, who was then on the General's staff, entered our cabin and announced in happy haste the arrival of the President and Mrs. Lincoln. We immediately proposed calling on them in their boat. The Captain volunteered to escort us. He had already seen them. I suppose the President's arrival was kept quiet for a purpose, but I was not satisfied, not being able to divest myself of the idea that I was somehow hostess, and so I urged not only a flourish of trumpets, but a grand salute to these guests, so distinguished and so honored.

Our gracious President met us at the gangplank, greeted the General most heartily, and, giving me his arm, conducted us to where Mrs. Lincoln was awaiting us. She received us most cordially, and as soon as a few words of greeting had passed, the President said: "Now, I am going to leave you two ladies together while the General and I go for a few moments to my room where we can have a little talk without being interrupted. Eh, General?"

On the departure of the gentlemen, Mrs. Lincoln politely pointed to the little sofa from which she had arisen and invited me to be seated. As I was standing near her, I seated myself beside her on this small sofa; then, seeing a look of surprise from Mrs. Lincoln, I immediately started up, exclaiming, "I crowd you, I fear." She kindly extended her hand to detain me, saying, "not at all." So I remained where I was for a few moments and then quietly took a chair near her. On my return to camp, in reply to inquiries as to my visit, I related this very awkward mistake on my part, and from this little incident innocently related, and, as I remember, casting blame on myself if there was any, saying, "I was a trifle embarrassed, or I would not have taken that seat," is woven the sensational story so recently published.[24]

NOTES

1. William Lum of Vicksburg was a prosperous merchant before the Civil War. Records indicating Grant's assistance to his widow, Mrs. Ann Lum, are in Union Provost Marshals' File of Papers Relating to Individual Civilians, Record Group 109, National Archives.

2. On June 5 and 13, 1866, the Cabinet of President Andrew Johnson discussed and finally decided to allow the claim of Madame Joseph Bertinatti, wife of the Italian minister, formerly Mrs. Eugenia P. Bass of Mississippi. John T. Morse, Jr., ed., *Diary of Gideon Welles* (Boston and New York, 1911), II, 522, 526. For earlier involvement in the claim of both Lincoln and Grant, see Roy P. Basler, Marion Dolores Pratt, and Lloyd A. Dunlap, eds., *The Collected Works of Abraham Lincoln* (New Brunswick, New Jersey, 1953–55), VII, 131, 149.

3. William Porterfield, born in Ireland, settled at Vicksburg, where he prospered in varied businesses and became associated personally and professionally with both Jefferson Davis and his brother, Joseph Emory Davis. According to local rumor, Porterfield's second wife, Julia Lyons, was the daughter of Joseph Davis. Information from James T. McIntosh, editor of *The Papers of Jefferson Davis*, June, 1974. An anonymous letter of August 28, 1863, accused Porterfield of treasonous talk. On September 13, Provost Marshal Loren Kent endorsed this letter with a request to expel Porterfield. Union Provost Marshals' File of Papers Relating to Individual Civilians, Record Group 109, National Archives. On September 30, U.S. Surgeon John Moore wrote to Grant's headquarters requesting revocation of the order banishing Porterfield; the request was denied. Volume 23, entry M626, volume 25, p. 565, Grant Papers, Library of Congress.

4. On October 16, 1863, Grant received orders from Washington to relieve Rosecrans and authorization, which he chose to use, to replace him with Major General George H. Thomas. *O.R.*, I, xxx, part 4, 404.

5. The battle of Chattanooga, November 23–25, 1863, may also be considered separate battles of Lookout Mountain and Missionary Ridge.

6. Both were raised in Georgetown, Ohio.

7. Peter M. Dox practiced law and served as judge in his native New York before moving to Alabama. He served as a Democratic U.S. Representative from Alabama 1869–73. He was a brother-in-law of Dr. Charles A. Pope of St. Louis, a close friend of the Dents. Sir Christopher Chancellor, ed., *An Englishman in the American Civil War: The Diaries of Henry Yates Thompson 1863* (London, 1971), p. 110.

8. Both Dr. W. A. Cheatham and his wife Mary, sister of Mrs. John Hunt Morgan, had been arrested in May, 1863, for corresponding with Morgan. *O.R.*, II, v, 709–10. Documents concerning the arrest of the Cheathams, including a copy of an intercepted letter from Mrs. Cheatham to Mrs. Morgan, are in Union Provost Marshals' File of Papers Relating to Individual Civilians, Record Group 109, National Archives.

9. In fact, Grant gave Major General William Farrar Smith an important command in the Army of the James, from which he was later removed after a clash with Major General Benjamin F. Butler. Julia Grant's unattractive account of Smith is almost certainly connected with his book, *From Chattanooga to Petersburg under Generals Grant and Butler* (Boston and New York, 1893). Smith argued that he had been removed from the Army of the James rather than Butler because Butler had

put pressure on Grant by threatening to expose his drinking. The point is discussed and rejected in William D. Mallam, "The Grant-Butler Relationship," *Mississippi Valley Historical Review*, XLI (September, 1954), 259–76.

10. Lewis S. Felt, a Galena merchant, became a close family friend of the Grants. Correspondence in the Elihu B. Washburne Papers, Library of Congress, indicates that Charles K. Rogers of New York City helped arrange the making of the sword; letters from Rogers of April 15, 16, 1864, discuss the presentation visit.

11. A picture of this sword is in [William H. Allen], *The American Civil War Book and Grant Album* . . . (Boston, 1894), p. [7].

12. See Chapter 5, note 13 for an account of the transfer of the Grant trophies to William H. Vanderbilt to repay his loan to Grant and Ward. The trophies are now in the Smithsonian Institution.

13. Sherman and Grant traveled together from Nashville to Cincinnati, discussing the coming campaign only so far as Sherman's occupation of Atlanta. Grant, *Memoirs*, II, 118–20.

14. As Grant recalled his plan, he intended to have Sherman restore officers removed in the West while Grant attended to others. The refusal of Major General Don Carlos Buell to serve under Sherman apparently canceled these plans. *Ibid.*, pp. 119–21. McClellan never received an offer of another command; Major General John Newton, once removed from command by Major General Ambrose E. Burnside, later resumed command in the Army of the Potomac, then served in the Atlanta campaign under Sherman; Major General George Sykes, relieved of command by Major General George G. Meade for slowness in following orders in December, 1863, served in Kansas through the close of the war.

15. Grant eventually won the sword, shown in [Allen], *Grant Album*, p. [7]. According to Rawlins, Grant was annoyed by his wife's action, apparently not because she voted for McClellan, but because she voted. Wilson, *Life of John A. Rawlins*, p. 425.

16. Julia Grant's cousin Louisa Boggs, wife of Harry Boggs, Grant's former business partner. See Louisa Boggs to Dr. Henry M. Whelpley, February 11, 1914, Missouri Historical Society, St. Louis.

17. For William Barnes, a Negro servant who had joined Grant during the Vicksburg campaign, see Jesse R. Grant, *In the Days of My Father General Grant* (New York and London, 1925), pp. 210–11.

18. The incident described is the capture of Fort Stedman, March 25, 1865. Meade's anger is also mentioned by Horace Porter, *Campaigning with Grant* (New York, 1897), p. 404.

19. The Confederate gunboats approached City Point on the night of January 23–24, 1865; Lincoln met the Confederate peace commissioners at Hampton Roads on February 3. The commissioners visited Grant at City Point before their conference with Lincoln.

20. Captain Richard M. Hewitt, Miles' Louisiana Legion, captured in 1863 and still at Johnson's Island in early 1865. For the Hewitt family, see Chapter 1.

21. Edwin L. Stanton attended Kenyon College, Gambier, Ohio.

22. Julia Grant here inserted in her manuscript a lengthy newspaper clipping discussing an article by Frank A. Burr in the New York *Press* in 1890. Burr based his account on an interview with James Longstreet, and most of the information had already appeared in Burr's book, *Life and Deeds of General U. S. Grant* (Philadelphia *et al.*, 1885), pp. 676–79. See also Longstreet, *From Manassas to*

Appomattox (Philadelphia, 1896), pp. 583–87. Longstreet, who originally believed that the idea of a meeting of wives originated with Grant, wrote more cautiously in 1896 about Ord's suggestion.

23. On March 20, Grant invited Lincoln to visit City Point, and Lincoln replied the same day that he would soon visit, accompanied by Mrs. Lincoln "and a few others." On March 23, Lincoln telegraphed that he would leave at one o'clock that day. Lincoln, *Works*, VIII, 367, 372.

24. Mary Lincoln had been quoted as saying to Julia Grant: "How dare you be seated, until I invite you." Adam Badeau, *Grant in Peace from Appomattox to Mount McGregor: A Personal Memoir* (Hartford, 1887), p. 362.

Chapter 5

I WILL TAKE this opportunity to relate several other incidents embellished by this same author. When attending one of the many grand reviews tendered the President on this memorable visit, I was most happy in the pleasure of taking Mrs. Lincoln in the General's ambulance to witness this pageant, always so enthusiastically enjoyed by me. At my request, General Grant directed two of his staff officers to escort us, one of them being the author of the stories published recently.[1]

As we were approaching the field, a lady on horseback passed us at full gallop, calling to me as she passed: "I cannot control my horse. He seems determined to join his mate, which the General (meaning her husband) rides," and dashing past, she was soon far in advance of our party. Mrs. Lincoln was somewhat disturbed by this and made many inquiries as to who the lady was. She thought ladies were not allowed in camp, to which I replied, smiling, "General Grant is much opposed to their being present, but when I wanted to come I wrote him a nice, coaxing letter, and permission was always granted."

Presently, we would see the equestrienne again dashing on, and Mrs. Lincoln seemed annoyed for fear she would join the President, but I assured her she would not, as the President was with General Grant. When we arrived on the field, we again saw this lady, now quite near the President and General Grant.

Seeing that Mrs. Lincoln was really annoyed by this, I asked an officer who was near us to ride over to Mrs. General Ord and, with my compliments, ask her to join our party, which she did immediately, feeling much gratified at the attention. I told her that Mrs. Lincoln and I both thought it would be more agreeable for her to be near our carriage, at the same time presenting her to Mrs. Lincoln, who received her most graciously.

On our return from this same review, General Ord, the commanding officer of the division, came up to us and said: "Ladies, the President and the General have been gracious enough to appoint me your escort back to headquarters." Always courteous and kind, he proceeded to present to Mrs. Lincoln and myself a great many of the officers as they passed our carriage.

A lady, the wife of one of his staff officers, riding up, he said: "Mrs. Lincoln, let me present Mrs. ———." Just then the horse wheeled and galloped back to the side of its mate, which the lady's husband was riding. The lady, feeling it a duty as well as a pleasure to be presented to Mrs. Lincoln and to explain her abrupt departure, gave her horse a smart stroke with her whip and brought him again alongside; then General Ord again started to present her. Again the horse wheeled and went flying back. General Ord, much annoyed and somewhat amused, said: "Mrs. Lincoln, that is a finely-trained horse. He will not let the lady leave her husband's side. I would recommend you to get one like it. If you would like I will try (growing quite radiant with the idea) to get him for you; he is just what you want."

All this time, Mrs. Lincoln was growing more and more indignant and, not being able longer to control her wrath, exclaimed: "What do you mean, Sir?" I quietly placed my hand on hers and said in an undertone, "Dear Mrs. Lincoln, he does not mean anything. He has only made an unfortunate speech. Do not be annoyed. He knows nothing of this morning's occurrence." Seeing Mrs. Lincoln was much fatigued, I requested the General not to present any more of the gallant fellows who dashed past, all eager to catch a glimpse of the wife of their beloved and honored President.

At another review of General Meade's army, a soldier broke from the ranks and, rushing forward, lifted up his hands in appeal, murmuring something in a foreign tongue. The poor fellow was soon carried off, and we were told he was crazy, but I feared he was a drafted soldier, that his family really needed his care, and that this was the cause of his petition.

One glorious spring morning, several days before the General's final departure from City Point when he went to meet Lee, he ascended the James River on his steamer accompanied by a number of his staff officers, President and Mrs. Lincoln, Admiral Porter, and several of the corps commanders stationed in the vicinity of Richmond. After ascending some distance above Haxall's Landing, we took a longboat —I think the gig from Admiral Porter's flagship (as the men who rowed were in sailor's uniform)—and ascended the James River so that we could look up through Dutch Gap Canal. As we rested on the waters here, looking up through the canal with field glasses, some of the officers turned their glasses towards the heights of the surrounding country. They said: "We had better move out from here, as they are looking at us from the heights with their glasses and might fire on us," to which remark Admiral Porter replied, "Oh, no! There is no danger. We are perfectly safe. These Southern fellows are all too gallant. They would not fire on a boat with women in it. These ladies' bonnets will protect us. We can turn and go back in safety." And we did return in safety.

As we approached our boat, to my amazement, if not to that of the balance of the company, we saw the heights all along the north bank of the James River were covered with cavalrymen, and across the river was a pontoon bridge, which had to be opened to let us pass through. This is the first time I ever saw a pontoon bridge. These were Sheridan's cavalry, who had arrived since we had passed this point going up the river. I do not know that Sheridan was with us as we went up the river, but I do know that he was with us as we came down to City Point again, as I came upon him in a sequestered corner of the boat reading from a voluminous scroll written on large office paper. He was eagerly and intently scanning this and, as I stood watching him, his face expressed intense eagerness, at times lighting up with a brilliant smile of pleasure and appreciative satisfaction. At length he came to the end, when I said: "Ah, General, I caught you reading a most interesting document. What is it? It cannot be a love letter, General, as no lady would use such paper as that." He smiled, rolled it up, placed it in his bosom and, with face beaming, approached me and whispered, "It is better than that, Madam. It is my order of battle written by your husband." I said: "It seems to give you great pleasure, General." "It does, Madam. It is magnificent."

For a day or two before the last movement of the army upon Richmond, we ladies, Mrs. Rawlins and I, were feeling some anxiety as to what we were expected to do or where we were to go. Mrs. Rawlins questioned me more than once on the subject, but the opportunity had not yet come for me to speak to the General, when on the afternoon before they left (all the officers were gone but two staff officers), the General turned to one of them and said: "Bowers, I want that chest of papers (pointing to the chest that always stood in the corner of his office) taken up to headquarters." Then I remarked,

[148]

"Why not leave it here with me?" The General said: "Oh, you cannot remain here, Julia." "No! then where?" The two officers had gone now, and the General said: "I have thought of that and decided that you and Mrs. Rawlins had better remain on the dispatch boat for the present, and if all my plans turn out as I hope and expect they will, I will then return with you to Washington." "But," he said, "if Lee should escape me—and I am desperately afraid he will move now before I am ready—and make his way to the mountains, there is no telling when this war will end, and in that case you would have to go home alone." But Lee did not escape, and what an escort I had back to Washington.

I remember what a glorious bright morning it was when General Grant and staff with President Lincoln (after bidding Mrs. Rawlins and myself goodbye) mounted and rode away to victory and to peace. I do not think I felt sorrowful; on the contrary, I think it was a feeling of—well, I will say admiration, as the leader of that cavalcade mounted and dashed away. I knew, or thought I knew, *my* General would return to me, believing as I always did, "the faithful soldier to be God's care."

The President returned that evening, calling to tell me he had left General Grant looking well and full of hope. Mrs. Rawlins and I had already taken up our quarters on General Grant's dispatch boat, which always was moored at the wharf in front of the General's headquarters, City Point, James River, Virginia. Then how interested we were receiving the news through the President from the front. The President was radiant when he told us of the fall of Petersburg, and I remember General H—— gallantly sent me a bouquet of flowers from the gardens of the captured city.

The weather was simply divine all this time, and I had letters daily from the General, always hopeful. Then one morning, to my great disappointment, I received one telling me he thought I had better return to the North. He did not say why, but I supposed he was thinking perhaps he would not get back as soon as he had hoped, but—mark this!—he did not say go home, only I had better go. So I decided that I would rather not go and did not, my decision giving Mrs. Rawlins great satisfaction as well, as she too thought it would be so lovely to go back with our husbands.

Again, while the President was on the James River, after the General had moved on Richmond, I went with a friend (Mr. E. B. Washburne, member of Congress from Galena, Ill.) to call on Mrs. Lincoln and her party: Senator and Mrs. Harlan and their pretty daughter Mary (who afterwards married the President's son Robert),

Mr. Sumner, the Marquis de Chambrun, and, I think, Mr. Seward.[2] As soon as I had entered and paid my respects, Mrs. Lincoln said: "Suppose we ask Mrs. Grant. Let her answer this important question." Upon inquiry as to the question, I was asked, "What should be done with the Confederate President Jefferson Davis in the event of his capture?" Happening to catch the friendly glance of the President just then, I repeated the question slowly and then said: "I would trust him, I think, to the mercy of our always just and most gracious President." This reply won me not a few compliments. The gentlemen all said it was a most diplomatic answer.

The President's boat, the *River Queen*, was anchored in the James River near City Point not a hundred yards from the boat where I was living. The President had lingered here to witness the departure of the army and to get the first news from the front. I saw very little of the presidential party now, as Mrs. Lincoln had a good deal of company and seemed to have forgotten us. I felt this deeply and could not understand it, as my regard for the family was not only that of respect but affection. The President had stood by my hero when dark clouds were in his sky, and I felt grateful. Richmond had fallen; so had Petersburg. All of these places were visited by the President and party, and I, not a hundred yards from them, was not invited to join them.

As I have said, the President and party had already visited Petersburg and had started early one morning on a visit to Richmond. The ladies of my party learning this proposed that we should take our boat and go up to Richmond also. After some hesitation, I consented. When we arrived at the landing, we took a carriage and directed the coachman to drive through the principal streets and past all the public buildings. I only saw that the city was deserted; not a single inhabitant visible. Only now and then we would meet one or two carriages with visitors from the North, coming like ourselves to see this sad city, and occasionally an old colored servant would pass along, looking on us as intruders, as we all felt we were.

I remember that all the streets near the public buildings were covered with papers—public documents and letters, I suppose. So many of these papers lay on the ground that they reminded me of the forest leaves when summer is gone. It was all so sad that I wished to return to the boat, where I at once retired to my stateroom and, feeling sad and weary, fell asleep. When I awoke, the boat still lay at the landing. I sat for a long time at the door of my stateroom looking out and listening to the familiar home-like twitter of the little river frogs and watching the bright stars looking down upon the broad calm river. I fell to thinking of all the sad tragedies of the past four years.

How many homes made desolate! How many hearts broken! How much youth sacrificed! How much treasure lost! And tears, great tears, fell from my eyes. For what, I could not tell. Could it be that my visit reminded me of my dear old home in Missouri?

I really must tell another story of this time, although it reflects most severely on my amiability. One morning, Captain [John S.] Barnes of the navy called. I asked if he would escort me to the President's boat, for though I had not seen much of them of late, I learned they would leave that evening and felt it my duty as well as pleasure to call and say farewell. Captain Barnes looked surprised and said: "Are you not going over tonight to the reception? Have you received no notice of it?" "No," I replied, "but I presume I will in good time." He looked at his watch with a doubtful air and said he would be glad to be my escort if I wished to call. I said, "no, not now. I will wait for the reception." As soon as Captain Barnes left, I sent for Captain [John W.] Livingston of the General's dispatch boat, said I wished to take a ride of twenty or thirty miles down the river, and asked if he could take me without inconvenience. He replied: "Yes, certainly; I am always at your service." I then wrote a note to Colonel Bowers, the only staff officer left at headquarters, and asked for the band to be sent to the boat, saying I was going to take a sail and wished to have the music. The steamer soon cleared her moorings and, swinging into the current, we had a delightful sail down the James River.

On every man-of-war we passed the yards were manned, which was an especial salute to me. Captain Barnes had arrived at headquarters when my note asking for the band was received and he had this done in compliment to me. About eight o'clock, as we were nearing City Point on our return, the captain of the boat said to me: "If you desire it, Madam, we have still time to go up the river as far as Haxall's Landing and be back at our moorings before eleven o'clock." I said I would like to go on. And as bad luck would have it, just as we were nearing the President's boat, the leader of the band came forward and inquired if there was any particular piece of music I wished played, expecting, no doubt, that I would order something patriotic. I coolly answered: "Yes, play 'Now You'll Remember Me.'" And we passed on up the river. When my boat returned, the kind President's boat had gone, and—well!—I regretted my ride up the river.[3]

One Sunday afternoon, Mrs. Rawlins and I, with half a dozen army and navy officers, were sitting in the cabin of our boat, talking over the probabilities of peace, when an attaché of headquarters breathlessly entered the cabin with flushed cheeks and beaming eyes and held up a sheet of paper, exclaiming: "Mrs. Grant, Madam, may I

[151]

speak with you for a moment?" I instantly followed him into the first open stateroom door and, closing it behind me, said, "What news?" for I recognized one of the telegraph operators. He replied: "Glad news! but you must not tell on me. It would cost me my head if old Stanton knew I had brought the news to you." He then rapidly read all that had passed over the wires to Washington: the surrender of Lee, the terms, etc. "Now, Madam, forgive me if I have done wrong, but I felt you must know as soon as anyone else, even the President. So I brought you the news." He went out, and I have never seen him since. I do not even know his name.

When I returned to the cabin, the officers urged me to tell them the news, but I was obstinate for full twenty minutes, when a shout went up along the bluffs, and cries of "The Union Forever, Hurrah, Boys! Hurrah!" then told them the glad tidings. The river was already full of boats with parties from different parts of the country, New York, Boston, etc., who had come to visit Richmond after the evacuation of that city. When the news of the surrender of Lee and his army reached them, they steamed alongside and came aboard to congratulate me and to tell me that General Grant would certainly be the next President.

This anticipation gave me no pleasure. I was always devoted to "le militaire," and my husband was commander-in-chief of this great and victorious army. I never wanted him to be President until he returned from his famous journey around the globe, and then I felt that by all rights he ought to have been chosen, but God willed otherwise.

The day (Monday) following that on which we received the news of the surrender was a little cloudy, and all at once at a given signal, every man-of-war, steamer, tug, or other craft that had a whistle began to blow it, and such a noise no one ever heard before. Each tried to outdo the other in volume and variety. Mrs. Rawlins came beaming to me and, taking both of my hands, exclaimed: "Are you not delighted that you did not go north when the General wanted you to? Now we will have the happiness of returning with our heroes."

When the engines had spent their steam or, I might better say, were out of breath, we began getting dispatches from the front, saying we could expect them for late dinner that evening. I at once informed the Captain and told him to order dinner for as many as he could accommodate. We ladies (Mrs. Rawlins, Mrs. General [Michael R.] Morgan, and myself) made our toilets and assembled in the saloon of the steamer to await the coming of our heroes. Every once in a while we would enthusiastically embrace each other and exclaim: "Only think, the war is over, and General Grant is the victorious general!"

We played on the piano and sang. Then one would play and the other two waltz gaily around the saloon. We watched the clock. It was growing late and no word of their approach. We sent to the office to inquire for news from the front. A reply came, saying that just as our messenger arrived a telegram came, saying, "Tell Mrs. Grant and party we will not be in as soon as we expected and cannot say at what time now."

It was nearly three o'clock A.M., and we were quite exhausted by our unusual excitement and vigil. We were now as despondent as we had been gay before and sat around feeling much wronged and neglected, saying, "Why do they not telegraph us?" We waited until four o'clock and then we consented to retire, but we did not undress, only went to our cabins to rest awhile, but "tell it not in Gath; publish it not in the streets of Askelon," we three wives of heroes slept. Yes, they came, and we were asleep! When I awoke, the sun was shining brightly. The General said: "You did not wait dinner for us." I explained, much mortified, but he smilingly said: "I'm glad you did retire. We hoped to be back sooner, but when we found we were unavoidably detained, I told them to inform you so you would not be kept waiting."

About fifty generals and other officers of high rank breakfasted with us that morning. I shall never forget how happy and satisfied they were—the grand, noble fellows! At table someone said: "General, of course you will go up to Richmond, will you not?" "No," sternly replied the General, "I will go at once to Washington." When I urged him to visit Richmond, he leaned towards me and said: "Hush, Julia. Do not say another word on this subject. I would not distress these people. They are feeling their defeat bitterly, and you would not add to it by witnessing their despair, would you?" I realized the delicacy and kindness of his decision and urged no more.

Some of the officers remained to visit the fallen city. The General and staff and a large number of other officers, and Mrs. Rawlins and I went to Washington on the General's dispatch boat. As we reached our destination that bright morning in our boat, freighted as she was with heroes, brave men, every gun in and near Washington burst forth—and such a salvo!—all the bells rang out merry greetings, and the city was literally swathed in flags and bunting. The sun shone gloriously, and the very winds seemed on a frolic, at one time proudly flinging the flag posted at the landing to the breeze, broadly spread as though to show that not a single star was lost from that blue field, thus spread broadly out quivering and murmuring a low gurgling laugh, then recoiling, hugging lovingly in its warm folds the stars—all there! all there! "Then blow ye winds and crack your cheeks." Our Union is safe. The General drove with us directly to Willard's and, as soon as he saw me comfortably located, went to the Executive Mansion.

Everyone was wild with delight. We received calls of congratulation all day. The city was illuminated that night. I went with Mrs. Stanton to the War Department, where we were joined by Mr. Stanton and General Grant. Mr. Stanton was in his happiest mood, showing me many stands of arms, flags, and, among other things, a stump of a large tree perforated on all sides by bullets, taken from the field of Shiloh. He was much interested in the preparations that were being made for the illumination of his department. He facetiously remarked: "They are going to illuminate at the Navy Department, I know, for they sent and borrowed two or three boxes of candles from my department."

Shortly after I returned to the hotel, young Stanton called to say Mr. and Mrs. Stanton would call for the General and me to ride out to see the city that night, and afterwards we were to go to their residence, where we would receive any friends who were in the city. As soon as the General returned, I hastened to inform him of this pleasant arrangement. The General said: "I am so glad. You will, of course, go with the Stantons and, as the President has asked me to do, I will accompany Mrs. Lincoln." To this plan, I protested and said I would not go at all unless he accompanied me. The General at once said, with a shadow of surprise, "I can first go out with you and the Stantons and, leaving you at their house, return and escort the wife of our President to see the illumination." This was all satisfactory to me, as it was the honor of being with him when he first viewed the illumination in honor of peace restored to the nation, in which he had so great a share—it was this I coveted. All of the great men of the nation who were necessarily in Washington at that time were assembled that night. Such congratulations, such friendly, grateful grasps of the hand and speeches of gratitude!

We retired at a late hour. As soon as the General awoke in the morning, I asked him earnestly if we would not leave for Burlington today. He said: "I wish I could, but I have promised Mr. Lincoln to go up this morning and with him see what can be done in reference to the reduction of the army." I pleaded earnestly, and he promised me that if he could possibly do so he would try and leave Washington that evening. Just then, a tap at our door brought a note from the President, saying, "Dear General: Suppose you come at eleven o'clock, instead of nine. Robert has just returned and I want to see something of him before I go to work." [4] The General said he was afraid that this postponement would prevent his getting off that evening, but on my insisting that I must go, he said: "Well, I will see what I can do. I certainly will go if it is possible."

At about midday, a rap at my door was followed, in answer to my "come in," by the entrance of a man dressed in light-colored corduroy coat and trousers and with rather a shabby hat of the same color. I remarked his dress; as he came in, I started up and said: "I thought it was the bellboy with cards. What do you want?" He reddened and, bowing, said: "This is Mrs. Grant?" I bowed assent. "Mrs. Lincoln sends me, Madam, with her compliments, to say she will call for you at exactly eight o'clock to go to the theater." To this, I replied with some feeling (not liking either the looks of the messenger or the message, thinking the former savored of discourtesy and the latter seemed like a command), "You may return with my compliments to Mrs. Lincoln and say I regret that as General Grant and I intend leaving the city this afternoon, we will not, therefore, be here to accompany the President and Mrs. Lincoln to the theater." He hesitated a moment, then urged: "Madam, the papers announce that General Grant will be with the President tonight at the theater." I said to this: "You deliver my message to Mrs. Lincoln as I have given it to you. You may go now." He smiled as he turned to leave. I have thought since that this man was one of the band of conspirators in that night's sad tragedy, and that he was not sent by Mrs. Lincoln at all. I am perfectly sure that he, with three others, one of them [John Wilkes] Booth himself, sat opposite me and my party at luncheon that day.

As soon as I received the invitation to go with Mrs. Lincoln, I dispatched a note to General Grant entreating him to go home that evening; that I did not want to go to the theater; that he must take me home. I not only wrote to him, but sent three of the staff officers who called to pay their respects to me to urge the General to go home that night. I do not know what possessed me to take such a freak, but go home I felt I must. The General sent me word to have my trunks ready and for Jesse and me to have our luncheon, and, if he could be in time, we would take the late afternoon train for Philadelphia.

It was in obedience to this that I was at late luncheon with Mrs. Rawlins and her little girl and my Jesse when these men came in and sat opposite to us. They all four came in together. I thought I recognized in one of them the messenger of the morning, and one, a dark, pale man, played with his soup spoon, sometimes filling it and holding it half-lifted to his mouth, but never tasting it. This occurred many times. He also seemed very intent on what we and the children were saying. I thought he was crazy. As we sat at table, I said to Mrs.

[155]

Rawlins in a low tone: "Be careful, but observe the men opposite to us and tell me what you think." After a moment or so, she answered: "Since you call my attention, I believe there is something peculiar about them." I said: "I believe they are a part of Mosby's guerrillas[5] and they have been listening to every word we have said. Do you know, I believe there will be an outbreak tonight or soon. I just feel it, and am glad I am going away tonight."

Afterwards, as General Grant and I rode to the depot, this same dark, pale man rode past us at a sweeping gallop on a dark horse—black, I think. He rode twenty yards ahead of us, wheeled and returned, and as he passed us both going and returning, he thrust his face quite near the General's and glared in a disagreeable manner. Mrs. General [Daniel H.] Rucker, in whose carriage we were, remarked: "General, everyone wants to see you." "Yes," the General replied, "but I do not care for such glances. These are not friendly at least." I noticed the General draw back as the man returned and came so close.[6]

We arrived without incident at Philadelphia. We went through the city and stopped at a large restaurant, situated near where we had to take the ferryboat to reach the cars for Burlington, N.J. The General ordered some oysters, as he had had nothing to eat since nine o'clock in the morning. Before they were ready for him, a telegram was handed him, and almost before he could open this, another was handed him, and then a third.

The General looked very pale. "Is there anything the matter?" I inquired: "You look startled." "Yes," he answered, "something *very* serious has happened. Do not exclaim. Be quiet and I will tell you. The President has been assassinated at the theater, and I must go back at once. I will take you to Burlington (an hour away), see the children, order a special train, and return as soon as it is ready."

On the way to Burlington, the General was silent and in deep thought. When I questioned him as to who could have done it and the object, he replied: "Oh, I don't know. But this fills me with the gloomiest apprehension. The President was inclined to be kind and magnanimous, and his death at this time is an irreparable loss to the South, which now needs so much both his tenderness and magnanimity." I asked: "This will make Andy Johnson President, will it not?" "Yes," the General said, "and for some reason, I dread the change."

We none of us retired for the night. Crowds of people came thronging into our cottage to learn if the terrible news were true. The General left for Washington while it was yet starlight. The first mail that sad morning brought a letter to General Grant. He having directed me to open all telegrams and letters, I read the following letter: "General Grant, thank God, as I do, that you still live. It was your life that fell to my lot, and I followed you on the cars. Your car door was locked, and thus you escaped me, thank God!" [7]

The whole land, now filled with lamentation and woe, had so recently been all joy at the restoration of the Union and peace. Our beloved and martyred President was dead, lay in state at the Capitol, and was at length carried in great sorrow and funereal pomp through all the principal cities from Washington to his old home at Springfield, Illinois. His bereaved widow, almost frenzied with grief, still lingered at the Executive Mansion, alone with her little son Tad. With my heart full of sorrow, I went many times to call on dear heart-broken Mrs. Lincoln, but she could not see me.

The first time the General came home, a committee waited upon him and informed him that the beautiful house presented to him by the loyal people of Philadelphia was ready for his occupancy, and they asked if he would not move into it. Of course, this was a happy event for me, and with joyful haste I made my arrangements to accompany the General to Philadelphia. When we arrived, we found a large party of charming, delightful people smiling their welcome to my hero and his family.

Well, the house was simply perfect in every part, not only amply and thoroughly furnished from attic to basement, but the closets were full of snowy fine linen, the larders and even the coal bins were full. I remember the beautiful glass and last, though not least, the quantity of fine silver on the table. For this last, I had been saving all of my pin money ever since the General had received the deed for the house on January first. I really felt a pang of disappointment, as now I need not buy it. My heart was full of gratitude for all this kindness and the appreciation of my dear husband, and it was a struggle to keep my tears from falling.

The next morning, Nellie was having her boots laced by the nurse when she looked up and said: "Mamma, when are we going to our home?" "Why, Nell," I said, "this is our home; we are going to stay here always. Those nice, kind ladies and gentlemen that received us yesterday gave this nice house to your papa, and this is our home." She looked up, rather mystified I thought, and said: "No, mamma, no, this is not our home. I have just come from there. Our house is a great, great house (with a struggle to say what it was like) like . . . like . . . the picture in my geography of the . . . the . . . Capitol in Washington; I know, mamma, I was there." "No, no, little girly, this is all ours. You have been dreaming, little one." She sat in thought for a moment and, with great delight, exclaimed: "Why, of course, I was dreaming, for I have been here ever since we came to the party" (meaning the reception on our arrival).[8]

Fred and Ulysses returned to school at Burlington. The General remained at home for a few days only, and we thoroughly enjoyed the many kind attentions shown us, when telegrams, many of them, all important, called the General back to Washington, and I felt very lonely with only the younger children. The General visited me often, but even before he would arrive telegrams would come from the War office calling him back, so that he could rarely stay even twenty-four hours, and sometimes not so long. So his visits were short and unrestful, and I was desperately lonely; and is it surprising that I should have been, after my four years in the field, surrounded as I was at headquarters by the all-absorbing subjects of the day, hearing the ordering and marshaling of troops, hearing the news from every quarter, being present at all those magnificent reviews, meeting all the distinguished men that daily visited headquarters.

After this life of absorbing interest for four long years, one could not expect me to be happy confined within the walls of my new home, lovely though it was. Well, I was not happy. Far from it, and it was with intense delight I read a letter from the staff officers sent me the morning after the arrival of the General on his last visit to me in my new home, telling me that hereafter the General could not come to me as often even as he had in the past. They urged that it was impossible for the General's home to be so far away from his headquarters, where, they kindly said, they missed me also, urging me to give up the pretty house and come with the General to Washington; that the General was suffering from the great pressure of business; that the corridors at his hotel were blocked by crowds before he was up in the morning, and that he must have a home where these petitioners could not penetrate.

This was just as I knew it to be, and when I went to the General's room, I told him of the letter and begged him to take me back with him, telling him how lonely I was. He replied: "It does seem that life is too short for us to live apart so, but what will we do with this house? When we accepted it, we promised to live here." "Well," I said, "we cannot, and you must give it back and tell them that we find it impossible. Anyway, for me, I cannot live here without you, Ulys; do take me back with you." And he did, taking Nellie, Jesse, and me back to Washington with him, stopping at Willard's. In two or three days, we took a house on Georgetown Heights.

And now the most magnificent pageant that ever occurred in the United States or any other country was in progress: the passing of the victorious armies up Pennsylvania Avenue in review before the President and the grateful people. The President was seated upon a platform and surrounded by his cabinet and members of the Senate and House of Representatives, foreign ministers, and many of the commanding officers. General Grant was there, and I sat near his side. As each division marched past with their faded and tattered flags borne proudly aloft, oh, what shouts went up! They thrill me yet.

How well do I remember when Sherman's men came tramp, tramp, tramping by, and Sherman arose to go to the front to review his glorious men. What a defiant and angry glance he shot at Stanton, who actually arose and offered his hand to Sherman, he having reprimanded that distinguished officer for giving too liberal terms of surrender to General Joe Johnston. General Grant was sent to Sherman's army by Mr. Stanton to receive such terms as he (Grant) had accepted from General Lee, but General Grant, always liberal to Sherman, insisted that Sherman be the man to receive General Johnston's surrender, and so it happened. Stanton had also sent an order prohibiting Sherman's army from entering Richmond.[9] Well, there was not the best feeling for our war secretary in the army that went "marching through Georgia." Sherman looked proud and handsome as his corps marched past. There was much admiration expressed at their wonderful marching, and not a little merriment when a foraging party (arranged specially for this occasion) passed laden with poultry, everyone even then being familiar with the popular song of "how the turkeys gobbled" and "the sweet potatoes even started from the ground" as Sherman went "marching through Georgia."

The house the General had taken was large but not comfortable, and I thought the rent very high ($2,500 per annum—a fortune to me), so we concluded to get a place for ourselves if possible. The General at once thought of a little place in the country—still longing for a farm—where he could pasture his horses and ride out to see the meadows grow green and the fruit ripen. He invited Commodore [Daniel] Ammen to help him to find a suitable place. They advertised, but did not use the General's name. Many answers came. I listened to all of their plans until the little pasturage had grown into a huge plantation of several thousand acres; then I am afraid I incurred the lasting displeasure of the General's old friend by asking rather impatiently: "Commodore Ammen, what do you know about farming? You tell me you have been thirty years at sea. Now if I were going to buy a ship, your advice would be invaluable, but really I do not think you can be good authority on farming." The Commodore, like the General, had always loved the country. He was much interested in it and was both hurt and surprised when I made my protest.

The plantation was far, far beyond the General's ability to pay for. I always had a horror of debt. Besides, it was a *home* in Washington we wanted. I might just as well have remained in Philadelphia at that lovely mansion given to the General as to go to a plantation in Maryland. Penelope had no idea of conforming to any such arrangement. No, indeed; so the country place was abandoned.

It was while we were in the house on Georgetown Heights that the General wrote his report of the army.[10] The authorship of this great state paper has been attributed to more than one of General Grant's staff. He wrote that report in our library in Georgetown Heights, every word of it himself. I know this, for I sat with him most of the time, and was kindly chided more than once for interrupting him. General Rawlins may have gotten together the exact numbers, dates, etc., which it was his duty to do, but nothing else. General Grant wrote his own reports, his own messages, his own proclamations; whatever they might be, he wrote them himself as he wrote his book, without assistance from anyone.

I was still looking with longing eyes at many of the handsome houses in Washington. All proved to be far beyond our purse, until one day an old acquaintance from St. Louis called and, happening to inquire what rent we were paying and thinking it large, said: "Why don't you buy a house?" Upon learning the reason, he at once offered to sell us a house on I Street and to give us ten years to pay for it. Well, I did a little sum in arithmetic about as follows: $2,500 × 10 = $25,000 and I decided at once, telling Ulys when he returned from his office and showing him my little sum with great pride.

I said: "You can pay nearly ten thousand right away, and the rest will be paid instead of rent." He said: "Yes, but the interest." To which I answered with convincing earnestness: "Do you not see? You pay eight or ten thousand dollars at once, and our rent for ten years would be twenty-five thousand dollars. So there is plenty left for interest." He laughingly said: "Why, you are a financier." We went with Mr. Corbin[11] to look at the house, and it proved to be most desirable: a large, four story, double house with large grounds about it, for thirty thousand dollars, and ten years to pay it in. I at once prevailed upon the General to purchase it, as I felt sure we could meet the payments. And only think! the gentlemen of the Philadelphia committee not only persistently refused to take back the house there, but insisted on our bringing all the lovely furniture to put in our Washington house and on our renting the house they had given us. Such are our American princes!

An upholsterer came down from Philadelphia and placed all the furniture, hung the curtains, etc., so that by the middle of January, 1866, we were snugly located in our lovely Washington home, from which time on we enjoyed—yes, we enjoyed—society, friendship, and love—and I really think they are divinely bestowed.

And this lovely house, this magnificent home, was a gift from New York to General Grant, and it is not the only expression of New York's appreciative generosity and magnanimity.[12] When General Grant and his sons surrendered in Wall Street and lay stripped of side arms, of everything—except their honor, thank Heaven!—New York's great papers, without exception I think, stood by him, and never a word against his or their fair names did I see; and then, too, did not New York's wealthiest citizen offer to restore at this sad time to the General through me all the property given to secure him against loss.[13] This generous offer was declined by me, though in yielding to this most proper impulse I gave up all the property owned by General Grant: some in Chicago, the four or five little houses purchased by him during his twelve years residence here in Washington, the pretty house presented to him in Philadelphia, and last, though not least, the dear old homestead in Missouri, White Haven. When I signed this last deed, it well-nigh broke my heart. My tears fell thick and fast; I could not help it.

Our receptions were brilliant. Our dinners (I do not know how my reputation as a good housewife came about, as I always felt that in that respect I was not as good as I should be) were fairly good and always pleasant. Our reception days were gala days indeed. The house would not hold our guests. The New York papers used to make wonderful cartoons of General Grant's house and surroundings on reception days and of General Grant's hand after the reception. We only *heard* pleasant words and *saw* smiling faces. We entertained many friends and many distinguished soldiers and statesmen. Our sons were going to school at Burlington most of the time, only being at home for the holidays, and were making good progress in their studies. Nellie and Jess went to school in the city.

On one occasion, the General and I were going out to dine, and Nellie and Jess were also going to a juvenile party. So they drove with us to their party, where Muller, their attendant, had already gone to meet them. On our way, the General casually remarked: "How was it, Jess, that you were punished today?" Jess looked up, rather sheepishly and surprised, and said: "Oh, I don't know why, but I did not like the way she punished me, though." The General inquired: "Did she whip you?" "No, I would rather she had. She made me sit among the girls" (with disgust). "Well, you liked that, did you not?" said the General.

"No, indeed, I prefer to sit with my own *race*." At this, Nellie pulled his sleeve and said: "your own sex, Jess." "No," Jess exclaimed, "I mean my own race," and, turning on Nellie, he said in no gentle tones: "There is just as much difference in girls and boys as there is in Africans and Europeans." "And which race do you consider superior?" the General asked. "The Europeans, of course," Jess replied. "Then you give the girls the superior race, of course," the General said. "No, I do not, either," replied Jess, looking sullenly out of the carriage window.

The General had no idea of the government of the children. He would have allowed them to do pretty much as they pleased (hunt, swim, fish, etc.) provided it did not interfere with any duty, but his word was law always. Whenever they were inclined to disobey or question my authority, I would ask the General to speak to them. He would, smiling at me, say to them: "Come, come, Fred" or "Nell" (generally), "you must not quarrel with mamma. She knows what is best for you, and you must always obey her." Again, I can remember Jess's loyalty to me when his little friends, the boys in the neighborhood, would be playing rather roughly with the boys from the valley, and Jess would entreat to be allowed to go and join them. His father would say, "Why do you ask mamma? Ask me, and I will let you go along. I think it is a good thing for boys to play together, even if they are rough. It teaches a boy how to take care of himself." But Jess indignantly declined this offer, saying, "No, I will not. You do not know what is best for boys, not near as well as mamma does." Yet he would insist on my consent and ask, "Why can't I go?" and would be very indignant if I said: "I am afraid you will get hurt," to which he would reply, "You had better be afraid *I* will hurt somebody."

The General used to have dreadful headaches about once in three or four weeks, and on those occasions he would return from his office, saying to me: "Oh, do not ask me to speak. I have a dreadful headache." I would seat him in his armchair, darken the room, call for a hot footbath with mustard, and, after bathing his feet, I would persuade him to take one of my little pills, when he would lie down and sleep; and always in an hour or two he would awake well and ready for a cigar. But—will you believe it?—when I would naturally feel that I ought to be commended for curing him and would ask him if I had not made him well nicely and quickly, he was ungracious enough to laugh and say: "You did not cure me. Why, I got well myself, did I not?"

The General was always fond of traveling. We therefore made many delightful journeys during the summer when he was at leisure. Wherever he went, he was met by thousands of his old soldiers and by thousands of citizens with cheers, banners, music, and, best of all, with hearty and heartfelt greetings. I could not, if I tried, tell of all the ovations given him at Baltimore, New York, Philadelphia, Boston, Cleveland, Cincinnati, Louisville, St. Louis, Galena—in fact, at every city on our route. We went over to Canada once and met the same kindly reception there.

I remember well a lovely ride through the White Mountains in a great chariot with some charming New England people. I remember especially the word "Welcome" was woven in fresh field flowers over the doors, and in many of the hotels the walls were decorated with evergreens, with great, green letters on the walls quoting some word of the General's or some dispatch from the field, such as "We will fight it out on this line, if it takes all summer," or "an immediate and unconditional surrender," or "I propose to move at once upon your works."

In Michigan, as we approached Detroit, where I had lived so happily when I was first married to Lieutenant Grant, as we passed through a town not far from there, Senator Chandler came towards me smiling (a little wickedly, I thought) and said: "Mrs. Grant, here is a nice question for you to decide. I have just now received the following telegram: 'The ladies of —— propose (if in order) to salute General Grant all along the line with a kiss.' Now, Madam, I am referred by General Grant to you as to the answer I am to return." With a mighty effort, I crowded back the vexation and, I might say, the dash of jealousy that sprang at once into my loving heart, and with an answering smile, said: "Oh, Senator Chandler, of course General Grant cannot decline so gracious a compliment, and as the General will be fully occupied greeting his old comrades-in-arms, I suggest and entreat you, Senator, to act as General Grant's proxy in this case." The Senator laughed heartily at my answer, saying it was both adroit and diplomatic, but added: "I do not believe the General would half like surrendering *such* a privilege to me."

My heartbeats had only just resumed their usual quietness when we rolled into the depot at Detroit, where the booming of cannon and the long, repeated huzzas of welcome started my heartbeats again, but it was only pleasure now. The great multitude that greeted General Grant, the long line of brave soldiers, the windows crowded with fair women waving their welcome, the flowers, the flags, the bunting that decked the beautiful avenue of that fair city, are not forgotten, no more than are the delightful rides I had long years ago alone with Lieutenant Grant along its beautiful, broad way behind his fleet, little steed Nellie Bly.

At length we reached the hotel, and General Grant was at once escorted to the balcony erected in front of the hotel, and there the mayor made his speech welcoming General Grant to his city, Detroit. The General returned his thanks in a few murmured words and, bowing to the vast crowd assembled there, turned and entered the house. This was not satisfactory to the assembled people. They wanted to hear General Grant speak, and shouted and called again and again. Our little seven-year-old son Jesse, who was with us, was so disturbed that his father did not or would not speak that he ran in and urged him to, saying, "Papa, the people want you to make a speech. Do try; you can if you will." And when the General said: "No, I will not," the dear little fellow rushed out on the balcony, and the crowd still calling out "a speech, a speech," Jesse mounted a chair and exclaimed, "I will make you a speech." As the crowd, which seemed to be in a most amiable mood, cheered, my dear little boy declaimed with great dignity and solemnity, and with as loud a voice as he could command, the speech he had heard his brothers recite of Casabianca: "The boy stood on the burning deck. . . ." And I am sure if General Grant had consented to speak and been ever so eloquent, he could not have received heartier or more enthusiastic cheering than did my little son Jesse, who felt now that he had vindicated his father.

While in Washington, I saw much of President Johnson's family. The ladies were always cordial and friendly with me. Mrs. [David T.] Patterson was a gentle, charming woman, as was also her sister, Mrs. [Daniel] Stover. Mrs. Patterson's little girl was a beauty, with large eyes and a wealth of golden hair. I saw much of the family at the Executive Mansion. Mrs. Johnson was a retiring, kind, gentle, old lady, too much of an invalid to do the honors of the house, which care and pleasure she gladly transferred to her two daughters, Mrs. Patterson and Mrs. Stover, but she always came into the drawing room after the long state dinners to take coffee and receive the greetings of her husband's guests. She was always dressed elegantly and appropriately.

At this time the President's chair proved to be no sinecure, Mr. Stanton hectoring and thwarting him in every possible way. I remember when at Doubling Gap, Pa., where General Grant had left me with the children for a change of air, we expected him time and time again and great preparations were made for him, but we were always disappointed, and at last he telegraphed me to come home. The General met me at Baltimore. When I asked why he disappointed us and told him of the preparations made for his amusement, he said: "Well, Stanton was hectoring the President, and I could not leave, as he feared some trouble." He said further: "I think matters are at a standstill, as I think I have pacified the President by explaining Mr. Stanton's manner to him."

The next morning, as we were about to start to church, a messenger arrived from the White House asking for the General's immediate presence. The General did not return until two o'clock, when he informed me that Mr. Johnson had appointed him secretary of war. He said Johnson had been thinking it all over, had worked himself up to a white heat of indignation, had made up his mind to remove Stanton, and had asked him if he would accept the portfolio of secretary of war. He said: "And I consented to do so, as I think it most important that someone should be there who cannot be used." He said further: "Stanton would have gone and on a double-quick long ago if I had been President. He was very offensive, voting 'nay' to every suggestion made by the President." [14]

After luncheon, we drove out to the Soldiers' Home, where Mr. Stanton and family were spending the summer. Mr. Stanton was absent, and, after waiting an hour, we started home on the road leading from the south gate of the Soldiers' Home to Seventh Street; there we met Mr. Stanton in his carriage. The General got out and stood on the step of Mr. Stanton's carriage and told him of the President's determination. Mr. Stanton exclaimed: "Ah, I expected it. He could do nothing else and keep his self-respect." The General told him also that the President had offered him the War Department portfolio and that he thought it best to accept, as in his (the President's) present humor it was difficult to tell whom he might appoint. The General said further: "I thought, Mr. Stanton, it was but just to inform you so that you might not be unprepared and might arrange your actions, papers, etc." [15]

I regret to say that the great war secretary entirely forgot this courteous act when a few months later he was reinstated by the Senate. He hastened to the office and took possession, thus entangling General Grant in a very disagreeable controversy with the President, who said that he (General Grant) had promised to keep the portfolio until he was relieved by the President. Whereas, when Mr. Johnson had himself suggested this plan, the General, apprehending some complication, had very respectfully replied: "Mr. President, the law is explicit on this subject," but Mr. Johnson seemed to think that the General should have kept the keys until he informed him of Mr. Stanton's reinstatement.[16]

When this controversy between General Grant and Mr. Johnson was at its height, a near but indiscreet friend of Mr. Stanton exclaimed: "Now Stanton has Grant just where he wants him," but he did not keep him there. To think of General Grant's veracity being questioned!

And now I must not fail to tell of how General Grant happened to be at the President's levee the evening of January 13, 1868, the night the Senate reinstated Stanton as secretary of war, every circumstance of which I so perfectly remember. I had some ladies visiting me who were very anxious to attend this levee, so I asked the General to be our escort. He, to my surprise, demurred, saying: "I would like to gratify you, but, really, under the circumstances, I do not think I ought to go." I, not knowing to what he referred, urged him, saying, "The ladies would be so disappointed, as we were all dressed to go." He then reluctantly consented.

Just as we were leaving the house, a messenger arrived from the Capitol with a note, which the General read by the gaslight in front of the house. The General hesitated again and said he really ought not to go, as he feared the President would look upon his presence as an expression of his sympathy. Not knowing the importance of this implied sympathy, we still urged our desire to go. On our way home, the General said he really felt embarrassed when the President grasped his hand so cordially.

The General went early the next morning to his office and to his astonishment found Mr. Stanton already in the war office.[17] Mr. Stanton never once remembered the courtesy, the etiquette, observed and strictly adhered to, when he was displaced and Grant appointed. General Grant went himself and informed Mr. Stanton, saying, "I thought you ought to know, so that you might remove your private papers." I remember most perfectly, too, when the General told him this in that little shady lane leading from the Soldiers' Home to Seventh Street, Stanton gave utterance to an expression, I thought, of displeasure.

NOTES

1. *Ibid.,* pp. 356–60. Lieutenant Colonel Horace Porter, who assisted Badeau in escorting the ladies, provides a discreet portrait of the outing in *Campaigning with Grant,* pp. 412–14. See also *Personal Memoirs of W. T. Sherman* (3rd ed., New York, 1890), II, 332. Although Julia Grant objected to Badeau's account, her own narrative basically confirms his representation of Mary Lincoln's irrational conduct.
2. Secretary of State William H. Seward arrived at City Point on March 30, 1865, then left on April 1 with Mary Lincoln for Washington. Earl Schenck Miers, ed.,

Lincoln Day by Day (Washington, 1960), III, 323–24. On April 5, Mary Lincoln returned to City Point with the family of Senator James Harlan of Iowa, the Marquis de Chambrun, and Senator Charles Sumner of Massachusetts. Also on April 5, Seward was injured in a carriage accident in Washington. Glyndon G. Van Deusen, *William Henry Seward* (New York, 1967), p. 411.

3. At this point in her manuscript, Julia Grant prepared an alternative passage to replace the last three sentences. "The dear, kind President's boat had left when I returned, and how unhappy and mortified I was when I learned that Mrs. Lincoln had been greatly disappointed at not having the band for her reception."

4. The note (in full) read: "Please call at 11. A.M. to-day instead of 9. as agreed last evening." Lincoln, *Works*, VIII, 411.

5. Confederate Colonel John S. Mosby then commanded eight companies of partisan rangers who had conducted numerous successful raids in northern Virginia and Maryland. About one year earlier, Mosby's troops had come close to capturing Grant in Virginia. Grant, *Memoirs*, II, 141–42.

6. In 1878, Grant told a reporter about a man whom Julia Grant thought tried to overhear their luncheon conversation, then approached their carriage. Grant stated that he later learned this was John Wilkes Booth. John Russell Young, *Around the World with General Grant* . . . (New York, 1879), II, 356. John Matthews, an actor and friend of Booth, was with him on the street as the Grant carriage passed loaded with luggage; Booth galloped off in pursuit. George S. Bryan, *The Great American Myth* (New York, 1940), p. 155.

7. Grant also spoke of this letter, "but how true the letter was I cannot say." Young, *Around the World*, II, 356. A similar letter, said to have been written years later, is described in Jesse R. Grant, *In the Days of My Father*, p. 40. At the conspiracy trial, Michael O'Laughlin was accused of attempting to murder Grant, but was acquitted. In his testimony, Grant made no mention of a plot on his life. Benn Pitman, *The Assassination of President Lincoln and the Trial of the Conspirators* (Cincinnati and New York, 1865), pp. 20, 37, 248. Booth, of course, had expected to find Grant at the theater with Lincoln.

8. Perhaps Julia Grant intended to indicate that her daughter had a premonition of living in the White House.

9. For the complex story of the Stanton-Sherman quarrel, see Benjamin P. Thomas and Harold M. Hyman, *Stanton: The Life and Times of Lincoln's Secretary of War* (New York, 1962), pp. 405–18. Stanton did not forbid Sherman to enter Richmond; Sherman refused to go there because Halleck, who commanded at Richmond, had been involved in the quarrel. Sherman, *Memoirs*, II, 374.

10. Grant's lengthy report of July 22, 1865, covering the last year of the Civil War, is most accessible in his *Memoirs*, II, 555–632.

11. Abel Rathbone Corbin, former editor of the *Missouri Republican* and St. Louis alderman, later married Grant's sister Virginia (Jennie) and acted as agent for Jay Gould and James Fisk, Jr., in the Black Friday affair discussed in the following chapter. Lloyd Lewis, *Sherman, Fighting Prophet* (New York, 1932), p. 604.

12. On February 15, 1866, Major General Daniel Butterfield sent Grant $105,000 raised by prominent New York City financiers: $30,437.50 to pay his mortgage and interest, $54,725 in bonds, and $19,837.50 in cash. A copy of the letter is in the William T. Sherman Papers, Library of Congress.

13. On May 4, 1884, two days before the collapse of Grant and Ward (discussed in Chapter 12), Ferdinand Ward induced Grant to borrow $150,000 from William H. Vanderbilt for one day to meet an alleged temporary emergency. Vanderbilt loaned the money to Grant personally; the check written by Ward the next day was worthless. After the firm collapsed, Grant voluntarily signed over to Vanderbilt all his real estate and personal property to satisfy the debt, and Vanderbilt later won a court judgment against Grant in order to protect the property from other creditors. In January, 1885, Vanderbilt offered to assign all the property to Mrs. Grant, except items of "historic interest," which were to be given to the U.S. government. Writing for his wife, Grant declined Vanderbilt's offer, except that part relating to property to be given to the government. Vanderbilt then proposed to create a trust fund with the remaining property from which the interest would be paid to Mrs. Grant. That same afternoon, Grant wrote a letter accepting the offer; later the same day, Mrs. Grant wrote refusing it. New York *Times*, December 10, 1884, January 12, 1885; Albert D. Richardson, *A Personal History of Ulysses S. Grant* (Hartford, 1885), pp. 584–95.

14. Grant may have spoken harshly of Stanton to his wife, but had advised Johnson of his belief that the Tenure of Office Act protected Stanton's place in the cabinet. George C. Gorham, *Life and Public Services of Edwin M. Stanton* (Boston and New York, 1899), II, 394–95. On August 11, 1867, Johnson ordered Grant to serve as Secretary of War *ad interim*, but Grant had known that Johnson was considering this move at least since July 31. Thomas and Hyman, *Stanton*, p. 548.

15. Edwards Pierrepont, who later served as Attorney General in Grant's cabinet stated that he dined with Stanton on August 11, and after dinner Grant came alone to Stanton's home to tell him of his removal. Badeau, *Grant in Peace*, pp. 139–40.

16. Johnson, who wanted to challenge the constitutionality of the Tenure of Office Act, believed that he had assurances that Grant would remain in the War Department until he informed the President otherwise; Grant believed that he had clearly informed Johnson of his intention to follow a Congressional ruling. Both understood that the U.S. Senate would insist on Stanton's reinstatement and that Stanton would at once seek to regain control. Stanton's conduct, then, could be considered tangential to the controversy between Johnson and Grant.

17. Grant arrived at the War Department an hour before Stanton. Thomas and Hyman, *Stanton*, pp. 569–70.

Chapter 6

O N ANOTHER OCCASION while General Grant was secretary of war
ad interim, the President wished to send him to Mexico on a
diplomatic mission,[1] which the General declined, saying, "Mr.
President, this is entirely a civil mission, and I really feel that someone
else would fill the position more to your satisfaction than I possibly
could. I therefore decline the honor which you wish to confer upon
me." Mr. Johnson ignored this modest protest and directed Mr.
Seward to prepare instructions for General Grant's mission to Mexico;
at a meeting of the cabinet later, the President opened the subject by
asking Mr. Seward if he had the instructions ready for General Grant.
The papers were produced, and then General Grant said: "Mr.
President, I thought you understood that I declined this mission."
Whereupon Mr. Johnson expressed great indignation and, with
elevated voice, and striking the table with his clenched hand with
considerable force, exclaimed, turning to his attorney general [Henry
Stanbery], "I want to know if there is anything in the commission of
the Lieutenant General that gives him the power to refuse to obey the
order of the President of the United States?"

The General at once calmly but firmly replied: "I can answer that
question, Mr. President, and without consulting your attorney general. I am an American citizen and I can accept or decline *any*
appointment the President may offer me." General Sherman was sent
on this mission to Mexico. I remember his saying to General Grant on
his return, "There was no mission, nothing to do. But after they failed
to get you out of the country, I was sent simply to save appearances."

[169]

Mr. Johnson now became involved in grave political troubles. The South needed and demanded much; the North watched his every move with jealous eyes. Too much precious blood had been shed, too much treasure wasted, for the great sin of rebellion to be too lightly condoned by the government so lately threatened. And it was now the impeachment trial took place. I felt very sorry for the Johnsons and was glad it ended as it did, and as I felt sure it would. I could not free myself from the thought that the trial savored of persecution and that it was a dangerous precedent.

There can be no harm now in my alluding here to the sentiment so prevalent about this time for a strong centralization of power, which was more than once talked of to me, citing more than one precedent for a man in General Grant's position seizing his opportunity. When I told the General all this, he was very indignant and said *he* would like to see anyone *try it*.

It was already constantly remarked that General Grant must be our next President, and I knew well that if any cabinet officer should try Grant as Stanton had tried Johnson there would be another impeachment trial, if that was what Mr. Johnson was tried for. It is certainly a very solemn act to bring the ruler of sixty millions of people, placed there by their voluntary votes, before a tribunal for trial as a criminal.

I was intensely interested when I was confidentially informed by my friend, Mrs. General Sherman, that the votes of [Senator John B.] Henderson of Missouri and [Senator Lyman] Trumbull of Illinois were uncertain. How this was learned, I will not tell. And I soon informed General Grant of this fact. He could hardly believe it, and I know he bravely defended both of these gentlemen when he heard them abused afterwards, saying such men could not be bought. They acted on their convictions and deserved great credit for proclaiming their convictions in the face of such overwhelming popular opinion, and we must believe in their sincerity.

The General was almost constantly surrounded by men of distinction and importance. Our home circle was almost broken up. The two older boys were in school at Burlington, Nellie and Jesse had tutors at home, and when we were not giving dinners ourselves, we were dining out. I remember a great ball at the French minister's and many others. Those four years are to me a pleasant memory of dinners, balls, and receptions, of pleasant people who said kind things, and some pleasant visits away from Washington.

In the winter of 1867–1868, I often heard that General Grant was to be nominated for the presidency. I gloried in his position as general-in-chief and preferred it to all others. A soldier had always been my ideal, and I could not bear the idea of giving up his military office for a civil one. The Republican hosts were hurrying to Chicago. We were alone in our chamber. I leaned over his chair and said to him: "Ulys, do you wish to be President?" He replied: "No, but I do not see that I have anything to say about it. The convention is about to assemble and, from all I hear, they will nominate me; and I suppose if I am nominated, I will be elected." "And then," I said, "if you are elected, do you think you can give satisfaction? The interests of the people are so widely different; to satisfy one section you must hurt another. Think well of all this, dear Ulys. Think of President Johnson. What a time he has had."

"Oh, Johnson!" he said. Then he earnestly repeated, "I do not want to be President, but I feel that if I am nominated I must accept as a duty and I feel, too, that if I am elected I can give to the widely separated interests and sections of the country more satisfaction than any other man. The South will accept my decision on any matters affecting its interests more amiably than that of any other man. They know I would be just and would administer the law without prejudice." And yet, I had the reputation of having urged the General to accept!

The convention met, and Grant was nominated. Then followed receptions of committees, regiments of soldiers, serenades, delegations from north, east, south, and west, and from every state in the Union. My poor flowers, in which I took such delight, were trampled and crushed under foot again and again, until at last I gave up replacing them and admitted the truth of the couplet, "Earth's brightest wreaths are oft made of fading flowers," but I did not mind the flowers now. I was intensely interested in the success of our ticket. I became an enthusiastic politician. No delegation was too large, no serenade too long.

The Democratic papers said: "General Grant was no soldier, had never won a victory." Would you believe it! They said: "Grant was not a soldier. It was true there had been victories when he had command, but it was all *luck*, not skill." Mr. Felt of Galena said these statements reminded him of a story of a woodman who chopped and split two or three cords of wood to the other men's one. When their attention was called to this, they said: "Oh, yes, but he is a lucky man." The General's luck, I think, was in his hard knocks. Only think of it! my soldier was no soldier! only a lucky man!

They said he was an inebriate and not even an honest one: that he did not pay for his drinks. Of course, I was filled with righteous indignation. One morning while at Galena, I read the following in a paper: "General Grant is now lying confined in his residence at Galena in a state of frenzy and is tearing up his mattress, swearing it is made of snakes." And there sat my dear husband, dressed in his white linen suit, calmly smoking and reading his paper and smiling at my wrathful indignation, saying, "I do not mind that, Mrs. Grant. If it were true, I would feel very badly, perhaps as badly as you do."

General Sherman said to me once, soon after the nomination, "Mrs. Grant, you must now be prepared to have your husband's character thoroughly sifted." "Why, General," I exclaimed, "General Grant is my Admirable Crichton. He does all things well. He is brave; he is kind; he is just; he is true." The General, smiling at my enthusiasm, said: "Oh, my dear lady, it is not what he has done, but what *they will say* he has done, and they will prove too that Grant is a very bad man indeed. The fact is, you will be astonished to find what a bad man you have for a husband." And I was astonished, but, like the General, I grew not to mind it.

The General was triumphantly elected and on March 4, 1869, was inaugurated President of the United States. General Grant left his residence on I Street in his own carriage accompanied by some friends. I know he did *not* ride up to the Capitol with the ex-President. He absolutely refused to do so. I went with a large party to the Capitol, where I heard the oath of office and listened with pride and emotion to the first inaugural address of my husband, the President. He stood for a moment, then bowed his acknowledgment to the wild huzzas of the great throng gathered around the Capitol. He received the greetings of a few friends standing near, then he turned and, hastening towards me, he stooped and kissed me on the cheek and, with a pleasant smile, handed me his *first* inaugural address. He passed on and drove in his own carriage to the White House. I returned with my party to our residence on I Street.

After the President had announced his cabinet, I think his first official act was to appoint his old friend and comrade-in-arms Sherman his successor as general-in-chief of all the armies.[2] This General Grant did in opposition to, in fact against, the earnest protests of many senators and members of Congress, among them Mr. [James G.] Blaine. They all begged him to pigeonhole this commission, which they said had been created for him (Grant), and he ought to keep it and occupy the position again when his term of office as President should expire. But the President said: "No, Sherman must succeed me. I shall send his name in at once, and I hope he will be confirmed without fail." And so General Sherman became general of the armies. It was Grant that made Sherman general-in-chief.

A week passed and our guests still lingered. I really felt loath to shut up my house, as we had enjoyed life there so much. One day, the General informed me that he had sold the house. I did not know he had even thought of doing so. On several occasions he had urged me to make ready to come to the White House, and I said: "It is impossible for me to make any arrangements with the house full of guests."

Imagine my surprise, then, when he informed me it was sold. "To whom, Ulys, and for what sum?" I asked. He mentioned the name and the sum ($40,000) with ten years credit. At this I protested and said: "Why sell this lovely home at all? Why not rent it, and then we will have it when you go out of office." He demurred. I then said: "Let us close it." To this, he only replied: "I have already sold it, I told you, and the matter is settled." "Then have *I* nothing to say in this matter?" I had enjoyed my independence too long to submit quietly to this, and like a flash it occurred to me that whenever papa had bought a piece of land, he was obliged to make his wife a handsome present to induce her to sign the deed or else the deed would be imperfect. With exasperating coolness, I said: "You have sold the house?" "Yes," he repeated. "But," I calmly asked, "if I decline to sign the deed, what will the consequences be?"

The General looked up with an incredulous laugh and said: "Oh, nothing. It would make no difference except it would be a little embarrassing to me; that is all." "Oh, is that so! Well," I answered, "I will not sign it."

At this, the General looked over his paper and said: "Very well, I will send word to Mr. Bowen that my *wife* will not *let me* sell the house." The dear General thought this shaft would annihilate me, but it did not. I said, as I left the room quite indignant, "Very well, you may do so."

He withdrew the sale, and the sequel to this little comedy was a great deal of abuse from the disappointed purchaser, who used it afterwards against the General, I was told, when he was candidate for President the second time,[3] and I also read a letter which I found among his papers since his death from the same disappointed person. The General never mentioned these facts to me, knowing it would grieve me. A few weeks after this, the house was purchased for General Sherman by some friends of his in New York. I did not hesitate to sign the deed this time, feeling keenly the silent reproof from the General on the first occasion.

I found the White House in utter confusion. I felt greatly discouraged, but after a few weeks things began to assume an appearance of order. The servants I had in my home were thoroughly demoralized. Perhaps they thought they were incapable of doing the work in the White House. I was forced to let most of them go, and took with me only my maid, a little girl from Galena; our housekeeper, Mrs. Muller, a most faithful and excellent woman; and faithful Albert Hawkins, our coachman, who is now serving his sixth term as presidential coachman to General Harrison.

Order soon came out of chaos, and by autumn the house was in beautiful condition. I love the dear old house and, if I could have my way, would never have it changed. Eight happy years I spent there—so happy! It still seems as much like home to me as the old farm in Missouri, White Haven.

After much thought and fatigue, I at last had the furniture arranged in suites, so that each room would have its own set. I found it scattered widely in the upper chambers. Chairs and lounges were recovered; the hall carpets, which were much worn and so ugly I could not bear to look at them, were replaced. I also had the reception room to the right of the front entrance thoroughly renovated to be used as a waiting room. We found it had been used as a rendezvous for messengers, ushers, and sweepers, into which they brought their lunch baskets. They also heated their luncheons and smoked their pipes there. These men were both astonished and chagrined when they received orders that thereafter they must appear in dress suits and white gloves. They must take their meals at home and would not be allowed to smoke while on duty at the Mansion; any infringement of the above orders would meet with instant dismissal. Of course, this was largely commented upon by the papers, but it made no difference. The men were well paid and there was no reason why they should not look as neat and respectable as those serving in the houses of private gentlemen.

I was somewhat annoyed by the fact that the grounds back of the Mansion were open to the public. Nellie and Jess, the latter just learning to ride on a velocipede, had no place to play, and I no place to walk save on the streets. Whenever we entered these grounds, we were followed by a crowd of idle, curious loungers, which was anything but pleasant. I inquired of the General if the grounds were public. "No," he said. "Then may I have the gates closed?" "Certainly," he said, and the gates were closed. Of course, a ripple of comment followed: "The Grants are getting a little too exclusive." But the children and I had that beautiful lawn for eight years, and I assure you we enjoyed it.

The first reception I held was in the Red Drawing Room. I felt a little shy. I had seen the ladies of the Johnson family receive there and I followed their example and stationed myself back of a white marble table, on which lay a large bouquet. Some of my acquaintances (among whom were dear Mrs. [William H.] Emory and Mrs. Blair) came in early and at once remonstrated, saying, "Mrs. Grant, you are not going to receive here! If you could only see the throng of visitors already waiting the opening of your doors! Come at once, do, to the Blue Drawing Room." To this I consented. A column of visitors began passing. They all looked happy and greeted me very kindly. I soon felt at home, as I knew nearly everyone present. Many inquiries were made for the President, "our President." After the first day, I prevailed on the President to assist me, which he willingly did. He came in at the last half of the reception and was usually accompanied by his cabinet officers, my reception day being one of his cabinet days.

One day as I sat in the library already dressed for my reception, one of the ushers appeared at the door and, bowing low, said: "Madam, if any colored people call, are they to be admitted?" I, after a moment's thought, said: "This is my reception day. Admit all who call." No colored people called, however, nor did they at any time during General Grant's two terms of office, thus showing themselves modest and not aggressive, and I am sure they, as a race, loved him and fully appreciated all that he had done for them.

The President's levees always seemed brilliant to me. The senators and representatives with their families, the diplomatic corps and their families, always in full dress, officers of the army and navy in full uniform, and all of the society people of Washington in full dress, made a gay and brilliant gathering. Madam [Antonio] Mantilla, wife of the Spanish minister, was, as Colonel Fred's wife said, "like a meteor" as she passed before us, so gorgeously dressed and with such magnificent eyes and beautiful complexion. The cabinet officers and their families, handsome men and women always dignified and well dressed, added to the scene, and the levees could not be otherwise than brilliant. I have visited many courts and, I am proud to say, I saw none that excelled in brilliancy the receptions of President Grant.

At first, I and my friends who were visiting me stood and received at the President's levees, but later I thought it would be civil to invite some of the ladies of the cabinet to be present. For instance, Mrs. Fish, wife of the Secretary of State, would stand near me while the members of the diplomatic corps were passing; and when the officers of the army and navy were passing, the ladies whose husbands were heads of these departments would, by previous invitation and arrangement, come to my side, and the lady who preceded her would retire and mingle with the company, thus making it easy and pleasant for me and also for the company.

The invitations were sent by my direction, and the ladies were invited to be present at the President's reception. I do not remember that they were asked to receive until after they arrived. I refer now to the official receptions on January first and the President's public levees. My receptions were always more informal. I always asked three or four ladies besides the young ladies of the household, who protested against standing there for three weary hours. They invariably deserted after half an hour or so with some young officer or diplomat, saying they would soon return, but I saw them no more. I could hear their merry laughter in the gay throng gathered in the room behind me. Once in a while, a lady (I suppose) would impose on my supposed good nature by attending the noon receptions without a bonnet, which would indicate that she was one of the receiving party. This little maneuver was never repeated by the same person.

I afterwards had the wives of the senators and members of the House, two or three from each house, also some of the ladies of the Supreme Court circle; and when an acquaintance from New York, Philadelphia, St. Louis, or other place visited the city, I generally invited her to receive with me, and they all seemed to enjoy coming.

Jacob and Demonet served all of the state dinners. As I remember these dinners, they were brilliant, stately, enjoyable, and most excellent. I have never seen any better, unless perhaps on Fifth Avenue, New York.

It is around our social private table that my memory still clings with the greatest pleasure. I can recall the bright, handsome faces of all of those brave, talented men. They are nearly all gone. Such repartee, such breaking of lances! such anecdotes and laughter!

The General enjoyed these evenings immensely, and papa, who was an uncompromising, old-time Democrat, I had to seat next to me so as to engage his attention when some anecdote was being related which threw the laugh on his party. I remember one occasion when Mr. [John W.] Forney, who was frequently our guest and who was always full of anecdote, related an incident that turned the laugh on an old friend of papa and a leader in his party. Papa at once came to his defense and said: "Mr. Forney, I should like to know when you changed your principles last, Sir?" Mr. Forney, without the least hesitation, replied with perfect equanimity, "Oh, Mr. Dent, at the same time all of these gentlemen did," waving his hand so as to include all at the table, "when our nation was threatened." It was rare, however, that anything unpleasant happened.

I am very fond of society and enjoyed to the fullest extent the opportunity afforded me at the White House. The President enjoyed it with me and always approved any pleasure I might propose.

We had a luncheon for all of the old people we knew, given in honor of my father, and I can assure you that party was one to be remembered. The witticisms, jests, and anecdotes of those old people can never be excelled. It is said old wine is the best. Old Mr. and Mrs. Frank Blair, Admiral and Mrs. [Samuel P.] Lee, Mrs. [Thomas] Ewing, Mrs. Baker, with many others, joined my father, the President, and myself.

Then I had a young people's luncheon, as I wished to know this charming part of our society, whom I could not meet except at my receptions, where I only saw them pass. The society circle was already so large that one rarely met a young, unmarried lady at dinner, and then we only attended a few dinners, as etiquette prohibited a general acceptance, and, of course, when we did go, only persons of high official rank were invited to meet the President. The young people's luncheon is a memory of dimples, smiles, gleaming white shoulders, of lace and flowers and tender glances—a pleasant memory to me.

Our summers were passed at our cottage at Long Branch, where the President enjoyed driving and gathered new strength and vigor for the ensuing winter's campaign in Washington. What a boon our cottage at Long Branch was to the President! Tired and weary as he was with his monotonous official duties, he hastened with delight, as soon as Congress adjourned, to its health-giving breezes and its wide and restful piazzas.

What glorious drives we enjoyed on that enchanting beach! Our children were with us here too, which was a great pleasure, as during this time they enjoyed their holidays and were happy in being at liberty to invite their young friends to pass days and weeks with them. And it was very pleasant to entertain our many guests that we gathered at this sweet, pretty cottage. My beloved and honored father enjoyed his last, declining happy years there. The General was always so, so lovely to my dear father, and papa was so proud of him, and I am sure this delightful sea air prolonged his life for years.

I remember a great ball given at the West End Hotel soon after our arrival at Long Branch, when the papers, describing the brilliant fête and, of course, the beautiful toilets of the different ladies, said as to Mrs. Grant's toilet: "We can only repeat Governor ——'s description of this distinguished lady's toilet—that it reminded him of a spray of dogwood in May." You see I was pleased with this pretty speech, since I remember it.

[177]

One morning whilst at Long Branch, the General came into my room and said: "Julia, I have a new conundrum for you." "Yes?" I inquired; then he said: "Why is victory like a kiss?" "Why is victory like a kiss?" I repeated and, as usual, gave it up. "Why," the General exclaimed, "it is easy to Grant." "Ah, that is charming!" I cried. "Is it original with you?" "No," he said, "yesterday at —— they were all asking conundrums when Miss —— gave me this, and I, like you, gave it up. But when she gave the flattering answer, I accepted the challenge with promptness and took the kiss. Yes, two of them. Do you not think I was right?" "Why, Ulys, how could you? I really think some girls very bold—dreadful." The General evidently enjoyed my annoyance more than I did his new conundrum, good as it was.

During our first four years at the Executive Mansion, we saw little or nothing of the children, excepting at Long Branch, as they were all busy at school. The General was fond of talking to them, and Jesse, who was never at a loss for an answer, was his especial delight. I remember Jesse was sometimes late for breakfast. This was one thing the General was particular about, and Jesse had been late more than once. He said: "Jess, how is this? Nine o'clock and you just down to breakfast? When I was your age, I had to get up, feed four or five horses, cut wood for the family, take breakfast, and be off to school by eight o'clock" (looking severely, if it were possible). Jesse was not the least disconcerted. He looked up smilingly and said: "Oh, yes, but you did not have such a papa as I have, you see." The General smiled and left the room, saying, "You are a saucy little rascal, Jess." And thus it was always. He never found fault with anyone; never with me, though I tried him sometimes.

Jess had two devoted little friends during his boyhood: Willoughby Cole of California[4] and Baine Dent (Jesse's cousin).[5] I never heard of any interruption to this friendship. Jess had a fire engine, and these three formed a most industrious and appreciative company. They really enjoyed fires, leaving in hot haste any study or lesson in which they were engaged to put on their fireman's uniform, fire up, and drag their engine to the scene of action. I had a very nice playroom made for Jess on the grounds near the house. In this they held debating societies and established a boys' paper, called the *K. F. R. Journal*, which was quite a success, I believe.

When the lamented, brave, and gallant Admiral Farragut died, the President was absent from the capital, but we all went up to New York to attend the funeral and to witness the pageant. Soon after the President's return to Washington, a letter was unearthed written by Admiral Porter to Mr. Welles, a former secretary of the navy, in which Porter reflected severely on the army before Fort Fisher and severely on General Grant.[6] This letter fell like a bombshell on Washington. General Grant felt dreadfully hurt, as he really thought a great deal of Porter, and Porter felt worse even than the President. He vowed he never wrote the letter, but there it was in his own handwriting.[7] It made the dear, gallant, old Admiral really ill. The General and I were speaking of him once, and seeing how grieved the General was at Porter's disloyalty to him, I said: "I do not believe Porter remembered he wrote that letter and really thought he was saying what was true when he denied its authorship. You know how eager Porter is to write, and at that time, you know, he was engaged in a fierce controversy with General [Benjamin F.] Butler, who wielded his pen so skillfully and sharply that Porter was utterly annihilated in the controversy. He did not remember the letter, I am sure."

General Grant smiled at the recollection of this Fort Fisher feud between Porter and Butler, and Porter's discomfiture. Though I must say I more than once about this time took exception to Admiral Porter's saying over and over again, "All now that old Welles wanted was a cap and he would be a regular old woman." At this, I was always indignant and begged him to keep all the superannuated old men to themselves. We women considered it a great disrespect to have them called old women, and I did not wish to hear him say it again.

As soon as Congress met, great anxiety was shown as to Farragut's successor. No one thought now that Porter's name would be sent in. I said one morning to the President: "Whom are you going to appoint admiral?" "Porter," he replied promptly. "Porter?" I asked, looking astonished. "Yes, Porter. I am not here, Julia, to dispense these rewards of the government at my pleasure. I am here to dispense them justly, and if Porter were my bitterest enemy I would give it to him just the same. The promotion is his by his own right, and he should have it. He has earned it gallantly, faithfully, and loyally, and I am happy at being able to confer it on him." And so Porter became admiral. And I say: would there were more men as broad as Grant.

In the early part of the General's first administration, Mr. and Mrs. Stanton called and asked for me. I was really shocked to find Mr. Stanton so changed. He looked pale and feeble. I was telling this to my husband when he said: "I will go at once to see him," and after dinner he called little Jesse to walk with him and went to Mr. Stanton's. When he returned, he said: "I am glad I went to see Stanton. I think it did him good. He is looking very badly." Jess also said: "Oh, mamma! Mr. Stanton looked so badly when we went in—just like a dead man, and he was all alone. He was so glad to see papa, but he looked very well when we said goodbye."

Soon after this, the surgeon general [Joseph K. Barnes] said, in reply to my inquiry as to Mr. Stanton's health, "He ought to go to Switzerland." I of course mentioned this to the General. He said: "Stanton is not able to go abroad. I am going to appoint him to the supreme bench. Judge [Robert C.] Grier is about to retire, and when he does I will appoint Mr. Stanton." And soon after, he was appointed. He was most grateful and seemed happy at receiving on the same day so many congratulations from his friends. The next morning, the papers announced his death.[8]

General Grant would often, when he had a caller who was interesting or important and who inquired for me, invite him to come into the library, which was my usual sitting room. One morning, I think in the autumn of 1871, the General entered, saying, "Julia, I have brought Mr. Horace Greeley in to see you." The old gentleman was rather old-fashioned looking, but his face was kind and, when lighted up by a smile, was beautiful. We conversed for a while, a half hour perhaps, when Mr. Greeley, looking at his watch, said he had an engagement and must say good morning. The General invited him to luncheon, but he declined, saying that he had come to Washington expressly to attend the funeral of his old friend, General Walbridge,[9] and that it would necessitate a hurried luncheon as General Walbridge's home was out of the city. General Grant then said: "Mr. Greeley, I am going to the funeral of General Walbridge and will be pleased to take you in my carriage." This was arranged, and Mr. Greeley then promised to come back to dinner with the President, which he did, and I remember they conversed on many subjects, both gentlemen seeming pleasantly interested. When Mr. Greeley bade us adieu, General Grant lighted his cigar and walked with him as far as the Arlington, where Mr. Greeley was stopping. The next I heard of Mr. Greeley, he was the opposing candidate for the presidency against General Grant. When I heard this, I told the General that Mr. Greeley had enjoyed his evening at the White House so much that he concluded he would like a term there himself, but the kind old gentleman never enjoyed that pleasure, for he died soon after the election, the excitement of which was too much for him.

In the winter and summer of 1871 and 1872, Fred was in Europe with General Sherman; and Nellie, who was now quite a young lady, nearly seventeen, was sent with some trusted friends to spend the summer abroad. How well I remember her coaxing me to let her take her one long evening dress with her, the dress having been made for her when she was, to her great delight, invited to be bridesmaid for her friend, Emily D—— of Philadelphia. When I demurred, she said: "Oh, do, mamma. Maybe Mr. [Robert C.] Schenck (our minister to

England) will invite me to tea." Well, Mr. Schenck did, and she had a great deal of attention and was presented privately to the Queen, who, Nellie told me, was very charming and gracious to her.

When Fred was accompanying General Sherman, the authorities everywhere insisted that General Sherman was accompanying the President's son. This was most embarrassing to the youthful Lieutenant, who tried in vain to correct what was to him an absurd and very embarrassing mistake. On the occasion of their reception by the Sultan of Turkey, Fred was compelled, much to his chagrin, to go in advance of his commanding officer, to be presented first to receive the greetings and the speech of welcome, all of which he had to reply to, and thinking that the Sultan was expecting him to say something more, he turned in desperation to our minister, Mr. [George H.] Boker, and said: "What else shall I say, Mr. Boker? I have said everything I can think of." Mr. Boker said instantly in a low tone, "Fred, ask him who cut his trousers." The smile that broke over the boy's face brought an answering one to the Sultan's, and ease was restored. It was Mr. Boker, our minister to Turkey, who told me this anecdote, not Fred.

When Nellie came back to me, she was no longer a nestling, but a young woman equipped and ready, ah, too ready, for the battle of life. How pretty and how innocent she was! How she enjoyed all the fêtes given in her honor! How happy she was! And soon, too soon, she spread her wings and flew with her handsome young English husband back to England. This nearly broke my heart, and I ventured to remonstrate by saying to her: "Nellie, is it possible you are willing to leave your father and me, who have loved and cherished you all of your life, and go with this stranger for *always?*" She looked up sweetly and, smiling, said: "Why, yes, mamma. I am sure that is just what you did when you married papa and left grandpa." But, after all, it has not been such a great separation, for she often visits me with her family.[10]

Nellie left us in May [1874]. In the following October, Fred brought home to us his sweet bride, Ida, and for two years she was honored and fêted as Nellie had been. On June 7, 1876, Julia Grant, my little namesake and granddaughter, was born in the Executive Mansion at Washington, and—would you believe it?—I, now a grandmamma, actually invited all of the fairies of my childhood days to come and confer their sweetest favors on this wee lassie, my namesake. And I believe they did, for now at sixteen Julia is as amiable as she is beautiful.

The winter before the marriages of Fred and Nellie, my dear father

[181]

passed away without suffering. The General and the gentlemen of our immediate household accompanied the remains to St. Louis by special train. My mother's remains were, by the General's wish, removed from the old farm at White Haven and placed beside my father's in Bellefontaine Cemetery in St. Louis.

Our eight years in the Executive Mansion were delightful, but there were some dark clouds in the bright sky. There was that dreadful Black Friday. The papers seemed to say I knew something of it, but I did not—only this. One day, while visiting a cousin at Washington, Pa., a banker there, I sat in the library writing letters. General Grant entered and asked: "Whom are you writing to?" I answered, "your sister." He said: "Write this." Then he dictated as follows: "The General says, if you have any influence with your husband, tell him to have nothing whatever to do with ——.[11] If he does, he will be ruined, for come what may, he (your brother) will do his duty to the country and the trusts in his keeping." I signed, "Sis." [12]

He said: "Seal and send the letter by the first mail." And I did. That is all I knew about it then. After the letter was sent, the General told me he had received a letter from his brother-in-law just before he came into the library, and supposing it had been brought up by one of my cousin's clerks, who always brought the General's mail, he then opened it and seeing it was from Corbin, glanced up at the man and said, "all right," meaning to dismiss the messenger and that there was no answer, who repeated, "all right?" The General nodded. Directly, General Horace Porter, then on duty with my husband, entered and asked the General if the letter he had just received was important. "No, it is from Corbin," General Grant said. "Did you read it carefully?" Porter asked. "Do you know it was sent by special messenger from New York?"

"No," the General said, "was not that one of [William W.] Smith's clerks?" "No," said General Porter, "what did you say to him?" "Nothing. I said, 'all right,' meaning there was no answer and that he could retire." Porter said: "Yes! the messenger said he would at once telegraph your answer 'all right.' "

The General said to me: "I have read the letter carefully now and I find it is an earnest plea for a certain financial policy, which you know he continually urges, saying if I will adopt it, it will make money plentiful and consequently make my administration popular. I always felt great respect for Corbin and thought he took much pleasure in the supposition that he was rendering great assistance to the administration by his valuable advice. I blame myself now for not checking this (as I thought) innocent vanity. It is very sad. I fear he may be ruined—and my poor sister!" And sure enough, when we arrived in Washington, the papers announced a fearful financial panic in New York, and, as I remember, the President did his duty, his whole duty, on that occasion.

I always flattered myself that I had rendered my husband and the country a very great service in advising the President to veto the all-important Finance Bill that was almost convulsing the country during General Grant's administration, but I find I had more than one rival in that honor. Two gentlemen have told me that they advised the President to do the same. But, to tell the truth, I think the President knew his duty quite well and would have fulfilled his duty in any case.

My advice came in this way. Once, when I went up to New York to attend to some fall shopping, I entered Mr. A. T. Stewart's magnificent business house on Broadway, between Ninth and Tenth streets. As I passed through, I met Mr. Stewart coming out of an enclosure which surrounded his desk. Mr. Stewart greeted me with unusual earnestness and, taking my hand, led me inside the enclosure, saying, "Madam, I want to speak with you. I want to know from you if the President intends to veto this most infamous bill." He hurried on to say, "The country's faith and honor is pledged, and surely the President will veto it." I answered with perfect good faith, "Yes, you are right, Mr. Stewart. The President will surely veto any bill that is infamous or any bill that would reflect dishonor on the country. You know that, Mr. Stewart." Mr. Stewart seemed satisfied with my assurance.

Then, when I returned to the hotel, I found several persons who were untiring in their attentions to me at that time. These people all began to talk to me about another bill which they said would bring great prosperity to the country, asking me if I knew if the President was going to sign it. I answered without the less hesitation, "Yes, of course he would, if it was to bring prosperity and good to the country. I was quite sure he would sign it." This answer also seemed to give satisfaction.

When I returned home to the Executive Mansion, I found letters about these same bills, asking if I would assure them and so forth. When I came to read the letters, I was rather confounded, for they seemed to refer to the same bill, only looked at from a different standpoint; one party urging that he should veto the dreadful bill, the others equally urgent that he should sign this bill that would shower prosperity and happiness upon the country. The President coming in just when I had finished reading my letters, and feeling rather mystified thereat, I inquired of him about the bills that were causing so much anxiety, telling him of what Mr. Stewart had said, and also what the persons said who called to see me at the hotel. I told him of the answers I had given both and reproached him for not informing me sometimes of state affairs, telling him how very embarrassing it was for me to be obliged to give such equivocal answers. I am sorry to say the General did not seem to sympathize with me, seemed rather amused at my dilemma, and repeated, to my great annoyance, that old story of "Know one woman by these presents."

I really felt much injured by his neglect to inform me on these important matters. When he saw that I was feeling really very much hurt, he said to me: "Would you like to know about this matter?" "Of course I would." We seated ourselves upon the sofa in that lovely old library, and he kindly and clearly told me the whole story of the government's embarrassment for funds to carry on the war and of the government's pledges to those who trusted and took its bonds. After listening to the end, I exclaimed: "Why, Ulys, it is your bounden duty to veto this bill. You will be burned in effigy if you sign it or veto it, and I would rather be burned for doing right than wrong." "Yes," he said, "my duty is very plain, and my duty will be done, though it does grieve me that doing my duty will bring ruin and desolation to so many homes." [13]

On one of our many delightful journeys out west, I can vividly recall the most interesting one to Salt Lake City. These people always interested me greatly. At Ogden, Brigham Young, the governor of Utah, came on our car. After the President had received and greeted him, the cars began to move, when the President arose and said: "I am anxious to see the country," and returned to the observation car. In the meantime, I had invited Mr. Young to be seated, saying, "I am at a loss to know how to address you, Mr. Young." He replied: "I am sometimes called Governor, sometimes President, and, again, General Young." "Oh, then as I am accustomed to the military title, I will call you the last." General Young, still standing, said: "Well, Madam, you will now have the opportunity of seeing this poor, despised, and hated people."

"Oh! no, General Young, not despised, not hated." "No?" he inquired. "No," I replied, "to the contrary, your people can only be respected and admired for their endurance, perseverance, and faith." I then added: "There is but one objection to your people, to you, General." To this he answered with emphasis and, I thought, with a slight dash of impatience, "Well, and without that we would not have the population we have." I said: "That is prohibited by the laws of the country and would have been wiped out long ago by the strong arm of the government except through charity for the young and innocent that would necessarily suffer, and, General, I have heard more than one of our most distinguished and conservative statesmen predict that now the railroad was bringing you in such close contact with all the country and the world, that this one and only trouble would die of itself."

Just then, a staff officer came from the President to ask General Young to join them in the observation car. When we arrived at Salt Lake City, carriages were in waiting for us. As we entered the gates, the street on either side was lined with rows of children, I should say three deep, the larger ones back, then the second size, and in the front row the little cherubs of Utah, all singing songs of welcome and literally strewing the President's roadway with flowers. Our visit here was most interesting. I went with two of the elders (who were, I think, members of our Congress; at least I had met them before at the Capitol) to the Temple.[14]

These gentlemen conducted me through that great Temple, had the magnificent organ play for me, and, as that great volume of solemn sacred music filled the Temple, I could not help kneeling with bowed head and my heart, always so susceptible to the power of music, full of tenderness, to ask God's blessing to these people. The gentlemen asked if I had offered a prayer for them. "Yes," I answered, "a good Methodist one."

As we left this wonderful city in the mountains, we found our car most tastefully decorated with flowers and fruits, and when we expressed our appreciation and pleasure, one of the gentlemen said: "There is a car full of the ladies of Utah on the train, going in your honor to accompany you as far as Ogden." I at once proposed that some of the ladies of my party should accompany me to their car, our car being so filled with flowers and fruits there was no room left for company. The gentlemen seemed pleased at the suggestion and readily conducted us to the car of the ladies, and we had a most delightful hour or so, exchanging a few words with almost all of these ladies.

During the time the papers were making such a howl about the third term, I followed the President into his office one Sunday afternoon, when one after another the cabinet officers arrived. I was a little surprised at all of them coming to call and also at their coming to the office. I inquired, "Is there any news? Why is it you have all happened to call today? I am sure there is something unusual." I asked this while the President was absent. He had gone to his room.

They assured me that they simply happened all to be of the same mind that day. Then I said: "You do not come by appointment?" General Grant coming in just then, no reply was made. Seeing they were about to enjoy cigars, I left the room, feeling sure there was something of importance to be considered. I was restless and anxious. I called to the General as I heard him dispatching a messenger nearly a half hour afterwards and said: "I want to know what is happening. I feel sure there is something and I must know." "Yes," he said, "I will come as soon as I light my cigar." After a moment, he entered smiling. I said: "What is it? Tell me." Then he said: "You know what a to-do the papers have been making about a third term. Well, I have never until now had an opportunity to answer." Then he told me of some resolutions that had lately been passed—I think in the Ohio Legislature.[15] "This gives me the much wished for opportunity of announcing that I do not wish a third term, and I have written a letter to that effect, and that is why my cabinet were here at my invitation." I exclaimed: "Did all of these men approve and advise you to send that letter?" He said: "I did not ask approval or advice. I simply read the letter to them. That is all." "And why did you not read it to me?" I exclaimed. "Oh, I know you too well. It never would have gone if I had read it." "Bring it and read it to me now," I said. "No," he said, "it is already posted; that is why I lingered in the hall to light my cigar, so the letter would be beyond recall."

"Oh, Ulys! was that kind to me? Was it just to me?" "Well," he replied, "I do not want to be here another four years. I do not think I could stand it. Don't bother about it, I beg of you." But I did feel deeply injured.

About this time, there was a widespread conspiracy to defraud the government, and I regret to say that rumor pointed to a member of our household as one of the authors. He was always civil and obliging and never officious. He never intruded either his presence or advice. I recall how shocked I was when a relative of his called and I approached him hoping for sympathy and an endorsement of my belief in our friend's innocence.[16] He emphatically denounced poor Babcock and declared his belief in Babcock's peculations. I felt so interested in the innocence of this gentleman that I urged the President to send either my son Colonel Grant or Marshal Sharp[17] with him to St. Louis, where he was tried. I was glad afterwards that he declined this courtesy tendered by the President.

It was I who protested against this same man's return to duty near the President. One day, whilst this man's trial was progressing, General Grant entered my room and said: "I really do not know what

Julia Grant in 1864. "This was taken by Brady in New York when I was on my first visit to N.Y. the spring that General Grant first came East."

Second Lieutenant U.S. Grant in 1843. An engraving based on a daguerreotype made soon after Grant was graduated from West Point. "As Lieutenant Grant was when I first knew him," wrote Julia Grant.

NELLIE GRANT, as "Old Woman in the Shoe."

Entered according to Act of Congress, A. D. 1864, by
NICHOLS & BRO., in the Clerk's Office of the District
Court for the Eastern District of Missouri.

Nellie Grant portraying "the Old Woman in the
Shoe" at the Sanitary Fair in St. Louis in 1864.
Nellie sold both the dolls and pictures of herself
to raise money for hospital supplies for the army.

Ulysses S. Grant, Jr.

Frederick Dent Grant

Grant's headquarters cabin at City Point, Virginia. "Jesse and I passed most of the winter of 64-5 with the General, returning with the victorious General and staff to the capital where we were greeted with salvos of artillery, flags, bunting, and smiling happy faces."

The Grant Family in 1865.

Julia Grant in the White House years.

Nellie Grant and Jesse Grant, February, 1868. "Jesse's first long pants."

"Our cottage at Long Branch....The light being intense, I am obliged to turn my face to the shadows." Colonel Frederick Dent sits beside his daughter.

Nellie Grant shortly before her marriage in 1874.

The Grant party emerging from the Bonanza Mines, Virginia City, Nevada. John W. Mackay stands at the far left, James G. Fair at far right, Ulysses S. Grant, Jr., next to his mother. Kneeling in front is Yanada, a servant brought by the Grants from Japan.

The Grants on their front porch.

John Russell Young, the newspaper reporter who accompanied the Grants through much of their journey around the world, had this photograph made at San Francisco for presentation as a souvenir to Mrs. Grant.

The Grants at Nikko, Japan. At the left of the second row is General Saigo
Isugumichi, next Itō Hirobumi. Mrs. Saigo is seated next to Mrs. Grant, and
Frederick Dent Grant just below his father.

Grant and Li Hung-chang.

Julia Grant in a photograph taken in San Francisco on September 22, 1879, just as she returned from her world tour.

The Grants and their son Frederick in a photograph taken in 1879.

I shall do. Every man in or near my office has been subpoenaed to go to St. Louis. I have no one left to look over my letters, and it is impossible for me to do that and attend to anything else." I said: "Tell [Marshall] Jewell and he will supply you with one of his efficient and confidential clerks." "Why?" the General asked. "Because I maliciously told him the other day that I spent most of my time reading letters from all parts of the country urging you to consent to become the standard-bearer again, notwithstanding that horrid letter you wrote." He eagerly asked me, "Is that so?" "Yes," I told him, "bushels of letters come, all with the same petition." The General laughed and said: "You ought not to have done that. See how it has inconvenienced me. Mrs. Grant, I think you are a—what shall I call you—mischief! Well," he said, "I will get even with you by not sending you any more of these letters to read."

The General at once decided to appoint our second son, Ulysses, to the position of private secretary and, sure enough, when General Grant mentioned his dilemma at a cabinet meeting, the far-seeing and most profound Postmaster General offered one of his own confidential clerks. The General told me I had rightly predicted; Jewell had offered to loan him a clerk. I said: "Ulys, how can you let that man stay in your cabinet?" He answered: "It is not time yet, but when the time comes he will go and with company, and on short notice, I can assure you." [18]

On the occasion of the visit of the Grand Duke Alexis, we ladies were greatly disappointed. Something had happened which made it necessary that the Russian Minister Catacazy should be recalled. I do not remember now why his recall was asked for by the Secretary of State; I suppose he was offensive in some way.[19] Our minister to Russia was either afraid to approach the powers at St. Petersburg on the subject or was dilatory, for the Grand Duke arrived and the obnoxious Minister still lingered at Washington. In order to entertain the handsome young Duke, the offending Minister had also to be received, and their presence together at this time was very embarrassing. So the Duke was simply received officially and no social entertainment was offered him at the capital. He traveled all through our country and was, I think, much pleased with his reception and with our country.

Then came the Emperor of Brazil [Dom Pedro], who insisted that he should not be entertained, that he came as a private citizen. When the Secretaries of State and of the Navy went to meet him with a private steamer, he positively refused their proffered attentions, and in no gentle manner, although he was told they had come at the request of the President. He arrived, therefore, in the midst of a crowd. He went to a hotel, where he left the Empress, and sped on to San Francisco. After having been in the country for several weeks, he came to Washington. He was in the city several days before he called on the President. At length the Brazilian Minister called and asked Mr. Fish, our secretary of state, when it would suit the President to receive the Emperor. He was received the next day at eleven A.M. He came and looked hot and rather dusty, having already that morning climbed to the top of the dome of the Capitol.

After he had been presented to the President, he said: "Am I not to have the pleasure of seeing the ladies?" The President answered: "Oh, certainly. We will find them, I think, in one of the drawing rooms." They found me there, surrounded by a party of ladies who could not be surpassed. There were Mrs. Fish, wife of the Secretary of State, my ideal of an empress; Mrs. [George M.] Robeson, wife of the Secretary of the Navy, a handsome lady and very clever; my daughter, Mrs. Sartoris, and my daughter-in-law, Mrs. Fred Grant, both young and charming. All of the ladies were beautifully dressed and looked cool and handsome. I thought the Emperor then realized he had missed a great deal in his pursuit of knowledge.

We met His Majesty again at the centennial in the spring of 1876.[20] He was invited to assist the President to start the great Corliss engine which put all the machinery in motion. The Empress of Brazil was invited, too, and did place her hand on the valve which started the great engine. I, too, was there on the platform with the President, the Emperor and Empress. I, the wife of the President of the United States—I, the wife of General Grant—was there and was not invited to assist at this little ceremony, which opened the centennial celebration of America's independence. I wonder what could have prompted this discourtesy to the wife of the President of the United States and, at the same time, this honor to the wife of a foreign potentate. Of this I am quite sure: if General Grant had known of this intended slight to his wife, the engine never would have moved with his assistance.

The Empress was escorted around the main building by the President. I did not like this arrangement, as I wished to walk with the President myself on that occasion. I walked with the Emperor and, feeling that I ought to call his attention to all that was good in our Republic, I pointed out to him as we passed, pyramids of tobacco all beautifully gotten up, and I said with pride, "Your Majesty, this is one of our greatest specialties." He replied, almost with disgust, "Humph, what is it good for?" I looked up with surprise and repeated, "good

[188]

for? Why," I said, "everything." "What?" he asked again. I said: "It is a great pleasure to smoke. Smoking quiets the nerves. If one is wakeful, it soothes one and promotes sleep. Smoking is a great assistant to digestion." I said all of this with the air of one who knew all about it. The Emperor repeated "digestion, digestion" with much force and then exclaimed, "Exercise, exercise, that is for digestion." I replied, with an air of great superiority, "Oh, Your Majesty, you are away behind the times. The whole energies of the United States are now bent upon inventing laborsaving machinery."

At this, he laughed heartily and almost dragged me to the Brazilian department and in triumph pointed out a beautiful glittering engine, saying: "forty horsepower, Brazilian." "What is it for?" I asked. He said: "an engine and forty horsepower, Brazilian," but he did not tell me what it was for. We met them again in England. The Empress, whom I liked best, seemed delighted to see me again.

At the centennial opening, the General and I were the guests of Mr. G[eorge] W. Childs, who took much pleasure in giving several magnificent entertainments to the many distinguished visitors then in the city. All of these we enjoyed. We were at our cottage at Long Branch during the latter part of the summer and enjoyed many trips to this wonderful and most instructive exhibition. I took much pleasure in selecting a piece of silver for the Executive Mansion and was happy in securing a piece entirely American in history, ideal, skill, and material. In that centerpiece I found something all our own. The artist had exquisitely wrought in American silver the beautiful story of Hiawatha. The piece consisted of a lake of mirrored glass surrounded by a border of grasses, rushes, and water lilies. Upon this lake, which was about twenty-four inches wide and thirty-six inches long, rested a light and graceful Indian canoe with a sail set, and in this canoe Hiawatha was reclining on robes of fur, all wrought in native silver. You can imagine the effect. I also had the pleasure of selecting for the Executive Mansion a magnificent bronze shield on which was wrought in honor of Milton some of the scenes from *Paradise Lost*. It was very beautiful and called the Milton Shield. These articles are still at the White House and are universally admired.

The summer and winter preceding the time for the nomination were full of anxiety for me. There was the trial of one of the General's staff officers, who, as I said, was always so conservative and efficient. Then came the impeachment trial of General [William W.] Belknap. Poor Belknap! His last wife was a widow, very handsome and with some little fortune of her own. She had postponed the marriage from time to time, hesitating to give up her liberty which was so pleasant to

[189]

her, but at length General Belknap declared this vacillation must come to an end. She named the day and, just before leaving for Kentucky where she was to be married, she sent for General Belknap and a mutual friend and, after some little pleasantry, she said: "Now I have named the day; I wish you to sign these papers in which you renounce any interest you might have in my property when I become your wife." Belknap felt much hurt at this request, as the mutual friend informed me. He said to his friend: "I wonder if she thought I cared for her bit of money?" He signed the papers, and they were married that autumn. For two years she enjoyed to the fullest extent possible her position, her beauty and youth, and the entire control of her little fortune.

The day before the dreadful disclosures, General Belknap and his wife came in to luncheon with us. He was very happy and said: "Well, Mr. President, the Inquisition has removed its weight from my shoulders (meaning the congressional committee which was then investigating some of the departments), and I am as happy as a boy with a new top. I am all right, Mr. President."

The next morning as we descended the stairs to our breakfast, the President said to his attendant: "Go up to my office and say I will not be there for an hour. I have an engagement I must keep," and, turning to me, he added, "I am going to give a sitting to Mr. [Henry] Ulke, who has been waiting so long for me." The President arose from the breakfast table before the rest of us were through and left the room. Almost immediately, a messenger came into the breakfast room, saying, "The President requests your presence in the Red Drawing Room, Mr. Ulysses, at once, Sir." Ulysses went at once, and we did not see or hear anything of them until luncheon, when the President came in and, after sitting silently for a few moments, said: "I have received and accepted the resignation of one of my cabinet officers." Of course, this was a surprise, and I asked if it were Jewell. "No. Wait until we get upstairs and I will tell you all about it."

He was called from the table, and I learned all from the New York papers of that morning, which were lying on my table when I went upstairs. The cruel, sad story was all there. Then red-mouthed rumor held high carnival at the capital. Guards were placed at Belknap's door. The President told me that when he left the breakfast room and was hurrying out to the front piazza, one of the messengers came running after him, saying General Belknap was in the Red Drawing Room and begged to see him.[21] The General said: "I cannot now, but will when I return." The man urged him, saying, "Oh, Mr. President, do see him before you go. He is in some trouble and looks very ill."

The General said that when he entered the Red Parlor, Belknap was standing resting his elbow on the end of the mantelpiece nearest the entrance door. His head was on his hand and he looked deadly pale. He was hoarse when he said: "Mr. President, I came to tender you my resignation. Accept it at once. Do not hesitate, Mr. President. For God's sake, do not hesitate!" The General said: "Certainly, if you wish it." And he sent for Ulysses. He directed Ulysses to write out his (the President's) acceptance of General Belknap's resignation as secretary of war. Ulysses did so and handed it to his father, who glanced over it and tore it up (thinking it rather curt, he said). He then wrote an acceptance himself. Belknap wrung his hand and said: "Thank you, you are always kind," and he hurriedly left the room. He had hardly crossed the corridor when two senators[22] entered and said they had come to warn the President against accepting Belknap's resignation, but it was too late.

As I said before, rumor ran riot. The poor lady who had been so admired was now subject to disapproval everywhere. The papers were full of dreadful things about these poor people. One day she wrote to me (I had been counseled not to go to her), asking me to meet her at some mutual friend's house, but I sent her word I could not do that, but for her to come to me, and to come without concealment in the daytime. She did—poor, pretty woman! And how changed she was. Her roses had fled. Her pretty, rosy, dimpled mouth now had its quivering lips drawn quite to one side. As she entered, I arose and, meeting her, threw my arms around her shoulders, and after a moment (tears were falling thick and fast from our eyes) I said: "You did not know you were doing such a great wrong, did you?" "Oh, no! no!" she replied. "I knew it was not just right after I became Belknap's wife, but the man sent me less and less each time, and I was in hopes it would stop altogether." I said: "Why did you not tell General Belknap? He would have made it right." She drew back and looked at me and exclaimed: "Tell Belknap! Why, he would have annihilated me. Oh, no, I could not." The Attorney General was announced—an unusual hour for a call, too. She hastily arose and left me.

The man who caused the trouble told this story: he was called to Washington by a subpoena. He arrived from New York on an afternoon train and went direct to General Belknap's. It was the same afternoon they took their last luncheon with us. When he entered Belknap's house, he found General and Mrs. Belknap in the drawing room. He said to General Belknap: "General, I am subpoenaed to appear before this congressional investigating committee." The General said: "Yes, what for?" "Well," he replied, "in regard to Fort Sill."

"Oh, yes. You did not go there after all, did you?" "No, I did not." "You allowed the original occupant to remain, did you?" "Yes." "And did you receive any remuneration?" "Yes." "That was not right, not permitted. The government is very strict about that," said Belknap. "Did you make a contract?" "Yes." "A written one?" "Yes." "Well," Belknap said, "my advice (he thought the man had come for advice) is for you to go up there and make a clean breast of it, every word, for they will get it. You cannot help yourself."

The man arose and said: "General Belknap, if I make a clean breast of it, as you advise, I will injure you. Yes, General Belknap, I will *ruin* you." The General held himself up and in his deep voice exclaimed: "How so? I guess not." Then the man ran over the whole story of how he had, ever since his appointment given him by Belknap, sent madam every quarter a portion of his gains, and how he had both the General's and madam's receipts.[23] Poor Belknap listened until he was through. His head fell upon the table and he shook as if he had received his deathblow. This man had been a business partner of Mrs. Belknap's first husband, and Belknap supposed the remittances were from her little fortune, which he had surrendered when he married her. We can readily see that he would not make inquiry into it and would, perhaps, feel mortification that he should be compelled to use it at last. I always felt much sympathy for General Belknap.[24]

It was an invariable custom for the General and the young people of the family to assemble in my bedroom when they returned from their walks or rides. I was generally lying on the bed resting among my pillows before making my toilet. The General usually sat near the head of the bed, smoking his favorite cigar. Fred, feeling sure of his welcome, stretched himself across the foot. Ulysses sat on a lounge at the foot of the bed, while Nellie and Ida took their comfort in great cushioned chairs. These half hours were the times we really enjoyed most and were about the only entirely private moments we had together. How pretty the young ladies were as they reclined in their cushioned chairs, radiant in the beauty of youth and full dinner dress. My maid protested against this custom and said: "Madam, you have always to dress in a hurry, and I cannot see how the General and all of them can be so inconsiderate of your comfort and your toilet."

It was President Grant's invariable custom to escort me, always calling at my door if I were absent from the assembled party, giving me his arm and conducting me to the table or the drawing room. If we had a lady friend visiting us and there was only the General present, he was my escort always, our guest walking in with some of the young ladies of the party. He always helped me first at table, no matter who

[192]

was there, and in these matters of etiquette he never failed, up to the day he was no longer able to go to the table himself. He often and often urged me to drive with him, suiting the pace of the horse to my timidity, as he knew I was afraid to drive at the same wild speed he liked so well.

I remember once, though, when General Grant was really cruel to me. It was during the holidays when all the young people of the family were at home. We were a gay party seated around the dinner table, happy and jesting, challenging each other to eat a philopena.[25] I accepted every challenge and was caught by almost everyone before I left the table. They all enjoyed my discomfiture, when the President arose, came around the table to me, and said: "Come, let us leave them." He was ready for his cigar now. As we ascended the stairs, the President said to me in a sympathizing tone, "Did they all catch you?" I answered in an injured tone, "yes." "Philopena!" he cried. I drew my hand indignantly from his arm and rapidly ascended the steps in advance of him. Then I met my son Ulysses, who had run up the back stairs on purpose to meet me, who, looking earnestly at me, said: "Mamma, did papa catch you too?" "Yes." "Philopena!" he cried. This was the straw that broke the camel's back, and I was ready to shed tears if I did not. I could count on no one now as my friend.

I see that a Miss North, an English lady, tells of dining at the Executive Mansion whilst General Grant was there and wondered that the Grants made such a fuss over her. Of any fuss, I was not conscious. The lady was introduced by either Lady Thornton, the English Minister's wife, or by the wife of the Secretary of State, and as the lady expressed herself as being so enchanted at having the honor of meeting General Grant and myself, and the pleasure she had had in looking down from the gallery at the Capitol and seeing all the distinguished men assembled there, I, remembering that we were to have several of these men dine with us the following evening, invited her to dinner. She comments on General Grant's manner, saying he sat silent, stirring his tea during the whole dinner. General Grant never took tea, even when he was ill, and tea was never served at dinner. As to General Grant's silence and lack of interest, I fear Miss North will have to attribute that to her own want of attractions.[26]

When the President, Roscoe Conkling, and I drove to the Capitol to attend the funeral services of our lamented Chief Justice, Salmon P. Chase, the Senate chamber was filled with the distinguished men of the country. When the officiating minister alluded to the mantle of the Chief Justice and invoked divine instruction as upon whose shoulders it should fall, I looked around and my choice, without hesitation, was

Roscoe Conkling. He was so talented and so honorable, and I must say that woman-like I thought the flowing black robes would be becoming to Mr. Conkling. He and I drove back to the Executive Mansion alone, and on the way I mentioned my impression and said to him: "Senator, if it were with me, I should know exactly where to place the robes of justice." I mentioned this to the General. He replied: "You have anticipated me, for I *am* going to offer the appointment to Conkling," and he did. Mr. Conkling's answer came *after some delay*, saying how honored he was by this evidence of the President's regard and confidence, but that his friends all advised him to decline.[27]

The President then offered the appointment to Senator [Timothy O.] Howe of Green Bay, Wisconsin. He also declined, for the reason that the legislature of his state was Democratic, and if he accepted this position (which he valued so highly) it would give his seat to a Democrat. Therefore, he also declined.

Soon after this, the President said to me: "I've half a mind to appoint [George H.] Williams to the chief justiceship. I wish to appoint a man to this most important position who has prospectively twenty years of life and health, and one who was present and familiar with the Reconstruction acts of Congress." The President thought only of the general good. When Senator Williams's name was sent up for confirmation, it was met with such fierce and bitter opposition from every quarter that the President in consideration alone for the Senator's feelings withdrew his name.[28]

There was much anxiety and uncertainty expressed throughout the country as to who really was elected President to succeed General Grant.[29] When Congress met to decide who had been elected, I was much interested and attended their sittings, but did not find much enlightenment. My policy would have been to hold the fort until another election could be held. The General said to me: "It is lucky you are not the President. I am afraid you would give trouble."

When I read in the evening papers that Louisiana had elected a Democratic governor, and yet her vote for President was to be counted on the Republican side, I felt it was wrong and incompatible. As soon as my toilet was finished (I always had the papers read to me as I was dressing), I hastened to the library with the papers in my hand, where I found the General and three or four senators. I hastened to the General and, pointing to the article, asked: "What does this mean?" He glanced at it and then at the gentlemen, and replied: "Why, it means just what it says. I am sure it is quite plain English." And I exclaimed, "Oh, Ulys, do you permit this?" "I? I have nothing to do with it. The whole subject is in the control of a committee of Congress, and Congress acts for and represents the people, the majority, and their decision must be satisfactory." Turning to the senators seated with the General, I again asked: "Can this be so?" "Yes, the President has nothing whatever to do with it, but, as you say, Madam, the two seem incompatible." [30]

For weeks before we left the Executive Mansion, I was much occupied in reading and burning old letters which had accumulated during our eight years there. Some brought tears and some smiles at this second reading, but all were consigned to the flames. I was very much occupied and much run down in health.

When Mr. [Rutherford B.] Hayes and family were en route to the capital, General Grant telegraphed them to come direct to the Executive Mansion, thinking to make it easier and more comfortable for them (coming, as they did, in such uncertainty). They declined this invitation, but afterwards accepted an invitation to dine with their party. The cabinet officers and their wives, the General and I with our brave sons and fair daughters—as we assembled in the Blue Drawing Room, it was a fair sight to look upon.

As we stood facing the center door, which was flung wide open, I saw Mr. and Mrs. Hayes enter. It is quite a little walk from the entrance through the vestibule, corridor, and into the drawing room, now all a blaze of light. The superb crystal chandelier was shedding its soft light upon the fair company assembled there for the last time. Mrs. Hayes was dressed in a handsome white silk. Her hair was arranged in Madonna style. She was handsome, I saw, as she approached with Mr. Hayes. She trembled a little as we stepped forward to welcome them, but this slight agitation soon passed as I said to her, "Mrs. Hayes, these ladies are all eager to be presented to you." We had a very pleasant evening. The oath of office was administered that night by Chief Justice [Morrison R.] Waite.

Sunday morning the young ladies and I were seated in the library when a gentleman was announced bringing me the message that Mrs. Hayes would be pleased to have me accompany her to the Capitol to witness the inauguration. I politely declined, when the gentleman said: "Madam, are you going to vacate the house while Mr. Hayes and party are at the Capitol?" *"No,"* I replied, "I am not." He looked at me as much as to say, "What in the name of Heaven are you going to do then?" He arose and said: "Then you will not go to the Capitol?" *"No,"* I said, "I have already witnessed two inaugurations."

Not till then did I think of our departure. I said to Nellie and Ida, "We ladies will remain here. General Grant will conduct Mr. Hayes to the Capitol, and we will be here to receive and welcome them. I will order a handsome luncheon, and on their return, General Grant will escort Mrs. Hayes, and Mr. Hayes will escort me, to the luncheon table. After that is discussed, we will return to the Blue Drawing Room and, as soon after as is graceful, we will make our adieux."

The ladies said: "Lovely! lovely! Mamma, what will you say when you make your adieux?" I replied, "I will say just what Buckner said to General Grant when he surrendered Fort Donelson, 'My house is yours.' " But I did not say it. I quite forgot it and only said: "Mrs. Hayes, I hope you will be as happy here as I have been for the past eight years."

Well, it all came out just as I arranged. I told General Grant before he left to go to the Capitol that we would remain, the Hayeses would lunch with us, and then we would take our departure. How pretty the house was! Flowers on the tables, the sunlight falling through the lace curtains; how sweet it looked! Nearly all of the cabinet people were present. Our little Julia was held high up for the first kiss from the new President.

Having made our adieux, we reached the front or north portico thronged with our old servants, all eager to catch a smile from their outgoing President and their kind employer. Remembering the demoralized state in which I found the servants when we entered the White House, I had ordered mine to remain until Mrs. Hayes was finally located and gave orders to the steward for luncheon and dinner, and for breakfast the following day, so that Mrs. Hayes might have no disturbance until she had rested from the fatigue of the inauguration ceremonies, thinking that in this way General Grant might entertain them another day.

General Grant's landau, with its four beautiful chestnut horses champing their bits, stood at the door ready to convey us to the residence of Secretary Fish, under whose hospitable roof we remained some two weeks, until after the birth of Mrs. Sartoris's son Algernon. All of this time was taken up by dinners, luncheons, and parties. We hardly had time to rest.

It was now time for us to start for the west. We drove to the depot, which was already filled with our many kind friends, who pressed forward to kiss and embrace me and pass some loving word. I bore it all stoically and smiled my thanks for their kind words. But when Michigan's tall Senator leaned over me and said: "Mrs. Grant, I wish to thank you, Madam, in the name of the Republican Party, for the propriety and dignity with which you have conducted and presided over the Executive Mansion during these eight years past," I did not say a word. I simply bowed my head. Oh, Senator! this straw was the lever which opened the floodgates of my heart. I bravely stood looking out, waving my scarf as we glided out of the depot, and when we had passed all our friends I quickly sought my stateroom and, in an abandonment of grief, flung myself on the lounge and wept, wept, oh, so bitterly.

The General, hearing my sobs, came in and with great anxiety asked what had happened. "Oh, Ulys," I cried, "I feel like a waif, like a waif on the world's wide common." "Oh," he said, "is that all? I thought something had happened. You must not forget that I, too, am a waif. So you are not alone." This was a consolation I had not considered, but, as I said before, the floodgates of my heart were open, and I wept on and on until I really think if all the tears I shed that night had been gathered in one great reservoir the ship of state might easily have floated safely on their bitter depths.

The General was received with unabated enthusiasm at every station en route for Cincinnati, where we were the guests of Mr. and Mrs. Washington McLean, who entertained us most royally for several days. Whilst here, the General and Commodore Ammen made a short visit up to Georgetown, the playground of their boyhood. From Cincinnati, we went to St. Louis, where we were again the recipients of wide and affectionate attention. Then on to Galena, dear Galena, who received us with open arms, as usual. Then to Chicago, where we were the guests of our son Colonel F. D. Grant. This was really delightful. The dinners, receptions, and serenades were many and charming. Then on to Harrisburg, where we were guests of our best of friends, Senator Don Cameron. From there to Washington, where our parlors were thronged all day long. And at night, it was like the President's levees.

NOTES

1. These events occurred in October, 1866, several months before Grant's service as Secretary of War *ad interim*. Apparently Johnson wanted to send Grant away from Washington in order to replace him as army commander with Sherman, believed to be more sympathetic to Johnson's Reconstruction policy. Welles, *Diary*, II, 621; St. George L. Sioussat, ed., "Notes of Colonel W. G. Moore, Private Secretary to President Johnson, 1866–1868," *American Historical Review*, XIX (October, 1913), 99–102; Badeau, *Grant in Peace*, pp. 40–41, 52–55; William B. Hesseltine, *Ulysses S. Grant, Politician* (New York, 1935), pp. 77–79.
2. Grant's nomination of Sherman as General of the Army was dated March 4, 1869; the Cabinet nominations were dated March 5. U.S., Congress, Senate, *Journal of the Executive Proceedings*, XVII, 3.

3. In 1872, Sayles J. Bowen, former mayor of Washington, threatened to sue Grant for $25,000 because of the cancellation of the contract for the purchase of the house. New York *Times*, July 29, 30, 1872; New York *Tribune*, July 4, August 27, 1872.

4. Son of U.S. Senator Cornelius Cole of California.

5. Baine Dent, born in 1856, son of Julia Grant's brother Louis.

6. In December, 1864, a U.S. expedition under Rear Admiral David D. Porter and Major General Benjamin F. Butler attempted to capture Fort Fisher, North Carolina, using Butler's plan to explode a ship loaded with some two hundred tons of gunpowder near the fort. After this proved completely ineffective, Butler was replaced by Brigadier General Alfred H. Terry, and the fort fell to an assault on January 15, 1865. Although Porter and Grant had worked closely together during the Vicksburg campaign, Porter was so angry that Butler had been permitted on the expedition that he severely criticized Grant in a letter of January 21, 1865, to Secretary of the Navy Gideon Welles in which he stated that Grant was "always willing to take the credit when anything is done, and equally willing to lay the blame of a failure on the navy." New York *Tribune*, December 5, 1870.

7. In a letter of December 3, 1870, to Grant, Porter said his first impulse had been to deny the authenticity of this letter, which he had forgotten, but he both acknowledged the letter and apologized for it. New York *Times*, December 6, 1870. Grant's nomination of Porter as admiral is dated December 5, 1870. *Senate Executive Journal*, XVII, 549.

8. Julia Grant's recollection that she urged her husband to appoint Stanton to high office is supported by a letter from Edwards Pierrepont quoted in Thomas and Hyman, *Stanton*, p. 628. Grant informed Stanton of his U.S. Supreme Court appointment on December 19, 1869; Stanton died on December 25.

9. Hiram Walbridge, whose military rank dated from an appointment in the Ohio militia in 1843, was a prominent New York City merchant, who served as U.S. Representative 1853–55, and died on December 6, 1870. The date of Walbridge's death provides the best guide to the date of Julia Grant's meeting with Horace Greeley, editor of the New York *Tribune*.

10. Ellen (Nellie) Grant's marriage to Algernon Sartoris was not successful, and they separated about 1890. Not long after Algernon's death in 1893, Ellen joined her mother in Washington.

11. Presumably Jay Gould and James Fisk, Jr., co-conspirators with Abel R. Corbin in arranging a corner on the gold market.

12. Corbin recalled the substance of the letter to be: "The President was greatly distressed at the rumor that your husband was speculating in Wall street, and hoped he would instantly disconnect himself with anything of that sort." Gould, who also saw the letter, testified that the substance of the letter ran: "Tell your husband . . . that my husband is very much annoyed by your speculations. You must close them as quick as you can." Corbin said the letter was signed "Sis"; Gould recalled the signature as "Julia." U.S., Congress, House, Committee on Banking and Currency, *Gold Panic Investigation*, 41st Cong., 2d sess., 1870, Report No. 31, pp. 157, 252.

13. On April 22, 1874, Grant vetoed the so-called inflation bill, which authorized the government to reissue greenback currency previously retired. Because the bill had

been designed to alleviate the distress caused by the panic of 1873, Grant originally inclined toward signing it. He later recalled that he had written a message favoring the bill; unconvinced by his own arguments, he then decided upon a veto. Young, *Around the World*, II, 153–54.

14. Actually the Tabernacle. The Grants visited Utah in October, 1875.
15. Grant responded on May 30, 1875, to a resolution offered in the Pennsylvania Republican Convention. Hamlin Garland, *Ulysses S. Grant: His Life and Character* (New York, 1898), pp. 431–32.
16. According to a note in Julia Grant's manuscript, the man was J. Russell Jones, Orville E. Babcock's uncle by marriage, an old Galena friend of Grant, who had recently served as minister to Belgium. Accused of involvement in the whiskey ring, a scheme to cheat the government of internal revenue taxes, Babcock went on trial in St. Louis in February, 1876. Although Grant submitted a deposition in Babcock's behalf, and Babcock won acquittal, Grant discharged him as secretary soon after the trial ended.
17. Dr. Alexander Sharp, U.S. marshal for the District of Columbia, Julia Grant's brother-in-law.
18. Postmaster General Marshall Jewell resigned in 1876. Jewell apparently earned the disfavor of the Grants by blaming 1874 Democratic gains on administration policy and by failing to use post office patronage to aid the Republicans in 1876. Hesseltine, *Grant*, pp. 371, 373, 409. In addition, Jewell supported Secretary of the Treasury Benjamin H. Bristow in his attack on the whiskey ring and was spoken of as a possible Republican Presidential candidate. Ross A. Webb, *Benjamin Helm Bristow: Border State Politician* (Lexington, Kentucky, 1969), pp. 154–55.
19. Count Constantin de Catacazy, described as "perverse, mendacious, and treacherous," participated in several complex and outrageous affairs described in Allan Nevins, *Hamilton Fish: The Inner History of the Grant Administration* (New York, 1937), pp. 503–10.
20. On May 10, 1876, Grant opened the International Centennial Exposition in Philadelphia.
21. Secretary of the Interior Zachariah Chandler accompanied Secretary of War William W. Belknap to the White House.
22. Justin S. Morrill of Vermont and Oliver H. Morton of Indiana.
23. Caleb P. Marsh entered an arrangement with the second Mrs. William W. Belknap in 1870 under which he would refrain from applying for the position of post trader at Fort Sill, Indian Territory, receive a $12,000 annual bribe from the current post trader, and divide the proceeds with Mrs. Belknap. She died the same year, and Marsh paid William W. Belknap until his marriage to the sister of his second wife; then the payments went to her. Because the arrangement lasted five years, Belknap received payment directly while a widower, and similar frauds concerning traderships were discussed in newspapers and Congress, historians have doubted Belknap's innocence. Nevins, *Fish*, pp. 804–10; John A. Carpenter, *Ulysses S. Grant* (New York, 1970), pp. 154–57. For the testimony of Marsh, see *Congressional Record; Containing the Proceedings of the Senate Sitting for the Trial of William W. Belknap* . . . (Washington, 1876), pp. 219–28, 236–43.
24. In fact, Julia Grant urged Cabinet members and their wives to call on the Belknaps. Nevins, *Fish*, pp. 808–9. Belknap was impeached but not convicted, primarily because many Senators believed they no longer had jurisdiction once Grant had accepted Belknap's resignation.

25. A game in which two people divide twin kernels of a nut, then must pay a forfeit for failing specified challenges.

26. Marianne North, an Englishwoman known for her paintings of flowers, traveled extensively in the 1870's in search of rare flowers. During her visit to Washington in 1871, Secretary of State Hamilton Fish took her to the White House, where she was invited for dinner the next day. "The President drank tea with his dinner, and had every dish handed to him first. He seemed an honest blunt soldier, with much talent for silence." She wrote that Mrs. Grant had invited her to dinner mistakenly believing her to be the daughter of the English Prime Minister, Lord North (1770–82). *Recollections of a Happy Life: Being the Autobiography of Marianne North* (New York and London, 1894), I, 73–76.

27. Grant's letter of November 8, 1873, to U.S. Senator Roscoe Conkling offering him the post of Chief Justice, and Conkling's vague refusal of November 20 appear in facsimile in Alfred R. Conkling, *The Life and Letters of Roscoe Conkling* (New York, 1889), between pp. 460–61. In January, 1874, friends unsuccessfully urged Conkling to reconsider. *Ibid.*, pp. 463–64.

28. George H. Williams had been an appointed Chief Justice of Oregon Territory 1853–57, U.S. Senator from Oregon 1865–71, and U.S. Attorney General since 1871. Opposition to his nomination as Chief Justice came from those who considered his legal achievements in Oregon mediocre, his conduct as Attorney General inept. Moreover, his wife flourished about Washington in a carriage bought with Justice Department contingency funds. Following the withdrawal of Williams, Grant nominated Caleb Cushing of Massachusetts. News spread that Cushing had written to Jefferson Davis to recommend a clerk shortly before the firing on Fort Sumter. Grant withdrew this nomination also, again unsuccessfully approached Conkling, then nominated Morrison R. Waite of Ohio, who was quickly confirmed. Nevins, *Fish*, pp. 662–65.

29. For the resolution of the dispute over the Presidential election of 1876, after which both Rutherford B. Hayes and Samuel J. Tilden claimed victory, see C. Vann Woodward, *Reunion and Reaction: The Compromise of 1877 and the End of Reconstruction* (Boston, 1951).

30. While Republicans and Democrats disputed the electoral votes of Louisiana in the Presidential election, Republican Stephen B. Packard and Democrat Francis T. Nicholls both claimed election as Governor of Louisiana. The electoral votes went to Hayes; then Republicans, including Grant, agreed not to use U.S. troops to support Packard, thus insuring the installation of Nicholls. *Ibid.*, pp. 192–202.

Chapter 7

O N MAY 17, 1877, General Grant and I, with our son Jesse and my maid, sailed from Philadelphia for England on the *Indiana*, one of the American line of steamers crossing the Atlantic Ocean. We were the guests of Mr. Childs of Philadelphia for several days previous to our departure. He entertained us royally. The General was so busy while in Philadelphia that I hardly had a glimpse of him. He received and shook hands with thousands. Every place wanted him, and he went everywhere.

On May 17, the General with a party of friends went on board a small steamer to go down to the *Indiana*. I, with a party of ladies and gentlemen, was also conveyed to the *Indiana* on another steamer of the U.S. Revenue Service. The wharves along the Delaware were literally lined with people whose shouts filled the air. The river was crowded with shipping and all sorts of small craft, all gaily decked with flags and bunting and crowded with enthusiastic people, who cheered and cheered with great heartiness as we passed. As we ascended the side of our good ship, we were met here too by a party, a multitude of friends, who came to say those sweet old words, "Goodbye and Godspeed." Well, of course, the General was at once carried to the ship's bridge by I do not know whom, and I was left to say the goodbyes. The ladies had been telling me all of the way down the river that they were going to kiss the General goodbye. How disappointed he looked when I told him of their intentions! He seemed to regret it deeply and declared that he missed all that was good and pleasant.

Our journey over was without incident—a little rough, that is all. I think the kind wishes sent after us for smooth seas had their effect. After a sail of ten or eleven days, we stopped at Queenstown, where many of our fellow passengers left the ship.

On May 28, we arrived at Liverpool. As it was on leaving America, so it was in England. The Mersey was filled with shipping and decked with flags. There was a perfect sea of faces as far as we could see in every direction, all looking towards us with kindly or interested expression. The Mayor met the General and delivered a speech of welcome, which was all written out, and which he read to the General. I must confess I felt some little apprehension when this speech, so elaborately gotten up, was read. I discovered very soon, however, that my anxiety was needless. The General's reply was most appropriate. We drove to the hotel. After resting for a few hours, we were driven out to the Mayor's residence, a handsome country place.

I must not forget to state that here at Liverpool we were met by the U. S. Consul General to England [Adam Badeau], who accompanied us to the hotel. As we sat in our drawing room, the Consul entered, bearing in his hand a slip of paper. He said: "General, you ought to have an aide-de-camp with you, and I have just written this cablegram from you to Sherman, asking that I be placed on duty with you during your stay in England." The General seemed annoyed and replied impatiently, "Oh, I do not wish to ask any favors from the government." The Consul urged and urged. He said: "General, you will, of course, receive many invitations and you have no secretary to answer them, and you know what a pleasure and honor it would be for me to serve you, in all things my chief." The General still said: "No, I will not ask it." The Consul still persisted and appealed to me for my influence, which I did not give. On the contrary, I said it would make our party too large, but when he told the General that it would not only be a pleasure but a great personal favor, the General yielded. The Consul left the room and in a few minutes returned, saying, "General, to make this a bona fide message from you, will you give me twenty dollars to pay for it?" The General handed him the amount asked for, and, of course, the request for an aide-de-camp was granted.[1]

We were entertained at a great banquet in the city hall given by the Mayor. We visited all places of interest and in a day or two left for Manchester, where we were again entertained and met by the member of Parliament for Manchester, Jacob Bright, and the Mayor of Manchester. A deputation of our American merchants resident here waited upon the General and welcomed him. At Leicester an address was presented in behalf of the Mayor, magistrates, aldermen, and council. At Bedford and intervening places the General was met with the same evidence of respect.

As soon as we arrived in London, we drove directly to Mr. [Edwards] Pierrepont's, who was then our minister to England. Our first dinner was with the Duke of Wellington at Apsley House.[2] We met a large and distinguished company at this dinner. The women were all handsome. After dinner, we assembled in a large drawing room or hall, quite as large as the audience or East Room in the White House. This hall was hung with trophies from the Peninsula, trophies of war gathered by Napoleon. This great house was presented to Wellington by the government for the single victory at Waterloo, along with wealth and a noble title which will descend throughout his line. As I sat there, I thought, "How would it have been if General Grant had been an Englishman—I wonder, I wonder?"

Mr. Pierrepont gave a brilliant fête to General Grant which was attended by England's noblest men and women. Not only the English, but all the foreign courts were represented, and many Americans were present. I was very proud of our Minister's wife, as she in her radiant beauty and arrayed in a superb gown of pomegranate-colored silk and lace stood beside General Grant and received the guests. I stood with Mr. Pierrepont and he presented the guests to me. My dress was also very handsome, a ruby velvet and cream-colored satin with pearls and diamonds for ornament.

The General and Jesse were presented at court. We dined with the Duke of Devonshire and attended a reception later. We also dined with Lord Granville, whom we knew in Washington, and with many other persons of importance. The General dined with Lord Carnarvon and Sir Charles Dilke.

We now went on a visit to Warsash, a few miles from Southampton, where my daughter and her husband were residing with his parents. This visit was full of interest to us. It was Nellie's home, and we were enchanted with both her friends and her home. This lovely English country residence is surrounded with places of historical interest, beautiful scenery, and charming drives. We had a sail on the waters nearby.

The freedom of the city of London was conferred on the General. The ceremonies attending this presentation were stately and unique. It is the highest honor that can be paid by this ancient city of London. Guildhall was especially prepared for the occasion, and eight hundred guests were invited to partake of the banquet given in General Grant's honor. Arriving at the Guildhall, the General was met by a deputation of four aldermen of the committee. They conducted the General to his place in the Common Council on the left hand of the Lord Mayor.

The Lord Mayor, Sir Thomas White, came in state from the Mansion House. A guard of honor stood near. At one o'clock, Mr. Scott, the chamberlain, addressed General Grant and said:

The unprecedented facilities of modern travel, and the running to and fro of all classes in our day, have brought to our shores unwonted visitors from Asia, as well as from Europe—rulers of empires both ancient and of recent creation; but amongst them all we have not as yet received a President of the United States of America—a power great, flourishing, and free, but so youthful that it celebrated only last year its first centennial. A visit of the ruling President of those States is scarcely to be looked for, so highly valued are his services at home during his limited term of office; you must bear with us, therefore, General, if we make much of an Ex-President of the great Republic of the New World visiting the old home of his fathers. It is true that those first fathers—Pilgrim Fathers we now call them—chafed under the straitness of the parental rule, and sought in distant climes the liberty then denied them at home; it is true, likewise, that their children subsequently resented the interference, well intended if unwise, of their venerated parent, and manifested a spirit of independence of parental restraint not unbecoming in grown-up sons of the Anglo-Saxon stock. Yet, for all this, there is furnished from time to time, abundant evidence that both children and parent have forgotten old differences and forgiven old wrongs; that the children continue to revere the mother country, while she is not wanting in maternal pride at witnessing so numerous, so thriving, and so freedom-loving a race of descendants.

After a good deal more lengthy address, General Grant replied:

It is a matter of some regret to me that I have never cultivated that art of public speaking which might have enabled me to express in suitable terms my gratitude for the compliment which has been paid to my countrymen and myself on this occasion. Were I in the habit of speaking in public, I should claim the right to express my opinion, and what I believe will be the opinion of my countrymen when the proceedings of this day shall have been telegraphed to them. For myself, I have been very much surprised at my reception at all places since the day I landed at Liverpool up to my appearance in this the greatest city in the world. It was entirely unexpected, and it is particularly gratifying to me. I believe that this honor is intended quite as much for the country which I have had the opportunity of serving in different capacities, as for myself, and I am glad that this is

[204]

so, because I want to see the happiest relations existing, not only between the United States and Great Britain, but also between the United States and all other nations. Although a soldier by education and profession, I have never felt any sort of fondness for war, and I have never advocated it except as a means of peace. I hope that we shall always settle our differences in all future negotiations as amicably as we did in a recent instance. I believe that settlement has had a happy effect on both countries, and that from month to month, and year to year, the tie of common civilization and common blood is getting stronger between the two countries. My Lord Mayor, ladies, and gentlemen, I again thank you for the honor you have done me and my country to-day.

After the conclusion of this speech, General Grant signed his name to the roll of honorary freemen. Then came the luncheon, after which there were many fine speeches and a very happy one from General Grant.

We dined one day at the Crystal Palace with Mr. [Thomas] Hughes (Tom Brown of Rugby fame) and a large party of ladies and gentlemen. Then there was a magnificent display of pyrotechnics; a portrait of the General appeared in flaming colors and then burned out, and when the Capitol appeared and met the same fate, the General facetiously remarked, "I hardly understand these English people. They have burned me in effigy and cheered me. Now they are burning our Capitol and apparently expect me to be pleased and happy." This caused quite a laugh.

We dined next at the Kensington Palace with the Marquis of Lorne and the Princess Louise, who is, I think, the Queen's fairest daughter. I remember she was much interested in the war then waging between Russia and Turkey. She had a large cardboard map of Russia and Turkey on which were located the exact positions of the two armies. She had little blocks of two colors, one for Russia, the other for Turkey. These little armies or blocks could be moved at pleasure whenever the news arrived. As the Princess and the other ladies returned from the dining hall, she consulted the map and at once began to move the little blocks. I said (thinking of the recent marriage of her brother to the Czar's only daughter), "Your sympathy is, of course, with Russia?" She glanced up at me and smiled, but did not reply. I did not know then that England's sympathy was with Turkey and was surprised to hear of it later.[3]

We drove out to Richmond Park to call on Earl Russell, who was a very old man and quite feeble. He was sitting in a rolling chair. He gave me a rose with a pretty speech and a kind smile. He and the General conversed for half an hour. His wife, who hospitably helped us to tea, was charming and interesting. We had known their son and daughter-in-law at home. They were both dead.

We passed a pleasant Sunday with Mr. and Mrs. [Junius S.] Morgan, Americans who had a lovely home near London.

On the 19th of June, we dined with the Prince of Wales at Marlborough House. I stop here to give a minute account of this entertainment as it has been so misrepresented by one who was not present.[4] As we entered the hall, the Prince came forward to meet us, coming about half its length. He greeted us cordially, taking the General by both hands. The Prince's greeting could not have been more cordial. He called for his two little sons that they might come now, saying, "My sons are very anxious to be presented to you, General," and two handsome young lads came running forward and were presented to the General and me. The two pretty children stood back after shaking hands with the General and took a good look at him. After a few moments' conversation, I inquired of the Prince, "Shall we pass on?" And we passed into the large and magnificent drawing room where many of the guests were already assembled: the Duke and Duchess of Wellington, Lord and Lady Ripon, Mr. and Mrs. Pierrepont, the Emperor and Empress of Brazil, and many others. When the Emperor retired, the Princess approached me only and made her adieux. I thought it a very magnificent entertainment indeed, and am sure the General was pleased also. The dinner was given to the Emperor, Dom Pedro, and we were invited to meet him.

On the 22nd of June, there was a dinner on Tower Hill, the Prince of Wales presiding, and several other members of the royal family were present. The Prince made a very cordial speech, which was heartily cheered, as was General Grant's happy reply.

We were invited to dine at Windsor Castle on June 27, to return on the 28th. We found carriages awaiting us at the depot and drove, of course, directly to the castle. We were received at the door by a member of the household and were conducted directly to our apartments. We occupied the Duke of Edinburgh's suite of rooms, which were very handsome. Soon after our arrival, Lady E—— called. She informed me that Her Majesty was not feeling well and had gone out, hoping the fresh air would restore her so that she might be able to be present at dinner.

After an hour's rest, we were surprised by a visit from the Consul General, who was now acting as aide to the General, and who was also of our party. He entered in the greatest excitement and exclaimed: "I have just had a call and am informed that neither Jesse nor I are to dine with the Queen, but with the household." The General said: "Rather good luck that, is it not?" "No," he said, "it is a downright insult and ought to be so considered." Soon Jesse entered and at once said: "Mamma, did you see my invitation to dine here?" I had not; I told him I had not even seen my own. Then he said: "Do you know, I think there is some mistake, for the Consul tells me he received a message that he and I are to dine with the household." I told him the household meant the maids of honor, the young officers, and pages. He replied: "Nonsense. What I want to know is if I had an invitation to dine here tonight or if there is some mistake; if I was not invited, then I want a carriage at once and I can return to London and still keep the engagement I so reluctantly broke to come here with you. Father, find out, will you?"

All this time, the Consul was striding up and down the drawing room. Mr. Pierrepont sat pale and anxious, as though this were a very serious international question indeed. I tried playfully to pacify Jesse, but only made matters worse by suggesting that they only looked upon him as a boy. He suddenly exclaimed: "Since I come to think of it, mother, did not father and you give a dinner especially in honor of the Queen's young son (Jesse said "youngster") when he was on a visit to America a short time ago?" "Yes," I said, "we did."

The General had already sent for the proper person, and when he came, General Grant said: "We fear there has been some mistake. My son, Mr. Grant, came down here under the supposition that he was invited to dine with Her Majesty. Will you make inquiry and, if there is a mistake, will you be kind enough to order a carriage for him, and he will return to the city at once." Almost immediately, this gentleman returned and informed the General that Her Majesty certainly expected Mr. Grant to dine with her that evening.

During the afternoon, two ladies called. The Duchess of Roxburghe and Lady E—— said they would call for me at eight o'clock, I believe. I was ready and was dressed in a black satin which was covered with Chantilly lace. The ladies were prompt, and as we walked up the corridor, one of the ladies said: "This corridor was built by George the Fourth (I think), the *only monument* of his reign." Then one of the ladies said: "Mrs. Grant, I hope you will not feel fatigued. Our Queen always receives standing." I at once replied: "Oh, I am sure I will not feel the fatigue. You must remember *I too* have received for the last eight years and always standing." We assembled in the corridor where the gentlemen joined us.

Soon after, the Queen entered, accompanied by Princess Beatrice and Prince Leopold. As soon as the Queen entered, she at once approached General Grant and shook hands cordially, saying the usual pleasant things welcoming him; then Her Majesty came to me and talked for quite a while, saying she had met my daughter when she was over some four years before. I said: "Yes, Nellie has told me of Your Majesty's kind reception, and she was so pleased with England that she has since become a subject of Your Majesty." Dinner was now announced. The Queen was escorted by Prince Leopold, Princess Beatrice by Prince Christian, and the General escorted Princess Christian. I do not remember who escorted me, but he was very pleasant, and I enjoyed the evening.

We were conducted through the castle on the following morning and shown the treasures which had been accumulating there for so long. I could not begin to describe all I saw. As we were passing through a magnificent hall, or perhaps it was a library, a fine portrait that hung over one of the doors was pointed out to me. It was one that England was proud of: a soldier, I think, as a martial cloak hung over one shoulder. He looked like a soldier and a noble one, too. A young lady who was accompanying us said in a low tone to a lady near me, "I have a mind to tell her he was one of my ancestors." I turned at this whispered remark and said: "I am sure you must be proud of him."

Mr. and Mrs. Pierrepont gave a dinner to the Prince of Wales, which was a brilliant event. They also gave a reception and a dinner on the Fourth of July, which were delightful. A day or two after this dinner to the Prince of Wales, which occurred, I think, on the 23rd of June, our Minister and his wife reluctantly consented to our becoming the guests of the Consul General, who had been urging us since our first arrival in London to become his guests. We were there from the 24th of June until the 5th of July. We were entertained constantly whilst we were guests of this gentleman by people wishing to do honor to my husband, so that I can only remember dining twice with our host at home.

On the morning of the 5th of July, we left for the Continent. After a pleasant run to Folkestone, where the General was met by and listened to an address of welcome from the Mayor, to which he replied, we took a steamer sent especially by these hospitable Englishmen and steamed to Ostend, where we were met by the municipal and military authorities, and also by an officer of the King's household, who offered us the use of the royal car to Brussels.

The gentlemen walked out. I did not accompany them as I was too fatigued and preferred to sit at the window and watch the quaintly dressed people as they walked to and fro beneath me in their wooden shoes and high caps. How the paving stones resounded as they pattered on them in these shoes. The General regretted that I did not go with them on their walk, as this was the first really *foreign* country we had been in, and it was very foreign.

We left the next morning for the Belgian capital, stopping on our way at Ghent. We visited all places of interest in this old city. I was shocked at seeing here a woman and a dog harnessed to a cart and actually dragging quite a heavy load. I saw this not only once but many times. Sometimes it would be a man and a dog. I suppose these animals are strong enough, but I did not like to see a man or a woman mated with them as burden carriers.

When we arrived at Brussels, the General called on the minister, Mr. A[yers] P. Merrill, whose illness confined him to the house. At noon, we visited the Hôtel de Ville. The authorities showed us all the objects of interest in this memorable edifice. The General was asked to add his name to the roll of illustrious names written there.

We dined with Mr. and Mrs. [Henry S.] Sanford, charming Americans living in Brussels. The next day, King Leopold and Madam de Winkersloot called on us at the hotel. The General had a long and interesting conversation with the King and found him both interested in and well informed on our national affairs. The King was absent from the city when we arrived and called on the General first on his return.

The next evening, we were entertained at the palace by His Majesty and the Queen, at which time the King said we could pay our respects to the Queen, return his call, and dine all at once. We passed through a number of salons and corridors and were presented to the Queen, who was young and handsome, as was King Leopold, a tall, noble-looking man. The Queen wore a lovely opal silk with lace. I wore a handsome white silk. I was very fortunate in having several handsome dresses with me, for I had no opportunity to have any made until we got to Paris.

General Grant and I went early to pay our respects, as His Majesty had proposed. After meeting the Queen, the General, Jesse, and I returned to the drawing room, where the company invited to the banquet was assembled. Soon after we entered, the King and Queen came. After they had passed quietly around and spoken a word or two to each guest, dinner was announced. The King escorted Her Majesty, General Grant escorted Mrs. Sanford, and Mr. Sanford escorted me. General Grant was seated next to the Queen and I next to the King, Mr. Sanford on my left.

We had been seated some little time when I noticed that not a sentence had been passed between Her Majesty and the President. In a low tone, I said to Mr. Sanford: "Do send word to Mrs. Sanford not to talk any longer to the General, so that he may look towards the Queen." "Oh!" Mr. Sanford said, "I dare not. I dare not." Growing desperate, I leaned slightly forward, spoke past the King in a voice subdued but distinct, and said, "Victor." The General did not look around until I said "General Grant." He at once looked towards me; then I said: "Do you know Her Majesty is a fine whip? Yes," I said, "King Leopold tells me she sometimes drives four-in-hand." After that, I had no more anxiety and thoroughly enjoyed the banquet.

The following day, we left for Cologne, making the journey in the King's railway carriage. The military governor called. We visited the cathedral (which I revisited last spring in 1889, and as I knelt in prayer under its lofty dome, I felt that in spirit my husband was there again beside me). We visited the bridges and made the tour of the Rhine as far as Bingen, "Fair Bingen on the Rhine," where we spent the night, and next day went to Wiesbaden; and on to Frankfort, where we were most pleasantly entertained. I remember especially the banquet at the Palmengarten, where one hundred and fifty gentlemen dined, and our walk around the garden afterwards. Many thousands were gathered there and all were eager to get a glimpse of the General.

I must relate a little incident which occurred at Bingen on the Rhine. I had retired, and the gentlemen had gone for a walk. My maid was in some distant room. I rang my bell, when a pretty little fräulein appeared. I said: "Send my maid, please." She curtsied, smiled, and shrugged her shoulders. I repeated, "My maid; send her please, at once." She repeated the pantomime but looked troubled. I said: "Parlez-vous Francais?" "Oui, oui, Madam," smiling delightedly. Then I said: "My maid; I want my maid." The distressed, troubled look returned. At last I thought of "femme de chambre"; then she darted off like a wild bird and soon returned leading my faithful attendant, who was beginning to grow a little restless, knowing she was wanted and, like myself, unable to inquire her way.

From Frankfort, we drove to Homburg-les-Bains [Bad Homburg], where General Grant was met by a committee led by ex-Governor [Marcus L.] Ward of New Jersey. While there, we visited the famous Roman camp at Saalburg, which is the finest Roman memorial to be found in all Germany. While there, the grave of a Roman soldier was opened. He had rested there for more than eighteen centuries. The bit of coin and the tear bottle, which were taken from the hand of the Roman soldier at rest in this grave, were given to me. In the evening, there was a dinner and a walk in the world-renowned gardens of the Kursaal, which were especially illuminated for the occasion, and the effect was charming. Then came the visits to some famous wine cellars and a dinner at some other garden.

Sunday, the 15th of July, we left for Heidelberg. We remained there all night and listened with pleasure to Wagner or Liszt—I cannot remember which—[5] who performed several of his own delightful pieces of music for us. I enjoyed climbing over that wonderful old castle on the heights above Heidelberg. Nellie had also been there and told me of it.

From Heidelberg, we passed through the Black Forest, a delightful ride, although I was disappointed in this. It was not a wilderness, nor was it dank and dark, nor did we meet any bandits or any adventure. It was only a lovely ride.

We remained several days at Lucerne. We enjoyed sailing on the lake, riding up Mount Righi, and seeing where William Tell had lived. Here we hired a large coach and four horses to cross the Tête-Noire mountain pass. This ride was delightful. We had our basket well filled with a tempting lunch and we loitered and lunched where we liked.

The scenery was wonderfully magnificent. We paused for a day or two at Interlaken, where we visited the Falls of Lauterbrunnen and the glacier fields. Just as we began to ascend the last height of Tête-Noire Pass, Jesse got out to walk. After walking some distance, he stopped at an inn and asked if any of us would have a glass of wine or ale. When he came out laughing, the General inquired: "What is it that pleases you, Jesse?" "Oh," he said, "I was badly sold. After much difficulty with my French, I made two very pretty girls understand what I wanted and as I was paying my score I inadvertently remarked, 'You are two very pretty girls.' This I said in English, supposing I might with perfect impunity. Then they smiled and replied, 'Yes, everyone says we mountain girls are all pretty,' and I left promptly."

At the falls, I met an old schoolmate. She was there like me, enjoying her first European trip. Her husband was a retired army officer. It was a great pleasure to meet her. Jesse and I ordered here a luncheon of broiled trout and English bacon. The General waited for his luncheon at the glaciers, where the courier had ordered it, and he had to be satisfied with a very poor one.

Another day, we had been riding since early morning and stopped at a deliciously clean-looking inn to refresh ourselves as well as to change our good horses. We had dined and I had indulged in a short siesta of twenty minutes, which always brings me up well and ready for any fatigue. The gentlemen had retired to a portico to smoke. I took my umbrella and proposed to my maid that we should walk on and let the carriage take us up. We passed out and on our way, up a slight incline until we reached the woods. There we stopped to rest and to await the coming of my party. I think we had walked fully a mile and a half. After resting and growing somewhat impatient, I remembered that I had not mentioned to anyone my intention on leaving and I sent my maid to see if they were coming. She soon returned and said: "The carriage is at the door, and Mr. Jesse is walking up the road. I waved my veil to him and he went back." Feeling well from my walk, I decided to have a little amusement and said to Bella: "I am going to hide. You tell them I am lost, that you do not know where I am." She said: "Oh, Madam, I couldn't say that, for it would not be true." "Well then, say 'When I went to see if you were coming, Mrs. Grant was on that bank. When I returned, she was not there.' That is literally true." Then I quickly hid myself behind the thick pine and hemlock boughs. I had only time to disappear when the carriage drove up. The General said: "Why, Bella, where is Mrs. Grant?" Bella, with her veil up to her mouth to hide her laughter, looked as if she were crying, as her face was red from the rapid walk. She answered as I had directed. The gentlemen leaped out of the carriage, began looking hurriedly over the precipice, and questioned poor Bella, who was nearly choking with laughter.

The General said: "Why, of course she has gone on up the mountain. Drive on at once." This brought me out of my hiding-place, as I had walked as far as was comfortable, and I said: "Oh, General, here I am." Well, I was severely reprimanded for thus needlessly terrifying everyone. I enjoyed it the more, asking, "What did you think had become of me?" "I could not imagine. Your freak for a walk was so unusual, and with Bella's tears, I did not know what to think. But the next time, I will drive on and leave you."

From here we went to Berne, where the General was entertained by the President and council of the Republic. I did not attend this dinner. There were no ladies present. I remember a queer old clock there, and we waited to see and hear it strike. The place looked substantial but it was not attractive to me. I think the weather was dull while we were there.

On July 26, we arrived at Geneva. This place was most interesting to us, being the place where our late differences or grievances against England had been amicably settled.[6] Geneva looked very lovely: like one of its own beautiful jewels in a setting of lakefront and background of emerald mountains. While there, the General laid the cornerstone of an American church, and there were speeches both eloquent and thrilling.

Our stay at Geneva was full of incident. We met many Americans. They all vied with each other in making our stay pleasant. We had dinners, evening parties, and lovely rides to villas in the country to tea, where we met many of our ever-charming countrywomen and men, who are head and shoulders above any others. I enjoyed visiting the shops. They were full of exquisite jewelry, pretty moss agate boxes, and all kinds of pretty nothings. It was hard to practice self-denial. I indulged in an agate box or two, which the General said were made of glass.

We enjoyed sailing up Lake Geneva several times and we visited the prison of Chillon. We again engaged a coach and four fine horses to take us on, finding it much more agreeable and but little more expensive than the diligence. As we dashed along some ten miles out of Geneva, we met a peasant going to market with a cart of vegetables and fruit, who nervously and hurriedly turned out for us, all the time calling out in a loud and angry voice and wildly and threateningly gesticulating. He seemed to think our coachman had tried to run over him. This was too much for Jesse. He stood up and shook his fist and called out: "You old simpleton, be quiet, or I will get out and thrash you in a jiffy." This had the effect of making the man wild with rage. Then Jesse arose, shaking both his clenched fists and his cane too. This pantomime went on until the General said: "Stop, Jess, that will do." After a few more wild passes in the air, and opening and shutting his mouth without uttering a sound, Jesse sank back on his seat as if exhausted with his gallant defense of the party and demanded a cigar. Having our own carriage, we could loiter when and where we pleased.

The Simplon Pass was grand in the extreme, awe-inspiring in its grandeur. We would alight and venture out on some dizzy height and look down through vistas of mountain gorges far out into a valley of glorious sunshine. Those scenes are as vividly photographed on my memory as if I had seen them but yesterday. The Yosemite is like those great mountains. Away up on this pass, we came to a broad and generous-looking edifice. It was a Roman Catholic monastery kept here to benefit passing travelers. We were received by some five or six smiling, rosy-cheeked young monks, who greeted us kindly and offered us their hospitalities, which were simple and good. These men stay there to succor those who might otherwise perish in the dreadful storms. I asked one of these young monks how they amused themselves during the long winter evenings, thinking I would send them some chessmen and a cribbage board and some cards for Boston, but he replied: "Amuse ourselves? We work always. That is why we are here. We are never lonely, never." And I believed him. These fine, noble fellows were literally living very near to Heaven.

We passed through a wonderful gorge down into Italy. We stayed all night at Domodossola, where the townspeople were having a fête to "Our Lady of the Snow." Then we went on to Lake Maggiore, where we spent several days sailing on the lake and making visits to many of the lovely villas in the vicinity. Thence on to Lakes Lugano, Como, and others, tarrying a day and night at nearly every place. We crossed the Alps again by the Splügen, and I think it was higher than the Simplon. At the summit, the General got out to gratify my whim and gathered me a few white pebbles. It was raining too. We arrived at Ragatz, where we remained for about ten days. I remember this place with great pleasure. We returned there later and remained for two weeks. We often walked five and six miles without fatigue and took long and lovely rides.

We now returned to England, going by way of Antwerp. We stopped two or three days in London and then went on to Edinburgh. The General was received with ceremony and with a hearty welcome and was presented with the freedom of the city, as well as at Glasgow, Inverness, Elgin, Wick, and Grantown, the home of the Grants. We visited Thurso and Dunrobin castles, where we were guests for two or three days. I remember the family of Sir [John George] Tollemache Sinclair. They were remarkably handsome, and his castle was an ideal home, romantically situated on the sea so near as to have its stony base washed by every wave.

We also visited Dunrobin Castle and passed several days there. The late Duchess of Sutherland was charming, and I was much interested in seeing the large company gathered there. We were met and received at the entrance, much as we used to receive our guests in the West, with a hearty welcome. The Duchess conducted me to my room herself and said dinner would be ready in an hour, but if I did not feel like dressing, not to do so, as I must be fatigued after a long day in the cars. Near the end of dinner each day, the piper entered and strutted round and round the table, blowing his pipes, which gave out a very shrill sound. The piper was dressed in Highland kilts, and so were the Duke and most of the gentlemen in the party.

We breakfasted with Earl and Lady Caithness, whom we had met at home. Their castle was quaint and very old. This lady firmly believed that the spirit of Mary, Queen of Scots had entered her fair form. Learning this as we went there, I said, as she handed me a picture of Scotland's Queen, "Oh, this is very good. When did you have it taken, Lady Caithness?" She was greatly pleased, of course, but it was inexcusable in me. But I thought it would please her, and it is kind to do this sometimes.

We visited the most northern house in Scotland, John O'Groat's, where the gentlemen gathered me a number of little shells from the beach, which they said were liberty caps (and they looked like them too) sent all the way from America by the Gulf Stream and left upon these shores.

General Grant regretted that he was unable to accept the invitation of Lord Seafield, who was the head of the Grant clan of Scotland. I regretted this also, but Lord Seafield's invitation clashed with others already accepted, and it was impossible to arrange a visit.

We visited many places in Scotland and were welcomed everywhere. We visited by special invitation, as we did all these places, Inveraray Castle, passing through Loch Lomond. The Duke of Argyll sent his carriage to meet us, but we did not enter it, as we had already started in our own conveyance. At the castle, which is a grand old edifice, the Duke and Duchess and the young ladies and gentlemen of the family met us at the doorstep with a hearty greeting. The Duke conducted the General to his room, and Lady Evelyn went with me to mine. She said: "Those rooms are Lorne's."

The members of the family were all most interesting. The Duke and the General had long conversations together, and I had the happiness of listening to many of these as I rode out with them. The Duchess, having had a slight stroke of paralysis, was something of an invalid and did not venture out with us in the carriage, though she went with us for a ride on the Duke's yacht. The Duchess seemed both proud and fond of her daughter-in-law, the Princess Louise, and pointed out to me a beautiful piece of bronze which the Princess had modeled, and again she called my attention to the drawing room curtains and said: "The Princess designed these for me. Do you not think them handsome?"

She called my attention to a beautiful portrait hanging in the drawing room and told me it was the mother (or grandmother) of the Duke of Argyll. "She was a famous beauty," she said, "and the artist has painted all the flowers in the garden in which she stands turning towards her, as they turn to the sun. A poetic and delicate compliment, was it not?"

Here, as at Dunrobin, the Duke and his sons came to dinner in Highland kilts and looked very handsome. The piper also played the bagpipes around the table and around the castle in the morning. I had the pleasure while there of meeting several members of the Duke's family, among them the Duke and Duchess of Northumberland. The Duchess was beautiful in a robe of rose-tinted silk. Lady Evelyn was simply delicious to look upon, as fair and delicate as a primrose.

On our return to England, we visited Newcastle, Sunderland, Sheffield, Birmingham, Leamington, and Stratford-on-Avon. At each of these places, General Grant was met by the dignitaries and authorities of the city and by thousands of the people with wild enthusiasm. My heart was filled with joy over this appreciation of my beloved husband, and from my heart, I said: "God bless England and her people."

I must tell of our visit to Newcastle-upon-Tyne. The reception and procession were glorious. It was a moving stream of red and blue banners, and all bore mottoes for the occasion. The vast throng cheered General Grant and Mrs. Grant. Speeches were made and replied to. The day was one never to be forgotten. A grand, glorious ovation!

We visited Warwick Castle. I should like to dwell there, it is so beautiful and so peaceful. But Kenilworth, historic Kenilworth, with its ivy-covered walls—the scene of Elizabeth's vanity, of Leicester's ambition and treachery, and of poor Amy's heart-breaking—I was doomed not to see, as I was entirely overcome with fatigue. I was compelled to sink down on a seat and, from a distance, like Moses, only look upon the land I had so longed to see from my earliest girlhood.

We made another short visit to Warsash House, Nellie's home. The General was received with honors at Southampton. From Warsash, we crossed the southern counties to Torquay to make a visit to our American friend, Mr. [Alfred D.] Jessup, who at once telegraphed and urged Mrs. Sartoris (Nellie) to join us, and she did. We had ten days of perfect pleasure with these charming and hospitable people, then returned to London and Nellie with us. We remained several days for the General to keep engagements at Bath and Birmingham. The General went without us and, on his return, said we had missed a great deal by not going.

We visited Brighton, December 20th,[7] and were guests of Mr. [James] Ashbury, M. P. This visit was full of honors for General Grant.

On October 24, we decided to make our long-postponed visit to Paris. It was the General's intention to have gone direct to Paris when we first went to the Continent in July, but our minister, Mr. Washburne, nervously urged that we should not visit Paris then, giving us a very important reason. He said: "The General's arrival might affect the elections," which were then taking place.[8] I thought it very absurd and could not see how General Grant's presence could affect French politics.

Mr. Washburne had gone when we arrived. Mr. [Edward P.] Noyes filled his place. Just before we arrived at the depot in Paris, General Noyes, General [Alfred T. A.] Torbert, and an aide-de-camp of Marshal (President) [Marie Edmé] MacMahon entered the car and, in the name of the President of the French Republic, the ex-President of the United States was welcomed to France. A great throng was waiting at the depot. I received two large bouquets of violets. They were tied with tricolored ribbons. I thought they were very sweet, but I felt somewhat conspicuous with the ribbons.

Our visit to Paris was delightful. We met many Americans who seemed proud of their countryman, General Grant, and left nothing undone to make our visit to this, their favorite city, a delightful one. I had a splendid time shopping. Mr. [Charles F.] Worth personally directed the fitting of my costumes, and Madam Virot attended me in person for any millinery I wished, and these were no small attentions, I assure you.

The President of France, that grand old soldier, President Mac-Mahon, and Madam MacMahon were unceasing in their attentions. After returning our visit, they gave us a grand dinner and often sent us their boxes at the opera, the theater, and the races. The latter we did not attend, as the great racing day is Sunday, and, of course, we did not accept this pleasure.

I could not begin to tell of all the entertainments given General Grant on our first visit to Paris, but with invitations from Frenchmen and our own dear countrymen, our time was wholly and most pleasantly occupied. My time was too much occupied; really, when I think of all the places I went to, it actually makes me dizzy.

I visited the tomb of Napoleon with a friend. I never read of his gallant deeds but it thrilled my girlish heart. We had been talking on indifferent subjects on the way, and when I ascended the steps, entered, approached the balustrade, and looked down upon the sarcophagus, I was seized with a violent shivering which was most alarming to me, and I can only account for it now as a feeling of sympathy. There lay Napoleon, not twenty steps from me in that great black sarcophagus.

The Paris I remember is all sunshine, the people all happy. All places of note were visited, of course: all famous art galleries and churches; Versailles, so rich in history; Sèvres, the famous porcelain and tapestry factories; and all places of historic interest in and around Paris. Many of these were visited with friends, but it would take a volume to tell this alone, and I must forbear.

The run from Paris to Nice, where we went to meet the ship *Vandalia*, was very fatiguing. Our courier had obtained comfortable quarters. The General and party were entertained by the Prefect, the American Consul, and many others. I remember with pleasure an entertainment at Villefranche, also a luncheon on our flagship, the *Trenton*.

General Grant, Jesse, Mr. [John Russell] Young, and I, with my maid, boarded the *Vandalia*, one of our men-of-war then cruising in the Mediterranean. The American government had placed this beautiful ship at General Grant's disposal during his stay in the Mediterranean. This was a great honor, and we appreciated it.

We arrived at Naples on December 17. The weather was unpropitious. We went ashore, however, and visited all places of note and rode through the city, visiting churches, the royal palace, and the museums. We enjoyed a lovely drive around the Bay of Naples. The sky was very blue and the atmosphere was also blue, which is caused, I believe, by the sulphurous smoke which is constantly arising from Mount Vesuvius. We made a charming excursion to Mount Vesuvius. We saw many mendicants; some of them followed us far up the mountain and got the remains of our luncheon. We had some fine wine on this trip, Lachryma Christi.

Our next trip was to Pompeii. We were happy in having the company of several young officers from the ship. It gave me great pleasure to stand in the very portico of the fair Greek Ione, and in imagination, beside poor Nydia, with upraised hands and eager look, her pretty head stretched far forward listening to treachery plotted against her beloved Glaucus.[9]

The shops of Naples were charming and were full of carved tortoise-shell, ivory, and coral. The General, very unreasonably I thought, objected to my buying a lovely coral handle for my parasol, but it was all explained when he entered one day with an exquisite one in his hand and said: "Now you see why I did not want you to buy one. I wanted to give it to you for a Christmas present."

On December 23, we arrived at Palermo, a lovely, romantic old place which looked very bright in its preparations for the Christmas holidays. We rode away up into the mountains. The ride was full of enjoyment and hazard, I thought, as only a short time before some wealthy person had been captured, spirited away, and held for a large ransom. I only found some rather pretty inlaid marble tables here.

The wardroom officers of the *Vandalia* gave a dinner on December 25 and were kind enough to say it was in my honor. They were always kind. This dinner is a very pleasant memory to me. The menu could not have been better, and the dinner was well served by their waiters, who wore white canvas jackets and black silk scarfs. The smilax was such a surprise and the pretty bonbons! You were very good, dear gentlemen and brave sailors, and I will never forget this, nor any of your kind attentions to me and mine.

We left Palermo with its Christmas bells ringing out merrily and steamed south. In the morning, we passed Stromboli. The sea had grown rough during the night, but we passed the rock of Scylla and the whirlpool of Charybdis without accident and into the Straits of Messina and to the city of the same name with its white domes glistening in the morning sun.

Then Etna came in view and remained with us during the day. The sea was calm, and we sat on deck watching the coming twilight, when two or three of the young officers came hurrying up to me and said: "Mrs. Grant, hasten and get out your cotton wool. We are nearing the Island of Calypso. Remember the fate of Ulysses of old. Take warning and bring out the cotton wool and fill the General's ears at once." "Oh," I said, "my Ulysses has no music in his soul. And am I not with him? Do you suppose that I, after such a lesson from dear old Penelope, would remain at home? No, indeed! I defy all outside enchantments." And so the fabled island was passed in safety. Not a single strain of music did we hear, save that of the waves as they dashed against and washed the sides of our gallant ship, which, on the afternoon of December 28, dropped anchor at Malta.

Then I heard "The Star-Spangled Banner" mingled with salutes fired. The Duke of Edinburgh called. His ship lay alongside ours. He sat quite a while. The Englishmen are handsome, and this one very.

The General called on the Governor of Malta in the evening. His name was [Sir Charles Thomas] van Straubenzee and he wore the order of the Grand Cross of the Bath. He received the General and party at the door of his palace, surrounded by his council and a group of gentlemen of Malta. There was a salute of twenty-one guns when the General left. In the evening, there was a state dinner given to General Grant and party at the palace, including a number of the officers of the *Vandalia*. After dining, we went to the opera. When our party entered, the company sang "The Star-Spangled Banner."

We breakfasted with the Duke and Duchess of Edinburgh, who had their three pretty, fair-haired children brought for us to see. They both walked with us through the fine orange grove around their residence. I thought the Duchess was a grand-looking woman. They were both certainly most amiable. We dined again with the Governor Sunday night, when he conducted me through the castle, telling me most thrilling legends of the castle, of the knights, and of the island.

We had quite a gale after leaving Malta. I was greatly alarmed and made some very important suggestions (?) to Commander [Henry B.] Robeson, our captain. I heard him enter his cabin and called out to him, "Captain, this is a stiff breeze." "Yes, Madam." "Captain, don't you think it would be well to drop anchor here?" "Cannot reach bottom, Madam." "Then don't you think we had better go back to Malta?" "It is just as far to Malta as to Alexandria, Madam." By this time, the General came to Captain Robeson's defense and called out from his cabin, "I think, Julia, if I were you, I would not make any more suggestions to the Captain. I really did not suppose you would take charge of the ship." The next morning, the sea danced and sparkled in the bright sunshine.

We arrived at Alexandria on January 5. The Governor of the district, the Admiral, the General, Pasha Beys,[10] the Consul General [Elbert E. Farman] and Vice Consul [Consular Agent Salvago], Judges [George S.] Batcheller, [Victor] Barringer, and [Philip H.] Morgan,[11] and the missionaries came on board to the reception, which lasted more than an hour, and as each official was received with his proper salute, which was returned, one might easily think we were bombarding Alexandria in place of making a pleasure visit.

The Governor welcomed General Grant in the name of the Khedive and offered him a palace in Cairo and a special steamer up the Nile. It is Eastern etiquette to return calls at once, and in the afternoon General Grant and Jesse, Commander Robeson, and a number of officers from the *Vandalia* were conveyed by the official barge to the shore. As this was an official visit, the *Vandalia* manned the yards and fired twenty-one guns. The salute was returned by the Egyptian war vessels. A guard of honor received the General at the palace, and the reception was most Oriental. Cigars and coffee in little jeweled cups were served.

There was a dinner and reception at the residence of our Vice Consul. The gentlemen enjoyed this, but I did not go, as I was not well and really felt a little timid about trusting myself at night on the tiny craft. The Captain's gig was used to convey us back and forth to the shore.

Next morning, we drove through Alexandria, looked up at Pompey's pillar and also on the obelisk that now stands in Central Park. The General and party, and the officers of the *Vandalia* assembled on deck and had their photographs taken.

[220]

The Governor of the province with his retinue met the General, and we took a special train for Cairo, which we reached in a few hours. There was a guard and a carpet for us to walk upon and a group of officers and civilians. The General recognized some old friends, among them General Loring and General Stone.[12] General Stone entered the car and presented the representative of the Khedive. This officer came to welcome General Grant in the name of His Highness. The General replied. General Loring came in, and he and General Grant greeted each other most cordially. General Grant asked Loring to ride with him, and General Stone rode with me.

We drove to the Palace of Kassr-el-Noussa, which was placed at General Grant's disposal by the Khedive. The General asked our Commander and one or two of the officers to reside in the palace during their stay in Cairo. The first evening, we dined quietly at the palace. The next day, the General called on the Khedive, driving over in the Khedive's state carriage, accompanied by his son Jesse, Commander Robeson, Mr. Young, ten of the officers, and Consul General Farman. This reception was even more ceremonious than that at the Governor's. The Khedive met the General at the foot of the stairs.

After this ceremony, the Khedive arrived at our palace, almost with the General, to return his visit. He also called on me at the same time. The General spoke in high terms of the American officers the Khedive had near him. General Stone was a classmate of General Grant at West Point.[13] He was always gallant and brave.

We found the Palace of Kassr-el-Noussa a charming residence. It was a large, two-story building with marble halls and fine stairs, situated at the end of a long, shaded roadway, and surrounded by a glorious setting of flowers and odorous plants. We had only to clap our hands and lo! a servant dressed in white approached with noiseless steps. The palace was full of beautiful ornaments of every description. The table service and the cuisine were most excellent. The dainty coffee cups, about the size of an eggshell, were held in filagree stands covered with jewels, as were also the jessamine pipestems through which the gentlemen enjoyed their after-dinner smoke.

The General had all the carriages he could possibly use. I had a beautiful little victoria drawn by a span of beautiful Russian horses with flowing mane and tails. I often used it with my two handsome syce[14] running ahead about twenty yards. The General dismissed his runners, saying it was inhuman, and wished me to do so, but I would not, as I liked to see them in their flowing white sleeves, velvet jackets, and full Greek skirts, with silver helmets and silver wands held high in air, flying as it were like Mercury before my phaeton. They really looked very handsome in the picturesque dress.

Judge and Mrs. Batcheller gave us a ball which was greatly enjoyed. Mr. Farman gave a large banquet at which we met many pleasant people. The Khedive intended giving the General a dinner and reception, but the death of the King of Italy, Victor Emmanuel, put his court in mourning, and all entertainments were postponed until our return from our visit up the Nile.

The Khedive assigned Sami Bey, a Circassian gentleman, to the charge of General Grant's party. He was with us at the palace and accompanied us up the Nile. We had also Emile Brugsch, one of the directors of the Egyptian museum. Without this gentleman our journey would have been a failure. As it was, we enjoyed every moment of it. We listened eagerly to his enthusiastic readings of the writings on the walls—and how patient and gentle this great scholar was! He was delightful and held us spellbound for hours. The General declared our trip would have been a failure without Emile Brugsch.

On January 16, we embarked on the *Zinet-el-Bohren*: that is, "the light of two rivers." We were met there by a party of our new friends, who brought flowers and sent kind wishes with us. We glided out into the river and were afloat on the historic Nile, where Cleopatra had floated so long ago in her boat with its silken sails and where she, no doubt, planned the seduction and destruction of those two great soldiers, Caesar and Antony. I never felt sympathy for Cleopatra. Mine was all for the men. I have seen more than one Antony fall, but our modern Cleopatra still lives on, not even having had the grace to take chloroform.

The *Zinet-el-Bohren* was a beautiful little steamer. My cabin was hung with amber and turquoise satin. The General's cabin was handsome too. The drawing room was also amber colored. The dining saloon was quite comfortable. We sat on deck all day long, listening to Brugsch and watching the emerald shores as we glided quickly past. The setting sun was always a thing to look upon and admire and remember.

On January 19, we arrived at Siut or Assiut. We met here some indications of our coming. Flags were out and a crowd on shore. Our Consul here was an Egyptian. He and his son came on board to welcome General Grant.

We rode to the town some distance back from the river. We rode through parched fields to the ruins on the mountains, then returned and went through a few of the bazaars. Large crowds gathered to see us. One little girl looked angry and kept repeating something. I inquired what she was saying, and Hassan said: "She said: 'You foreign devils. Why do you come here?' " I did not think the crowd looked friendly and now I knew their temper—as straws show the direction of the wind. They said: "Their ruins were much despoiled by the Christians."

We were invited to an entertainment at the house of Wasif el-Hayat, our consul. As we neared the house, a perfect blaze of light flashed out. Men were drawn up in rows like soldiers, holding blazing torches, and over the door were the words, written in flame, "Welcome, General Grant."

We found the house handsomely furnished in Oriental style: couches, lounges, and pillows were plentiful and of fine material, and with Eastern rugs on the floors. The dinner was simply regal: at least twenty courses. Our greatest surprise was a beautiful speech of welcome to the General spoken by the Consul's son. He was educated at Beirut at the mission school. Dr. [George H.] Cooke wore his uniform and was taken for General Grant. I did not like this joke.

In the early morning, we were off again. I forgot to say that we met Mr. Joseph Drexel's dahabeah, and I did wish Madam was of our party, she was so charming. Also at the town of Girgeh, where we arrived January 21st, we found Admiral [Charles] Steedman and Mr. Davis of Boston in their dahabeah, and they said they were having a splendid time. We had a pleasant call from them, but the wind sprang up and they had to leave.

We started early in the morning for Abydos. After getting animals and escort, we started, followed by a multitude of Arabs: men, women, and children. Our escort continually repeated "good donkey" and shyly begged us to buy their bits of old pottery, scarabaei, and bits of mummy cloth. I was obliged to order Hassan to tell them they must not annoy me, for if they did, they should not have baksheesh when we returned.

Abydos was built on the edge of the Libyan desert, and the road to the great oasis leads to it over the mountains. Our road was over dusty and desert fields, but the air was pure and the sky blue. Abydos is one of the oldest cities of Egypt. It dates back to Menes, the first Egyptian king, who, Brugsch said, reigned 4500 B. C., long before even Abraham went to Egypt. The temple is very fine, and the Khedive is now raising it from the sands. Here in the temple is a stone which was found in 1865 which gathers up the threads of Egyptian history and gives us an unbroken chain from long before the time of Moses up to Seti I.

This is a grand temple, and we were all thrilled by the enthusiasm of Brugsch as we wandered from wall to wall, reading the writings.

Brugsch said that it was supposed the god Osiris was buried near this temple. We went from ruin to ruin. I rode my donkey; the gentlemen walked. The sands looked like molten gold in the blazing midday sun. The walk had sharpened our appetites, and we feasted in the temple—this temple sacred to Osiris—drank the Khedive's health, everybody's health, and were merry and happy.

Then Brugsch told us of Salib, an Arabian, who had been working for many years on the excavations. We went to his house for coffee, and while there I rested while the gentlemen smoked. I enjoyed an hour's sleep and returned to the gentlemen refreshed and ready to start.

As we were coming over the desert on our return, Lieutenant [William A.] Hadden proposed we should all sing. Remembering there was something said of "Afric's golden sands" in that sweet old hymn, "From Greenland's Icy Mountains," I proposed that, and we all sang it with great fervor. Then Hadden proposed "John Brown," which was also sung with great gusto. We sang "Rally Round the Flag, Boys," "The Star-Spangled Banner," and last, "I am Dying, Egypt, Dying."

Hadden said the first hymn would have started a revival if we had only a camp meeting. The last song, "I am Dying, Egypt, Dying," set them (the young gentlemen) to thinking what a muff old Antony was (I suppose), for they were silent for a while. Then directly, they all began chatting pleasantly and complimenting me on my endurance and continued cheerfulness. And what do you think they said I was? "A brick, a regular little brick." This I was to suppose was a compliment—was it?

We had ridden quite twenty miles on our donkeys over the burning sands and were glad to be on our pretty little steamer again where we could rest for a while. One could not but reflect here on the emptiness, frailty, and vanity of the works of man. Egypt, the birthplace, the cradle of civilization—Egypt, the builder of temples, tombs, and the great pyramids—has nothing, nothing left her. Except the very few, her people live in huts built of cornstalks without a roof and subsist almost entirely upon farinaceous food. Egypt, with the fangs of that relentless vampire—debt—fastened at her throat cries out in despair, as did Marc Antony when encircled by the arms of that cruel Circe, "I am dying, Egypt, dying, Ebbs the crimson life-tide fast."

NOTES

1. No such telegram from Grant to Sherman has been found, but on May 30, 1877, Badeau himself telegraphed to Sherman: PLEASE ISSUE FORMAL ORDER PLACING ME IN ATTENDANCE AS ARMY OFFICER ON GENERAL GRANT DURING STAY IN ENGLAND WITHOUT PAY [.] 362 ACP 1876, ACP Files, Record Group 94, National Archives. On May 31, Sherman replied to Badeau: SECRETARY WILLING YOU ATTEND GENERAL GRANT, BUT REGARDS YOU AS CONSUL GENERAL—NOT SUBJECT TO FORMAL ARMY ORDERS. *Ibid.*

2. The Grants met Arthur Richard Wellesley, the second Duke of Wellington, son of the victor of Waterloo.

3. In 1877, Russia declared war on Turkey following Ottoman success in crushing insurrections in Bosnia (supported by Serbia) and Bulgaria. The British, their traditional support of Ottoman integrity now strengthened by interest in the Suez Canal, eventually decided to send a fleet to Constantinople. Before it arrived, Russia and Turkey agreed on an armistice.

4. Badeau, *Grant in Peace*, pp. 275–80, discussed this evening as an affront to the Grants since they were not received as having royal status. Grant discussed the matter with John Russell Young. "Some of the newspapers at home invented a story to the effect that the Prince of Wales had been rude to me. It was a pure invention. I cannot conceive of the Prince of Wales being rude to any man." *Around the World*, II, 161.

5. Richard Wagner and his family met the Grants at the Hotel Schloss in Heidelberg. *Times* (London), July 19, 1877; Robert W. Gutman, *Richard Wagner: The Man, His Mind, and His Music* (New York, 1968), p. 392.

6. On May 8, 1871, Great Britain and the United States concluded the Treaty of Washington, which provided an international tribunal to settle U.S. claims resulting from the wartime activities of the British-built Confederate raider *Alabama*. The tribunal, which met in Geneva, rendered a well-balanced decision which smoothed international relations.

7. Actually October 20. Julia Grant here repeated an inadvertent error in Young, *Around the World*, I, 123.

8. On June 30, 1877, Elihu B. Washburne wrote to Grant urging him not to visit Paris because "if you do not call on the President, the Republican papers will say it is because you are not in sympathy with his *Coup d'Etat*, and if you do call upon him the reactionary papers will claim that it is to signify your approval of his action." John Russell Young Papers, Library of Congress. President MacMahon had recently dissolved the Chamber of Deputies during a test of strength over control of the government.

9. Characters in the novel *The Last Days of Pompeii* (1834) by Edward Robert Bulwer-Lytton.

10. Young, *Around the World*, I, 230, refers to part of the welcoming committee as "the admiral and the generals, pachas and beys. . . ."

11. The function of the three American judges, who heard cases involving foreigners, is discussed in Jasper Yeates Brinton, *The Mixed Courts of Egypt* (New Haven, 1930).

12. Major General William W. Loring and Brigadier General Charles P. Stone served in the Civil War on opposite sides. Blamed for the U.S. defeat at Ball's

Bluff in October, 1861, Stone was imprisoned for six months without formal charges, then released, but was never given independent command. Loring, whose war record was clouded by a controversy with "Stonewall" Jackson, had commanded troops opposing Grant at Vicksburg. Loring and Stone were the most prominent of some fifty American officers employed by Ismail Pasha, Khedive of Egypt, to improve his army. See William B. Hesseltine and Hazel C. Wolf, *The Blue and the Gray on the Nile* (Chicago, 1961).

13. Grant graduated from West Point in 1843; Stone in 1845.

14. *Syce* is a Hindi word meaning attendant.

Chapter 8

O UR NEXT stopping place was Keneh, where the gentlemen went ashore, bought some pottery, and called on the Governor and the German Consul. I did not leave the boat.

Thebes, mighty Thebes, was next. We had all read of it and heard of it from Brugsch until we thought we knew it well—with its temple, its obelisk, its colossal Memnon—yes, we knew it all now, from our gentle and cultivated friend and companion.

The Nile widens and sweeps around Luxor. The great ruined castle or temple of Rameses stands on the promontory formed by this bend in the Nile. As we approached, we saw that the dahabeahs were in gala dress with flags. The inhabitants of Luxor were assembled on the shore, which is high here, and they looked picturesque in their flowing robes and white turbans. The Consul saluted us from the top of his house. He came on board our boat at once to welcome General Grant. The salute was fired from the housetop by five or six soldiers with muskets.

In the early morning, we were ready to start for Thebes, once famous for its riches and splendor. The statues of Memnon that used to give out music when the sun rose—I had read of them long years ago at the old farm—well, they were silent enough now, having been broken, I was told, by the shock of an earthquake; they sang no more. As we lingered near these colossal statues and viewed them with wonder, the young gentlemen amused themselves by climbing upon the arms and shoulders and making measurements. I remember that Jesse standing under the chin at the base of the throat could just touch the underpart of the chin with his umbrella held as high as he could reach.

Then on to Thebes, followed by troops of Arabs offering to sell us all kinds of relics and slender girls carrying on their heads water jugs as tall and slender as themselves and looking like the Egyptian statues in bronze we see at Tiffany's. Followed thus, we wended our way over long, undulating sand hills and plains to the temple of Medinet-Habu. This temple, Brugsch told us, had an inner chamber evidently occupied by Rameses and shows something of the homelife of the Egyptian kings. The gentlemen all wished to visit this chamber, scaling the walls to see it. The General, on his return, told me he wished I had gone, as I would have seen how the husbands of old were waited on by their wives, who held lotus flowers to their lords to enjoy the perfume while they played—perhaps draughts or perhaps Boston.

After partaking of a fine luncheon, always a feature of the Khedive's princely hospitality, we rested for an hour and then enjoyed the long, delightful ride over Egypt's golden sands back to Luxor, where the Consul had a fine dinner prepared for the General. The General felt tired and worn-out by our day's excursion and sent word that he would not be there. This made the Consul so unhappy that the General reconsidered and went. We all attended it. The dinner was long. We had the native music. Jesse volunteered some instruction in this, but without great success. After dinner, we were entertained by some dancing girls, neither graceful nor pretty.

A word more of the temple of Luxor with its dark corridors into which we deeply penetrated, the feet sinking ankle-deep in its sand-covered floors. The corridors and chambers were all magnificent in dimension. Two colossal statues lay prostrate and half-buried in dust and sand, almost hidden by a growth of woods and deadly nightshade. I was told these were Rameses and his Queen. They were immense and were cut from some hard flint-like stone not unlike the great boulders we have in our mountains in America.

The next day we visited Karnak, situated about two miles down the river. This temple is approached by a wide avenue on either side of which are sphinxes about twenty yards apart throughout the entire length. The temple is a wilderness of columns, some ten and twelve feet in diameter. Many of these are broken and fallen now.

We seated ourselves and were photographed. Then, climbing over the huge blocks of stone, we visited the sacred lakes. Coming into the temple again, we lunched, drank the Khedive's health and the health of all at home. Here a pretty little Egyptian boy took a great fancy to Jesse and hung about his knees, smiled, and placed his hand on Jesse's arm. When Jesse asked him if he would go with him, he said: "Yes, take me with you, kind gentleman."

The next day we started for Assuan, which was to be the end of our journey up the Nile. This was the most flourishing place we saw after leaving Cairo. We called on the Governor, a splendid man over six feet in height. He was dressed in pure white linen and wore a red fez.

At Assuan we all shopped. I spent quite a good deal of money buying ostrich feathers and found them to be a perfect nuisance when I came home. They were not pretty and they needed finishing, and I knew not where to send them. So my feathers were all lost to me and my friends. Let me give a bit of advice here. Only buy what you need. You can get everything in New York better and cheaper than you can import it yourself.

In the morning, we started for Philae. Just before starting, the General received a dispatch from [Charles G.] Gordon Pasha, who was then governor general of the Provinces of the Equator. He welcomed the General, and the General returned his thanks. We mounted and were off. The General had a fine Arabian steed, furnished by the Governor, and with royal trappings. I had a lovely white donkey, richly caparisoned. We rode some eight miles over rough roads, but the atmosphere was perfect.

We at last reached beautiful Philae nestled in the trees. The columns were slender and beautifully carved. The capitals of these columns were ofttimes wrought to imitate ferns and were perhaps of green marble. They could not have been painted, as they still kept their color. We walked through the temples and then to the cataract or first falls, and saw the natives dash down them on bits of wood and come out uninjured. I was quite fatigued when I returned, as I had ridden sixteen miles and had walked a good deal at Philae and the falls.

On the way back to Cairo, we stopped for the gentlemen to visit the tombs of the kings. I did not go ashore. We also stopped at Karnak to see our friend the Consul, who came aboard and took coffee with us. At Siut, we heard the news of the war and from home through some missionaries.

We reached Memphis on February 3 and found General Stone waiting for us. We visited the ruins of Memphis and the Serapeum, or the tombs of the sacred bulls. To reach the latter, we followed up the bed of a dry stream between two mountains, then ascended the mountain until we reached a cavern or opening in the mountainside. Descending a long road which you could drive a Fifth Avenue omnibus down, we reached a great hall. On each side were chapels or alcoves large enough to hold huge granite sarcophagi, large enough to let tables into with room to seat four or six men around them. In these sarcophagi were placed the sacred bulls called Apis. The halls were filled with smoke from the lamps and lights, and I was glad to be in the fresh air again.

The next morning, we arrived at Cairo, bade adieu to our boat's crew, and went again to our beautiful home, Kassr-el-Noussa, feeling glad to see again the pleasant people we had met there. Some of the ladies suggested that it would be agreeable to the Khedive if I would ask to be presented to his wife. I took the hint at once and made a formal request to that effect.

The time was appointed. I was accompanied by the Vice-Consul's wife, a fair Greek woman. As we were driving to the palace, I told her how much we had enjoyed our journey up the Nile. She said: "Do, Mrs. Grant, tell that all to the Princess. It will please her so to hear it from you." I was helped out of the carriage and up the steps so lightly by two very large black men that it required no effort from me.

At the door we were met by two more elaborately dressed men of large stature. They were black Nubian eunuchs. In the hall and all the way up the stairs, which were entirely covered with beautiful Turkish carpets, were two rows of lovely women standing side by side, leaving a passageway for me. These, I suppose, were the attendants of the Princess. They were dressed simply and prettily, but to my regret, not in Turkish or Egyptian style but in French.

I was ushered into a grand drawing room covered with gold embroidery, mirrors, and gilt furniture. Directly, the Princess appeared with her two ladies, wives of some of the high officials—ministers of state and treasury, I think. These last spoke French and a little English. My friend spoke French, Greek, and also English. After our first greeting and we had all had coffee in the tiniest and daintiest of cups in jeweled filigree stands, I told the Princess of our glorious visit to Egypt, of our beautiful vessel, and of our journey up the Nile. I purposely dwelt upon the lovely vessel with its silken curtains, saying I was sure "The historic and famous vessel of your beautiful Cleopatra was not more luxurious than is your *Zinet-el-Bohren*." This delighted her. She evidently knew about Cleopatra and her magnificence and power. Our adieux were made, again I was lifted into our carriage, and we drove home.

The next morning, the Khedive's state coach or drag, with six horses, came for us to drive to the Pyramids. The drag and the horses were superb. We had two postilions or outriders. General and Mrs. Stone and the Consul General went with us and our party. After a delightful drive of two hours, I should think, through a broad and shaded avenue, we arrived at the Pyramids. I will not attempt to describe this world-renowned monument. The Sphinx is so grand, so calm, the Pyramid so majestic in its magnitude, and the whole so awe-inspiring in its majesty and loneliness.

We visited Heliopolis, where Moses studied. We walked back and forth, as he did, and pondered over his career. This spot is marked by a fine obelisk like the one in Central Park. We went to the place where Pharaoh's daughter found the baby Moses in the rushes. Then in one of our rides we visited the spring of sweet water where Joseph and Mary rested with the child Jesus in their flight into Egypt. I drank of the water, bathed my eyes to rest them, and gathered some leaves from the drooping boughs of the sycamore tree that shaded this sacred spring.

Then came the Khedive's banquet to General Grant. The Khedive met us at the foot of the palace steps and, giving me his arm, escorted me to the drawing room. The salon was already filled with guests, among whom were Count [Ferdinand] de Lesseps and wife. I soon requested the Khedive to conduct me to the Princess. He murmured, "Oh, Madam, it is not the custom of the country." The Khedive does not speak much English, but he made me understand that much.

The palace was quite imposing with its wide corridors and superbly large rooms. I thought them all as large as the East Room at the White House. They were lighted by forests of wax candles which shed their soft light upon us. On the same floor as the drawing room, there was a garden with flowers, trees, and fountains, where we walked and lingered.

As our time in Cairo was about up, the General went to say goodbye to the Khedive, and I to the Princess. I was again lifted from my carriage and up the palace steps by the Nubian eunuchs. The same lines of female attendants were in the hall and up the great flight of stairs to the door of the audience chamber. The Princess was there to meet me with her two handsome young friends. This time when coffee was brought in, two handsome girls entered, bearing between them a large rod upon which was hung a beautiful embroidered cloth, which I noticed was held up so that we could not see the making of the coffee. This was moved back and forth so as to show its beautiful coloring and rich embroidery of gold, green, and purple.

When I told the Princess how disappointed I was not to see her at the banquet, she repeated through her interpreter just what the Khedive said: "Oh, it is not the custom of our country." I at once declared it to be a very hard and unjust custom, and added, "In

America we would not consent to such an unjust custom. We always were present at the entertainments given by our husbands if any ladies were." I am afraid in saying this I left the apple of discord for the Khedive in the heaping basket of delicious fruit on the table in front of us.

The Princess was kind enough to admire my gown, which I had brought from New York. It was a carriage costume of sapphire-blue velvet with silver fox trimming, with a little muff of the same. The latter she took in her hand and inquired what it was for. I replied that "It is so cold in winter in America that this little article is necessary to protect our hands, but here where you have such balmy weather, really perpetual spring, this little bit of one's dress is not needed." She thrust her little hands into it and seemed to admire it. She inquired: "Where do you go from here?" "To Constantinople, Athens, Rome, and Paris," I replied. "And how do you go?" she asked. "On board the *Vandalia*, an American man-of-war." "And are you the only lady?" she inquired. "Yes," I said, "the only woman excepting my maid." She clasped her little hands and turning their backs inward, raising them so as to cover her rosy mouth, thus elevating her pretty dimpled elbows, and looking oh, how much, with her great eyes, exclaimed: "Madam, I envy you, I envy you." And now at this date, whilst I write, this fair Egyptian is as free as was I to wander where she cares to and has already visited each and all of the delightful capitals I mentioned with her Khedive.

The next day, we left by special train for Suez, where we remained for a day looking over some very interesting docks. The day following, we went in a special boat through the Suez Canal, stopping over one night at Ismailia, where a dance was arranged for us by our host and hostess, a young Englishman and his wife, who were lately married. They were most hospitable. The next day we proceeded on our way and late in the afternoon arrived at Port Said, where we at once went aboard our now beloved ship, the *Vandalia*. We were delighted to meet again our friends on board, and they were kind enough to say they were most happy to have us with them again.

We soon steamed out to sea and in a day or two, I forget exactly how long, we reached Jaffa and were landed—at great peril, I thought. We had to pass between two great jagged rocks in our little boat, and the sea rushed and roared fearfully. I was terribly frightened and lost no time, when our little craft was carried up on the crest of the waves quite near the high rough landing, in leaping ashore almost without help.

Jaffa is a poor place and very dirty. However, the people looked quaint and picturesque in the same old style of clothes as worn in the days of Simon Peter and Tabitha. We stopped at the house of the American Consul, who kept a small hotel which was quite neat. The oranges were the best we had yet tasted. We left it to the Consul to procure our transportation, which, to say the best, was miserably poor, and I for once remonstrated. I think Cook's dragoman would have done a great deal better for us.

The day was glorious; the plains were sparkling with lilies, scarlet anemones, and the roses of Sharon, and the orange trees were bending low under their loads of golden fruit. We passed on, now in a mist, until evening, when we stopped in a hard rainstorm at Ramleh. We were, of course, taken to a hotel belonging to the Consul's friend instead of to a convent, where I could have slept comfortably and partaken of the shewbread and lenten food. I wished to go like any other pilgrim to the Holy Land and to Jerusalem.

The Prefect, having been informed of the General's arrival, had a score or more of soldiers at our gate early in the morning and offered them to the General as an escort, but the General declined the courtesy. So on we traveled towards Jerusalem. It was about two o'clock when we passed over the mountaintop and saw far down in the valley a long low row of buildings with a portico along the front. On this and around the house were assembled a large number of people, looking bright and gay with many flags. The consuls of all nations were assembled there with their flags and pennants; also, an escort of one hundred and fifty men at least, dressed in the gorgeous uniform of the Turkish Governor, with silver helmets, bearing their flags, and mounted on fine horses. This great show surprised us. They came from the Governor with fresh horses for General Grant and family, and said: "The Governor thought your horses must be weary from your long ride."

The General was delighted at getting a fresh horse and was impatient to be off, but I was rather timid about mounting the one sent for me, a great, fiery, dappled-gray stallion. I was hesitating and was making some little trouble about mounting when the General impatiently accused me of affectation, saying, "Do mount and do not be absurd, Julia." I did mount and sincerely wished as I did so that the horrid brute would run away with me, dash me over a precipice, and thus cause my husband to remember with regret his want of sympathy. Affectation, indeed! But I was not thrown over the precipice. I arrived safely, without even a jolt, though my horse would not allow anyone to ride near me, as he would kick fiercely if anyone approached within a yard of me, feeling no doubt that he was carrying

[233]

some precious burden—at least, one unusual to his back—as every once in a while he would turn his head and look me squarely in the face with such an intelligent and amused look. I thought he meant to say, "Do not be afraid, no one shall approach you."

The high waters of the Ajalon had carried away the bridge, and I was again much frightened at having to pass through this turbulent and dangerous water. I hesitated on its bank, when a young Egyptian soldier (I think) leaped from his horse and taking my horse by the bridle near his head, wading up to his middle, led me safely across the Ajalon.

As we climbed this very, very rough mountain road, I saw the cavalcade which surrounded General Grant far in advance of me. I had purposely tarried with the young officers, still feeling some indignation at the General. As I looked ahead, I thought of long years ago, when I had a strange vision or daydream. I was awake, sitting with my mother and sisters at the old farm, White Haven. I was reading aloud, a pleasure we always enjoyed at home. As I said, I was reading aloud *History of the Conquest of Mexico* by [William H.] Prescott. I was just where Cortez makes that gallant and cruel dash upon the capital when I was interrupted by the entrance of a servant making some inquiry. I sat back in my chair to rest, I do not know how long, when directly I saw a mountain with cliffs and precipices, draped in overhanging clouds. Moving out of this cloud came a cavalcade of miniature horsemen with silver helmets, spears, and pennants and bright flags fluttering in the breeze. I saw them all so clearly, these horses and men, scarcely more than eighteen inches high, the horses champing their bits and tossing their tiny heads to loosen their reins as they wound up the rugged mountain road in solemn procession.

And now I saw the same again as we crossed the valley of Ajalon and wound our way up the mountainside. But now my husband, General Grant, was in the advance, escorted by this gorgeous, gleaming pageant, entering Jerusalem. Every detail of this brilliant sight before me was so exact in every feature—the rugged mountain, the cliffs, the overhanging clouds, the silver helmets, the glittering lances, and gay banners—all, all were so exact with my daydream of long years ago that I cannot help but tell it here.

There was a double row of soldiers and great crowds assembled on each side of the road as we neared the city. The General's head was bared nearly all of the time in acknowledgment of the salutes as we passed.

We went through a large gate and then through a small one (the needle's eye), then under the walls of the tower of David. It was here

King David (poor human king) first saw the ewe lamb of Uriah the Hittite bathing in the pool (poor ewe lamb!). We passed on through narrow, slippery streets to our hotel. The morning brought sunshine and a great throng of petitioners to the door, quite like the crowd assembled around the door of a newly-elected President. Calls of ceremony were received and returned by the General and the gentlemen. A band of music was offered and an escort of soldiers, all of which were politely declined. I wished to have the band play during dinner, as it gave pleasure to our party as well as to the people in the street.

We all assembled, deeply interested, to visit the places so familiar to us and so full of sacred import. I mounted one of those faithful little donkeys sent me by the Pasha. He also sent General Grant his own fine Arabian steed with housings of gold embroidery. We went to many churches. There seemed to be three or four of different denominations clustered near the Holy Sepulchre. In the latter, I was privileged to enter a small white room, a single lamp hanging from the ceiling. To the right of the entrance was an elevated platform about two feet in height, all of white marble. Beside this I knelt in prayer, and with an appeal for pardon, I threw my arms far over its cold surface, laid my cheek upon it, and kissed it again and again, but there was no response, no emotion in my heart. I came out, bringing with me the relics I had pressed upon the Sepulchre, and passed on with the party into another church.

We entered a large, dark, dingy room, in the center of which was a large marble post about four feet high. The floor was of black and white mosaic in radiations from the center. A very beautifully featured priest, robed in black with a white turban, hastened on before me and, placing his hand on the post, earnestly looking at me, said: "This marks the center of the earth." I should have laughed outright, but he was so earnest I had not the heart to, and I only said, as if awe-struck, "Really! May I place my hand upon the post also?" I was permitted to do so.

We went up over the hills to the village of Bethany, where Mary and Martha lived, now an old tumble-down rookery. We looked down into the tomb of Lazarus; then we entered a chapel supposed to be located on the site of the Ascension, now a place of worship for the Mussulman. We climbed to the top of the minarets and had a fine view. We went to the chapel erected over the spot where our Saviour taught the Lord's Prayer. We went into a beautiful chapel built by a princess for her tomb on which is the Lord's Prayer in thirty-two different languages.

While the others were looking over these, I observed a placard on which was this notice, "Anyone who will say a prayer for the soul of Pope Pius IX will receive absolution" (this in substance). Seeing this in this holy place, I at once knelt and was aroused by hearing the General say, "You see, Young, Mrs. Grant is taking all the chances."

The following day, we visited the Garden of Gethsemane. I was disappointed in this, having pictured to myself a garden of flowers and vines (passion flowers), and birds hovering in safety in the grand old trees. There were no birds, no vines, a few poor little marigolds, but the grand old trees were there. As we wandered from one to another, I was wondering under which one Christ had knelt, and as we approached the third one and stood around, I was seized with a violent shivering and felt deep emotion. I knew now. This was the tree under which our Saviour knelt! I fell upon my knees and burying my face in my hands, I pleaded for mercy—mercy for me and mine.

As we returned to the city, we passed the tomb of Absalom. This tomb of Absalom seemed to bring me nearer to the Bible days than anything else. I fell to thinking over King David's lamentations over the death of Absalom and the words I had committed to memory in the little log schoolhouse in the backwoods of Missouri long years ago, "Would God I had died for thee, O Absalom, my son, my son!"

The gentlemen went to dine with the Governor. I was too fatigued, and there were no other ladies.

The next day we mounted and started on a ride over the hills to Bethlehem. It was cold and promised rain, but we kept on and were overtaken by a hard shower. We sought shelter in a stone structure built against the tomb of Rachel. We reached Bethlehem and took luncheon and a rest in the Greek chapel. We afterwards visited the manger in which the infant Jesus lay, also the cave into which the innocent little children were thrown. We passed a chapel in which pious and holy monks dwelt, where we made some purchases of carved pearl and ivory trinkets and beads made of olive wood. Then we mounted and returned over the hills to Jerusalem, stopping only to get a cup of water from the well where Jesus sat and asked the Samaritan woman for a draught of water.

In the morning we left for Jaffa, where we again went aboard the *Vandalia*, lifted our anchor, and were soon off again on the blue waters of the Mediterranean. We went to Smyrna, where we met Admiral [William E.] Le Roy on the flagship *Trenton*. Calls were exchanged, and with the official calls made at Smyrna, our time was fully occupied. We visited the ruins at Ephesus and the Temple of Diana. Excepting the General, we were mounted on donkeys and had an interesting day. The General had a magnificent mount. I was rather overcome with fatigue and was glad to return to the ship. Official farewells were said, salutes exchanged, and we were off again, steaming up the coast of Syria.

On the 1st of March, early in the morning, we were called up to look upon Mount Ida. "Aurora, now fair daughter of the dawn, Was sprinkling with rosy light the sparkling sea." I think it was here we procured the *firman* or permit to enter the port. Perhaps it was at San Stefano where our Consul, Mr. [Eugene] Schuyler, General [Alexander] Chambers, and Captain F[rancis] V. Greene of the army came aboard to greet us.

We arrived soon after the Treaty of San Stefano was completed.[1] As the General was escorted up to the American Legation, the streets, doors, and windows were filled with people who were looking earnestly and eagerly towards the General. The official from the Legation (a Turk, I think) said to General Grant: "You see, General, how eagerly they look after you. I suppose there is no harm in telling you they think and say, 'He has come to save us, but why did he not come six months ago?' "

Mr. [Horace] Maynard gave a very pleasant reception to the General, at which we met some old acquaintances. The General, Jesse, and some others were received by the Sultan. The General told me the Sultan looked very melancholy. No wonder! The Russians were still before their gates.

The Sultan's ministers gave the General a dinner, and we dined and attended a soiree at the residence of one of the foreign ministers. They were very hospitable to us. I remember Madam asked me several rather trying questions with the idea, perhaps, of encouraging me to converse. After dinner, when the ladies had returned to the drawing room, I being weary was rather quiet, when our hostess said with a pleasant smile: "Mrs. Grant, now that you have seen nearly all the countries of the Continent, how does America compare with them?" I felt rather helpless to answer this. There were several ladies looking towards me. Glancing up, I saw a beautiful crystal chandelier which shed its soft light over the large and rather gloomy room and I repeated: "How does America compare with other countries? As that chandelier is to this room, so is America to other countries." She smiled and said: "very good, very good."

Then she said: "Mrs. Grant, how does the cuisine in foreign lands compare with that in America?" "Oh," I said, "I think fairly." "Indeed?" she replied. "Oh, yes, fairly," I said; "You must remember the vast extent of our territory and our facilities for bringing together our viands. We have a continent to draw from. Our salmon and trout come from Oregon and Maine; our seafish from the two great oceans; our beef, mutton, and game from our vast prairies; our vegetables and fruits—why, our country is a great garden producing everything. Then our chefs have originality and license. For instance, when we purchased Alaska, our chef at once produced a centerpiece for the President's table consisting of a great block of ice upon which rested a great white polar bear looking down upon another lying at its base, made of ice cream." I told her we often had roman punch and bischof glacé served in goblets and boxes made of ice. She appeared incredulous, but I assured her it was true. She asked how it was done, but I could not tell her. I simply knew the fact, and that it was done in the kitchen.

After a moment, she said hesitatingly, "Mrs. Grant, do tell me how it is. I have often heard that men are elected to Parliament, or Congress rather, who are already married to women quite humbly born. How do they know how to conduct themselves in this unexpected position? Why, we have heard that a man was sent to Congress whose wife had once been a factory girl."

I waited for a moment and then looking up at her, said: "In America, we are all equal. Our school system is most liberal; the humblest and poorest woman or man has the same facilities for education as the wealthy. The factory girls are not so badly off. At Lowell, Massachusetts, one of our manufacturing towns, General Grant told me once he was so pleased to see the young women so comfortably situated: for instance, four or five young girls hire a house, giving each a chamber, and with a bathroom, dining room, and little parlor. When their day's work is over and they have dressed and dined, they assemble in their little parlor and read the periodicals of the day. Afterwards some of them play on the piano or organ, which are not infrequently a part of their furniture. Then the young men call; sometimes even it is the proprietor's son, sometimes the proprietor himself, and if the girls are pretty and modest, they may hope for anything. Our men in America are very independent. They select their own wives. They like beauty and intelligence, and generally think *their* wives have both. But they must always be amiable and chaste."

Our hostess said: "This is a charming picture you have drawn, but who, pray, does the work, the menial work, cooking, etc., in this ideal home?" "Oh," I replied, smiling archly at her, "oh, that is done usually by one of your own fair countrywomen." She laughed heartily at this reply, but she did not question me further.

[238]

We visited the bazaars, where I supplied myself with amber beads, filagree cups for Turkish coffee, and a great deal of embroidery. We also went to the Treasury where I saw great bowls full of pearls, rubies, diamonds, emeralds, and housings for horses entirely covered with jewels.

The city was full of sick troops. St. Sophia, the finest mosque in Constantinople, was turned into a hospital. Jesse told me not to go there, as there were five or six soldiers lying dead with typhoid fever. As we left Constantinople, Captain Greene came with an invitation to General Grant from the commander of the Russian forces encamped just outside the gates of Constantinople to breakfast with him. The General declined, however, and said to me and those present, "I cannot. It seems so heartless. I have but just now clasped the hand of the Sultan and I cannot step outside the gate and breakfast with his foe."

We steamed out through the Dardanelles and soon reached the Gulf of Athens and the port of Piraeus, about six miles from Athens, where we were met by our Minister, General John Meredith Read, and a party of Americans and Grecian officials. I can yet see the throng, the carpet spread from the landing to the cars, a little girl handing me a great bunch of violets, but I did not like the idea of going to Athens in the steam cars.

Our Minister gave us a superb banquet, entertaining as well a number of navy officers, a large number of Americans, and all the diplomats in Athens. A grand reception was given by the King and Queen of Greece. This fête was very brilliant. King George and Queen Olga were both young and handsome. The Queen wore a rich, white, corded silk; around her slender white throat was a band of rare jewels, and a tiara crowned her pretty head. She was young and graceful. The King lunched with the General and the officers of the *Vandalia*.

We did so much—I cannot tell all! Sunday morning we visited the Acropolis. We entered the grounds and after walking around, seated ourselves (General Read and family were with us) upon the steps of one of the temples. After resting awhile, General Read pointed out the place where poor old Socrates died in prison. I ascended the steps and looked out to sea, whence the fated ship returned to Athens which signaled the death of Socrates. I stood looking out to sea and called to my mind those very lines from my old history lesson. Even the picture returned to my mind. I could see Socrates lying on a bed of straw and quietly drinking his death draught, a bowl of hemlock.

The General said to me, "Come, we are going now." Then I

inquired, "What temple is this?" General Read said: "Why, did you not know? It is the Temple of Victory. The eagle has alighted there and has never left his perch." I at once asked the General to come up and stand by me in this Temple of Victory. The party moved on. I urged again. The General still declined, threatening and pretending to leave me. I still insisted, saying, "Come up. It is a little thing to yield, and I so much wish it." Then he suddenly turned and rapidly mounted the steps; coming close to my side and taking my hand, he exclaimed, with ill-suppressed merriment, "I am here, my Xantippe." Of course, I tried to release my hand, but he held it fast and enjoyed his triumph and that wicked speech to me.

The Parthenon and the Acropolis were illuminated the next evening in honor of the General. It was a wonderful and beautiful sight. The great battlefields of Greece were visited, including the plain of Marathon. We all consulted our little volumes, the *Iliad* and the *Odyssey*, which had not been read by me since my girl days at the old farm, White Haven.

It was growing late in March, and we had engagements which hurried us to Rome. We were welcomed to Rome by many friends from America. Our Minister, Mr. [George P.] Marsh, and our Consul General [Charles J.] McMillan were indefatigable in their attentions to General Grant. Mr. Marsh entertained us many times with dinners and receptions. They were most brilliant. General McMillan devoted his whole time to General Grant.

The General, Jesse, and I were received by His Holiness, Pope Leo XIII, in his private apartments. He looked very impressive and exalted in his quiet dignity and robed in white. He thanked the General for the kind reception he had given his emissaries sent to America, and gratefully referred to the General's having appointed two roving Roman Catholic chaplains in the army. At my request, the Pope blessed my little diamond cross, a present from the General on our twenty-fifth anniversary.

We were presented to the Pope by [John] Cardinal McCloskey. After the reception, we wandered through the Vatican and were greatly interested. We visited St. Peter's many, many times and were rapt in admiration and wonder as we gazed upon the magnificent arches and domes. I was a trifle disappointed, however, not to find the fountains at the entrance flowing, as had been promised the Empress Anne when she had the honor of turning these waters on for the first time they ever flowed. She was told these fountains should flow on through all eternity. At least, so I have read somewhere.

The General visited the studios of the American artists, and many of them gave him teas and receptions, throwing open their rooms filled with works of art and objects of virtu. Our distinguished American sculptor, Mr. [William W.] Story, gave him a most brilliant reception.

King Humbert and his lovely Queen, the fair Margherita, were very kind and received us at the earliest moment after their mourning for the late Victor Emmanuel. They also gave us a magnificent dinner. We were very happy here, as we saw our daughter Mrs. Sartoris daily. She was here to spend the winter in Rome with her husband and his family. They came to meet us, they said. We met Nellie at all of the entertainments, and Mr. and Mrs. Sartoris, Sr., were very hospitable to us.

We were also much pleased at meeting our fair countrywoman, Countess ——, née Constance Kenney of Washington, who was affectionately kind to me. She escorted me to call on the Queen, whom she seemed to revere and love. Her husband, the Count ——, held some important position near King Humbert. I was happy to find her so pleasantly situated.

We visited all places of interest. I remember a morning spent in roaming through the Palace of the Caesars, beautiful rides in the vicinity of Rome, and a happy day passed in riding over the Campagna.

We enjoyed the statuary and the paintings so much. I wished so much to possess a piece of this statuary that I fear I committed the sin of violating the Tenth Commandment. I did not make my wishes known to my husband, knowing well that he could not afford to gratify such a wish, but I did petition for his beloved features cut in stone cameo, and this wish was cheerfully granted when I told him how much I wished it.

One day, as we were driving to the races, we passed up the Appian Way, and I called his attention to the fact that this road was the one over which many of the Roman heroes and emperors had passed in triumph. "Only think," I exclaimed, "over this Appian Way, Aurelian passed in triumph, followed on foot and in chains of gold by the fair Zenobia, the Queen of Palmyra."

The General said: "Do you not think, though, that this is far better—with you and me sitting side by side without any heart-burnings or care of any kind?"

"Oh, yes, of course," I said. I then reminded him that Zenobia's villa was somewhere in the vicinity and begged to have a drive to it, which we did in a few days. The General invited General [Charles F.] Ruff, a retired army officer, and his wife, who was an old schoolmate of mine at Mauro's in St. Louis, to accompany us. We had a delightful drive to Tivoli, and after we had refreshed ourselves with fruit and wine, the gentlemen smoked, and my friend and I sat in the temple which overlooks the fair Campagna and thought with pleasure of the power, the beauty, the triumphs of Zenobia; and, with regret, realized that she was but human after all when she chose life and this beautiful villa instead of death like a heroine, as *we* would have had her do. On our way back, we visited Hadrian's villa.

We reached Florence April twentieth. Nellie was with us. Mrs. Sartoris, Sr., so kindly suggested this arrangement, thinking it would give us great pleasure, which it certainly did. While in Florence, we were the guests of Mrs. [Louisa] Graham, an American lady, who lived there in a delightful villa. This lady was princely in her hospitality and most amiable. I remember too a charming little dinner from our Consul, Colonel [J. Schuyler] Crosby. Of course, the General was here, as everywhere, met at the station by the city officials and appropriately received and welcomed. We had lovely drives, visited statuary, picture galleries, and churches.

The shops here were bewitching. I indulged in the extravagance of two beautiful mosaic tables. Notwithstanding I sent them all properly invoiced and signed by the American consul at Leghorn, to whom I paid the legal fee—alas, these, my pretty tables, which had cost me so much of my little pin money, so much care in selecting, were confiscated at the Customhouse in New York by our government. My pretty tables had been lying in the storerooms of the Customhouse as long as the law allowed, and *sometimes it seems the law is very stringent.* We had already arrived at San Francisco and would soon have been near enough to attend to the custom tax—but no, the time was up and my pretty tables were sacrificed for the government duties. Our rich and great government saved its duties, but I lost my pretty tables, and there was no help for it. My son offered to redeem them from the mean fellow who purchased them, telling him that his mother had selected them herself and with much care—but no, he would not give them up, saying that his wife thought they were very handsome, too. He ought to have had his head broken—but no, one could not expect this one man to be greater than a whole government.

The Pitti Palace was visited with intense interest, as we saw the wonderful works of Raphael, Tintoretto, Salvator Rosa, Rubens, Carlo Dolci, and Del Sarto. We visited a beautiful palace in the country near Florence filled with wonderful curios which had been collected not for pleasure but for sale by the lord of the manor. Since then, all of these pretty things have been sold at auction to the highest bidder and many can be found now in the New York shops.

We left Florence on the 23rd and arrived at Venice, "Beautiful

Venice, Queen of the Sea." We were met at the depot by our Consul and a number of Americans who welcomed us warmly. Then came the authorities with their speeches of welcome. The hotel was very good, and Nellie and I enjoyed the gondolas and the nightly serenades greatly.

We went just where we wished: shopped; visited all the old curio shops, the Venetian glass factories; fed the myriads of pigeons in the Piazza di San Marco; visited the Doge's Palace, and listened to the bloodcurdling stories of the Bridge of Sighs. Nellie attended two or three parties; I did not. We daily threaded the canals in our gondolas and passed under the Rialto. We went again with the General and by moonlight. How many, many pleasant memories I have of this.

Nellie and I induced the General to go with us on a visit to the Armenian convent where Lord Byron wrote his *Childe Harold*. We were escorted through the convent by a very affable young priest. We at length reached a room in which hung a portrait of Lord Byron, one that was familiar to me. I recognized it. The priest said this was the room he wrote *Childe Harold* in and this was the table he wrote on.

I expressed great pleasure at being in the room. The priest asked if we would like to see Lord Byron's autograph. I said I would be delighted. A great book was brought out and the real signature examined. Then looking up, I saw General Sherman's photograph and recognized it. The young priest was delighted that we were so interested and said: "We have General Sherman's autograph, also the autograph of the son of the President of the United States of America. Would you like to see it?"

"Of course I would," I said. The General was, all this time, growing impatient. The page was soon found and there, sure enough, was "Lt. F. D. Grant, Aide-de-Camp etc., to General Sherman."

I looked up and asked: "Would you like to have General Grant's autograph?" He replied, "Oh, indeed we would." I then said: "This is General Grant, the late President of the United States." The man was overcome, fell into the background, and said: "If we had only known, the Bishop would have been here to receive Your Excellency. I hope you will pardon our ignorance. You should *surely* have been received as we would wish to receive such a distinguished man." The General was quite put out with me for mentioning his name and said: "Now you have destroyed the day. We shall have no more comfort."

We left Venice on April 26 and arrived at Milan on the 27th, where we were met by the Prefect and Syndic with much ceremony and great respect. We remained here three or four days and were much interested in all we saw.

We left for Paris. The Exposition had been opened three or four days when we arrived. We visited it many times with pleasure and some fatigue. Invitations were showered on the General and party, and it was impossible to accept all. Nellie enjoyed her visit here very much, and we had the felicity of meeting our friends the Beales from Washington. We had many happy excursions together. Nellie was obliged to say goodbye and return to England.

Soon after, the General and I started for The Hague. Our Minister, General [James] Birney,[2] met us and conducted us at once to his house, and we were his guests during our stay at The Hague. We met here a number of diplomats we had known in Washington. There were several delightful entertainments for us here. General Birney was most hospitable, and I must not fail to mention a delightful breakfast given to the General by His Royal Highness, Prince Frederick, at his countryseat near The Hague. Here we met some charming and distinguished people. After breakfast, the Princess Mary took me in her carriage to visit a model farm of the Prince of which he was very proud and which he had been telling us about. The Prince accompanied General Grant. This house was old-fashioned and there was nothing in it, implement or furniture, under three hundred years old.

I took much pleasure in a little shopping at The Hague. To my great delight, I procured twenty Apostle teaspoons, getting two, then one, then three, and so on until I had secured twenty. I wanted the General to remain longer that I might make up my two dozen, but no, he would not.

We all enjoyed our visits to the museum, where we feasted our eyes on the wealth of pictures there of Van Dyck, Rubens, and others, but the General lingered longest before Paul Potter's bull. He thought it wonderfully fine.

Amsterdam was our next stopping place. We were much interested in its canals and quaint buildings. We here visited and spent the best part of a day at a model farm which, I am happy to say, was being mowed by one of Mr. [Cyrus] McCormick's mowers brought from Chicago, driven by a skilled driver from Illinois at the good wages of five dollars per day. The General said: "That is high wages for this country, is it not?" Our host said, "Yes, but it is better than sending to America for another blade and stopping the machine, which I would have to do if I did not have this man. If anything breaks, he can mend it."

We visited a menagerie while at Amsterdam, a very wonderful one, and the only one we visited whilst abroad. The sloth was disgusting in its lazy movements, the hippopotamus equally repelling with its greedy jaws widespread, and the great coils of serpents were horrid. I remember once when walking with some friends in Paris we passed a cage which contained a pair of elephants which had just been fed. The male had already finished his portion and was looking sullenly at his mate, who quietly and generously gathered large bundles of hers and threw them to her lord without even turning her eyes in his direction. He quietly munched the largest part of Mrs. Elephant's dinner without once nodding his thanks, thus showing he was from the East.

A visit was made to the city of Rotterdam. A superb banquet was given to the General by the burgomasters. He deeply regretted that I did not go, but I could not, as I wished to try to make up my two dozen Apostle spoons. The General was much interested in a piece of engineering which unites Amsterdam with the North Sea.

From Amsterdam we went to Hanover, where our second son Ulysses had spent a year studying German. This was sufficient to make us tarry. We were again welcomed by the authorities and by Americans living here for the purpose of giving their children the benefits of studying German in its purity. I can call to mind some stables where there were some cream-colored horses with flowing white manes and tails, and a garden where a former king had held court.

We learned here that our Minister to Berlin, Mr. Bayard Taylor, was coming to meet General Grant. He met us sixty miles from Berlin. In Mr. Taylor we found a charming gentleman. We went at once to a fine hotel with large, airy rooms.

The next morning, Prince Bismarck called. I do not remember whether General Grant called first or not, but the Prince called and came again in an hour with the Princess (his daughter) to call on me. We had the pleasure of being presented to the Crown Prince, Frederick, and his Princess, Victoria.

When we dined with them at the new palace, the General and I were presented in a private room adjoining the beautiful shell room, where we met them again and assembled for dinner. The dinner was early. We took coffee after dinner on the stone balcony facing the east, looking out over a beautiful lawn and a grand old forest. When the Prince and the Princess entered the room where General Grant and I were, we simply arose and bowed, but they advanced and shook hands in a very cordial manner. We did not have the pleasure of meeting the Emperor and Empress while in Berlin. The Emperor was confined to his bed with wounds received at the hands of some fanatic who had attempted his life, and chains were fastened across the entrance at the palace to prevent noise.

After we returned from the new palace, we attended a reception at the English Minister's. Lord Beaconsfield [Benjamin Disraeli] was present, as he was a member of the great European Congress then in session at Berlin to adjust the Treaty of San Stefano. Mrs. Taylor and I returned home, worn out by the excitement of the day.

We dined with Prince Bismarck at Radziwill Palace. Nothing could exceed the cordiality of our reception by this great and most distinguished man. I enjoyed every moment spent in his company. His family, the Princess and her son and daughter, were equally agreeable. I shall always remember this visit with the greatest pleasure. The dinner was early, as usual in this country. The Prince conducted me to the table, and the Princess took General Grant's arm, and she and the General sat opposite us at table, which brought us all quite near together and made conversation possible. I can remember even now much that was said.

After dinner, the Prince gave me his arm and asked if I would like to see where the Congress was sitting. I replied that I would. We entered the large room in which there was an immense table, long and wide. The Prince pointed out to me the seat of each member of the Congress. As he finished doing this, I looked up at him and inquired in a mystified manner what the Congress was meeting for, and seeing his look of surprise, I said hurriedly, "Oh, I know. It is about Russia and Turkey. But what has Germany to do with that?" He laughed outright and said: "Well, to tell the truth, Russia has eaten too much Turkey, and we are helping her to digest it."

We had the pleasure of meeting here several young gentlemen we had known in Washington at the German legation. When we made our adieux, the Prince and the Princess accompanied us to the entrance where our carriage stood. The Princess took my wrap from the attendant and wrapped it affectionately around my shoulders. When I gave my hand to Prince Bismarck to say farewell, he bent low over my hand and kissed it. I said, laughing, "If that were known in America, Prince Bismarck, every German there would want to be kissing *my* hand." The Prince, still holding my hand in his great palm, looked down admiringly upon it and said: "I would not wonder at all at them." I was, of course, enchanted with Prince Bismarck.

We went from Berlin to Hamburg, where the General was received with great hospitality. I remember with much pleasure a garden party and the very agreeable people we met. I was not present at a Fourth of July entertainment in the country given by some Americans. The General said it was very pleasant. He made a little speech.

Our next stopping place was Copenhagen. Our Minister, Mr. Cramer,[3] received us and insisted upon our going at once to his house, where he entertained us hospitably.

The King and Queen were at their country place and were kind enough to send word that we should be presented when we came to dine with them, thus saving us a long ride. This was most agreeable to us, as it gave us time to visit the Castle of Elsinore and walk through its ghostly corridors. We also went to the willowy brook where poor Ophelia drowned her grief. Rosenborg Castle was also visited with much interest. From this latter, we went to the Thorwaldsen Museum.

We next drove out to call by appointment on the Crown Prince and Princess. The Princess, a handsome, stately woman, was the granddaughter, I believe, of [Jean Baptiste Jules] Bernadotte, and a descendant from my ideal woman Josephine. The Prince had his two pretty little sons brought in to shake hands with the General.

The next day was appointed for the presentation to Their Majesties and also for the dinner. After a pleasant drive of about an hour, we arrived at a modest but very pretty villa, much resembling Brentwood, a pretty villa near Washington. We were at once ushered into a large drawing room in which a number of guests had assembled. They all spoke to us and greeted us cordially. The Queen entered directly, dressed very simply in black silk. She looked rather delicate but handsome, as we expected to find the mother of two of Europe's fairest queens.

The Queen spoke to the General first and gave him a cordial greeting with some pleasant remarks. Then she came to me and greeted me in the same cordial manner. She was simply charming to me in every way. After a moment's pause, I said to her, "Madam, in addressing you, I think I must be greeting the happiest mother in all Europe." She looked rather inquiringly at me, and I added, "To be the mother of England's future Queen, of the future Empress of Russia, of the King of Greece, and of the future King of Denmark, I think you ought to be not only a proud but a very happy mother."

The Queen regarded me with a pleased expression while I was making these remarks and exclaimed: "I am, I am!" And she really seemed to be as she graciously passed from one to another, making some pleasant, kind remark to each of her guests. We had a charming evening and then rode back to Copenhagen.

We left Denmark about July 11 and went aboard the ship for Christiania. In the evening, the vessel stopped at Gothenburg, and we were surprised to witness the ovation to General Grant. A large delegation was waiting to take him up to dinner, but the General declined and said he would rather drive through their city, which preference was readily granted, and we accompanied these gentlemen on a drive through the city. We drove out to some pretty little cottages that lay along a fine road. Each had a little enclosure and a parterre of bright, gay flowers. Our escort seemed to take much pleasure in showing these ideal homes for their poor, for such they said they were. These homes were self-supporting, and three or four were added each year.

I could not sleep that night. The sea was rough and the waves dashed against the sides of the ship like great battering-rams. Remembering from my schoolbooks that Norway's chief export was timber, I at once came to the conclusion that one of their immense rafts was afloat, and I was sure it was thudding against our ship. I aroused the General and told him of our danger. He impatiently requested me not to awaken him again. I left him to his fate and went on deck to inquire of the Captain, who was composedly walking up and down the deck. I felt rather frightened and out of place, but as the Captain neared me on his return, I timidly inquired, "Captain, is there anything the matter?" He promptly answered, "nothing." "Then," I asked, "what is making that terrible thudding sound against the ship's side?" "The waves from the North Sea," he answered. "Then it is not a timber raft?" "No," he said. Then I went downstairs out of the moonlight, or rather out of the beautiful twilight of this season.

We arrived at the capital, Christiania, at about twelve o'clock, July 13. There were not less than ten thousand people gathered on the landing to welcome General Grant. King Oscar was absent when we arrived. The General received a message from him to the effect that he would return in four or five days to his capital, when he would be glad to see the General.

Our Consul, Mr. [Gerhard] Gade, a Norwegian gentleman whose wife is an American lady, advised the General to take advantage of the time thus afforded to see as much of the surrounding country as possible. The advice was followed. A large pair of horses and a commodious carriage were hired, and the General invited Mr. Gade to accompany us on our trip. This gentleman was most agreeable and interesting, and related many historical reminiscences as we passed along.

We had many pleasant changes in the way of traveling. The karjoler[4] I was delighted with and insisted on driving myself, but the little scamp who rode behind me managed my steed by some magic. A low whistle always started my pony off at full speed downhill, and a low guttural sound made him stop and walk slowly uphill. I scolded the boy more than once and took his long switch from him, but just the same he directed his horse's gait though I held the reins.

We saw beautiful lakes, cascades, and green hills or mountains, and drove through such delicious pine woods, the odors of which still linger with me. I have very vivid recollections of the heaping plates of delicious mountain strawberries and cream, and the slices of brown bread I invariably ordered when we stopped for refreshment. I told the General that this must be the ambrosia upon which the gods fed. He teased me by saying, "Yes, no doubt. I see it is making you very stout." He knew well that this thrust would stop the ambrosia for that day at least.

On our return, the King received the General and at once returned his call. He gave the General a banquet in the evening. I remember a charming ride to Oscarshal, a former country residence of the King, but now the property of the town of Christiania. While on this country ride, I purchased some pretty filagree silver buttons and two or three very old silver cups.

We were soon on our way for Stockholm, where we arrived on the 24th of July. We had apartments in a very delightful hotel. The General was warmly welcomed as usual, and everything was thrown open for our inspection. We passed one or two days there very pleasantly.

It was near sundown when we went aboard the ship at Stockholm. Every vessel in the harbor was gaily dressed in flags; ours was, of course. Every prominent point, every little island, was flying an American flag. Salutes were fired from cannon, muskets, toy guns, and even firecrackers. The bay was fairly in bloom with American flags. Every little boat (and the water seemed covered with them) carried little American flags, but the best of all was a long rowboat full of young ladies, looking like so many laughing Hebes. It came up until they saw they had attracted our attention. As they paused, they drew in their oars and with one motion threw their arms high over their heads, clasped their rosy hands, and floated in silence past the General, giving him as they thought, no doubt, the salute of "present arms." This was really a very pretty tribute to the General, and I waved my handkerchief to them in acknowledgment of their graceful interpretation of this military salute. Goodbyes were said, anchors were hoisted, and we were afloat on the "Baltic's broad billow."

The ship ploughed its way through a sea of glass. The sun sank from sight and the long twilight followed. The General and I sat alone on a secluded part of the deck. He smoked and smoked. I chatted and even sang a song or two. I sang for the General my little song of the Baltic:

> Day has gone down on the Baltic's broad billow,
> Ev'ning has sigh'd her last to the lone willow;
>
> . . . .
>
> Rise, gentle moon, and light me to my lover.[5]

[249]

And when at length I was weary and said I would retire, he remonstrated, saying, "How can you weary of this beautiful sight? Only look out on this calm sea and rest here. Do not go to sleep. You will never see this again." After another half hour, I retired, and the next morning we arrived at Helsingfors.

NOTES

1. The Treaty of San Stefano, ratified March 23, 1878, ended the war between Russia and Turkey. With the Russian army before Constantinople, Turkey conceded several Asiatic provinces to Russia, recognized the autonomy of Bulgaria, and granted independence to Serbia and Rumania. Other European powers reacted to the Treaty of San Stefano with a round of international negotiations which culminated in the Congress of Berlin. This congress, in session while the Grants were in Berlin, modified the treaty.
2. James Birney, a son of the antislavery leader James G. Birney, was prominent in Michigan Republican politics before Grant appointed him minister to the Netherlands in 1876. The error in referring to him as general may have arisen because he had two brothers who attained that rank in the Civil War.
3. Since Michael J. Cramer married Grant's sister Mary, it is surprising that Julia Grant wrote so little of this visit.
4. This small buggy is discussed and pictured in Young, *Around the World*, I, 449–50.
5. "Rise Gentle Moon," words by J. R. Planché, music by J. Barrett, in S. Baring-Gould, *English Minstrelsie* (Edinburgh, 1895), III, 66–67.

Chapter 9

WE WERE RECEIVED by an enthusiastic crowd of citizens and the city officials. The General and I were alone, having only my maid and a courier. We were conducted up to partake of a sumptuous breakfast. I do not remember whether it was at the hotel or at the city hall, but it was very fine. We remained at Helsingfors several hours and were driven out to the park, of which the people were justly proud. We also saw a fine church with columns of porphyry. I noticed a green, hazy atmosphere prevailing, much like the blue atmosphere which hangs over Naples. I had seen this phenomenon once before in the Allegheny Mountains when we visited General [Thomas L.] Kane. We were escorted back to the ship with music and by people bearing garlands of flowers. We enjoyed the same beautiful calm sea and lovely twilight we had on the previous night.

We arrived at St. Petersburg at about seven A.M. We found our Minister, Judge [Edwin W.] Stoughton, waiting to receive us and were driven at once to a very large, handsome hotel where we were soon most comfortable. The General made all the visits etiquette required of him and was pleased with his interviews with the Czar, the Crown Prince, and Prince [Aleksandr] Gorchakov. I think he breakfasted with the latter.

I had the pleasure of being presented to the Czarina, the second daughter of the Queen of Denmark. I had told the Queen I was going to Russia and asked if I could take any message to her daughter. She said: "You must take her my very best love." Of course, I conveyed this sweet message when I was presented. The lady was slender and graceful, and received the message from her mother with a pleasant, happy smile.

I do not remember much about this palace except that the salons were perfectly immense and the floors of inlaid woods. I was presented to another of the Czar's sons and his daughter-in-law, a Princess of Mecklenburg. She proudly brought in two of her baby children for me to see. The Grand Duke Alexis, who had quite recently visited America, was absent at some distant post.[1] The Empress also was absent, having gone to the south of Russia for her health. Her birthday occurred whilst we were in St. Petersburg and was celebrated with great pomp and splendor. Here, as at almost every place we visited, an officer was appointed to escort General Grant and party, to accompany us everywhere, and to give us every possible facility for seeing all that was interesting.

I remember the interest with which I viewed at the Peterhof the charming rooms of the Duchess of Edinburgh, only daughter of this great house. These rooms were draped simply in pretty chintz as sweet and pretty as her lovely self. The Peterhof was full of interesting matter: the old carriage built by Peter the Great, the implements used in forging different parts of this, the little leaded windows to the carriage, and, in fact, everything ever used by this indomitable, this great man. I could not help drawing a comparison between this great man and another great man I knew.

Whilst at the Peterhof, the fountains were made to play for us, and how beautiful they were! It would require pages to tell of all the rare and beautiful things we saw at the Peterhof, but I must not forget to mention some lovely teacups with handles of natural coral. How I tried to procure some like them, but I was never fortunate enough to see any more.

The Winter Palace is indeed magnificent. Whilst we were there, some renovation was being made in parts of the palace. The different great halls we saw were magnificent in dimension and splendor of decoration. The floors were of inlaid wood of wonderful beauty. The walls were of mirrors or else of tapestry or frescoing relating some historical event in the nation's life. Then great, gilded columns supported the lofty ceilings, all exquisitely frescoed. The corridors, and we passed through many of them, were, I am sure, not less than thirty feet wide, as down each side about twenty feet apart stood the most superb vases gathered from all parts of the world, mounted on stands from four to seven feet high, made of onyx, lapis lazuli, porphyry, malachite, or superb Sèvres, and everything else to correspond. Here again in this great palace I stopped to admire the apartments of

Russia's fair Princess. The bath here called forth my special admiration. It was a bath for a goddess, and I could but wonder that she could consent to leave such surroundings.

We also visited a place where many wonderful jewels were shown us—great ropes of pearls, rubies, and diamonds—but these I did not care for. One sees so many; they cease to dazzle. I now only remember the exquisite crown of the Empress, who, poor lady, was then far away from home in pursuit of health.

We found the magnificent churches—with their columns of porphyry, malachite, and lapis lazuli, and the balustrades of solid silver—crowded with devotees prostrating themselves until their foreheads touched the floor. We saw in the churches many caskets containing the remains of loved ones of the late war. These were entirely covered with faded flowers, but these again were covered with fresh flowers. Nearly every woman wore black.

We went out to see a great warship, and as we neared it a salute of seventeen guns was fired. As the firing ceased, our Minister said (I thought with some surprise): "Madam, they are saluting your husband." I quickly replied, "Oh, no, that salute is for you, Mr. Minister. General Grant's salute is twenty-one guns always." For a wonder, I had counted the guns.

We now left St. Petersburg by rail for Moscow. Judge and Mrs. Stoughton accompanied us. I only remember we passed over vast, uninhabited plains, making only two or three stops, and these stops were at mere station houses. The food was not nearly so good as we get at similar stations at home.

After a fatiguing journey, we arrived at Moscow: the city of churches, the city of bells, the city where Napoleon's downfall began. At Moscow, as at St. Petersburg, we had an officer detailed to escort us to all places of interest. We visited the Kremlin and viewed its treasures, not least of which was a beautiful portrait of the Empress Elizabeth astride a superb charger. I do not wonder at her power. She was beautiful, as I saw her then. The great bell, the red gate, the Treasury filled with beautiful things—all these we viewed with pleasure.

I must not forget to mention some curious Russian spoons I bought here, our polite military escort kindly indicating the best shops. These pretty coffee and teaspoons had in each bowl an etching of some one of the many churches or castles of Moscow and had twisted handles, curious if not quite pretty. I secured here also some more pretty trifles in malachite, also several very fine specimens of enameled wood and a portfolio.

[253]

We met and dined with the Governor, Prince [Vladimir] Dolgoruki, and his niece, who knew my son Lieutenant Grant when he visited Russia with General Sherman. They both made many inquiries for him and for General Sherman. I remember how intensely interested this lady was in the health and welfare of the soldiers of Russia; and it seemed to me that these people, all those I met, were so earnest, so patriotic, in their devotion to their country. The men were usually tall and nobly-formed. The women too were handsome. I was very happy to have such fair representatives of our own country as the Stoughtons, both so handsome and noble-looking.

From Moscow, we went by special train to Warsaw. I remember this as a bright place, full of sunshine, and remembering *Thaddeus of Warsaw* that I had read so long ago, inquired for his home, but to my regret could receive no information regarding him. I remembered afterwards that it was only a novel I had read and not a history.

After resting for a day or so and seeing the city and many of its beautiful suburbs, we passed on to Vienna. Here our most accomplished Minister, Mr. [John A.] Kasson, met us and escorted us at once to his house. Mr. Kasson was occupying a fine palace and lived elegantly. He gave several dinners in honor of his guests. General Grant dined with the Emperor and with Count [Gyula] Andrássy. The Empress was absent in Ireland hunting. As it was late in August, all persons of rank were out of the city and it was pleasantly quiet. Of course, we visited all places of interest in the vicinity. I remember a delightful day spent upon the blue Danube.

From Vienna, we went to Ischl, a most charming place, and stopped at Hotel Elizabeth, situated on a rushing water course. Our handsome rooms fronted on this, and it was very pleasant. Mr. Kasson joined us here, which gave General Grant much pleasure. How many long, delightful rides we enjoyed at lovely Ischl! I well remember the one to Wolf Hausen and another to a lovely lake. In fact, every day we enjoyed a different ride and all beautiful. I remember too how I enjoyed the long and most interesting conversations of these two gentlemen as we rode over mountain and through valley.

The ride to Salzburg was long. We rode all day. The wife of the innkeeper on the mountaintop where we stopped for luncheon was, I thought, a most beautiful woman, and the gentlemen agreed with me. We arrived at Salzburg about four P.M. and before reaching our rooms had met a dozen or more Americans. This always gave us pleasure. They are such cosmopolitans that they really feel at home wherever they are. Whilst at Salzburg, a message was received from the Emperor of Germany saying the Emperor was well enough now to see General Grant. So the General and Mr. Kasson left Salzburg and went by rail to some watering place to meet the Emperor. They returned next day to Salzburg, where I had remained with my maid for the much-needed rest.

From here we went on to Ragatz, where I insisted on remaining for a fortnight. Here we met some delightful Americans: Mr. Payne from Cleveland, Ohio, and Mr. Schumaker of New York.[2] What long walks the General and Jesse enjoyed with these gentlemen! I, too, became quite an expert in walking, once taking a walk of six miles from our hotel up the gorge to the baths of Pfäfers and back again, quite six miles.

It happened in this way. One bright morning, the General and I started for a walk up the gorge. The road was clean and firm from a hard rain the previous night. We had been walking quite a while, I chatting away all the time, when the General remarked: "Why, you are walking finely this morning. Do you think you can walk to the Halfway House?" (just one and a half miles from our hotel). I replied, "Yes, of course. I do not feel the least fatigued." He said: "If you feel tired when we get there, we will rest awhile, have a glass of ale, and I will get a carriage for you."

We walked on and on; then the General said: "I think we ought to be getting near the Halfway House, do not you? Are you not tired?" "Not in the least," I said, walking on. Then the General exclaimed, "I do believe we have passed the Halfway House. We have, for we are at the baths." And how we enjoyed the surprise! A surprise to me but not to the General, for when he asked me if I could walk as far as Halfway House, he knew we had already passed it. He was forever playing such practical jokes on poor me. He said it would be so fine for me to be able to say I had walked six miles once, and so it has been my one brag.

From Ragatz, we went to Paris for a short time, then on to Spain, remaining for a night at Biarritz. The next day, we went to Vittoria, where by special invitation the General dined with Alfonso XII, the young King of Spain. From here, we went to Madrid, arriving there October 28. We looked at its famous pictures and visited the Escurial, which was of intense interest to me as we saw there so many things in some way connected with Ferdinand and Isabella and with Columbus. We also saw there the sarcophagus of the beautiful but ill-fated young Queen Mercedes. It was covered with bright flowers for poor Mercedes. Mr. and Mrs. [James Russell] Lowell gave us a delightful dinner and reception, and General Grant dined with the King's cabinet officers. The court was in deep mourning for the late Queen and, of course, all entertaining was necessarily informal.

While we were at Madrid, Alfonso arrived from his military

inspection. As he passed through the square in front of the Hotel de Paris, the square was thronged with people. As he entered the square, passing under our window, we all greeted him in American fashion. We ladies waved our handkerchiefs, the gentlemen took off their hats and bowed. As he passed us, he returned our salutes by waving his hand to us. He passed the entire length of the square without receiving one word or expression of loyalty. As he passed out on the other side, he was fired upon by some vile assassin, but he escaped without injury.

We went from Madrid to Lisbon, a beautiful city said to have been founded by Ulysses when he went wandering after the fall of Troy, leaving his Penelope at home. Our stay there was pleasant and full of interest. We were much pleased to meet and be entertained by Their Majesties, King Louis and his beautiful Queen. The Queen, then only thirty-two years old, presented to me her two sons, handsome youths, the eldest just sixteen and the other a year or two younger. The Queen looked more like the sister than the mother of the tall lads who leaned so lovingly over her chair. She was very lovely in her gown of rich mauve silk and her abundant beautiful hair, plaited in coils around her queenly head. This fair young creature was the daughter of Victor Emmanuel, King of Italy. I remember this reception by Their Majesties of General Grant as a most brilliant one, the King and Queen being surrounded by a concourse of brilliant courtiers in rich uniforms and many fair women.

As we were leaving the palace after having been received by the King and his Queen, one of the gentlemen of the King's suite came to the General and said: "General Grant, this is the birthday of the ex-King Ferdinand, King Louis's father, who would be gratified and pleased if you would call." The General said he was not only willing but would be much pleased to call. We were at once escorted to the ex-King's palace. As we entered the drawing room, we were met by a handsome, stately woman, who at once approached and, taking the General's hand, said in the most charming manner, "General Grant, I am a countrywoman of yours, and I am so happy to welcome you to my house." Just then, the ex-King entered and, after welcoming us, said: "General Grant, let me present to you and Mrs. Grant, my wife, your countrywoman." [3]

We had a delightful call. The palace was full of beautiful things, the choicest and loveliest I saw while I was away. I remember particularly a kneeling figure by Thorwaldsen; it was so pure and chaste. I could not help admiring the lover king who abdicated his throne to enjoy the society of this truly beautiful woman. He showed me some finely decorated plates he was painting for her. He was, I should think, about sixty-two or sixty-three years of age, and the lady was about ten years his junior. They were both handsome and happy with the prospect of many long years before them. He had presented his wife with a beautiful palace, Cintra, about ten or fifteen miles out of the city, where we all made a lovely visit. This is one of the most beautiful palaces I remember and, like their residence in Lisbon, is overflowing with all that heart could desire.

We had the honor and pleasure of dining with King Louis and his Queen at the palace, when we met many of the court. King Louis conducted me to the table, and I suppose General Grant escorted the Queen. They sat exactly opposite the King and myself. I enjoyed the dinner and especially the conversation of my interesting young host. I remember he was much interested and seemed to take great pride in the work he was then engaged upon, translating Shakespeare into his own language of Portuguese, a copy of which he presented to General Grant.

Ex-King Ferdinand was present at this dinner, and when I inquired how the countess was, the dear, kind old lover smiled and beamed like a boy of seventeen and exclaimed rapturously, "Is she not a darling?" Of course I assented, and she really was charming. From this dinner, we attended the opera, where we again met King Louis and his Queen. She was, of course, dressed as she was at dinner, in a robe of rich white silk, and such wonderful pearls adorned her slender throat.

We found Lisbon delightful and full of interest. I sent home a plane tree from Lisbon. This beautiful tree was a favorite of Cyrus, who used to hang chains of gold on its beautiful boughs.

We left Lisbon in the evening and soon reached Cordova. In all of these places, General Grant was received by the officials with great marks of respect. Our hotel at Cordova was very fair. I remember an exquisite bedstead made of gilt which was in my room. It was hung with lace. I not only enjoyed this, but then and there decided to get one just like it. I also remember a delicious conserve made of the petals of the tuberose, surely a dainty food. The Moorish mosque with its forest of columns and the old Roman bridge were very interesting. It was a great pleasure meeting Mr. and Mrs. [Robert R.] Hitt from our own state of Illinois at Cordova.

From here, we went to Seville. After a delightful ride about Seville, the General remarked to me, "The Duc de Montpensier[4] lives here, and I am going to call and write my name in his book." The General had hardly returned before the Duke called and invited us to breakfast the next morning at twelve. We went and had the pleasure of meeting the Duke and the Duchess and their son and daughter.

The young lady was very handsome, tall and graceful, with a gorgeous complexion. The son was still a lad of, I should think, not more than ten or twelve years. We sat down to table in a large, pleasantly lighted room, which looked out upon a garden full of roses (December 6th) and flowers. The table with its delicious viands and, above all, that distinguished and agreeable company is one of the pleasant memories of Spain.

After breakfast, the Duke and General Grant sat and smoked, and the Duchess escorted me through the halls of San Telmo, pointing out the things she particularly valued. She paused before a beautiful portrait of her daughter Mercedes, touched me gently on the arm, then passed quickly on as if afraid of showing her emotion. A lady who was with us called my attention to a very handsomely embroidered chair or divan and said the Duchess did it all herself. The furniture in some of the chambers was very old-fashioned, quaint, and pretty. We enjoyed the walk with the Duke and Duchess through the lovely grounds and gardens of San Telmo. We came upon the young son, who was busy in his little garden, which he had enclosed by tying ropes from tree to tree. The Duke, taking hold of the rope, said: "What is this rope here for?" "To mark the ground you gave me, sir," the lad promptly replied. The Duke said to me, "I only gave him permission this morning and you see he has already taken possession." San Telmo and its gracious and charming inmates, beautiful Seville, and the Guadalquivir, whose silvery course we followed, are pleasant memories.

We now directed our steps towards Cadiz on the seacoast, where we remained for a few days awaiting a steamer. The General was called on by the officials and a review was given him. The women of Cadiz were graceful and beautiful.

From Cadiz, we went to the Pillars of Hercules or Gibraltar, where we were glad to learn that our good ship the *Vandalia* was en route for home. Captain Robeson sent his gig to the steamer to take us ashore. Just as it arrived, one came from the Governor of Gibraltar, Lord Napier,[5] to perform the same friendly duty. The General took our American gig which had performed the same service for him so often before and so well. It was done well this time, for the waves ran high.

We enjoyed Gibraltar. We met many distinguished men, soldiers mostly, and women also. Lord and Lady Napier did a great deal to entertain the General. They gave a brilliant reception, a magnificent banquet, and a military review. I enjoyed the review particularly. The General accompanied Lord Napier on horseback. I was with Lady Napier in her carriage. The General dined at the officers' mess several times. We saw our own officers from the *Vandalia* quite often. While at Gibraltar, we were the guests of the American Consul, who gave several enjoyable parties to the General and the officers of the *Vandalia*. I must not forget our ride up and around the Rock of Gibraltar. What a wonderful fortification it is! I realized then as we climbed up its dizzy heights of solid rock what my old neighbors meant to infer when they used to tell me that it was as impossible for General Grant to take Vicksburg as it would be to take the Rock of Gibraltar. The English are fortunate in securing the key to such a number of strategic points.

From Gibraltar, we went to Malaga on an English revenue cutter. Our Captain Robeson could not venture to use the *Vandalia* a few hours without orders. Lord Napier kindly sent us on an English ship, as there was no regular steamer between these ports. We rested one night at Malaga, started early for Grenada, and, on arriving, rested at the Hotel Washington Irving.

We went to the Alhambra, to the churches and places of interest, and into the crypt which contains the remains of Ferdinand and Isabella. The General and I had entered the church together. The others of our party passed on as I lingered to look at something. They entered the crypt before us. So, entering last and the General in advance of me, we were the last to leave, as we could only move single file around the caskets lying side by side. I had reached the head of the caskets, the last visitor had passed out, and the General was halfway to the door, when I called to him, "Ulys, here are Ferdinand and Isabella." "Yes, I know," he said, "come on." "Oh no! let us linger a while, do! It was this woman who enabled Columbus to fit out his ships for the discovery of America." The General here called: "Come! Come!" "Only think," I said, "they have been lying here side by side for nearly four hundred years. Let us stop and reflect." The General said: "Come on, or I will leave you and will shut the door after me." Of course I went then, and he said to me, "I knew that threat would bring you."

But soon revenge was mine. Soon we entered a large room in which there were closets filled with church embroideries. The priest took a great deal of pleasure and pains in showing these to me. After seeing two or three, the General said more than once, "Come, they are all alike. Let us go on," and, "Now have you not seen enough of them?" But no, to tease him I exclaimed, "Oh, no, they are all different and very beautiful."

I told the kind old priest how interested I had been in touching and seeing the casket containing the sacred remains of Ferdinand and

Isabella; that every child in America knew the story of the jewel box of Isabella and of all she had done to aid the great navigator Columbus.

The priest was so pleased to hear this that he asked: "Would you not like to see that little jewel box?" Of course I would, and the whole party moved into an inner room, this kind, good man leading the way. We all stood around until the casket was taken out of a doubly-locked closet with iron doors. It was silver, about eighteen inches long, eight or ten inches wide, and deep, with a rounding top or lid, and ornamented in repoussé. It was perfectly white and looked as though it had just come from Tiffany's. The box was opened, and I put my hand into its depths again and again, telling the party to do the same. The General was skeptical about a great deal he saw abroad and said to me in a whisper: "It looks very new."

Then the good priest asked if I would not like to see Queen Isabella's crown. Indeed I would. He unlocked another dark chamber and brought forth the crown. It was silver, but it looked like iron and perhaps it was; Isabella was a stern and austere woman. But there were no jewels in this crown, and I was disappointed. He held it up a moment for me to see and, smiling, said: "May I place this crown upon *your* head?" "Oh, yes," I said, bending low to receive the crown, which he placed on my head. And placing the scepter in my hand, he said: "It is fitting that Queen Isabella's crown should rest upon the brow of America's first lady, if it is only for a brief moment." I held the scepter up and, with an air of command, waved it towards the gentlemen; then Mr. Young, shading his mouth with his hand, said to me in a loud whisper, "I am going to telegraph to the *New York Herald* that Mrs. Grant is here in Europe trying on crowns." I at once asked the kind old priest to remove the crown, saying, "It is too heavy for my American head, too heavy."

After this, we returned to the hotel and had a pleasant evening talking over our day's sightseeing. We started early the next morning for Valencia, pausing for a few hours in several quaint old places. We tarried at Barcelona for three or four days. Governor Blanco was very attentive, and we saw much of him. He entertained us at dinner and at the theater. He not only entertained the General but told him to invite any Americans in Barcelona he desired to be with. Throughout Spain the General was treated with the utmost consideration, and we brought from that sunny clime only the most charming memories. Barcelona was a busy, bustling place, very like an American city.

From there, we went to Pau, where we remained several days and enjoyed meeting some of our countrymen. I learned the night before we left that Mrs. Abraham Lincoln was there and I was very, very sorry we had not learned this sooner, as it was now too late to make her a visit. We had our tickets and our train, a party was going with us, and we could not at this late hour change our plans.

After a long, cold ride of not less than thirty-six or thirty-eight hours, we reached Paris. The General having decided definitely to return home by way of India and China, we found we had plenty to do. Our engagements, we found, would occupy all of our time. President and Madam MacMahon, having previously entertained the General at dinner and at the opera, now gave him a magnificent banquet, and Mr. Waddington, the secretary of state,[6] gave him another. At the President's banquet, I sat, of course, next to the President. Count de Lesseps sat next to me and interpreted for us.

During dinner, I noticed a stand full of bonbons about as large as an English walnut and very pretty. Taking one in my hand, I asked the President what it was. He took it from me and, giving it a twist, opened a little box which was full of comfits and, bowing, offered it to me. I helped myself and he did also. Then closing it, he returned it to me. I said: "Mr. President, I will take this little box to America and will tell my friends that the President of France and I ate sugarplums together from it." He was a grand, handsome soldier and ought to have been elected President again. He always conducted me to the door, took my wrap from the attendant, and placed it around my shoulders. Madam MacMahon was equally charming. Our Minister, General Noyes, and other Americans gave us elegant and brilliant dinners. That of Mrs. J[ohn] W. Mackay was simply regal in its appointments.

The General thought he must make a visit to Ireland before leaving for the East. We had intended doing Ireland very thoroughly on our way home, but our change of plans would leave out this very interesting country. The General decided to go now and to leave me in Paris. I at once petitioned my daughter and her family to make me a visit. The General willingly assented and telegraphed for them at once, and soon Nellie, her husband, and her golden-haired, dimpled, rosy boy were with me. Nellie and I had a perfectly lovely time doing our Christmas shopping, receiving our acquaintances, and going out to parties. The General was much pleased with his visit to Ireland.

Christmas came on Monday,[7] and on Saturday the General said: "Julia, have you ever been to Tiffany's house in Paris?" "No, I have not." "Come," he said, "I will take you. It will be well worth your while to go. Get your wraps and I will go with you." I did as he wished though it was a great interruption. He evidently thought it would give me great pleasure, and of course I did not let him know anything to the contrary.

We went, and a great many beautiful things were shown us. Tray after tray of jewels were shown. In the first tray was an exquisite jeweled butterfly, with diamond wings, ruby eyes, and body of glittering topaz. When I saw it, it was fastened to a hairpin of gold by a golden spiral wire, the butterfly quivering and flashing at every motion. It could be made into a pendant or a brooch as well. When I learned the cost of it, I at once laid it down as I thought it beyond my purse, but I returned to it again and again. The General said: "You seem to like that." "Yes," I said, "now that I look at it again, it does not seem so expensive. I am always buying flowers and feathers for my hair. I think there would really be an economy in getting it, but it seems a great sum to pay for such a bauble." "Yes," he said, "it is a great deal of money. Shall we go now?" "No," I said, "let me think if I can buy this. I really need it." By this time we were near the door, and the General, looking at his watch, said: "My time is up. I have an engagement and must go now."

We began to descend the stairs when I suddenly came to the conclusion that it really was very cheap; in fact, a bargain. The General refused to turn back, said he was superstitious about turning back, and reminded me that I was about to make a purchase on Saturday, which he knew I was always superstitious about. "Wait until Monday," he said, "and if you still wish for it, you can come and get it." I replied, "Monday is Christmas and it may be sold." "Oh, no, there is no danger of that," he said. I submitted to this proposal but indulged, I am sorry to say, in some very hard thoughts against men in general, feeling them all, to say the least, unappreciative.

Christmas morning came, and the very first thing I saw on sitting down to breakfast was this very same beautiful butterfly with love from my dear husband. Think of his kind thoughtfulness for me! He was always so forgiving, so charitable to my faults, and so generous to me.

Our party for India had assembled in Paris. Our dear Nellie had said farewell and returned to her home in England. Our party consisted of the General, myself and maid, Colonel Frederick D. Grant, Mr. [Adolph E.] Borie, Dr. [John] Keating, and Mr. John Russell Young. Farewells were said to our many pleasant acquaintances in Paris, and after a tiresome, cold journey of one night, we arrived at Marseilles, where we remained for a day and then embarked on a French steamer, *La Bourdonnais*, on the 24th of January. Several friends came to see us off and to wish us smooth seas. They were soon waving us a last farewell. The sea was rough at first—a disappointment to me. The ship was rather poor, and so was the fare. My maid was very ill. The next day, however, the weather moderated, and we sat on deck, where, much to my delight, we found some charming Americans, including two or three from my old home, St. Louis. They went as far as Alexandria with us.

We again saw Naples and Vesuvius, which was now sending out not only black smoke but an angry, lurid, red flame, which we watched far out at sea. We arrived at Alexandria on January 29 and met there our Consul and our friend General Stone. These gentlemen accompanied us to Suez, where we had to wait a day for the English steamer *Venetia* of the P. & O. line to Bombay. We went on board at sundown, and General Stone and Mr. Farman stayed with us until the last moment. The ship was a magnificent one, and every apprehension disappeared when I saw its size and power.

The deck was thronged with passengers, all strangers to us. The next morning, our party assembled and took possession of a spot on deck near the stern. This was ours during the voyage. There was a cool, soft, balmy breeze blowing from Arabia's shore, which lay to our left, low and sandy and entirely destitute of vegetation. Our good ship ploughed the waters on its way with but little motion.

I reclined on a steamer chair entirely comfortable, with only a pale light-blue cashmere shawl for a wrap over a light-gray cashmere dress, and a wide-brimmed hat with a long blue gauze veil to wrap twice around my neck. My traveling dress for this trip to India was both pretty and comfortable. I had a skirt and long sacque of gray cashmere of the same style as that now called matinee.

I sat in a steamer chair all day long near the gentlemen of our party; my maid read to me, and the gentlemen played Boston, a game they were much interested in. Fred used to grumble dreadfully, as he much preferred to read.

The sea was perfectly smooth; there was only the long, white, plume-like line made by the ship's prow as she glided through the Red Sea. We all gazed with interest on Mount Sinai, and one of the party, Mr. Young, read the nineteenth and twentieth chapters of Exodus to us as we steamed by this hallowed spot.[8] One morning we found ourselves at Aden, built upon volcanic rock, it seemed to me. All I remember of this place is the swarm of black natives swimming around the ship to catch the coins thrown to them by the ship's passengers. I bought some very pretty polished shells and a basket or two.

The ship was very clean and the table fairly good. Over each table was a punka, or hanging fan, which was kept in motion and which gave us a breeze while we were at table. The weather was growing warmer, but my light shawl was still comfortable. I began to know some of the ladies. We exchanged a few words of greeting in the morning and good-nights on retiring. I used to pity the poor children who were left entirely to the care of their ayahs (Indian nurses), who usually had a baby also to care for.

I was well entertained. Some one of the gentlemen remained near me and was ready to read to me or otherwise amuse me. It was generally by reading some nice book. One great amusement was looking for the Southern Cross. The moonlight in the Indian Ocean is a grand sight. We had religious services on Sabbath morning by a young English minister who was going to India as a missionary—I think. His wife was with him. The gentlemen amused themselves by making bets on the ship's run, and whenever any of our party joined in the betting, they invariably won the pool and always gave it to the charity box.

The ship's crews were interesting. They moved about with catlike tread. They were slender, lithe, and tall, and looked well in their long, white gowns, with scarlet girdles and turbaned heads. I never saw such sad faces. They never smiled and never showed any interest in anything. How long must this bondage continue? Will it be obliterated by a short, bitter struggle like ours, when my hero arose and with the blood of the nation's brave men and his own strong arm washed from our country's escutcheon its one shame? Or will it continue until England crumbles as did another great power long years ago? Poor India! Thy pathetic face haunts me yet!

Our journey across the Indian Ocean was long but not wearisome. On the contrary, it was delightful. The gentlemen said it was warm, but I did not suffer. I never do. The gentlemen said: "Of course not, when you are always keeping cool." The North Star was forgotten. We only watched for the Southern Cross now. How beautiful and large the stars were in that southern sky! The Milky Way seemed so near. What glorious moonlight we had! The Moon, as she walked in beauty across her starry azure field, conquered us all, yes *all*, with her soft, beaming light. We were all quiet as we sat out on deck looking out upon the beautiful sea.

The morning we arrived at Bombay, an American flag was floating from one of the masts. It was a pleasure to see it, although it was upside down. No one noticed it but our party, however. The flag was made by some of the ladies on board the ship when they heard that there was none on board to fly for General Grant. They were very nice to do this, and we all appreciated the fine compliment.

We had decided to go to India so recently that not even our Consul (we thought) knew we were coming. We made our arrangements to go to a hotel and from there arrange for the future. As soon as we neared Bombay, we saw the shipping in full dress. All flags were flying. As we passed the English flagship, a gig came alongside with an officer bearing Admiral [John] Corbett's welcome to General Grant. A moment later, another boat came alongside bringing Captain [John S.] Frith, military aide to Sir Richard Temple, Governor of Bombay. Captain Frith brought letters from Sir Richard welcoming General Grant and offering him the use of the government house at Malabar Point.

At nine A.M., we bade adieu to the many pleasant acquaintances we had made on board the *Venetia*, went aboard the government yacht, and landed at the Apollo Bunder. There was a great crowd and a long line of troops drawn up to receive the General. They presented arms and the band played our national airs. The General passed with uncovered head. We entered the state carriage and were driven to Malabar Point.

This is the Governor's headquarters. We entered a grove of mango trees, then passed into a court filled with beautiful flowers, around which were clustered the bungalows of the officials. The General and I occupied Sir Richard's, who was, I am sorry to say, absent on some military duty. His bungalow was charming, surrounded as it was by wide, cool piazzas, which were enclosed by hanging mats. Two or three times a day a native came and threw water upon these mats, which kept the air cool and delightful. Our bungalow was furnished in carved wood lounges, tables, and chairs. Fine Indian mats were on the floors. The lounges had cushions made of silk, in which was woven much gold and silver. The tables held many fine and interesting books. Some beautiful shells lay on the shelves, and there were flowers everywhere. Across the court were the audience hall and the dining hall. To this we were always escorted by a retinue of natives dressed in long scarlet robes, girdled with white and gold. On their heads they wore white and gold turbans. They carried umbrellas to shield us from the sun's hot rays, and at night they carried lanterns in case we needed them. The other members of our party were located in the other bungalows.

Our time was much occupied in sightseeing. I remember with deep interest our visit to the Elephanta Caves. We went across the bay in a yacht. It was a lovely ride, and we afterwards climbed a long flight of stone steps—over two hundred, I should think. Groups of natives met us, who danced and capered around us, and begged us to buy the gold and green beetles. These natives were almost nude, poor things. I bought a great many more beetles than I wanted. This cavern, or temple, for such it evidently was, was most interesting to us all. The entrance was, I should think, quite sixty feet wide and twenty high, supported by two massive pillars which divided it into three passageways, wide and deep, presenting an endless vista of immense pillars cut in the living rock. Opposite the entrance is a bust supposed to represent the Hindoo trinity: that is, Brahma, Vishnu, and Siva. The heads are large and well cut, the headdresses curiously ornamented. Some of the columns of this temple were broken and defaced by the Portuguese, I was told, during their occupation of the island.

We attended by invitation a Parsee school, where we listened with pleasure to the young ladies and children recite in their studies and were delighted with the pleasure and facility they evinced in gratifying us. And I must not fail to say they were all very lovely representatives of their handsome race. From the school, we were conducted to the home of a distinguished and influential Parsee, where we were refreshed by a cup of the delicious coffee these Eastern people know so well how to make and dainty sweetmeats, after which, as an expression of esteem and friendship for General Grant, they hung around his neck and mine chains of roses and gave the General a pretty little desk of carved sandalwood, and to me they gave a pretty red Indian shawl.

While at Malabar Point, the merchants often brought beautiful gold and silver filagree work and superb jewels for me to look at and select from. I remember a girdle of pearls of three strands, four feet long. Every eight inches there was a superb emerald, through which passed the three strings, and then the pearls began again. At the end of the strings of pearls they were made into a large loop and came back into a still larger emerald, thus forming a tassel of pearls with an emerald knot. These pearls were as large as filberts, and this was to be thrown around the neck, tied on the breast, and allowed to hang loose. I saw many others just as magnificent. It would have made the hearts of some of our millionaires' wives turn green with envy to have seen the magnificent jewels these barbaric maharajahs and independent princes were hanging all over and around them. There was a great exhibition of jewels at the Governor's house at the reception after the banquet to the General. They were simply dazzling to me.

A young officer was presented to me while we were at the government house named Major [John Henry Rivett-] Carnac. When his name was mentioned, I repeated "Carnac?" "Yes," he said, "you have no doubt been visiting my ancestral halls in Egypt, Mrs. Grant. See," he said, "my signet is like that on the great temple." And, sure enough, there on his signet ring was the sign of Osiris. I laughingly told him, "I too could trace my family far back. As my brother General Dent used to tell me, Dentatus, the Roman tribune, was an ancestor of our family, the Dents. He was celebrated down to the latest times as one of the noblest specimens of ancient Rome, and as a verification of this assertion my brothers all carry roman noses. My brother Fred told me Dentatus invaded Britain with Caesar; that is how we happened later to be of English descent. But at last, finding Britain too small, his descendants emigrated to America." The Major bowed to the magnificence of my ancestral tree.

We had a delightful visit to Bombay and were driven to the train in the state carriage accompanied by Major Carnac, who represented Sir Richard Temple. A guard of honor was at the station. It presented arms and lowered its colors as the General alighted. We bade goodbye with many regrets to the charming English people at Bombay.

Our next stop was Icbulpur,[9] where we remained all night in order to visit the marble rocks nearby. We rode out to them the next day. It was interesting to see the natives in their little vine-covered houses near the roadside. After several miles in carriages, we had our first experience in elephant riding. The first elephant knelt at a word from his mahout, or driver. The General with Mr. Borie and one or two others besides myself mounted the steps and seated themselves lengthwise on the platform. At a glance, I saw that the best seat was in front exactly back of the head of this superb animal. I seated myself on a cushion, letting my feet hang over the platform. I thus had the gilded balustrade both as a protection and support to hold to and was saved from all inconvenience from the animal's motion. The huge beast arose and walked off with a measured, stately tread. I enjoyed my seat now, seeing far ahead of me, and enjoyed more my authority over the mahout, whom I chided more than once for his cruelty in the management of the brute. After two or three miles, we came in sight of the Nerbudda River, which is held in high esteem and is supposed to have the power of washing away the sins of the natives. We went in small rowboats over the river. The view was very fine. The pure white marble cliffs rose abruptly from the calm depths of this beautiful river, seeming almost to reach the blue sky and catching the last rays of the setting sun. So dazzling were they as to remind me of some enchanted palace. Our tiffin was awaiting us in a bungalow nearby. We saw the Hindoo temple where many pilgrims come to bathe.

Our return from this interesting visit was much more pleasant, as it had grown cooler. From here, we went on to Allahabad and were met at the station by the Lieutenant Governor, Sir George Couper, and Colonel [Henry A.] Brownlow, a distinguished young officer whose acquaintance we were happy in making on shipboard en route for India. They conducted us at once to the home of Sir George, where we made a short but very pleasant visit. As we came out of the cars at Allahabad, what should I see but a beautiful slender girl (as I thought) reaching up to take the General's hand. She was radiant as Aurora herself in her rose-colored trousers, with tunic and turban of fleecy gauze, bound and looped with bands of pearls; around her beautiful shoulders and slender neck hung these radiant gems; and then the eyes, such wonderful eyes, as were raised to welcome the General. Well, to use a sea phrase, I felt as though there were breakers ahead and decided I did not like the custom of this country, where young ladies came out so early and in such an effective costume to meet my Ulysses, even if I were with him. And, of course, when presented I was not nearly as cordial as I might have been.

I was much mortified when I learned that this was the young, independent Prince of all this part of the country. Learning of my mistake, he called on me later in the day dressed in a suit of black velvet knickerbockers, with large diamond buttons. When I first saw him, he was my exact ideal of Lalla Rookh.[10] One day while we were dining with this young Prince, he told me he was soon to be married. I asked if his intended bride were beautiful. He said: "I hope so, but I cannot tell, as I have never seen her." I told him his story was like that of Lalla Rookh. He did not know the story, and I took much pleasure in sending it to him from Calcutta.

From Allahabad, our next stopping place was Agra, where General Grant and I were the guests of Mr. [Alexander J.] Lawrence. He and his fair young Scotch bride were most hospitable and seemed to take much pleasure in pointing out everything of interest. All kinds of beautiful curios were brought to us here for me to select from: garnets, carbuncles, mosaics, sandalwood carvings, and a soft, green stone beautifully carved.

Of course, we visited the Taj and admired it as everyone does. We went again to view it by moonlight. Everyone says it is the most beautiful building in the world, and I suppose it is. Only I think that everyone has not seen the Capitol at Washington! We entered the vast dome, enriched with exquisite carvings in which the lotus flower predominated, and which contained many Arabic inscriptions. From the center of the dome an ostrich egg, the symbol of maternity, was suspended by an invisible thread. In the center are two tombs carved and inlaid with precious stones (not jewels). Around these tombs runs a marble balustrade carved to resemble lacework, into which the lotus flower is introduced. This balustrade is to protect the tombs from a too near approach. As we left the Taj, the gardener gave me some lovely roses. Fred told me that the Taj is most certainly the tomb of our favorite, Lalla Rookh, and begged one of my roses. I suppose he wanted to send some of its sweet petals as bearers of sweet messages to his dear one at home.

The palace of Akbar, now used as a fort, must have been magnificent. It originally covered an area of four square miles.

From Agra, we left for Jeypore [Jaipur], where we arrived late in the evening. The country we passed through en route reminded me of that lying near Salt Lake City. We were met at the depot by His Highness, the Maharajah of Jeypore, and Dr. [Thomas H.] Hendley, the acting English resident, and were conducted at once to the English residency, escorted by a company of Jeypore cavalry.

It was arranged that we should visit Amber, the former capital, now a deserted city—the great-grandfather of the Maharajah having told him in a dream to move his city, and he did. We were all ready early in the morning. We drove through the city and some miles beyond in carriages. The roads grew hilly and rough, and we were delighted to find elephants and palanquins awaiting us. I and my maid each took one of the latter. Mr. Borie took the third, as he did not like the motion of the elephant. I had eight bearers, who skipped on right cheerily. As we passed the low fences covered with wild vines, many in bloom and giving out delicious odors, I felt quite exhilarated with my ride and, looking up, saw the palace with its columns and long line of walls following over hill and dale, away down into the valley and appearing again, passing on and on, with every few hundred yards a white minaret in which to station a guard.

I thought of Lalla Rookh and began to sing quite distinctly and without restraint the "Feast of Roses."

> Now sunlight dies and over
> The valley reigns delight,
> And happy is the lover,
> That wanders here tonight.
>
> For every heart uncloses,
> And old and young arise,
> To hail the feast of roses,
> And bless it as it flies.

How I wish you could have seen the amazement of my bearers! They nearly dropped me; they stopped so suddenly to look up and back.

Supposing it must be familiar to them, I kept on singing this, one of my favorite ballads.

My little party reached the deserted palace a short time before the others came up. We waved to them from the heights. Just as the rest of the party came up, a sacrifice was made which, however, I did not witness. The palace was very fine. One of the halls was supported by large pillars of amber-colored marble. Another was prettily decorated with bits of mirror inserted so as to resemble a flower. I have seen the same effect in the ceiling in a very grand house on Fifth Avenue, where we find everything beautiful and rare.

As we returned to the city, we visited the mint where their money is coined. The General bought me three or four pieces. We went to the royal stables. The General said the horses were very fine. We saw the caged tigers (man-eaters) and passed into the palace to see the nautch girls dance; I was disappointed in them. I had quite a little talk with one of the Maharajah's suite. He spoke English and wore a flowing cloak like that worn in Spain.

When our call was over, the Maharajah hung a chain of roses and another of jasmine around my shoulders. He did this also to the General and the other members of the party. He also placed one of gilt cord and silk over my shoulders and seemed greatly pleased when presenting to each of us a little guide book of Jeypore. I think he was very proud of this book and gave it with great satisfaction. Another ceremony was the sprinkling on us of attar of roses, which was brought in in little golden cups.

We bade him farewell and hastened back to the government house, where dinner was ready and the delightful merchants were waiting to show me the most beautiful things. We each selected some souvenirs of Jeypore in the form of enamels and garnets, Mr. Borie being the chief purchaser.

While at Jeypore, Colonel Grant went on a boar hunt. Starting very early, they drove out to the jungle, where horses were in readiness. There were sixteen horsemen, camels, bullocks, and carts in the cavalcade. The Colonel ran down his first boar, speared him, and had similar success with the second one. He also shot an antelope and was very proud of his trophies, two pairs of boar tusks and a set of antelope horns. These he brought back in triumph to carry home to his pretty wife Ida.

We drove to the station to return to Agra by way of Bhurtpur. We wished to arrive early, but it was nearly noon before we reached there, and a vast concourse of people had assembled to meet the General. The Maharajah himself dressed in state. He was a handsome,

[270]

haughty, stern-looking man who never smiled. He brought his little son to meet the General. He was a pretty, dimpled boy.

We breakfasted with the English officer, Major [Charles] Grant. The Prince did not breakfast with us, as it was not allowed by the customs and religion of his country. After breakfast, the Maharajah returned to us in state, and a long, ceremonious interview, abounding in cordial interchanges of expressions of good feeling, passed between him and the General. He presented to me and the General brushes resembling a horse's tail, cut from ivory with beautifully carved handles. To each of the others he gave one made of sandalwood. They were all shattered to pieces before we reached home.

After these ceremonies, we drove to the station and after a ride of a few miles, we stopped and found carriages drawn by camels waiting to escort us to Futtipur-Sikri. This was our first experience with camels, and we were not enthusiastic by any means. We traveled over sandy plains for miles, following a road parallel to a red stone wall. It was quite dark when we turned into the enclosure we had been following so long. Here were the ruins.

The General, Mr. Borie, Dr. Keating, and I were quartered in the Burbul House, which is supposed to be the home of Akbar's daughter. It is a two-story, temple-like pavilion, finished with carvings of the most exquisite delicacy. We entered the pavilion through an open doorway, which was covered with mats, as were the windows. The partitions were made by hanging mats over poles which extended the length of the room. From the first floor, which we occupied, was a flight of white marble steps leading to the upper rooms. The frieze on the floor I occupied was a deep flounce of about four feet, resembling a flounce of exquisite lace, carved from white marble, and gave a marvelous effect. These were the rooms of Akbar's daughter, no doubt, but her couch must have been of ivory and her floor covered with leopard skins, with incense always burning. We could easily imagine this.

Our couches were rather hard, and as I was told that leopards and tigers sometimes roamed into these hallowed ruins, I felt rather uneasy, especially with only a mat hanging over the entrance. My uneasiness grew into real terror when, in the small hours of the night, one of our party sleeping on the other side of our mat partition had a nightmare and howled like a whole cageful of tigers. I started up in great terror; then I heard a thud and a suppressed remark: "Wake up. What in the thunder are you bellowing that way for? You will frighten Mrs. Grant to death."

The next morning, we walked over to see some tombs that were wonderfully carved and covered with exquisitely embroidered covers. We saw men jump from a wall eighty feet high into a pool of water. We also drove to the Kutab, or tower, one of the wonderful things in India.

We had a delightful ride back to Agra, and there we made our adieux to the pleasant people we had met on our previous visit and, in the cool of the morning, we left with the sounds of booming cannon in our ears to go to Delhi. The ride was warm and tiresome. The General was, as usual, received by the authorities with military honors and with expressions of great respect. We were conducted to Castle Ludlow, where we remained during our visit to Delhi. The remainder of the party went to the hotel. After a bath and a few hours rest, I was quite refreshed and ready for dinner.

We visited the Palace of the Moguls with its peacock throne; it is now a fort. The peacock throne was literally studded with beautiful jewels; it was valued as high as $30,000,000; no trace of it now remains. We saw Humayun's tomb and heard the tragic story of the siege of Delhi in 1857. We also inspected the Kutab, or great dark tower. It looked like iron.

Mr. Borie found a merchant who asked but one price and recommended him to us. We were very happy at this discovery until Mr. Borie, as well as the rest of us, learned to our cost that he had taken good care to make ample profits. I bought from a merchant who came to the government house a gorgeous set of jewelry—necklace, bracelets, and earrings made of filagree gold and set with superb carbuncles—for my daughter Nellie. I also got several shawls and some camel's hair cloth for dresses. I also got several rampur chadors[11] to bring home to my friends; they are always pretty and acceptable.

We next went to Lucknow. The ride was extremely fatiguing. I could not sleep and was entirely worn out when our train stopped. The usual ceremonies were gone through, and we were driven to the residence of Judge W[illiam] C. Capper, whom we had met on the *Venetia* and who had given us a pressing invitation to visit him.

After my bath and a cup of tea, I fell back on the bed utterly exhausted. My maid called the General, who at once sent for a doctor, who assured me it was only fatigue and I needed rest. After the General and the doctor left, I called my maid and said: "I am very, very ill and they do not know it. I wish to tell you, before it is out of my power to do it, that if the worst happens say to General Grant that I told you to tell him that if I died here under no consideration was he to take me home. It was my wish to be buried right here at Lucknow."

Of course she protested. She did not think me so ill and all that, but

I made her promise. I did not want to mar the pleasure of the little party, thought what a nightmare the taking home of my remains would be to them, and made my wish imperative. Of course I appeared at breakfast next day, well as usual. Mr. Young came smiling and said: "How kind and thoughtful you were." He said it reminded him that he might do me a service and that he had spent several hours in drawing up my will, which he at once proceeded to read to me in a solemn manner, willing away the little treasures I had bought in India, giving to himself the lion's share.

The General bought for me, because I was too ill to look at them, two beautiful silver cologne bottles and a silver tête-à-tête set for my room at home. A grand ball and a banquet were given to the General. The doctor advised rest for me, and I was glad to have it. Our new friends and the military escorted us to the depot. A line of not less than a hundred elephants dressed in gorgeous trappings stood along the road and, at a word of command from the head mahout, they raised their trunks high in the air as a salute to General Grant.

We were now en route to the famous sacred city of Benares. We arrived in the evening and were received with great honor. The government representative and the military were at the depot; the roadway was hung with lanterns. We were taken to the government house, where a delicious dinner was in readiness, after which we sat upon the wide veranda enjoying the cool evening breeze. I retired soon and left the gentlemen smoking. In the very early morning, we had our little breakfast and started on our round of sightseeing.

The General and I each had a handsome chair carried by four bearers, but the General surrendered his to Mr. Borie. A ruby velvet umbrella was over my head, embroidered in gold and silver and set with glittering stones. It was a feast day with the natives, and we went at once to a very beautiful temple, all gilded. As I left my chair, a large gentleman of the party with a flowing beard and broad shoulders gave me his arm. I cannot now recall his name.

We ascended the steps of this beautiful temple. The court, the temple itself, and the steps were crowded with people. We entered and passed by a shrine, near which stood a beautiful young man who seemed to be exhorting the people to greater enthusiasm. This young priest was very handsome. He was a Brahmin. As we approached, he held up a wreath of marigolds strung on a thread and offered it to my escort, who threw up his head and, with great scorn, exclaimed: "No!" The young Brahmin's beautiful countenance changed its expression to that of a demon. I smiled, leaned forward, and motioned that I would like to have one. I asked again and bent forward to receive it, when his face lighted up and he placed two of those pretty emblems about my neck, which made me an object of interest to the sacred cows and, as I passed through the court going out, two of these little creatures came up and nibbled at my wreaths, causing many kind smiles to fall on me, as it was considered a good omen. I was a little startled at the near approach of these cows. The women smiled and by nodding their heads indicated to me that there was no cause for fear; they would not harm me; and throwing their white muslin scarfs around the necks of these gentle little creatures, drew them quietly and caressingly away. Some of the party told me that the people were saying the episode was a good omen for me.

We visited some temples built on the Ganges. We ascended the steps and towers and sat for a half hour watching the pilgrims as they bathed in the sacred waters, prince and pauper side by side. As we were beginning to feel the sun's hot rays, we returned home and found the piazza filled with an offering to General Grant of meats, fruits, vegetables, sugar, coffee, tea, spices, and the confections of the country. This was a custom of India and, in fact, of all Eastern countries, and was carried out at nearly every place we stopped. They were always received with much ceremony and, after the donors departed, were turned over to the servants of the house where we were guests.

We also found some beautiful Benares brass work on exhibition, brought there to save us the fatigue of hunting it up in the bazaars. We enjoyed this greatly. Colonel Grant secured some of the very finest pieces. Mr. Borie told the Colonel he was the best shopper in the party as he always bought the best, while I, following a favorite axiom of our merchant prince A. T. Stewart of New York, always bought the *most* and best I could for my money.

General Grant received a communication from the Viceroy[12] at Calcutta inviting him to visit at a certain time. The General was obliged to decline, as he would have been obliged to cut short the best part of his visit to India. The Viceroy postponed his departure for Simla and arranged that the General could have a few days with him.

On our way to Calcutta, a messenger arrived from the independent Prince of Deccan bearing an invitation to General Grant to visit his domain. The invitation was beautifully illuminated on parchment and tied with ribbons and golden cords. The messenger looked like a sheik, dressed in flowing robes of soft, fine, white muslin and a turban of white and silver. The invitation was declined, as we had just time to arrive in Calcutta to meet the engagement with the Viceroy of India.

We arrived at Calcutta in the early morning after a long and fatiguing ride from Benares. Our Consul General and an aide-de-camp to the Viceroy with a guard of honor of Bengal troops met us at the depot. We drove to the government house in the state carriage. The house was not unlike our own White House, only it was much larger. Our baths and the chotahasaire[13] were in readiness, which was very acceptable to us after our long journey. There was a banquet and a reception in the evening. We had already met Lord Lytton and the beautiful Lady Lytton.

Each day brought its banquet and different guests. The independent princes and maharajahs looked very magnificent in their flowing robes of soft silken texture and their wonderful jewels. Lady Lytton was spirituelle in her beauty and very charming. I had heard others speak of her amiability and beauty, and I was not disappointed. We had a garden party at Barrackpur on the Hoogly River under the banyan trees which gave delightful shade. Sir Ashley Eden was with us and did the honors for the Viceroy, who was very busy with war affairs in Burma. The General and Sir Ashley Eden, with many high officials, attended the convocation at the Hindoo college. The General's visit to the Viceroy being over and our ship the *Richmond* not yet heard from, we were pressed to become the guests of Sir Ashley Eden, the lieutenant governor, and a most charming and hospitable host. Our short stay at his stately mansion will ever remain a pleasant memory to me. The garden party on his beautiful lawn was a brilliant affair: the music was fine; and the refreshments, fruits and ices, were served to the guests under a marquee, which was most agreeable.

The General learned that the *Richmond* had not passed Suez yet, so he determined to take a steamer for Burma. We bade adieux to our delightful English friends with great regret. We owed them much for the delightful time we had on our visit to India. We embarked that night, and morning found us floating over those smooth summer seas, all as well and as happy as if it were to last always. We sat on deck and talked over India and the pleasant people we had met. We all agreed that the English were very fine people; in fact, almost as fine as Americans.

NOTES

1. John Russell Young, however, stated that the Grand Duke Alexis called on Grant at St. Petersburg, reminisced about his visit to the U.S., and expressed regret about the death of General George A. Custer. *Around the World* I, 468–69.
2. Since Henry B. Payne of Cleveland, a wealthy industrialist, was a prominent

Democrat who served as Congressman (1875–77), his traveling companion may have been John G. Schumaker, a Democratic Congressman from Brooklyn (1869–71, 1873–77). Jesse R. Grant, Jr., identified Payne's companion as Mr. Schoonmaker of Newburgh, New York. *In the Days of My Father*, p. 239. In that case, John Schoonmaker, a merchant of Newburgh, is probably meant. New York *Times*, January 2, 1904.

3. In February, 1836, Queen Maria II of Portugal married Ferdinand of Saxe-Coburg-Gotha, who fathered eleven children and served as regent (1852–55) after his wife's death until his oldest son Pedro V came of age. In 1869–70, when Europe sought a successor for Isabella II of Spain, Ferdinand emerged as a contender. In the meantime, he had taken as his mistress Elise Hensler, daughter of a German pianist who had taken her to the United States for musical training. Under pressure to abandon either his ambitions for the Spanish throne or his mistress, Ferdinand chose to marry Elise, later given the title Countess d'Edla. Francis Gribble, *The Royal House of Portugal* (Reprint of 1915 ed., Port Washington, New York/London, 1970), pp. 237–45.

4. Antoine, Duc de Montpensier, son of King Louis Philippe of France, married the Infanta Luisa of Spain, uniting the French Bourbons or House of Orléans with the Spanish Bourbons. Their daughter Mercedes, wife of Alfonso XII of Spain, died in 1878, shortly before the Grants visited Spain.

5. Robert Cornelius Napier, Baron Napier of Magdala, a veteran of Indian campaigns, had commanded the British force in Abyssinia in 1868.

6. William Henry Waddington, son of an English textile manufacturer who settled in France, served as minister of foreign affairs 1877–79.

7. Christmas day in 1878 fell on Wednesday.

8. The location of the Biblical Mount Sinai remains a matter of speculation.

9. Although Julia Grant here follows the name given in Young, *Around the World*, I, 624, the party more likely stopped at Jubbulpore. Young stated that the Grants stayed at a hotel, and Grant wrote on March 15, 1879, that he had been at a hotel only once in India—at Jubbulpore. Badeau, *Grant in Peace*, p. 514.

10. *Lalla Rookh* (1817), an Oriental love story in poetry and prose by the Irish poet Thomas Moore, enjoyed great nineteenth-century popularity.

11. A large cloth suitable for covering the head and upper body made in the Indian state of Rampur.

12. Edward Robert Bulwer-Lytton, Baron Lytton, went to India in 1875 as governor-general and viceroy. A poet who wrote as Owen Meredith, he was the son of the author of *The Last Days of Pompeii*.

13. Probably *chota hazri*, from the Hindi for small breakfast.

Chapter 10

T HE STEAMER *Simla* was very comfortable. It had a broad deck
with heavy awnings and many easy chairs. Best of all, I had a
bath connected with my staterooms which I enjoyed greatly,
bathing three times a day in a beautiful porcelain bathtub in water
from the Gulf of Bengal, warm and clear. There was one other lady
passenger on board. She was from the island of Mauritius, where the
scene of the charming little story of Paul and Virginia is laid.[1] Captain
Franks of the *Simla* was a very efficient young officer and did his
utmost to make us comfortable.

March 19th found us at Rangoon. The shipping was dressed in
bunting, and our own little *Simla* was covered with streamers. The
landing was covered with scarlet cloth, and the English and American
flags were intertwined for decorations. Mr. [Charles] Aitchison, the
commissioner, came on board accompanied by Mr. Leishman, the
American vice-consul, and bade the General welcome to Burma.

We drove to the government house, a handsome, commodious
residence in a forest of trees and flowers. We had a banquet and a
reception at the government house, and a grand banquet and ball at
the American Consulate. Our American Consul had been compelled
to return home, as the consulate fees would not support him, and the
consulship had been turned over to an English merchant. Although
we are a nation of tradespeople, our laws do not permit a consul to
engage in trade—oh, no! He might grow rich, and we are too grand
to let a poor consul have a chance to support himself. So he has to go
back home and surrender the office to England, whose patriotic

subject invariably fosters English trade and shoves out our trade, lets America's cotton and shipping interests go to the wall, and grows rich. If an American should chance to get rich while in such a position, a committee would be assembled at once to find out how he became so.

While I was at Rangoon, a ship's captain from Maine told me he had been there for several months trying to get a cargo or clearance papers and could not. Yet almost every week from eight to ten English vessels sailed with clearance papers from our Consul, who also, I think, held the same office for England. I am not finding fault with this man, who was so very civil to us, but I do find fault with a policy that hampers our foreign trade.

The Governor of Hong Kong, Sir [John] Pope-Hennessy, told General Grant of the immense increase of trade with China in cotton goods that was cut off by the Exclusion Act.[2] The Chinese, who were so friendly to our country, are now almost ready to make war against us, and if they should come we would find them no despicable foe.

We saw the heir apparent of the throne of India while we were at Rangoon, also his daughter and her husband, a handsome Chinese Prince. They were here in exile: the Mogul for being a Mogul, and the Prince for heading a revolt in his own country. The Chinaman was handsome and stalwart, but the Indian looked weak and effeminate, even dissipated.

The daughter, the Indian Princess, was permitted to come to the reception at the government house and to look down from the balcony upon the dazzling scene. She reminded me of a delicate flower upon which the sun had never shone. I went to the balcony and sat with her when I had grown weary of the reception. She expressed pleasure at my attention, poor little thing, and admired my gown, my jewels, rings, and the jeweled butterfly (my pretty Christmas present) in my hair. Her attendant, anxious I should see the pretty things her mistress wore, coaxingly drew down her silken veil and pointed with delight to the enameled band that encircled her fair young brow. The band was not pretty, but the eyes beneath were wonderfully beautiful. The little Princess was so shy—like a fawn.

I must tell of an adventure I had while at Rangoon. Mrs. Aitchison accompanied me to my room and, as she was bidding me good-night, casually remarked that it would be best for me to put my trinkets and rings out of sight as there was a large monkey of the orangoutang species about. He was harmless but had the habit of taking and hiding away everything bright that he found. I said: "You do not mean that he can come up here to my room?" "Oh, yes! He scales every wall and climbs to the highest treetops, but he is perfectly harmless. Hark! You can hear him bellowing now. He is harmless—quite." But this did not reassure me, and in the night I heard something scrambling on the wall. I ran into the General's room and hid myself in his bed next to the wall. He was sound asleep and unconscious of any danger.

I must tell another monkey story. One day we were riding—at Agra, I think. There were a great many monkeys climbing over the trees. There were four gentlemen in one carriage, and Lady Roberts[3] and I with two gentlemen in another, when dear Mr. Borie called out, "See, see, only see all of these monkeys." The gentlemen, who saw them plainly, turned around and asked: "Monkeys? Where, Mr. Borie?" "There, there, right before you in that tree. Fifty of them. Don't you see?" They looked, but looked as though they did not see anything, and exchanged sorrowful glances, sighing deeply. Mr. Borie grew very excited, pointed vehemently with his cane, and exclaimed: "Damn it all. Do you pretend to say you do not see any monkeys?" They still pretending not to see anything, Mr. Borie turned and called back to me, asking if I saw any monkeys. Of course I did. He pretended to be very indignant, saying, "They want to make out I only imagine I see them." Mr. Borie enjoyed the joke immensely and, as we drove past the clubhouse, got out and in a hopeless manner said: "Mrs. Grant, I am going to put another peg in my coffin." That is what the gentlemen say in India when they take a drink of brandy and soda. We were all, Mr. Borie included, most temperate.

Whilst at Rangoon, we visited some very fine temples, all with gilded domes and great bells. So large were they that the gentlemen of our party marveled as to how these people ever placed them. We visited the bazaars, which everyone must know is a pleasure always, whether in New York or Burma. Colonel Fred and I secured a few table covers, not fine but very gorgeous in coloring, with bits of glass sewn on them. But the markets were the most interesting to me. The women were simply beautiful: all slender, generally of medium height, with complexions like new wheat. Everyone must know this beautiful coloring—a rosy brunette—and such hair, such eyes, such teeth. Ah, they were fair to look upon. The women seemed to be the vendors of all market stuffs; great mounds of grain, rice, and new wheat (which suggested to me the coloring of the women) were on sale, and on each mound always a bunch of fresh flowers. Nor did these fair daughters of Burma forget to deck their own glossy and abundant braids with the same lovely blossoms.

From Rangoon, we crossed the Bay of Bengal to Moulmein, where the General was received with honors. Colonel and Mrs. Duff were our hosts and were very civil and hospitable, entertaining us at dinners and breakfasts with other guests to meet us.

I can only recall our visit to the woodyards of Moulmein and the wonderful sagacity of the elephants, who were the chief workmen at these yards. These brutes seemed to have human intelligence. A great chain was fastened to one of their feet. They would walk past a great huge log of teakwood, let the chain drag not quite past the log, then, with one tusk for a lever, hoist the log on the chain and, with their trunks, take the hook at the end of the chain, fasten it securely, and walk off with their loads to the pile of logs. Taking one end, they would hoist it up and place it securely, then take the other end of the log and do likewise. They would then walk off and look to see if it were placed straight, turning their heads first to one side and then to the other, and if it were not in line they would (and did) walk up to the end of the pile and push the log they had just carried further on and a trifle back. Their intelligence is wonderful!

From Moulmein, we went to Penang. Here I positively refused to leave the boat. The General and some of the party went with an escort of honor up the mountain to a reception and dinner by the Governor. The General said I had missed a great deal by not going. They had hardly left, however, when the wife of the Chief Justice came on board and insisted that I should go and stay all night with her. The next morning, we rode over the island and saw nutmeg orchards and coconut trees growing in great forests. We secured a bunch of Penang canes for our old friend Commodore Ammen.

The General made the best speech here I ever knew him to make. The landing was covered with the usual scarlet cloth, and after the English authorities had welcomed the General, the Chinese also gave him a reception and in the speech of welcome asked why America refused the same home and liberty to Chinese emigrants she offered to the rest of the world. The General's reply was most diplomatic and was, as near as I can remember, in these words: "It is true the United States has made laws discouraging emigration from China, but Chinese emigrants are sent by contract and become, as it were, slaves for the time being. You must remember the great struggle the United States has just passed through, in which there was so much precious blood and treasure lost, to wipe out slavery. You must not, therefore, expect the United States to tolerate even temporary slavery on her shores." [4] This speech pleased me intensely, as I had often wondered why this difference was made.

From Penang, we went to Malacca. The General was met by the naval commander and driven to some ruins. I did not go ashore. We arrived at Singapore early in the morning. Our Consul, Major [Adolph G.] Studer, and two or three of the government officials came to welcome the General. We were conducted to the government house and were received most hospitably by the acting Governor, Colonel

[Archibald] Anson, and Mrs. Anson, and also by the Maharajah of Johore. Our stay in Singapore was full of engagements for dinners, receptions, and garden parties.

We made a delightful trip to Johore, where we were entertained by the Maharajah at his residence in a charming manner. We were also entertained by the Maharajah at dinner at his city residence in Singapore, a house full of all the beautiful baubles money could buy. An important Chinese merchant named [H. A. K.] Whampoa gave the General an immense and magnificent banquet. His gardens were grand and well worth seeing.

There was some mistake as to the time the boat left, and we were detained several days longer than we intended staying at Singapore. We expected the *Richmond* daily, but she still loitered. The General, having received an invitation from the King of Siam to visit him, decided he could accept and still be back in time for the *Richmond*, so engaged ship for Siam. On the morning of April 14th, we saw land, and at ten A.M. the royal yacht was in sight, with some four or five of the high officials, accompanied by our Consul, Mr. [David B.] Sickels, on board. They came, of course, to meet the General and convey him up the river to the capital, Bangkok.

As we left our ship in one of the small Siamese boats for the yacht, we were nearly washed under the wheelhouse of the yacht, which was so near that I, with great presence of mind, put out both hands against the white walls of the wheelhouse as it came down, and forced back our little craft. So near was the descending monster, for such it seemed to me, that it only just did not touch, that was all. The next instant, our gig shot past the gangway, and we all leaped on board glad to have escaped a dreadful accident.

We found a delicious luncheon awaiting us on the yacht for which we all showed our appreciation, shared as it was with a half-dozen or more young Siamese noblemen, who also came to do honor to General Grant. As we ascended the river, the rain came down in torrents, but we could see the shores which were low and green and, as we neared the city, some hundreds of little boats moored safely along its banks. I was told many people in this country lived in houses built on boats, which seemed to me very pleasant.

We were received with great ceremony on landing. The Minister of Foreign Affairs advanced and welcomed the General. He was accompanied by a brilliant retinue. We entered carriages and were driven to the Palace of the Suranrom, the home of His Royal Highness, the Celestial Prince. As we drove past the barracks, the troops were paraded and a salute of twenty-one guns was fired.

Reaching the palace, a guard was drawn up and a band played our national airs. The Minister of State again met the General at the gate of the palace and conducted him up the steps, at the head of which stood His Royal Highness, surrounded by a brilliant suite of young Siamese noblemen. His Highness gave me his arm and escorted the party to the salon, where they were all presented to His Highness, who later conducted the General and me to our apartments.

Visits of ceremony were made to the King and were returned by him. The King conducted me through his audience hall, which was furnished in French fashion. As we ascended the hall, he paused before a marble bust and, pointing to it, said: "Do you recognize it?" "Of course I do," I said; "It is General Grant. Where did you get it?" "I had it made in Paris and I had the model destroyed so that no one could have one just like it."

When we passed on to another salon, the King led me up to a sweet-looking little lady and said, "my consort." We shook hands, and she led me to a sofa where we seated ourselves. Directly, a person entered bearing a salver on which were several Siamese curios, or specimens of fine Siamese work. There was a toilet set for a lady in pure gold. This Her Majesty presented to me. It was really beautiful. The King handed the General a gold cigar case and Colonel Grant a bowl for cigars.

We had a reception at the palace we occupied and a superb banquet at the King's palace. The young princes were all handsome and were dressed in court dress, which was very beautiful. Across the breast of the Prince who escorted me to the table was a broad, pink scarf, like the blue one worn by the Grand Duke Alexis when he visited Washington. It was most becoming to the delicate, peach-like complexion of the Prince. He was charming as well as handsome. This young Prince turned to me and said: "Madam, I wish you to know how much we appreciate this visit from General Grant, how honored we are in having the privilege of seeing him and hearing him speak."

The King conducted General Grant to table. The General and I sat next to the King. As I recall it, the dining hall was a vista of white marble columns. From the distance came native music from guitars and lutes, I suppose. The effect was delightful.

After dining, we assembled in the audience hall again. I was taken to an inner room where I met the young Queen. It gave me great pleasure to take from my arm and fasten on her wrist a lovely little gold and enamel bracelet in the form of a serpent, which I told her was a fine specimen of American workmanship. I also asked her to accept a little crystal and gold watch, one of those in which you can see all of the works, which I was wearing and thought curious. She was much pleased, and I hung it on her girdle. She would take it out, look at it, and hold it to her ear to hear it tick.

We had a lovely excursion up the river in a fine steamer. We went as far as the steamer could go. Then we went aboard a pretty, wide flatboat with an awning over it, under which we sat in easy chairs. This flatboat was drawn by a small tugboat. The river was lovely. It was wide and as clear as crystal. Its shores were covered with flowering shrubs, lofty palms, and other large trees, from which hung long columns of vines falling to the water's edge; great clusters of brilliant orchids (scarlet, purple, and white) hung from the drooping branches; all were in full bloom and were reflected again from the clear depths below.

As we swiftly glided up this lovely river drawn by the energetic, panting, little tug, the fishes leaped high in the air—they were so startled—and fell back again into the clear depths. It was like a shower of pearls to see these little glistening, quivering creatures leaping and falling again, sometimes on deck at our very feet. Poor little things! I wonder what they thought we were. This beautiful river with its flowery shores and its glittering, shimmering inhabitants was my ideal river in or near the Garden of Eden. Away up this river, we visited a deserted city, and while there our Consul gave me a panel of wood exquisitely inlaid with mother-of-pearl. I have it hung in my home now.

Bidding these hospitable and delightful people farewell, we returned to Singapore on April 27th. Our tardy ship had not yet arrived. The General, greatly disappointed by the nonarrival of the *Richmond*, determined to take passage on the French steamer *Irrawaddy*. We only had time to transfer to the ship when she steamed out of port. The gentlemen regretted their inability to call on their friends in Singapore, as it was late at night when we arrived and very early when we left.

There were many passengers on board, and we were much pleased and entertained learning who they were and whence they came. The gentlemen did not let me grow weary, as some one of them was always ready to read to or chat with me.

As we were steaming up the river (having reached Cochin China) on the way to Saigon, whence the Governor had sent a telegram asking the General to be his guest during his stay at Saigon, the General, Mr. Borie, and some others were sitting in a group near me when I heard a snap and felt a slight, unusual shiver of the ship. I started up and exclaimed: "Did you hear that and feel the motion?" "No, no." No one had heard it, and I was requested to be quiet. I insisted that they should tell the Captain something was broken; but no, it was not their business. The Captain would find out if anything were wrong. Just at that moment, about thirty men came running up on deck with axes and began cutting and splitting the vessel's decks, and our mammoth ship began to plunge and stagger like a drunken beast. Everyone was frightened. There was confusion for a while. I had quite a good deal of satisfaction in telling the gentlemen, "I told you so. I knew something had broken." The ship's rudder chain had snapped asunder, which was the reason for her bad behavior. Fortunately, this was soon remedied, and we proceeded on our way.

We found the Governor's officers ready to direct us to his house, where we dined with a large party. A night's sleep ashore was very grateful to the General. The next morning, there was a beautiful breakfast, many guests, and flowers and fruits. After breakfast, we drove through Saigon, returned, rested, had another dinner and a large reception, and went back to our ship. It was so intolerably warm that night I could not rest.

In the early morning, we were off again for the China seas. As we turned towards Hong Kong, the weather grew cooler, and when we arrived in Hong Kong Bay, the shipping was dressed in flags. Governor and Mrs. Pope-Hennessy met us and took us to their house, where they did everything to make our visit agreeable. His carriages were in waiting, and we drove through a long line of soldiers and Chinese police up to the Governor's house, a beautiful and commodious residence on the heights. Salutes were fired, the band played our national airs, and the church bells rang merrily. Everything was gay and bright, and everyone smiled a kind welcome. We found one of our men-of-war here, with its full complement of the very nicest men in the world, and we were very glad to see them. Dinners, receptions, and garden parties were given to us, and I had many lovely drives with Madam Hennessy in her pretty phaeton, behind her fleet little steeds, Puck and Ariel, and how we sped along over the smooth, wide roads.

On May 5, we went aboard the U. S. ship *Ashuelot* to go to Canton. As we approached the forts, a salute was fired from a line of Chinese gunboats, which was returned by the *Ashuelot*. A gunboat carrying a U.S. flag accompanied us up the river to Canton. It was late at night when we reached the city. Our Consul, Mr. [Charles P.] Lincoln, told the General that the entire population had been at the landing for hours waiting to see him and were greatly disappointed at his nonarrival.

The General was treated with the greatest consideration and distinction. Bulletins were posted all over the city announcing that the

"American King" would soon visit Canton on a friendly visit to the Viceroy, and the Viceroy commanded all the people to be quiet and orderly as the "American King" passed through the streets, and that any Chinaman failing in this or showing any disrespect to General Grant or any of his party would be severely punished.

Ceremonial visits were exchanged between the General, the Viceroy, and the Tartar General, at which there was a great deal of court etiquette to be gone through. Service at table is very ceremonious. The Chinese chefs, you know, are the most accomplished in the world. The General and his party dined with the Viceroy. I did not, as it is not a custom in China for ladies to appear on such occasions, but the Viceroy had a very fine dinner prepared for me and had it served at the Consul's. I had only just got up from a very elaborate luncheon at the Consul's, to which our missionary friends were invited, and could not even taste of the dainties the Viceroy had sent to me. He also presented to me two pieces of very finely worked jade about the size and shape of a postage stamp.

I was greatly disappointed in my visit to Canton, as I had to see people nearly all of the time and did not have an opportunity to see anything of the city. I did manage to get one afternoon for shopping and had to get things at first sight without much chance to select.

We sailed down the river, after saying goodbye to our new acquaintances, and stopped at Macao, a Portuguese town. It was dismal and dark. The General walked out in the rain to see the place and saw "Welcome to General Grant" written over many of the doors.

On the evening of our return to Hong Kong, the Governor gave the General a fine banquet. Friendly toasts to our respective countries were drunk. Mr. Hennessy was a most hospitable gentleman, and I hope yet to have the pleasure of meeting him and his accomplished wife in my own country. Mr. Hennessy is a patriot, a statesman, a philosopher, a philanthropist, and a charming Irish gentleman.

We came in sight of the forts of Woosung on May 17th. They fired salutes of twenty-one guns, which was remarkable as the Chinese salute to *all* ranks is three guns. The *Ashuelot* returned the salute, and all of the gunboats joined in until the air was as full of sulphurous smoke as if a naval bombardment were in progress.

The *Monocacy* of our navy, dressed from stem to stern, was soon seen coming towards us. She lowered a boat and brought a committee of citizens to meet the General. Mrs. [R. W.] Little and Mrs. [Chester] Holcombe came to meet me. They lunched aboard our ship.

The *Ashuelot* steamed slowly up the river, receiving and returning salutes. We were constantly stopping to meet small boats bearing

[285]

Chinese delegations with great red cards for the General, which were interpreted by our accomplished acting Minister, Mr. Holcombe. All the shipping in port was in full dress with yards manned, and the men cheered as we passed. Another salute was fired as we landed. The way was covered with scarlet cloth, and the entire shore was crowded with people dressed in holiday garb. The houses, lampposts, and trees were hung with flags, flowers, and lanterns. The General and party were conducted to a large hall full of people, and the ceremonies were gone through.

The General and I were then escorted to a carriage, but the horses grew dangerously restless, and Lieutenant [William S.] Cowles, who commanded the U.S. Marines, ordered them to be taken out, and the carriage was hauled by the men along the embankment to the house of Mr. [David H.] Bailey, the consul, whose guests we were during our visit to Shanghai.

Sunday, we went to church. Monday was passed roaming through the city and making calls. In the evening, we dined with Mr. and Mrs. Little and after dinner went to the house of Mr. and Mrs. [Ewen] Cameron, where we had a large reception and witnessed the beautiful illumination and torchlight procession from the windows and balconies. This illumination was wonderful. On almost every house words of welcome were seen in flaming letters, and thousands of lanterns shed their soft light in the darkness. The shipping was also illuminated, and China, the land of pyrotechnics, entirely overwhelmed us by its great display this night. I cannot do justice to this great ovation. It was simply grand!

On May 21st, our dear old friend Mr. Borie sailed for home. Dr. Keating thought it best, as it was beginning to grow warm again. We remained a few days longer at Shanghai. We had an agreeable dinner at the house of Chief Justice [George] French, a beautiful ball at the club, and a charming garden party at the country residence of Mr. and Mrs. [Francis B.] Forbes. It was delightful to see their family of lovely children and their pretty home so far away from their own country, and yet they were very contented and happy.

On May 24th, we left for Pekin, the capital. Our Minister in charge, Mr. Holcombe, was anxious that the General should lose no more time, as they were expecting General Grant at the capital. As the *Ashuelot* neared the Pei-ho River, a Chinese gunboat drew up alongside with Consul General [Owen N.] Denny and other officials on board. They came aboard the *Ashuelot* with hearty greetings for the General. As we neared the forts, salutes of twenty-one guns were fired, then returned by our gallant ship. The ships and junks were dressed in flags, and the men-of-war manned their yards. The shores were lined with thousands and thousands of people. A line of Chinese gunboats was drawn up, dressed, and yards manned. Banners waved and cannon boomed, and it was all magnificent. Everything now seems tame to me after the wonderful, wonderful pageants I witnessed in General Grant's honor in every country in the world, from Philadelphia to Philadelphia again.

As we neared Tien-tsin, the yacht of the Viceroy [Li Hung-chang] came alongside with a party of two or three mandarins on board, who brought the Viceroy's card to General Grant. Several of the ship's officers met the Viceroy at the gangway and at once conducted him on deck. After being presented to General Grant, he was presented to Mrs. Holcombe and to me. We then had tea. There was much ceremony on leaving the ship; great crowds followed our party to the Consulate. The General and I were carried in chairs covered with yellow silk. The Dennys were very kind and polite to us, and we found terra firma quite a pleasant change. The next day, General Grant visited the Viceroy. He was conveyed to the palace in the Viceroy's yacht and had a guard of honor from the marines of the *Ashuelot*. Every junk on the river was flying bright flags and had crowded decks. The banks were literally covered with people. A guard of troops presented arms as the General entered the palace grounds amidst the firing of guns and the beating of gongs.

The visit was, of course, full of ceremony and good feeling. A day or two after this, a ceremonial dinner was given at the yamen.[5] Toasts were exchanged, our most accomplished fellow citizen, Mr. [William N.] Pethick, acting as interpreter. The Viceroy arranged to have a photograph taken, and the whole party was photographed.

There was a dinner and a garden party at Mr. Dillon's (the French consul). The Viceroy dined with us, which is, I think, an unusual occurrence, but he seemed to enjoy it very much. General Grant escorted the Viceroy to the table, and I went with Mr. Dillon. We sat opposite each other. There were several ladies present besides our hostess. The Viceroy most gallantly admired our fans and said they were the most beautiful he had ever seen, which was a great deal to say in China, a country where fans are universally used. The fête was a brilliant affair with a grand display of fireworks and Chinese legerdemain.

We now proposed to visit Pekin higher up the river, one hundred and fifty miles from Tien-tsin. The journey had to be made in small boats. After considerable preparation, we hired quite a flotilla of queer flatboats. The General had a nice large one with two cabins and a dining room, and also another boat in which our cooking was done. It was really good fun. We were constantly hailing each other, running races, inviting each other to dinner, and getting out to walk by the shortcuts. It was always very pleasant in the evening. Once as I sat dressing my hair in my little cabin, I glanced up at my mirror and was startled by seeing the reflection of three smiling, eager faces, almost at my shoulder. They disappeared as soon as I turned, and I began to think I must have been dreaming when the white headdresses appeared again. Their curiosity got the better of their sense of propriety. They were about to take their seats and see how I dressed my hair, but I did not like company at such a time and frightened them away with a flourish of my hairbrush. They disappeared like a flock of partridges, and I did not see them again. I learned later that they all lived in the underpart of our boat.

The journey was so primitive and so novel that I could not help enjoying it. The General and I enjoyed the quiet of the deck as the young people made the shortcuts across country to meet us again. They were quite exhilarated and gay after their scamper. The General was quite proud of himself for having thought of Boston baked beans for our mess and enjoyed the repeated commendations he received for his thoughtfulness.

When we arrived at the head of the Pei-ho River, where we left our boats and began the overland journey, the General had a fine horse to ride. I had a palanquin made of slender bits of straw running perpendicularly with narrow intervals, with a drapery of yellow silk. It was very light and cool. When I took my seat, my maid brought me two bottles of claret to put in under the seat for me to drink in place of water. I was glad to get them. When we had gone about halfway, a halt was made for a rest. The gentlemen were gray with dust and red from the heat. They came to me and were astonished to find me quite comfortable and free from dust. They were more than happy when I got out my two bottles of claret, stipulating a single draught only for myself.

Our party consisted of General Grant and myself, Colonel Grant, and Mrs. Holcombe; Mr. [Charles W.] Deering, Mr. [Charles] Belknap, and Mr. [Augustus L.] Case, [Jr.], officers of the *Ashuelot*; Mr. Young, Mr. Pethick, and Mr. [Charles E.] Hill, who very kindly acted as admiral of the flotilla. After a long, weary ride, we arrived at the gates of Pekin. The walls around the city were very high and very wide, and one might feel safe indeed if on the inside. We noticed that the people here were larger than at Canton and Shanghai. The streets were wide and unpaved. They were very dusty. We were glad to see our dear old flag floating over the Legation, as this was our haven of rest. We were the guests of Mr. and Mrs. Holcombe while at Pekin.

The first evening, a number of American residents called on the General. Also the Chinese cabinet officers called and welcomed General Grant in the name of Prince Kung, Vice-Regent of the Empire, the Emperor being then a mere lad. The General saw Prince Kung the next day. The General and party left our residence about noon and went to the palace of the Prince Regent. After being received by the Prince, they were conducted to a table covered with Chinese delicacies such as bird's nests, plover's eggs, and shark's fins. Our gentlemen had just finished luncheon and could not take any of these delicacies.

They told me on their return that the Prince asked Fred if he were married and if he had any children. Fred told him, "Yes, one—a daughter." The Prince said, showing much sympathy, "Oh, what a pity." Dear little Julia, we do not agree with Prince Kung; we are very proud of our little girlie.

The Prince returned the General's call very promptly. As there were some of the officers of the *Richmond* off on a holiday at Pekin as well as those from the *Ashuelot*, the General invited all of them to assist him in receiving Prince Kung, whom he found to be an earnest and able man. The General seemed impressed with the Prince's ability. The gentlemen said to me: "His voice was low and impressive, his manner most captivating." The Viceroy had already made a deep and lasting impression on General Grant. They discussed matters of state with the General and seemed to feel great anxiety for the stability of the friendship between the United States and China. I only wish their hopes may be realized. It is a great loss to our country to lose the friendship and commerce of a great nation like China. All European nations are fostering her friendship and encouraging her bitterness towards us. We will discover our mistake too late, I fear.

The day after this interchange of ceremonies, there came from Prince Kung, who represented the government, some handsome presents to General Grant: several vases, not large but fine, old, and rare; specimens of Chinese shoes, so small they were and wrought in gold on scarlet cloth; sheaths for dirks and knives; tobacco pouches, etc. We enjoyed immensely examining the curious things Mr. Holcombe allowed the merchants to bring inside the court, or, as it is called in Eastern countries, the compound of the Legation, where we could view them with comfort. I was fortunate enough to secure some fine bits of jade, some enamels, fine embroideries, and, best of all, two large, beautiful, blue cloisonné vases, which last nearly exhausted my purse, but I have now the pleasure of seeing them in my drawing room. I also bought several fine, dark, sable skins.

On our return to Tien-tsin, we had more entertainments, garden parties, and dinners. I must try to give a correct account of the entertainment given to me by the wife of the Viceroy Li Hung Chang. It was a great honor and a *very* unusual one. I think there were six ladies invited: Mrs. and Miss Denny, Mrs. and Miss Dillon, a missionary lady who interpreted for us, and myself. I cannot recall what I wore, but the other ladies were all prettily dressed. The ladies assembled at the U. S. Consulate, where the Viceroy's chairs were sent to convey us to his residence. These chairs were hung in yellow silk. We had a mounted escort, dressed in yellow, to escort us from the Consulate to the Viceroy's yamen. When my chair, which went in advance, arrived at the court of the yamen, the bearers ascended a few steps; then there was a great flourish of trumpets, and my chair was rested on the stone floor of a grand vestibule which was spanned by a fine arch. As my chair was lowered, the curtain was gently lifted, and a voice said: "Madam, you have arrived at the yamen."

As I stepped out of my chair, the door near me rolled back, and I saw a Chinese lady and her attendants before me. The usher simply said: "Lady Li—Madam Grant." Lady Li took my hand and welcomed me in a dignified but cordial manner. She stood inside of the doorsill, which was unusually high, and she tried to assist me. She took my arm, and with her attendant walking on her other side, we walked through a long corridor to the library, where upon a lovely, little, simple table of natural wood was a teapot, cups, and saucers of dainty blue china. The library was also in plain wood. The shelves and upright pieces were all of the same undressed wood as the table; that is, without either lacquer or varnish. The books were in rolls like manuscript, tied with dark, silken cords. The floor was polished, and on it lay a rug of soft, white matting. The appointments were exquisitely elegant and simple.

When I had finished my cup of delicious tea, Lady Li took my hand and led me to the drawing room, where the other ladies of our party soon assembled and were presented to our distinguished hostess. I do not remember whether this room was as elegantly simple as the library or not, but I think not. Two young ladies, a daughter of Lady Li and a son's wife, were now presented to us. The Chinese ladies were dressed in the costume of their country, with long jackets very beautifully embroidered and skirts of rich material. Their hair was elaborately and beautifully dressed. Madam was dressed in a more matronly manner than her daughters. They were all refined and elegant in feature, in manner, and in dress.

[290]

The table was similar to ours and handsomely furnished, with many flowers; at each place, there was a variety of glasses and a pretty porcelain plate filled with nuts, which the Chinese ladies were constantly tasting between the courses. I liked this custom so well that I have adopted it. We had a course of European food and cooking, and then a Chinese course, alternately. Out of compliment to my hostess, I partook only of the Chinese courses. The bird's-nest soup was served in a small bowl. It was so delicious that I ate the whole of mine and was entirely satisfied.

Madam Li was astonished that when she proposed to drink my health in a glass of sparkling champagne I only tasted it. She turned to the missionary lady, who was our interpreter, and said she wished to drink my health. I said: "Yes, I know that, fully understood you, and have acknowledged your compliment by tasting of your delicious wine." Lady Li said: "I have been told that it is the custom to take the full glass when one's health is drunk." I said, laughing, "Oh, no. That is not so. What I did is our custom. If we finished the glass, I am afraid we should stay all night with Lady Li."

After dinner, Miss Dillon and Miss Denny played on the piano and sang a few ballads; they even waltzed. Whilst this was going on, a handsome young son of the Viceroy entered the drawing room. He was remarkably handsome. He had no beard and looked like a lovely girl. He wore a long, pale-blue silk gown, which was very becoming, and his hair hung down his back in a long, single plait. It was now time to make our adieux. Farewells were said, and wishes that we might meet again were exchanged. When we arrived at home, we found a roll of pretty China silk for each lady as a souvenir of our visit to Lady Li.

We left our kind friends at the Consulate that night and went aboard the *Richmond*. In the early morn, she lifted her anchors and steamed down the Pei-ho. The shipping was again gaily dressed; crowds lined the banks, gazing with interested faces upon the *Richmond*. The Viceroy had gone down on his own yacht. After General Grant had received all honors, the Viceroy was received aboard the *Richmond* with similar honors. Our naval officers were in full dress uniform and were a handsome lot of men. The Viceroy was much interested. He examined the ship and its workings. Li Hung-chang seemed loath to part with General Grant and was almost affectionate towards the General. He spoke of the friendship of the United States as dear to China and begged the General to use his influence in behalf of his people in America. The parting was most friendly, and as the Viceroy descended to his yacht, the band played our national airs, the yards were manned, and the *Richmond* fired a parting salute to our distinguished friend, the Viceroy of Tien-tsin.

The *Richmond* hoisted her anchors and slowly steamed through the smooth blue waters of the China Sea. We followed up the coast as far as the end of the great Chinese wall, which we reached about noon. We all went ashore. I gathered some shells and pebbles. The wall is high and wide, but I do not think it would have hindered our Sheridan. If he could not have passed through, he surely would have climbed over it. The day was glorious. A marine registered our visit on the wall with a brush and white paint.

We had smooth seas all the afternoon and night, and in the morning we arrived at Chefoo, a port which is the Newport of China. The General was again the recipient of many honors. The landing was handsomely decorated with the flags of all nations. There were great crowds of people, as well as a double line of Chinese soldiers, stretching from the landing up to the Consulate. General Grant and I were carried in chairs amidst firing of cannon, beating of gongs, and other national music.

We arrived at the Consulate, where we had luncheon. The General met the Chinese officials and went over the town. In the evening, there was a brilliant ball at the house of Mr. and Mrs. [C. L.] Simpson. At midnight, we were conducted back to our ship with great ceremony, received salutes, and returned them, late as it was. We could not let China outdo us in civility.

In the morning, the sea was very rough. The gentlemen teased me a great deal because I wrote them a note from my cabin telling them of a very dangerous rock that was located somewhere in the China Sea. I had heard the young officers of the *Ashuelot* tell of it and of its location, and I feared from the wild way we had been drifting about that we must be nearing it, and begged they would consult the chart.

The next morning, the skies were clear, and we were making our way through lovely green islands. On the 21st of June, we arrived in the Bay of Nagasaki, where the tall, white cliffs, capped by a luxuriant growth of vines and pines, were reflected in the clear, deep waters below. The *Richmond* ran the Japanese flag to the fore and fired a salute of twenty-one guns. The forts and gunboats in the harbor sent up the United States flag and gave it a like salute, then fired twenty-one guns for the General. The U. S. Consul, Mr. [Willie P.] Mangum, came on board to welcome General Grant. Directly, a vessel approached with Prince Dati [Date Munenari] and Mr. Yoshida [Kiyonari] (whom we had known in America as Japanese minister), who were received with the usual ceremonies. Prince Dati was the Mikado's representative; Mr. Yoshida had been called home from the United States to be present at the time of General Grant's visit. It was a great pleasure to meet him again, as he had been an old friend of ours in Washington. Prince Dati was a high officer in the Emperor's government. He was most loyal to the Mikado's government and had, I was told, laid aside his great rank and domains in order to serve the Emperor. Prince Dati was as accomplished as he was loyal. We all held him in high esteem.

At one o'clock, General Grant, Colonel Grant, and I were escorted on board the Japanese barge by Prince Dati and Mr. Yoshida. As we boarded the Japanese vessel, salutes were fired, yards were manned, and cheers greeted us as we passed slowly towards the landing, which was covered with red cloth. Lines of troops were formed, and great crowds gathered to see the nation's guest.

Soon after landing, we took our seats in jinrikshas about the size of an infant's perambulator. Each one of these had for this occasion two men to a carriage; only one is needed usually. In these beautiful little vehicles, which had been sent all the way from Tokio for us, we were conducted to our residence about one mile away. The streets were beautiful, adorned with flags, flowers, and lanterns, and the crowds bowed low as the General passed. A beautifully furnished house was prepared for our use. The U. S. Minister, Mr. John A. Bingham, came from Tokio to meet us.

The Governor gave a grand dinner to General Grant, which I did not attend, as it was for gentlemen only. The citizens of Nagasaki gave a *real* Japanese dinner, which lasted several hours. The menu was wonderful both in novelty and variety. In addition to music by young ladies, the beautiful butterfly dance was performed—not by professionals but by the young ladies of the town, I was told. Then followed a short scene in which there was a forest and a lake and a fisherman who caught fish which were served alive on our table. When I mentioned this to a Japanese gentleman as something shocking, he smilingly said: "I am sure you serve live oysters as a favorite course on your tables in the United States, do you not?" It was so, but we had never thought of that.

> O wad some Pow'r the giftie gie us
> To see oursels as others see us!
> It wad frae mony a blunder free us

As we rode home, the town was brilliantly illuminated with arches of lanterns, flags, flowers, and bonfires. This entertainment was a great honor and was appreciated as such by all.

We saw everything there was to be seen at Nagasaki. We attended the Exposition, where I bought a few pretty things: a desk, a few plaques, and some pretty tortoiseshell articles. I also bought a handsome set of black china decorated in colored flowers, but this I unfortunately lost, as it was claimed, after our return to New York, by one of our party who also had ordered or bought a set.

The Governor requested the General and me each to plant a tree in memory of our visit to Nagasaki. This was done before a large company. The Governor said that Nagasaki intended erecting a monument to commemorate General Grant's visit, and if the General would write an inscription it should be engraved on the stone in English and Japanese. The General wrote as follows:

> Nagasaki, Japan.
> June 22d 1879.
> At the request of Governor Utsumi Tadakalsuu Mrs. Grant and I each planted a tree in the Nagasaki park. I hope that both trees may prosper, grow large, live long, and in their growth, prosperity and long life be emblematic of the future of Japan.
>
> U. S. Grant
> Julia D. Grant.[6]

We re-embarked on board the *Richmond*. Prince Dati remained on his own ship, but Mr. Yoshida and other gentlemen escorted General Grant to the *Richmond*. We were accompanied still by the *Ashuelot* and, since entering the Japanese waters, by one of their splendid gunboats, commanded by Captain Ito.

It was dark and cloudy when we put out to sea, but the next morning was glorious. The Inland Sea of Japan is a dream of loveliness. To appreciate it, you must see it as we did. Three ships were in company: the flagship *Richmond*, a Japanese man-of-war, and the gallant little *Ashuelot*. The *Richmond* had a fine band and a noble group of officers, all bent on being as happy and as bright as the sparkling sea and the glorious day itself. I wish I could tell how happy we were as we sat on deck surrounded by friends, listening to the band's best efforts, and watching the young officers signaling the morning greetings to our sister ships.

In the evening, we always came to anchor and then visited from ship to ship. We dined in state on board the flagship. General Grant gave two dinners to the officers of the ships and his guests. The Japanese officers also gave a large dinner or two. The ships were all dressed and illuminated with Japanese lanterns hung all through the rigging. It was like a fairy scene. Those three beautiful ships as we saw them against the sky, the young moon and the bright stars, and the rippling sea around us added to the beauty.

Can I ever forget the many civilities and kind attentions we received from these charming people? The fireworks from the Japanese ship were beautiful. We rarely stopped at any of the villages, as the cholera was making its appearance, and the Japanese authorities were afraid of it. We had a view of the hills and mountains which lay on either side and upon which lay some picturesque villages.

Great preparations were made to receive General Grant at Hiogo, but we were not permitted to land, as the scourge had already reached there. We came to anchor, and our Consul, General [Julius] Stahel, came out to see us, as did the Governor, who informed the General that a palace was ready for his reception and he hoped yet to have the honor of a visit from him. A committee also came out with an invitation for the General which, of course, was declined. The illuminated city looked beautiful as we saw it from the sea.

A sad accident happened one morning. A young sailor far out on the bowsprit of the *Richmond* fell overboard. Everyone saw him. He caught a rope which is left out for such a purpose, but this only turned him so that his face headed forward, his mouth filled with water, and he sank. The lifeboats were quickly lowered, but he never rose again.

The *Richmond* came to anchor in the Bay of Sumida [Suruga]. This bay is not an open port; that is, ships are not allowed to anchor there. We were there as guests of the Emperor. This bay and its surroundings are beautiful. We enjoyed seeing some fish that had been caught to show us. They were placed in troughs, or vats, filled with clear water. Some of them were strange and beautiful. I remember one with fins which looked like the wings of a butterfly, rivaling in coloring even our most beautiful ones.

We visited a teahouse; that is, a house where they prepare tea for export. It was very interesting to watch the pretty little Japanese girls picking and assorting tea. As we passed through the villages, long rows of children, all well-dressed in their native costumes, came out to increase the pageant. These dear little creatures bowed low as the General passed, but I noticed they all, Eve-like, took a long side-glance after he had passed. With their bright eyes, glossy black hair, and silver-gray dresses, they reminded me of the swallows I used to see at home. As we passed up the roads in our jinrikshas, a delightful odor of burning sandalwood was in the air. I suppose it was burned in the temples.

[295]

The roads were perfect and were shaded by overhanging and interlaced boughs of great trees. There were many really pretty, quaint, little cottages along the roadside, each a picture in itself. We bowled over these fine roads and, at about noon, arrived at Shiguoka [Shizuoka]. Visitors rarely come here, and as we rode through the streets, they were as eager to see us as we were to view them. The town was pretty and clean. The bazaars were full of beautiful Japanese lacquerwork.

After luncheon, we had some wonderful fireworks in the daytime. One of the pieces was a remarkable one. It made a sort of cloud in the sky and shot out fans and ribbons. Then another rocket burst, and a young woman appeared, deliberately raised her umbrella, then walked with stately and measured step across the sky. This one, I was told, represented the "Girl of the Period." And again, when the cloud burst and cleared away, behold a gigantic man appeared striding across the sky, dressed in black, on his head a stovepipe hat, and in his hand a huge satchel, representing, I suppose, a carpetbagger going south, or, mayhap, an American globe-trotter.

We all enjoyed the day and rode back to our ship, which steamed towards Yokohama, which came in view about ten o'clock, July 3rd. Admiral [Thomas H.] Patterson's flagship, the *Monongahela*, thundered out her salute of twenty-one guns in welcome to General Grant.

As we neared the harbor, the Japanese escort passed in ahead of our ship. The *Richmond* and the *Ashuelot* entered the harbor slowly. The flagship fired its salute to General Grant first. Then the *Richmond* saluted the Japanese flag. These were returned by the forts and ships, and the roar of cannon continued for nearly an hour. The guns of Russia, Germany, France, and England thundered out their welcome to General Grant. The General received calls from the various officials on the deck of the *Richmond*. It was a brilliant scene, as all were in full dress and some of the uniforms were gorgeous. When the Imperial barge came alongside, General Grant and I, escorted by Prince Dati, Mr. Yoshida, Colonel Grant, and several of our navy officers, passed over the side and went aboard the royal boat.

As soon as the General went on board the barge, the *Richmond* manned her yards and fired a salute. The Japanese, English, French, and Russian men-of-war did likewise. We steamed slowly to the landing, and as the smoke cleared away, a magnificent sight met our eyes: gallant men-of-war with the yards manned, flags flying, their quarterdecks crowded with officers and sailors in full uniform, the music, the cheers repeated again and again. Can I ever forget it? As the General reached the landing, the Japanese bands played our national airs.

[296]

The princes and high officers of Japan were there to meet him. We were taken by special trains to Tokio, which we reached in less than an hour, and found a vast crowd assembled at the depot. We entered the Emperor's private carriage, which was in waiting. We were escorted by a troop of cavalry and drove through long lines of infantry, which gave the General "present arms" as he passed. The streets were decorated with arches of evergreens and flowers, and, of course, were crowded with citizens. The carriage drove on and on until, with a flourish of trumpets and beating of drums, we halted at the drawbridge of the Emperor's summer palace, the beautiful Enriokwan [Enryōkan].

July 4th was selected by the Mikado as the most suitable for his audience with General Grant, and this was the day for which the arrangements were made. Early in the afternoon of that day, the General and I, with Colonel Grant, Minister Bingham, Admiral Patterson, Commander [Andrew E. K.] Benham, Mr. Young, and a number of others drove out to the palace—a long drive over bridges and across moats. We were surprised at not finding the palace full of beautiful cloisonné, lacquerwork, and embroideries, but there were none of these. It contained the simplest furniture. The salons, however, were lofty and wide. We entered the audience hall, at the end of which Their Majesties were standing. The Emperor was dressed in uniform, the Empress in a court robe of ruby velvet over a white silk skirt. Her hair was dressed in beautiful, wide plaits arranged in a large bow on the back of her head. On her forehead she wore a small jeweled coronet or, rather, an aigrette, resembling the end of a peacock feather. The Empress was young and fair and delicate-looking. She said a few words of welcome to me through an interpreter, to which I made a suitable reply.

On this occasion, I wore a lovely, rich, mauve silk gown made by Worth, demi-train, trimmed with exquisite Brussels lace. My pretty hat was a dainty cluster of flowers and lace, and as I looked in my mirror after dressing, I was, I assure you, in full sympathy with the modern philosopher who says, "A pretty gown gives the greatest peace of mind to a woman."

This ride to and from the palace was, as I have said, long and fatiguing, and it required some patriotism and more courage for me again to enter the carriage for another long ride to attend the dinner given by our American friends to welcome General Grant on this same evening, the Fourth of July.

NOTES

1. *Paul et Virginie* (1788), a novel by Jacques Henri Bernardin de Saint-Pierre, was set in Mauritius, where Bernardin had lived for three years. A friend and disciple of Jean Jacques Rousseau, Bernardin incorporated ideas about the advantages of natural simplicity in his popular romantic novel.
2. As the Grants toured Asia in early 1879, the U.S. Congress passed a bill prohibiting the landing in the U.S. of more than fifteen Chinese passengers from any single ship. On March 1, 1879, President Rutherford B. Hayes vetoed this effort to control Chinese immigration as a violation of the 1868 Burlingame treaty with China. Negotiation of a new treaty in 1880 which permitted U.S. restrictions led to the Chinese Exclusion Act of 1882. In his annual message to Congress, December 7, 1874, President Grant had stated that most Chinese immigrants came to the U.S. under contract to persons "who own them almost absolutely." In particular, Chinese women were "brought for shameful purposes," and he urged remedial legislation. U.S. Congress, *Congressional Record*, 43rd Cong., 2nd sess., 1874, pt. 1, 4.
3. Probably Nora Bews Roberts, wife of Sir Frederick Sleigh Roberts, commander of the Punjab frontier force, who was then engaged in campaigns in Afghanistan.
4. Grant's speech at Penang received coverage in the *Straits Times* (Singapore), April 5, 1879.
5. The office (sometimes also the residence) of a Chinese official.
6. The text of this note has been altered to agree with a photocopy prepared in 1931 at Nagasaki, now in the Missouri Historical Society, St. Louis. Julia Grant's signature does not appear on the original. The name of Governor Utsumi Tadakatsu is thus transliterated in his dinner invitation of June 22, 1879. Grant Papers, Library of Congress.

Chapter 11

—◆—

T HE DAY WAS one we celebrate at home, and the Americans living at and near Tokio had arranged to give a dinner and ball that night. It was a very nice affair, and we all enjoyed it greatly. Speeches were made—good ones too—and toasts were drunk. The General and his party left soon after dinner, but we learned that the others remained until the wee small hours.

On the seventh, the Emperor ordered a military review for the General, which was very interesting. The Emperor was present and conversed with General Grant. After the review, we drove to the beautiful Shiba Palace near the sea, where the Emperor gave the General a regal breakfast. The Emperor met us in a large salon and conducted the General to the breakfast room.

During this delightful repast, the Emperor conversed much with the General. His Majesty expressed a desire, I was told, to have a long conversation with the General, and it was arranged to take place after our return from Nikko. The foreign ministers and their wives were present at the breakfast. The table appointments were superb. During our stay at this palace, fountains were playing so as to water the shrubbery and to cool the air. I was gratified at meeting here again our good friends Mr. and Mrs. Pope-Hennessy. They seemed like old friends to me.

The view from the palace windows was grand. A beautiful lake was near, the banks of which were covered with beautiful, emerald-green grass and flowers. The air was kept cool by the falling water from the fountains. The ride from here to our beautiful palace, Enriokwan, was not long, and I was glad to reach its cool shelter, where I could lie on a couch and rest. I was very tired but was much interested by all I saw and heard.

The Japanese ladies, pretty, bright, and happy, reminded me of so many singing, chirping canary birds, nodding their pretty heads, fluttering and flapping their airy wings. They were so gay, so gentle, so pretty, and birdlike in their brightness and cheerfulness.

The days were occupied in receiving visits from officials, receiving and returning social calls, and visiting the bazaars in search of curios. The merchants brought everything to the palace, but it was very pleasant to go out ourselves sometimes and pick up things not brought to us. We always had company to dinner: the princes and their wives, the officials, and often the officers from our good ships. We also had often Mr. Yoshida and Minister Bingham and their families. We roamed over the beautiful grounds, rowed on the miniature lakes, fished from the bridges, and looked over the novel and beautiful merchandise brought there for our inspection. We were there during several fête days. The feast of lanterns was a wonderful sight. There was a tournament and races. The paraphernalia of the horses was rich but too heavy. We were seated under a mammoth umbrella.

There was a special theatrical entertainment given in honor of General Grant where all the pretty actresses were dressed in American flags made of crepe, and their dresses were very pretty. The actresses said they would play in honor of General Grant and declared they would not receive any remuneration for their services. The General ordered a handsome red cloth drop curtain for their theater as an expression of his appreciation of the compliment. This performance was attended by all of the royal princes and their ladies, all foreign officers in port, and many native officials, all in full uniform. The occasion was long remembered in Tokio and by all present.

An entertainment was given at Yokohama by the merchants and officials which, if possible, surpassed all others in the decorations, the feast, and the good feeling. I enjoyed my visits to the shops and ordered embroideries, quilts, and embroidered silk double gowns.

We enjoyed the visit to Nikko, eighty-two miles away through this lovely land of flowers and finely cultivated lands. We paused and rested at charming little villages. We had a carriage, but I liked the jinriksha and rode a long distance in one which had been taken for me in case I got tired of the carriage and wanted a change. The road was beautiful and good. Great trees, said to be over three hundred years old, spread their interlaced boughs over our path and formed a grateful shade, and they were full of forest birds. As the General and I rode along under this beautiful arch, I said to him, "Look up and see this arch. St. Peter's does not compare with it. It is so lofty and so graceful." "Yes," he said, "I have been admiring it. Some of these trees are very, very old."

Our party consisted of General Grant and I, Colonel Grant, Prince Dati, Mr. Yoshida, and Mr. Tateno [Gōzō]. When we arrived at the shrine of Iyeyas [Iyeyasu], we went to the temple, listened to the music, and looked upon all the relics of the heroes buried near.

We were domiciled in the houses of the priests of the temple. They were exquisitely simple. The houses were of plain wood, unpainted and unvarnished, and were one story in height, with a long range of rooms and a piazza running the whole length of the house which fronted towards the south. In front there was an extensive and beautiful lawn, with a lake filled with fish which were daily fed by me. The lake was bridged over in two or three narrow places. The distant mountains, the valleys, and the great trees added to the beauty of the scene, and the roar of the rushing river added music to it.

General Grant had many visitors from the capital and held long and earnest conversations with them. "It was at Nikko that General Grant met the representatives of the Japanese government who came to speak to him officially of the difficulty between China and Japan on the Loochoo question." [1] I am now quoting from John Russell Young in his book, *Around the World with General Grant.*

This conference, which may some day have historical value, took place on the 22d of July. General Grant had intimated to the Japanese government, on his arrival in Tokio, that he had received a communication from the Chinese government which he would like to present officially to the Japanese cabinet, if he could do so without appearing to interfere in their concerns. The Emperor sent Mr. Ito [Itō Hirobumi], Minister of the Interior, and General Saigo [Saigō Tsugumichi], the Minister of War, to receive the statement. Mr. Ito presented the case of Japan at length, contending that Japan's rights of sovereignty over Loochoo were immemorial, and going over the whole question. When Ito had finished, General Grant said that he had been anxious to have this conversation with the Japanese government, because it enabled him to fulfill a promise he had made to Prince Kung and the Viceroy, Li Hung Chang. He had read the Chinese case and studied it. He had heard with great interest the case of Japan. As to the merits of the controversy he had no opinion to express. There were many points, the General said, in both cases, which were historical and could only be determined by research. His entire interest arose from his kind feeling toward both Japan and

China, in whose continued prosperity America and the entire world were interested. Japan, the General said, had done wonders in the past few years. She was, in point of war materials, army and navy, stronger than China. Against Japan, China, he might say, was defenseless, and it was impossible for China to injure Japan. Consequently, Japan could look at the question from a high point of view. At the same time, China was a country of wonderful resources, and although he had seen nothing there to equal the progress of Japan, there had nevertheless been great progress.

And how true this prediction of General Grant has proved. He was a philosopher and a wise statesman as well as a great soldier.

We made a picnic excursion to a famous waterfall, as renowned as our Minnehaha. We were overtaken by a terrific thunderstorm but were unharmed. On our way back to Tokio, great ovations were given us in every town and village through which we passed. We made a detour in order to visit Kanagawa, with its fine silk factories. We crossed a beautiful, wide, shallow river where, instead of being rowed over, we were drawn in boats by fishermen who waded, dressed only in a fringe of rushes around the waist—very picturesque and certainly very appropriate for a water dress.

On our return to Tokio, we visited the schools and all places of interest. The old palace, the home of the last tycoon, was very interesting, and the grounds were beautiful. There was to be a new and more substantial modern palace built for the Emperor.

The festival at Uyeno [Ueno] was one of the last and most important of all the entertainments during our stay in Japan. Extensive preparations were made for it; the streets were most profusely decorated. It took place on the 25th of August. Several of our naval officers lunched with General Grant, and after luncheon we drove from our residence, Enriokwan, through the streets in the state carriages for about three miles, escorted by a troop of cavalry. The escort was considered necessary, as some malicious foreigners had started the rumor that the livers of all the cholera patients who died in the hospitals were to be taken out and sold to General Grant for a thousand dollars each, as he wanted them for talismans.[2] The ride was exciting and interesting. We rode for quite three miles through streets decorated with flowers, long lines of lamps, and the flags of the United States and of Japan.

As we approached the park, there was one vast sea of faces, all eager to get a glimpse of General Grant. As we entered the park, our carriage passed slowly through a long line of infantry which presented arms, and the band played our national airs. A committee requested General Grant and me to each plant a tree, which we were happy to do. A tablet recording the event, engraved both in English and Japanese, had been prepared beforehand. Soon after the General arrived, the trumpets signaled the approach of the Emperor, who came in honor of General Grant—an unusual attention from a Japanese Emperor. The Emperor was driven to his marquee, where he received General Grant and afterwards all of the foreign ministers. There were feats of horsemanship, music, and a good deal of visiting among the gentlemen, who came to converse with the ladies. Then there was a superb dinner; all of the cabinet ministers and many others were present.

Then we drove home, or to our lovely Enriokwan, which was beginning to seem like home to us. The way was beautiful, enchanting, with its thousands of lamps, flags, words of welcome written in light, and the myriads of human faces eagerly pressing forward, anxious to see the man for whom all this was done. They were all reading the life of General Grant which had been printed in Japanese and distributed throughout the country.[3] I often saw the young attendants at our palace reading these little books eagerly.

Admiral Patterson gave an entertainment on the *Richmond*, but I was too fatigued to attend. Again, we had a long, delightful journey over the mountains, through long shady roads, over hill and dale, to visit a beautiful cataract. We rested two nights going and returning. I was very happy as we went flying through the meadows of tall grasses, spangled with great, beautiful Japanese lilies and pinks. One of my jinriksha men would dart off and gather great sprays of these beautiful flowers, often ten or twelve lilies on a single stalk, lay them in my lap, and seem much pleased that I enjoyed them. I was singing nearly all of the time and was gleeful and happy. I had grown so accustomed to the presence of the gentlemen that I felt quite at my ease with them—grand, noble fellows they were, all of them.

We stopped at the sulphur springs, and I enjoyed a lovely bath which had been heated away down in some subterranean furnace. We also tarried by a lovely lake where an American officer who was on duty in Japan was spending his vacation with his family. I had had so much exercise that I begged the General to let me remain here all night while he went on a visit to Hakone, a place nearby. The General had a lovely visit and regretted that I had not accompanied him. While at this summer resort, I had delightful walks through groves of old trees and also visited several temples in the vicinity. The priests seemed so gentle, so pure, and so near to their God—and so it seemed at all of these holy shrines we visited.

It was beginning to draw near the time for our departure for home. Our orders for embroideries, etc., had to be looked after, and all of the pretty things already purchased had to be packed. Each day brought new temptations, as the merchants came each morning with new fabrics and more curios. Their Majesties, the Emperor and Empress, sent us many beautiful and valuable souvenirs of our visit: rolls of superb silk, vases, cabinets, and several very fine photograph albums. The Governor of Hakone sent us some beautiful presents. I have all of mine yet, of course, but General Grant's are now in Washington.

Our last days at the lovely Enriokwan were so full of kindnesses from our friends, new acquaintances, and our exalted host and hostess that my heart is too full to write of them. We had dinners, receptions, and teas. I can recall vividly the evening we passed at the countryseat of Prince Dati. His charming residence was situated by the sea, whose murmurings come back to me even now to remind me of that delightful evening. There was also a dinner at the Prime Minister's, Prince [Sanjō Sanetomi], and we had a charming time with the many distinguished people who were present. There was also a grand dinner and reception by Mr. Mori [Arinori], whom we had known as the Japanese minister in Washington, now vice-minister of foreign affairs. Mr. Yoshida and Mr. Terashima [Munenari] also gave beautiful dinners. I got to know Madam Saigo quite well. She was with her husband, General Saigo, when he visited the General at Nikko. The General thought highly of General Saigo's ability. Our Minister, John A. Bingham, and Admiral Patterson also gave elegant entertainments.

General Grant had his farewell audience with the Emperor on Saturday, after which all entertainments ceased. We were fully and pleasantly occupied on Saturday and Sunday in receiving calls from the official dignitaries and their families, officers of the navy, and others; in wandering around over the grounds again; and in visiting the pretty Japanese teahouses scattered through the grounds. The many incidents of these last few days are so crowded in my mind that I fear I cannot do them justice.

Monday, we made the trip to Yokohama, where the very last pretty thing was secured. Tuesday, the day we were to have sailed, was a gala day. Our Japanese friends arranged a farewell dinner.[4] Our guests were several of the Japanese cabinet officers and their wives, our Minister, Mr. Bingham, Mr. Yoshida, Admiral Patterson, Captain Benham and ladies, and our party of four. The table was, as usual, covered with beautiful china and glass, and exquisite Satsuma vases filled with the loveliest of flowers. The viands and fruits could not have been surpassed in any country. Toasts were passed with great good feeling. After dinner, our number of callers grew into a reception, and we had a brilliant evening. I cannot recall a more glorious one than this, our last in Japan, in our lovely residence at Enriokwan. Several of the royal princes and their wives called in full dress, all of the cabinet officers and their families, all the foreign ministers, and, lastly, the officers from our four ships, all in full uniform. This formed a galaxy of rank, beauty, and youth in dazzling array. The salons were superb and decked in flowers, the music was fine, the lawn was hung with lanterns, and wonderful fireworks added to the effect.

At last, all felt the time had come to say good-night and goodbye. General Grant and I, the Colonel, Mr. Young, and a few others sat on the pretty veranda until quite late, talking over the delightful evening, Japan, and the Japanese. We were loath to leave this charming Enriokwan and these charming people.

Early next morning, as the General gave me his arm to take me to the breakfast room, he said: "You must take your last look at these beautiful things and these pretty rooms; we must be off at once, for you know the tides will not wait for you." I did take a last, long, loving look at my pretty bedroom, with its low windows looking out on a rose garden, and tarried for a few moments in the exquisitely decorated drawing room, over the walls of which were thrown lovely fans. The salon was lovely. An artist had spent much time and talent in its decoration. I will not attempt to describe it further than to say that it was Japanese and very beautiful. I took a last look out at the lovely grounds and said farewell to Enriokwan.

The General called for me, the Imperial carriages were at the door; so, bidding a smiling farewell to our faithful attendants, we entered the coaches. Accompanied by Prince Dati, many high officials, and friends, and escorted by the cavalry and infantry, we drove slowly to the depot through long lines of troops and crowded streets. Mr. Iwakura [Tomomi] escorted me into the Imperial car, where I found Mrs. Yoshida and Mrs. Mori, who went with us to Yokohama. As the train moved out slowly, the troops presented arms and friends waved goodbyes. The General stood on the platform and raised his hat in a farewell salute. As we sped past the stations, we saw crowds assembled but did not stop at any place until we reached Yokohama, where we found the crowd as large as on our first arrival. The Governor and the troops were there, and the band played our national airs. The Governor escorted us to a carriage, and we drove to the Admiralty wharf, where we found Admiral Patterson, Captain Benham, and Commanders [Robert] Boyd [Jr.] and [Mortimer L.] Johnson waiting for us. We remained at the Admiralty for luncheon. The General went aboard a barge accompanied by these gentlemen, while Admiral [Sumiyoshi] Kawamura escorted me.

[305]

We moved away amid the roar of cannon, music, the flashing of fireworks, and the loud huzzas and shouts of farewell. We were received on board the *City of Tokio* by Commodore Maury. During the short time we had to say goodbye, the deck of the *City of Tokio* was crowded and made a brilliant scene. The officers of the U. S. squadron came, as did friends from Yokohama, among them princes, noblemen, ministers, and others, whose guests we had been and who had entertained us so royally. It was hard to say all we wished at parting in the short time we had. Many of our Japanese friends went on board a Japanese man-of-war which escorted us far out on our way to sea.

As we passed our U. S. ships, the yards were manned, and each ship fired a salute. The officers came to the quarterdecks and waved farewells. God bless them all, the dear, nice fellows! Our Japanese friends accompanied us for two or three hours. At last, the roar of a gun was heard, and we knew that this was farewell, farewell indeed. We all hastened to the side of the ship to wave our final adieux. The yards of the Japanese man-of-war were manned, the sailors sent up ringing cheers, and the ship slowly turned around and sped back to Yokohama. We waved our scarfs and handkerchiefs and stood and watched until they were far, far away. Their princely hospitalities and many kindnesses were fully appreciated by all of us, and we had only kind words to say of our Japanese friends. Our grand ship, the *City of Tokio*, swept bravely and majestically on, her prow "in the deep bosom of the ocean buried" as she glided over the calm waters of the Pacific.

The weather was like our own glorious Indian summer. Our accommodations were luxurious. The General and I occupied the Captain's cabin on deck, which was commodious and elegantly furnished. One half hour was devoted to a promenade each morning and evening, and upon the spacious decks we made the acquaintance of our fellow passengers. The gentlemen smoked, and I retired to my cabin and nestled down on my couch among soft pillows while my faithful and kind maid read to me from *Les Misérables*.

Thus day followed day, until one morning Colonel Grant made his appearance and said: "Mamma, can't you devise some way of keeping father up on deck?" "Why, yes," I said, "but why, Fred?" "Well, I am so eternally tired of playing Boston, and it seems to me that father will never weary of it, and I am sure the other men are tired too. Why, mother, I am afraid I will grow like one of those holy men of India in a sitting position. I am so stiff that I can hardly stand straight now. Can't you keep father?" "Of course I can, but I see well enough what is the matter with you, Fred. Your father is beating you every time. I see that."

So when the General came for his morning walk, I inquired, "Have you read Hugo's *Les Misérables*?" "No," he replied, "I started to read it on the James River but was interrupted so frequently that I only read a few pages." I said: "I am reading it now and have just finished the first volume. It is intensely interesting and powerful. Just read the first fifty pages and you will hardly be willing to put it down until you have finished it." He replied, "Well, I will. Give me the first volume, for I am heartily tired of playing Boston and, after I have my cigar, I will begin it." He soon sought the shelter of my cabin wall to read, and he read all day long and the next day and the next, until he had finished the first volume when I was but halfway through the second, but he did not know that when I surrendered it to him, saying, "I am so happy to have suggested the book since it has proved so interesting to you." I finished it months afterwards at home.

So the time passed. As we neared home, the lady passengers began to grow a little nervous in regard to the dutiable articles they had in their baggage, and I was questioned not a little as to what I had to declare. I was quite disturbed for a moment, then I laughed and replied, "I have been around the world; it is quite impossible for me to remember all that I have, and I shall leave it to the customhouse officer to find out what I must pay."

At last it was announced that in half an hour we should see land. We ladies, womanlike, hastened to our cabins for fresh gloves, veils, etc., then joined the gentlemen, who were standing well forward on the deck, glasses in hand, watching eagerly as Columbus did for the first sight of land. What a shout went up when our beloved shores came in view! Then we saw a procession of ships which approached in pairs, separated as they neared us, passed on either side of us, closed in again after they passed, and escorted us in through the Golden Gate to San Francisco.

I wish I could give some idea as to my feelings as these vessels passed laden with my own beloved countrymen. Our son Ulysses was among those who boarded our vessel. As they neared and passed us, they rent the air with their shouts of welcome, while the bands played our own beautiful and stirring national airs. The decks were white with waving handkerchiefs. The smiling faces and the familiar melodies filled my heart with joy. We entered the Golden Gate to the roar of artillery, the smoke of which entirely obscured everything.

From the pier, we drove through vast throngs of people who greeted the General with enthusiastic cheers again and again, and which were renewed as my carriage passed until I was compelled to half-rise many times in acknowledgment of their hearty and glorious welcome. This great ovation continued with us even to our entrance into the luxurious apartments assigned to General Grant and his party at the Palace Hotel by hospitable San Francisco.

The day which followed our arrival was gloriously bright. Every moment of General Grant's time was taken up in receiving delegations, committees, and the different officials of most royal San Francisco. Where shall I begin to tell of the ovations in that beautiful city?

There was a sumptuous dinner followed by a large reception given by Major General [Irvin] McDowell at his headquarters. In answer to my inquiry as to what I should wear to this midday dinner, Mrs. McDowell suggested a black silk. This was most satisfactory to me, for although I love to see gay, bright dresses on those around me, I prefer the simplest costumes for myself. But when the company began to arrive, I did feel a pang of regret for my husband's sake. Imagine how a plain little wood quail or gray dove would look in a garden full of gay parakeets and gorgeous birds of paradise. Well, that was my situation. But it was all right. When I expressed my regret to General Grant that evening at not having worn one of my many gayer dresses, he said: "Oh, your dress was entirely proper for the occasion. You are always well dressed."

The headquarters was thronged with the elite of the Pacific Coast, and no country I had seen could have assembled a more distinguished-looking or handsomer company. Next came the reception at the magnificent residence of Mr. Charles Crocker. The house was palatial, and as General Grant and I stood with our host, fair hostess, and their daughter, and received nearly five hundred guests, all superbly dressed, looking and feeling the happiness and independence so plainly stamped on their handsome faces, I felt very proud of America and Americans.

Next was the wonderful entertainment at Belmont, the residence of Senator [William] Sharon. The guests were conveyed there by special trains. We remained all night. The ball was magnificent. Over one thousand guests were present. The refreshments were such as California alone can supply, and the wine flowed like water.

The morning after this entertainment, we drove to the residence of Mr. [James C.] Flood at Menlo Park, where about twenty of our party breakfasted. How handsome our host looked and how proudly he held himself as he presided at that table fit for the gods themselves. And all this he had earned with his own strong arm.

Then we dined at Millbrae, the residence of Mr. D[arius] O. Mills. We were all conveyed by special train, and as we entered the grounds and saw them beautifully illuminated, it seemed like fairyland. The

[308]

host, his gentle wife, and fair daughter received us most cordially. The mansion was filled with all good taste could suggest. The table appointments and the decorations throughout excelled any I had yet seen—and I had seen a great deal that was beautiful. Then there were campfires, fancy balls, and army meetings. I was quite worn-out and attended but a few of these. The General enjoyed them all.

We had quite a delightful ride to the Yosemite Valley, stopping at Stockton overnight. I was rather shocked at some remarks made by the General at Stockton. In reply to oft-repeated assertions of persons who said they used to know him, had mined with him, camped and messed with him at Stockton, he replied that this was the very first time he had stopped at Stockton for more than an hour. He had only passed through and stopped long enough to get luncheon and for the stage to change horses, so it was quite impossible for him to have done any camping or mining there.

On our return from the Yosemite, I prevailed on the General to let me join him up in front with the driver. He consented, and soon I thought the coachman was driving entirely too fast either for safety or comfort and I remonstrated. The man only smiled at my timidity and continued his dangerous and alarming speed. As we turned a sharp promontory where the road had been widened by building a dry wall and filling in with mold, our horses swept around, and just as the stage rounded the point, the wheels cut so near the wall that it gave way, and the stage careened towards the frightful precipice below. At that instant, the driver, who was really most skillful, drew up his flying steeds. I did not stop to see what was going to happen; I leaped to the ground. I was safe if no one else was. But when all was made right and they were ready to start again, I behaved very badly and refused to enter the coach again. The General remonstrated but to no effect. Then he asked me what I proposed doing. "Walk," I said. "It is ten or twelve miles to where we stop," he urged; "Do not be so unreasonable, Julia." "No, I will not; I cannot get into that thing again."

Fortunately for me, just then two gentlemen drove up in a buggy with a span of fine horses. They generously volunteered to take our seats in the stage and to let the General drive me in their buggy over these grand, rugged mountains. I liked this and know the General enjoyed it too, for he told me so. It is with no little pleasure I look back to this time when I behaved so badly and refused to enter the stagecoach again, thereby securing such a charming ride with the General all by ourselves. And how pleasant it was bowling over those grand hills! He said I had behaved very badly and he feared people would think he did not have me under proper discipline, to all of which I ha! ha! ha!d gaily and asked again and again, "Are you not glad I was so bad? See what a nice ride we are having."

We had a delightful sail up the coast to Portland; that is, we had a pleasant party, but the sea was rather rough. I remember how the ship tossed and pitched. I said to the Captain: "I fear you have not placed your ballast just as it ought to be. You should have it distributed more widely." The General was surprised at this speech and said: "Really, Mrs. Grant, I was not aware that you knew how to ballast a ship." "Nor do I," I replied, "but if you will remember, when we were coasting along the Spanish shore, the ship behaved exactly like this one. It careened over and returned with a thud. Well, I heard two Englishmen talking about it and they said that the ballast was too much in the center of the ship and it was very dangerous." The Captain said: "There is a great deal in what you say, Madam, and as soon as we get into port I will see that all is made right."

On our arrival in Portland, we were happy in meeting and being welcomed by many old acquaintances, who entertained us with cordial hospitalities. We were greatly interested in our visit to Fort Vancouver, where General, then Captain, Grant was stationed so long. His little office house, now protected by a substantial fence, was pointed out to us as an object of interest. Our ride up the Columbia River was enchanting. The beautiful scenery on both sides of this broad, majestic river; the view in the distance of Mount Hood, lifting high his hoary head; the very, the more than pleasant, the delightful company of old army friends made this visit one to be remembered.

It would take a volume or a poet to tell all one feels when one first visits our beautiful Far West. The magnificent, the infinite sweep of plain; the majesty, the magnitude of the mountains; the very forests here are heroic in their grandeur; and the Pacific—one must fall prostrate on first beholding its majestic grandeur. How its billows rush on, gathering force and height (and rage too, it seems) as they near the limit of "Thus far shalt thou go and no farther"; then they lift higher and higher their wrathful heads and with one great bound fall broken and sobbing at the feet of those calm, majestic mountains.

And I must add here too that this grandeur was not confined to the mountains, the plains, the great forests, the fruits and the flowers, but the men and women also were of a superior character and physique. This could not have been imagination on my part. Surely with such surroundings one must become godlike. Nor do I wonder now that General Grant had hoped with such anticipation for a station on the Pacific slope.

Our visit to the capital, Sacramento, was very delightful. We visited

[310]

many beautiful homes. I was too fatigued after the day's sightseeing to go to a proposed dinner, so it was decided that it would be for gentlemen only; but after resting and a siesta I felt quite well enough, and the ladies proposed that we should surprise the gentlemen and take dessert and coffee with them. They were kind enough to say they were not only surprised but delighted.

Towards the latter part of a reception tendered to the General, a colored woman entered and was announced as Mrs. Jones. She came up and, holding out her hand, said: "Miss Julie, I do not believe you know me. I am Henrietta, or Henny, as you used to call me at home." I took both of her hands now. She was one of our old slaves my father had sent with my brother G. W. Dent long years ago to nurse his (my father's) grandchildren. I was very glad to see Henny and told her to come to my room the next day, but I never saw her afterwards.

When we left San Francisco, the General was escorted to the depot by many thousands. The men formed in line with lighted torches, singing "He's a jolly good fellow." I was so enthusiastic that I felt like getting out and joining them. Goodbyes were said, and we were off again.

We reached Lake Tahoe the next day. It is a beautiful lake high up in the mountains. I remember the terrific speed at which we crossed this lake. The woodwork around and near the machinery fairly scorched from the fierce fires kept up to increase our speed. It was torture to me. There was a lovely little village nestled on its eastern shore where we were refreshed and, I think, stayed all night. We had a flying drive down the mountainside, along which was one of the many flumes for conducting water to the mines. The rapidity and power of this aqueduct was marvelous. It carried away a piece of timber thrown upon its surface like a flash of lightning.

We arrived at Virginia City, the richest mining center of our El Dorado. We met here Mr. and Mrs. [James G.] Fair and Mr. J[ohn] W. Mackay. We visited the mines, going far down into their depths. What cruel, hard work this mining is. Surely, it is pleasanter far to "wear the gem than delve the mine." The General made a wager with Mr. Mackay that I would not venture down the shaft. I came out all equipped for a descent into its gloomy depths and was just about to reconsider when Mr. Mackay said to me in a low tone, "Don't give up going. The General has bet money that you would back out." I calmly stepped on the platform. The General looked surprised and said: "We descend one thousand seven hundred feet. Are you going?" "Yes," I said, with a look of reproach and triumph. So the General lost his wager when he bet against me.

[311]

I took a drive with some ladies to a fish lake, or preserve. It was here I first heard the telephone, and having messages answered by voices many miles away seemed uncanny. We met here our greatly esteemed friend Senator [John P.] Jones and his charming family.

Our next stopping place was Carson City, the capital of Nevada. Our stay here was very pleasant. The place looked bright and prosperous. The house we stayed in was so pretty, and the people were charming. The table was excellent, and my room was refined and exquisite in its appointments. I was loath to leave it.

Our next stop was at Cheyenne, but we only remained a few hours. We were taken in a coach and four up to the Governor's house for a collation, which was most enjoyable. But it seems the citizens had prepared a luncheon and expected General Grant to lunch with them at the depot where they could all see him and shake hands with him. They waxed very wroth and hurled anathemas at the Governor and at the President for sending them such a Governor who did not know his ―― (I will not say what kind of business, for indeed I heard some sulphurous swearing).[5]

Omaha was our next stop, and we met a great many of our old army friends, which was always a great pleasure to both of us. Then on to Burlington, where we were received with real affection. Then on to Galena, dear Galena, where we were at home again in reality. The return here was like our return after the war. The entire town was decorated as on the previous occasion, and everything was done that could be done to welcome back their citizen, General Grant.

After a week's rest, we went to Chicago. The ovation there was marvelous. The city was crowded to its utmost. Many friends came from the East to meet the General and to participate in and to witness this magnificent pageant. I cannot help repeating the sad old song, "Earth's gayest wreaths are made of fading flowers." In a short twelvemonth all those bright wreaths were withered; the fine speeches spoken there were changed.

From Chicago, we went to Indianapolis, Louisville, Cincinnati, and Harrisburg on our way back to our starting point, Philadelphia, where our journey around the globe was completed. After the magnificent pageant on that occasion, we were the recipients of many, many beautiful and hospitable attentions. Dear loyal Philadelphia!

General Grant concluded to visit the southern states, Cuba, and Mexico, after resting in Philadelphia for a week or two. General Sheridan and Mrs. Sheridan, Colonel Grant and wife, and Miss [Katherine (Kitty)] Felt of Galena joined us, and we started for the South, tarrying for a few days at Washington as the guests of our dear friends General and Mrs. Beale.

As we journeyed through the South, our reception was most cordial. Everything was done that could be to make our visit pleasant. In the different cities, arches were erected, and the line of march through the town was decorated with flowers and evergreens. All were polite and cordial. The General and his party were entertained at dinners, etc., at Jacksonville, St. Augustine, Savannah, and many other places. Our rooms were full of delicious fruits and beautiful flowers. I was not very well and did not attend any of the dinners. There was a beautiful ovation at Key West, but we ladies did not leave the ship.

After a run of some hours, we arrived at Cuba. Our ship was at once boarded by an officer of the Captain General's staff, who arrived in a specially fine gig, his men all gaily dressed in the national uniform. He came with the Captain General's compliments to conduct General Grant and party to the Governor's Palace. This was a pleasant surprise to us all, as we had intended and fully expected to locate ourselves in some one of the hotels—in which we were told there was not much choice. Of course, this invitation so cordial and agreeable was accepted, and what a lovely time we had! The palace was delightful in its spaciousness, its handsome furniture, and most generous and luxurious hospitality.

The gentlemen were all so very kind and attentive. I still hope to have the pleasure of meeting again and returning in some way the attention of these charming gentlemen. Nothing was left undone that could in any way promote our pleasure or happiness. Dinners, balls, and receptions followed in rapid succession. Excursions into the country to coffee, sugar, and tobacco plantations were all most interesting, especially our visit to the longleaf tobacco plantation where there were several hundred slaves. Cuba had not yet severed the shackles of her slaves, but this followed soon after. I remember the gallant and handsome young Governor of Consolatia [Consolación del Sur], who accompanied us part of the way back to Havana, telling them that night in an eloquent speech that Spain, the mother country, was making all haste to loosen their shackles. I remember how weird it all looked! Four or five hundred slaves standing under the torchlights listening to this kind promise, which was soon carried out too. We traveled in volantes, a carriage resembling a victoria, only much larger and with a front seat for the driver. These vehicles were always drawn by three horses abreast. General Grant always rode with me and, of course, I liked that. Our visit to Consolatia was a very interesting experience. The hospitalities could not well be surpassed.

We visited the springs and baths at Santiago [San Diego de los Baños] and had another lovely visit to Matanzas, where we met many charming people living in magnificent luxury, their toilet and chamber service not infrequently being of pure silver, and from them we received much delightful hospitality. We remained in Cuba until after the carnival. How loath we were to leave these really delightful people. If one of us happened to admire anything, they would say at once, "It is at your disposition. Do accept it, I pray." But, of course, we never did.

Soon after the carnival, we took a steamer for Vera Cruz, where we arrived at about ten o'clock one bright morning. We were met here by our old friend Mr. [Matías] Romero and by the authorities, who came out to the steamer in small boats in very much the same order as the ships at San Francisco. We drove through the town and were then taken to the house of an official where a fine collation was served, of which we partook with no little enjoyment. Late in the afternoon, we entered the special cars tendered the General by the authorities and started for the City of Mexico. We passed through the loveliest scenery imaginable. The country was beautiful. The people in their pictur-esque sombreros and costumes were very interesting. The tall coconut trees, the pineapple, the broad leaves of the plantain, with the vines and flowers of gorgeous hues made our journey one of ever-changing pleasure. The mountains were grand and imposing, and the broad tablelands were entirely different from the lowlands both in atmos-phere and in vegetation. At every hamlet there was some demonstra-tion of welcome.

As we neared Orizaba, a beautiful city nestled close under the great snow-crowned peak of the same name standing like a huge sentinel, it seemed to me as if the sun's last rosy light lingered to lovingly kiss the many white towers and minarets that pointed heavenward. I enjoyed a rest here. In fact, we all did and literally enjoyed the speech attributed to the Mexican when he welcomes you to his house: "My house is yours." And so it was at Orizaba. We had a large, fine house built around an inner court which was filled with trees, flowers, and birds. The people were gentle and civil, and we were entertained with some lovely music from the young ladies and gentlemen of Orizaba. The place was very attractive to me. I thought I should like to remain. The cool mountain air was so delightful, the skies were so blue, and it was all so restful.

The next day, we passed on to the City of Mexico, a city so renowned in history, which I had eagerly studied when a child, and from which, as a woman, I eagerly awaited the news when *my* Lieutenant was there. And now I was to visit this place which had interested me for so long in various ways.

We arrived at night and were escorted to the palace of Mineria by

[314]

the rural guard, all carrying torches. The effect was very fine and imposing. The palace of Mineria is a magnificent building used as a school of mineralogy. Our apartments were furnished perfectly and our salons were spacious. Most of them were as large as the East Audience Room at the White House.

I cannot begin to recall all that was done for us in that beautiful city. Mr. Romero, our good and trusted friend, Mr. [Ignacio] Mariscal, and, in fact, all those in authority were unceasing in their attentions. We visited all places of interest, and there are many of them: the halls of the Montezumas, the Cathedral, and the Art Museum. There we found many Murillos, others of the old masters, and many of native production which showed rare talent. I remember one I thought very fine. It is about a twelve-inch canvas and is a portrait of a lady and her pet dog. The little creature is following along and catching at her train of some rich, green fabric. The lady is looking over her shoulder at her little pet. The sheen on that gown and every detail were executed perfectly.

I remember with great pleasure the entertainment given in General Grant's honor at the palace by President [Porfirio] Díaz and our many interesting visits to the palace; the ball given by the city, another by Mr. Mariscal, again another by Mr. [Thomas] Braniff, and many others by persons in authority. At these balls, I remember how the dancers seemed to glide or float; the music and motion were enchanting.

The visit to Puebla was delightful, and they told me most interesting. For some reason I did not go. We visited the Cathedral of Mexico and the Church of Guadalupe, and went to look upon that marvel of antiquity, the Calendario Azteca, and other wonderful relics of the past. Then we viewed with admiration the statues of Carlos the Fourth and of the great Columbus.

There were many historical and lovely villages in the suburbs of the city. They all brought to the General some interesting reminiscences of the Mexican War. Here was the wall around Molino del Rey where the General (then Lieutenant Grant) found my brother Lieutenant Fred Dent wounded and faint from loss of blood. The General refreshed him from his canteen and dragged him to a place of safety close under the wall. Nearby the General pointed out about the spot where he once backed up a cart against the same walls, thus making a scaling ladder, enabling him with a few followers to enter the Mexican works, which soon surrendered. From here he led us on to the famous San Cosmé Gate, where he rendered such signal service in capturing a church cupola and placing in it that fierce, howling little howitzer which brought dismay to the besieged Mexicans and a glorious brevet to my Lieutenant. We saw the beautiful town of Tacubaya, where Lieutenant Grant was quartered so long and where, no doubt, his loyalty to one at home was severely tested, although he did not say so. Oh, no! But I had my thoughts.

Then there was the romantic old Church of Guadalupe, situated to the north of the city, where a marvelous apparition appeared. There were beautiful suburban villas, so luxuriously and beautifully furnished. We also visited the beautiful Chapultepec, where our troops had such a fierce hand-to-hand conflict and where they stormed the heights. I remember reading of it at the time it occurred. It is now a military school and a summer residence for the President. We all thought the situation and buildings surpassingly beautiful as we looked down from the heights upon the broad plains, villages, and lovely plantations, now so rich with their burdens for the coming harvest. While there, I registered my name in a book kept for that purpose. I wrote, "If Rasselas had been here, he would surely have been content." [6]

Then there was the magnificent drive over three miles in length along a well-kept esplanade, shaded on both sides by fine trees and guarded by cut-stone balustrades, with stone seats placed at intervals on which the weary foot travelers could rest while the more fortunate drove up and down in their drags, landaus, phaetons, and victorias, as the young gallants rode by on their prancing steeds. These young men were quite charming to look at. They were richly dressed in black velvet cut in the fashion of their country, which is both becoming and picturesque. They wore broad sombreros to shade their handsome faces. Their horses were superbly caparisoned and had flowing manes and tails which almost swept the ground; they pranced and curvetted, generally following closely some carriage which contained a closely-veiled señorita who did not, I am sure, lose a single glance from those handsome eyes, nor miss a motion of the prancing steed. One really felt as though he were enjoying in reality the days of knight-errantry. This beautiful road is quite as wide and imposing as the Élysée in Paris. Along it are many fine equestrian statues and fountains.

We took a run down to the great volcano Popocatepetl, which the General had visited with a large party of young army officers thirty years before but did not succeed in scaling. So, of course, we did not attempt it now.

The ladies of our party found much pleasure in collecting some beautiful specimens of opals and pearls brought from the Gulf of California. We paid more than one visit to the Monte Pio [Monte de

[316]

Piedad], where we saw some rare old gems. I remember one ornament especially, composed of large, pear-shaped pearls and diamonds; the pearls, three or four of them, were as large as plover's eggs. All were large and might well have belonged to the jewel case of a Cleopatra. We saw also a wonderful collection of old silver and beautiful old fans. Of the latter, I secured some specimens. It was a great pleasure to visit the old curio shops and to find such wonderfully pretty things. They had some fine specimens of Mexican onyx; a magnificent buffet of this wonderfully beautiful material was presented to General Grant. It was much broken, however, in transit to New York, and when it was put up, I had the broken parts replaced by Hess and Co. of New York with ornamental woods, for which I paid five hundred dollars out of my pin money. It is now in Washington with the other gifts presented to General Grant.

After another visit to the cathedrals and to the halls of the Montezumas, our farewells were said, and we started on our return well pleased with Mexico and its charming people. I think we stopped again at the restful little city of Orizaba.

We sailed for Galveston, Texas. The Gulf was rough and boisterous. I spent most of the time in my cabin. We received much attention at Galveston. We met many army officers, which is always a pleasure.

I remember a large dinner at which General Sheridan was called upon humorously to explain what he meant by some very strong statements he had made on a former occasion, expressing emphatic disappreciation of Texas.[7] "Well," he replied, "you see, . . ." he hesitated, "I had just come off of a long journey tired, dusty, hot, and thirsty as the . . . well, as thirsty as you Texans always are, and two or three of those infernal newspaper fellows came abuzzing around me and wanted to know what I thought of Texas. Well, you see . . . I was hot and thirsty . . . and was not feeling just as chipper as usual, you see, and I think I said I thought Texas *was hot, very hot,* as hot as (General Grant suggested) Tophet. Yes, that is what I said—Tophet. I did not say the other name, did I?" "No, no, no. You said Tophet, that is what you meant," came a chorus of voices, and Sheridan was received into full fellowship and sympathy with the boys again.

From Galveston, we visited San Antonio. This place was most interesting to me on account of the tragedy enacted there in the beginning of Texas's stand for independence, which I dimly remembered. As we were starting, the railroad officials cautioned the General against going on the platform of the car, as they said you could not always predict how the Texas boys would act, but the General went out at the very first station and was greeted with hearty cheers and a great tossing up of wide-brimmed hats, and so it was over the whole route until we again reached the Gulf.

It was very pleasant to visit this army post, where we met again our old friend General Ord and his charming daughter, who soon after this married General [Gerónimo] Treviño, Mexico's war secretary. This was a brilliant match for our General's pretty daughter, but, if rumor be correct, General Ord himself could claim lawful descent from King George of England.[8] Ord was brave and noble enough to have *been* a king himself.

Whilst at San Antonio, we enjoyed some delightful drives over the plains, literally covered with wild flowers which filled the balmy air with their fragrance. To my astonishment, we visited some fine old Spanish ruins that had once been monasteries. It seemed too bad to have these fall in ruins. We had a charming visit to the house of Mr. B—— far out on the plains at the head of the San Antonio River where there were grouped many springs, and here, far from the "madding crowd," these charming people had stopped and not only pitched their tent but planted their vine and fig tree. Their flower garden was the most beautiful we saw on this journey.

General and Mrs. Sheridan and Colonel and Mrs. Grant left us at Galveston. General Sheridan felt that he had been absent from his headquarters at Chicago long enough. General Grant and I with Miss Felt went by steamer to New Orleans, where the ovation was quite equal to that in my dream of long years ago at the old farm while I was reading George Sand's *Consuelo* for the first time.

We were met by a delegation of gentlemen at some distance from the city and escorted to the riverbank, where we took a steamer and crossed the Mississippi in a cloud of blue smoke from the artillery salutes. This beautiful city was in holiday dress indeed. Every house was dressed in bunting, roses, and jessamine. The streets were crowded with gaily dressed people, bands of music were playing, and carpets were spread from the steamer to our carriage—just as I had seen it in my dream.

The hospitalities here were many and delightful. So the General told me, as I was anything but well and only attended one or two of these entertainments. These I found delightful and regretted having missed so many. I remember with much pleasure the ride down the Mississippi on a splendid steamer to view the jetties built by the distinguished engineer and our townsman, Captain [James B.] Eads of St. Louis. The drive over the famous shell road was more than delightful. Also the visit to the cemetery was very interesting, where the strange spectacle is presented of the graves made above ground.

The same thing occurs near Jerusalem, just outside the gates as you pass the cemetery on the road to Gethsemane.

I remember well, too, a great banquet given to General Grant at New Orleans. He was greatly pleased by the sentiment and good feeling shown on this occasion. The guests presented him with an album with their names subscribed as a souvenir of the pleasant evening. Well, even pleasant things have an end, and it was so with our visit to New Orleans.

We traveled on through Mississippi, being greeted at every stopping place with most eloquent speeches. At Little Rock, Arkansas, where we were for two days only, there was, I remember, a reception and much cordiality. Then on to our own state, Illinois. Well, to use the figurative and eloquent language of the famous Indian chief Red Cloud, the people that met and greeted General Grant were in numbers as the "grass of the plains." We finally arrived at Galena, where we remained, except when absent on occasional visits to Colonel Fred, who was stationed in Chicago on General Sheridan's staff.

NOTES

1. The island chain extending some 600 miles between Japan and Taiwan, called the Loo-choo or Ryukyu Islands (both spelled in a variety of ways), had paid tribute to both China and Japan for centuries. The Meiji restoration in Japan (1868) led to a more aggressive foreign policy, including gradual steps (1871–79) toward absolute sovereignty over these islands. While Grant was in China, Li Hung-chang and Prince Kung asked him to mediate the resulting dispute. After discussions with Emperor Mutsuhito and key Japanese officials, Grant advised the Chinese to withdraw some threatening communications and to appoint commissioners to negotiate with the Japanese on this issue. Both sides accepted Grant's advice and began protracted negotiations, which culminated in Chinese acquiescence in Japanese control of the islands. Because the dispute had been resolved without bloodshed or foreign intervention, Grant received the thanks of both nations. Payson J. Treat, *Diplomatic Relations Between the United States and Japan 1853–1895* (Reprint of 1932 ed., Gloucester, Massachusetts, 1963), II, 98–104, 126–27, 141–44, 177–81; George H. Kerr, *Okinawa: The History of an Island People* (Rutland, Vermont, and Tokyo, 1958), pp. 381–92; Hyman Kublin, "The Attitude of China during the Liu-ch'iu Controversy, 1871–1881," *Pacific Historical Review*, XVIII (May, 1949), 213–25; Richard T. Chang, "General Grant's 1879 Visit to Japan," *Monumenta Nipponica*, XXIV (1969), 379–83.

2. Young, *Around the World*, II, 570, discusses this rumor as circulating at Yokohama, not Tokyo, and mentions no threat to Grant from the people of either city. On August 4, 1879, however, John A. Bingham received an anonymous letter

protesting the expense to Japan of entertaining foreign dignitaries which contained a threat to assassinate the officials responsible and also the visitors—including Grant. Bingham to William M. Evarts, August 16, 1879, Dispatches from U.S. Ministers to Japan, Record Group 59, National Archives.

3. A translation of a charmingly inaccurate Japanese biography of Grant by Kanagaki Robun appeared in *Century Magazine*, L (July, 1895), 435–46.

4. Since the departure of the *City of Tokio* had been postponed, the Grants returned from Yokohama to Tokyo, where the dinner took place. For Grant letters mentioning the delay, see Badeau, *Grant in Peace*, pp. 518–20.

5. When the Grants reached Cheyenne, Wyoming Territory, only one of six members of the welcoming committee met the train, and Governor John Wesley Hoyt was not ready when the party reached his house. To add to the embarrassment, a delegation from Colorado was ready and willing to entertain the Grants. Some Wyoming Republicans accused Governor Hoyt of snubbing Grant. Chicago *Tribune*, November 1, 1879; T. A. Larson, *History of Wyoming* (Lincoln, Nebraska, 1965), p. 136.

6. The hero of Samuel Johnson, *History of Rasselas: Prince of Abissinia* (1759) flees imprisonment in a "happy valley" in search of fulfillment. Disillusioned by all he finds in the outside world, he finally returns to the valley.

7. Sheridan was supposed to have said, "If I owned Texas and Hell, I'd rent out Texas and live in Hell."

8. In 1785, George, Prince of Wales, married Maria Anne Fitzherbert. Since he was then too young to marry legally without his father's consent and this marriage to a Roman Catholic would have barred the Prince from the throne, this marriage ceremony was ignored when the Prince married Princess Caroline of Brunswick in 1795 and when he succeeded his father as King George IV in 1820. Whether the Prince and Mrs. Fitzherbert had any children is uncertain, but James Ord established a family tradition that he was the son of George IV. Shane Leslie, *George the Fourth* (London, 1926), pp. 198–200. Ord, brought to the United States as a small child, was educated at Georgetown College, served in both the U.S. Navy and U.S. Army during the War of 1812, and was the father of Edward O. C. Ord.

Chapter 12

---◄●►---

W E WERE at Galena when the Republican Convention met at Chicago, and how can I describe that week of suspense for me! I did not feel that General Grant would be nominated, although I had been with him on his triumphant journey through the country from east to west, from south to north, and knew the people wanted him. They all told me so, but *I knew* of the disaffection of more than one of his trusted friends. The General would not believe me, but I saw it plainly.

During the week through which the balloting continued without change of vote, Mr. J. Russell Young came over to Galena, and General Grant wrote a letter to his friends Senators Conkling, [J. Donald] Cameron, and Logan, and directed it, I think, to Cameron, who was, in a certain emergency and with the consent of the other two, to use the letter for withdrawing General Grant's name from before the convention. Mr. Young was unwise enough to read the letter to me, and I then told him to tell Senator Cameron *not* to use that letter.[1] If General Grant were not nominated, then let it be so, but he must not withdraw his name—no, never.

It had been arranged that General Grant should go to Chicago on Monday night and from there to Milwaukee to attend the annual reunion of the Grand Army of the Republic. How I entreated him to go on Sunday night and appear on the floor at the convention on Monday morning—but no! He said he would rather cut off his right hand. I said: "Do you not desire success?" "Well, yes, of course," he said, "since my name is up, I would rather be nominated, but I will do nothing to further that end." "Oh, Ulys," I said, "how unwise, what mistaken chivalry. For heaven's sake, go—and go tonight. I know they are already making their cabals against you. Go, go tonight, I beseech you." He only said: "Julia, I am amazed at you," and he went to meet some visitor and to talk over the probabilities of the morrow. The result is known to all.

We went to Milwaukee as arranged and attended the meeting of the Grand Army. After our return, we took a trip to Manitou Springs, Colorado. The General was followed there by several persons who desired his name as business partner, all of whom he declined. He was also offered the presidency of the Panama Canal Company in the United States with a salary of twenty-five thousand dollars per annum. He declined this also and said he did not believe it practicable, for which he incurred the enmity of those who had the stock to dispose of. We returned to Galena and met on our way many friends who grieved because General Grant's name had not been chosen by the Republican Party.

The General and I were invited to go to Mentor.[2] The General went, but I would not go. We decided to go to New York for a time, the General to do all he could for the success of the Republican ticket, and I went because he did. All along the route as we passed to the east, the General was greeted with the wildest enthusiasm; great crowds gathered and cheered at every station. I remember as we paused at one station, a town in western New York, great crowds gathered about, half of whom were in uniform; all surrounded our cars eagerly calling for Grant. A gentleman coming in laughingly told the General of how he, knowing that a great Democratic meeting was just assembling and hearing that General Grant would pass through the place, had taken the liberty of sending a messenger to the hall to announce in a loud and telling voice, "Grant is at the depot." "And you see how it is, General; the meeting is broken up for today anyway."

When we arrived in New York, a grand torchlight procession was tendered General Grant, grand in its extent. General Grant and Senator Conkling worked hard for the ticket, and our party triumphed again.

We made arrangements at the Fifth Avenue Hotel for accommodations for the winter. General Grant was poor. With an income of less than six thousand dollars per annum, we found it difficult to meet even the very liberal terms made for us by the proprietor of the Fifth Avenue.

My second son, who had been taken into partnership with

Ferdinand Ward, was most successful. Mr. Ward and a Mr. [James D.] Fish seemed to be the firm. Ulysses, feeling that he could easily spare one-half of his share of the profits made by Mr. Ward, offered in the generosity of his noble heart to divide it with his father, whom he so honored and loved. When the General told me of Ulysses's offer, I asked: "Did you accept it?" "No," he said, "I cannot accept it. He has a family, and I am not willing to." I thought the General's voice expressed emotion and said at once, "You can pay for your interest and then you will be under obligations to no one. Accept the offer of one-half of his interest. Let me telegraph that you will." I did so, and that evening my son came in, his face radiant with the good news he brought. He said he had received my telegram and had read it to Ward, who generously proposed to increase the stock to four hundred thousand dollars and to take General Grant in as an equal partner. So this partnership began which ended so disastrously. It swept every dollar from all the members of our family in any way connected with it.

In the spring of '81, our old friends Mr. A[nthony] J. Drexel and Mr. G. W. Childs of Philadelphia telegraphed the General that they wanted to see him and asked him to appoint an hour. The General telegraphed them to come and dine with us at the Fifth Avenue. They came, and as I was dressing to meet them, the conviction flashed across my mind that these gentlemen were going to present to me the fund they had been raising for General Grant, of which we knew through the papers. I hastily banished this conviction as unworthy and went to meet our friends, who soon asked me if I knew what they had come for. I replied, "well, yes. The papers have told us all about your kind interest in the General." "Oh," they said, "do you know what we have decided to do?" "No," I replied. Mr. Childs said: "We have decided to present this fund to you to purchase a home with." I am sure I turned deathly pale. I was so startled that I did not respond until Mr. Childs asked: "Is not that nice?" I said: "Oh, yes, yes indeed, but talk with the General first. See if he approves." "Oh, no. We have decided it is to be yours. The General has nothing to do with it. It is yours, and what is yours is the General's."

So I was to have a beautiful home, all my own, and how happy I was all that summer looking for a house and selecting paper, furniture, etc. After many delightful sails from Long Branch to New York to find a suitable house, we at length decided upon one situated on East Sixty-sixth Street. It was a much larger and a more expensive house than we had intended (or had the means) to buy, but it was so new and sweet and large that this quite outweighed our more prudential

[323]

scruples—unfortunately, as later I had to pay out of the proceeds of General Grant's book a mortgage of fifty-nine thousand dollars on it. And how happy I was all that autumn in ordering the making of my handsome hangings, the opening of my boxes, and the placing of all the souvenirs collected during our long and eventful journey around the world. What pleasure I had in taking out and expressing to my friends the lovely, soft, white rampur chadors, the bits of carved ivory, lacquer, and cloisonné. I really think it is more pleasure to give than to receive.

How handsome my home was when all was finished, and I had the supreme pleasure of a visit from my son Fred and our darling Nellie. How happy our Christmas was! The children said there was nothing left for them to give me. I had everything, but the General thought of a little traveling clock that not only struck the hours but the quarters and halves as well. I have it now each day and night beside me, and it never fails me.

Fred and his family and my daughter Nellie with her husband and children were spending the winter with me. Ulysses and Jesse were both married and keeping house in the city. I think my happiness was quite complete; we dined with them or they with us every few days. Having so many acquaintances and friends, we took great pleasure in having some of them visit us nearly all the time. Dinners and receptions followed in quick succession, and how regally New York entertains. In our journey around the world I saw nothing that excelled them in magnificence or elegance.

How well I remember one evening when the General and I were going to a dinner given to the General at one of the palaces on Fifth Avenue. I, of course, wore one of my handsomest gowns, made and designed for me by Worth. It was a superb silver brocade, elaborately trimmed in front with flounces of point lace. The jewels and so forth were in keeping with this beautiful gown. As I descended the stairs with the General, Harrison [Terrell], the butler, came with a message from the young ladies, who were having a gay, large dinner themselves that evening, to come in and show myself. Feeling quite satisfied with the expressions of approval I received from the gay and partial young people assembled there, I turned to accompany the General to the carriage, when he said to me, "Mrs. Grant, Julia," looking at me with a very puzzled expression, "can you tell me how old, old ladies get before they put on caps?" I did not answer this question but gave him a look. When he pressed for an answer, I simply replied, "Really, I cannot say. I don't know anything about old ladies."

I was often annoyed by some persons and the papers also stating that General Grant was no conversationalist: in fact, a sphinx. All of this I knew to be untrue, having known him over forty years. I found him to be the most interesting man I had met in all that time, and I am sure I have met and conversed with a great many distinguished men. But I must confess that I had to resort to a little strategy sometimes to start him off when I wished him to be especially interesting to others, and this plan I confided to several of the General's friends, who often used it with great success. I would begin to tell something with which I knew he was perfectly familiar and would purposely tell it all wrong. Then the General would say, "Julia, you are telling that all wrong," and seemed quite troubled at my incompetency. I would innocently ask, "Well, how was it then?" He would begin, tell it all so well, and for the remainder of the evening would be so brilliant and so deeply interesting.

One evening, when General Grant had returned from a gentlemen's dinner party and was telling me of the events and bright witticisms of the evening, as he invariably did, he said: "I am afraid I have ruined myself in the estimation of President ——, who sat next to me at dinner." He continued, "Mr. —— at once began talking of books, mentioning one or two familiar names, and I—well, I looked as though if I had read that particular book I had forgotten it. After a while, he made some allusion to a character of Dickens. I was equally ignorant of poor little Oliver. So the old gentleman gave me up, and I enjoyed the rest of the evening." [3] I was sorry to hear of this and said, "You will hear of this, remember!" The General replied, "Oh, well, I went there to enjoy myself and I am not willing always to sacrifice my pleasure." And, sure enough, within a year after General Grant's death, Mr. —— did announce to his class that General Grant was no reader, citing the above incident as evidence. I tell this in justification of General Grant, who read aloud to me many hundreds of books to save my poor eyes.

Seeing in this morning's paper that General J[oseph] E. Johnston is very ill reminds me of a little incident that occurred during Mr. Arthur's administration. General Grant and I were in Washington on a visit, and I happened to be present when General Grant was asked to endorse or urge the appointment of Mr. —— for city commissioner in place of Mr. [Josiah] Dent of Georgetown, who was an old and esteemed friend of my family. I do not know why Mr. Dent was being replaced—perhaps he resigned. When I learned that the applicant was of the same politics as the majority of the other members of the commission, I remembered clearly and with some bitterness that majority of the county judges in St. Louis when Captain Grant was an applicant for a little office (city engineer) for which he was so well fitted and for which he was defeated by that most unjust majority.[4] I at once exclaimed, "If Mr. Dent is retired, why place in his stead a man differing in politics and sympathy? Washington is the capital of the United States, the South as well as the North. The people of the District must have a representative who will vote for their interests sometimes." "Yes," the General said, "that is only just," and he at once suggested the name of Joseph E. Johnston and urged his appointment, but Johnston did not get it.[5] The administration discovered some insurmountable obstacle.

This reference to General Joe Johnston reminds me of a conversation I had with the General at the time of General [John B.] Hood's death [1879], when he remarked, "Hood was a gallant, brave fellow." I said: "But, Ulys, he was not loyal to the Southern cause, was he?" "Why, yes," he replied, "why do you ask me that?" "Well," I replied, "for this reason. Once at your headquarters during the last winter at City Point, when news came that Hood had been placed in command of some army, you said, 'ah!' with seeming great satisfaction and glanced smilingly around at the officers, who returned your glance knowingly. I at once came to the conclusion that this man was not true to his cause, else why should this change give such evident satisfaction to the Union side? I never alluded to this before, for I was both mortified and surprised to think you would avail yourself of this equivocal advantage, having heard you only a few days before indignantly refuse and dismiss a person who proposed a plan for capturing Jeff Davis at his home in Richmond and bringing him inside the Union lines a prisoner bound and gagged, saying, 'I cannot approve of it. We are not kidnappers.' "

The General said: "Yes, I remember both the incidents you speak of, and my satisfaction at Hood's being placed in command was this. He replaced General Joe Johnston, who was a most careful, brave, wise soldier. But Hood would dash out and fight every time you raised a flag before him, and that was just what we wanted. Hood was just as ready to fight as your brother Louis was when your brother Fred would place a chip on his shoulder and call Louis's attention to it."

How happy we all were in our new home for that first winter and another and another, until the distressing and cruel accident to the General, who, while reaching up to give his coachman a Christmas present, slipped on the icy pavement, dislocated his hip, and never passed a well day afterwards.

The General and I had anticipated a gay, bright winter. We had sent out invitations for four large dinner parties in January. All had accepted. When this dreadful accident occurred, Dr. [Benjamin] Fordyce Barker told me I must withdraw all my invitations, as the General would not be able to be present at dinner for a long time.

He was ill during the winter, and early in March we left for the South in search of sunshine. The change proved most beneficial to the General, and on our return we lingered for a week in Washington, where we were the recipients of the widest hospitality. At least I was, the General declining every invitation as he felt unable to sit long at table. Dear Washington, how I love you, with your beautiful, broad, generous streets and blue skies! The sun shines always there for me. While in Washington, the General went downstairs on his crutches to be present for a few moments at a great dinner. How the men shouted at his entrance! How they stamped and shouted and cheered when he arose to say a few words to them!

And so it was everywhere. When I told some old friends that I had prevailed upon the General to come to Washington in place of going farther south, they seemed much pleased and said I was a better politician than the General. They were glad he had come to Washington, as it was rumored and believed by many that the General's health was broken, his mind shattered, and he never could do anything again. He was a little lame now, but otherwise in excellent health. While we were in Washington, there was a good deal of talk about General Grant's name being again brought up before the Republican Convention, and it disturbed me not a little.

One night whilst there, I dreamed that I looked down upon a great throng surging up the avenue leading from Pennsylvania Avenue towards the White House. In the midst of this throng of moving people was an open carriage drawn by four prancing horses, and seated in this carriage with his pretty wife beside him was one dear to me.[6] The carriage drove on and stopped at the portals of the White House. The trees were green and the air was balmy as I looked down on that pageant. After that, I gave no more thought to the subject, as I knew General Grant was not to be there, nor was I.

Hardly two weeks after our return, the failure of Grant and Ward came like a thunderclap. It was a great shock to my family, as they all believed they were not only prosperous but wealthy. A few days before this dire announcement, the General had said to me, "Julia, you need not trouble to save for our children. Ward is making us all rich—them as well as ourselves—and I have been thinking how pleasant it would be for us to make our impecunious friends (several of whom we were then helping) independent, get them comfortable little homes, and make them allowances. I would like to, and I am sure it would be a great pleasure to you." How rudely was this anticipation broken! Imagine the shock to us, who thought we were independently wealthy!

Fortunately, I had no small bills. I was still following my early precepts by paying my bills at the end of the month. This saved me a world of trouble and distress. It was solely the business transactions of Grant and Ward which disturbed the General, and I soon realized that when money is at stake there is little room for charity. My sons had already ordered their summer supplies of groceries, wines, cigars, etc., and at once ordered them returned as they could not pay for them. They had not enough to pay carfare. Even the quarterly dividends arising from the munificent fund presented to the General by the city of New York had been subtracted from his deposit. The fund, fortunately, was a trust fund.

We were literally without means when a gentleman from Lansingburg, N.Y., sent the General five hundred dollars, saying, "General, I owe you this for Appomattox." The General acknowledged this and said to the gentleman, who was a stranger to us, that his timely thoughtfulness had been a great relief to him.[7] The gentleman then sent a cheque for one thousand dollars, telling the General to consider it a loan to be repaid at his convenience.

A friend [Matías Romero], a foreign minister to our country, also brought one thousand dollars as a loan to the General. This latter was paid within a month, as I was fortunate enough to be able to dispose of one of the two little houses I had in Washington, and it gave me great pleasure to send to our friend in Washington a cheque for his generous loan.

The following winter, the General sent with pleasure and with expressions of gratitude a cheque to Mr. Wood of Lansingburg for the one thousand dollars. This was a portion of the money he earned by writing articles for the *Century*. The five hundred dollars sent by Mr. Wood I paid from the first proceeds of my husband's book. Captain Eads, the distinguished engineer, also generously offered to assist the General in this, his hour of misfortune, but the General did not find it necessary to make use of the privilege placed at his command by Captain Eads.

We decided at first to rent my little villa at Long Branch, but the rent offered was so small that we decided to occupy it ourselves and have some of our family with us, a very happy arrangement for all. It was during this sad summer that the fatal malady first made its appearance in General Grant's throat. There was a plate of delicious peaches on the table, of which the General was very fond. Helping himself, he proceeded to eat the dainty morsel; then he started up as if in great pain and exclaimed: "Oh my. I think something has stung me from that peach." He walked up and down the room and out to the piazza, and rinsed his throat again and again. He was in great pain and said water hurt him like liquid fire. This was the very beginning of his throat trouble. I always thought it was a sting from some insect in the peach. He preferred to bite and eat this fruit without paring it and said that "It spoiled it to cut it with a knife."

His throat continued to be sensitive, and I begged him to see a physician, but he said: "No, it will be all right directly, and I will not have a doctor." So it continued for weeks until Dr. [Jacob M.] Da Costa was called in for some of the family, and I asked him to look at the General's throat, saying that he had been complaining of it for some time and I felt a little uneasy. As soon as Dr. Da Costa saw the General's throat, he recommended immediate attention. This was early in August, I think, but the General did not consult Dr. Barker until late in October. All that summer was spent by my dear husband in hard work: writing, writing, writing for bread.

We returned to our home in New York early in October. It was not until the twentieth of October that the General consulted Dr. Fordyce Barker. It was then that he realized for the first time that his malady was of a serious nature. The General did not inform me of the physicians' opinion of his trouble for some time after he had learned it. I then went myself to the specialist and learned the dreadful truth but still could not believe the malady was a fatal one. I asked again and again if it were not curable and was answered that there had been instances when it had been cured. Then hope returned to me. My husband was healthy, temperate, strong. Why should he not be well and strong again? And down in my heart, I could not believe that God in his wisdom and mercy would take this great, wise, good man from us, to whom he was so necessary and so beloved. It could not be, and I surely thought he would recover.

The General was now (in January) closely confined to his room. The specialist came to him instead of his going to the specialist, as he insisted on doing as long as he was able for the reason that it saved expense. The General found this confinement most irksome and concluded to write his memoirs.[8] Happy, happy thought for him! How many weary hours were thus occupied, and with what earnestness he began and with what perseverance he continued to the end this writing, writing, writing for bread.

All this sad, weary winter and up to the very last, we had the daily and sometimes nightly visits of our dear friends Bishop and Mrs. [John P.] Newman. Their sympathy and spiritual consolation was a great comfort to the General and to us all. The General in his big chair, with his head thrown back on the cushion, his eyes closed and his hands clasped before him, listened devoutly to the prayer of this pure and great divine. And then dear Mrs. Newman—we all still kneeling—repeated, with downcast eyes and clasped hands, some one of the beautiful Psalms. Shall I ever forget these beautiful Psalms? Shall I ever forget the kindness and sympathy of my dear friends Bishop and Mrs. Newman?

Then Mr. Romero, our old, old friend, would come up from Washington, walk quietly into the room, and sit with the General. How eloquent was his silent devotion! But then the sympathy we met with from every source cannot be written: kind messages and great bouquets of flowers sent from the hothouses of friends, little boxes of trailing arbutus gathered from beneath the snow and sent from far and wide by schoolchildren with loving messages to the General. Beautiful letters came from many schools offering prayers for his recovery, and this same prayerful petition was offered by every denomination throughout the country. But love and skill and prayers availed not. He was taken from our midst.

The General's memoirs occupied every leisure moment. He even wrote at night sometimes when sleep would not come to him. It was a happy thought that suggested that book. He worked on and on in his labor of love, his health gradually failing. Sometimes it would receive an impetus from some outside event: once when Congress failed to put his name on the retired list, and again when an old staff officer who was at the time sharing his hospitality proved his base ingratitude.[9] These events gave him attacks it was hard to rally from.

The weather was rapidly growing warmer, and after consultation with a number of our most renowned physicians, it was decided that General Grant must leave the city at once and go to a cooler locality. A kind friend, Mr. Joseph Drexel, offered the General a cottage on Mount McGregor. This cottage was not only comfortably but elegantly, yet simply, furnished with everything that one could wish for. Within five hundred yards of the cottage was a fine new hotel, from which our table was daily served.

How grateful it was to the General, as he sat resting from his writing on the wide, cool piazza, to see the hundreds of people who daily passed the cottage with uncovered heads, all anxious to get a glimpse of him. How many old friends called to take his hand in theirs for the last time! I remember well a visit from General Simon Buckner. How affected they both were! As General Buckner took General Grant's hand at parting, the only words were "Grant," "Buckner." Many came to him to say a last word: Sherman, Ingalls, Sheridan, [Charles S.] Hamilton, Hilton,[10] Beale, [Jerome B.] Chaffee, and too many more to mention. Many delegations also came, but these my son Colonel Grant always received.

The General could not be induced to rest long on the piazza. He was so anxious about his book, so afraid of not being able to finish it. After sitting awhile with us, he would take out his little tablets and write, "It is very pleasant to be here, but I must go to my writing or I fear my book will not be finished." And so he wrote on and on. General Grant, the savior of our Union, General Grant, commander-in-chief of 1,000,000 men, General Grant, eight years President of the United States, was writing, writing of his own grand deeds, recording them that he might leave a home and independence to his family.

As I write the above, my thoughts go back again to Apsley House, where General Grant and I dined with the Duke of Wellington, its magnificent halls all decked with war trophies, to the three million pounds sterling and the great title conferred by a grateful government, and I cannot help wondering what England would have done for Grant had he been an Englishman.

He seemed to rally for a while in the cool mountain air, and our hopes revived. He wrote on and on in his love's labor. He finished his book about July the nineteenth. His work was done, and to our dismay he grew rapidly weaker and weaker, and on the morning of July the twenty-third, he, my beloved, my all, passed away, and I was alone, alone.

For nearly thirty-seven years, I, his wife, rested and was warmed in the sunlight of his loyal love and great fame, and now, even though his beautiful life has gone out, it is as when some far-off planet disappears from the heavens; the light of his glorious fame still reaches out to me, falls upon me, and warms me.

NOTES

1. According to Badeau, *Grant in Peace*, pp. 321–23, Young, believing that Grant could not be elected, visited him in Galena to persuade him not to allow his friends to nominate him at the Republican Convention of 1880. Over Julia Grant's objections and without her knowledge, Grant finally wrote a letter to Conkling withdrawing his candidacy. But, after visiting Grant, Young wrote to John Hay that while Grant was "indifferent" about the nomination, "There was only one consideration that prevented his withdrawing his name absolutely, and that was the belief that he could be the means of ending the 'miserable sectional

strifes' between the North and South." Hay Papers, Brown University, Providence. A letter printed in newspapers written by Grant to Conkling, dated May 2, 1880, expressing a desire to decline another nomination and urging Conkling to end his feud with James G. Blaine so that one of them might receive the nomination, may well be spurious since it does not reflect Grant's style or sentiments and is datelined New York at a time when Grant was in Galena. *Americana*, VII (September, 1912), 848–50. In 1897, in response to continued comment about Grant's offer to withdraw, Frederick Dent Grant wrote that Young delivered to him in Chicago a letter advising his supporters to withdraw Grant's name if they could also persuade Blaine to withdraw. Frederick Grant delivered the letter to Conkling. George S. Boutwell, *Reminiscences of Sixty Years in Public Affairs* (New York, 1902), II, 271–72. In the Conkling Papers, Library of Congress, is a letter from Grant to his son Frederick, June 8, 1880, concerning a proposed visit by Conkling to Grant after the convention. This letter was forwarded to Conkling by Frederick Grant after the convention had already nominated James A. Garfield. Thus the question of whether Grant's principal supporters ever received instructions to withdraw his name remains undecided.

2. Garfield lived at Mentor.

3. In the manuscript, Julia Grant identified the questioner as "Elliott," perhaps indicating President Charles W. Eliot of Harvard. Frederick Dent Grant later recounted much the same story, placing it at New Haven and identifying the questioner as "Professor S." "My Father as I Knew Him," New York *World Sunday Magazine*, April 25, 1897.

4. See Chapter 2.

5. When the term of Josiah Dent as commissioner of the District of Columbia expired in July, 1882, President Chester A. Arthur nominated Joseph R. West of the District of Columbia to the office. General Joseph E. Johnston, who had served in Congress as a Democrat (1879–81), received no federal office until appointed commissioner of railroads by Grover Cleveland in 1885.

6. Perhaps this means that Julia Grant dreamed that her son Frederick would be elected President.

7. Grant's letters of thanks to Charles Wood appeared in the New York *Times*, August 5, 1892.

8. As he completed four articles on individual campaigns for the *Century* during the summer of 1884, Grant decided to write full-length memoirs. Badeau, *Grant in Peace*, p. 563; Robert Underwood Johnson, *Remembered Yesterdays* (Boston, 1923), pp. 216–18; Thomas M. Pitkin, *The Captain Departs: Ulysses S. Grant's Last Campaign* (Carbondale and Edwardsville, Illinois, 1973), pp. 12–16.

9. On May 7, 1884, Senator George F. Edmunds of Vermont introduced a bill authorizing the President to appoint Grant a general on the retired list. The Senate quickly passed the bill with near unanimity, but the House took no action during that session. U.S. Congress, Senate, *Congressional Record*, 48th Cong., 1st sess., 3910, 4096. By January, 1885, Edmunds had learned that President Arthur believed that any bill authorizing him to appoint a specific individual infringed on executive powers, so he introduced a second bill, quickly passed by the Senate, authorizing the President to appoint an additional general to the retired list. *Ibid.*, 2nd sess., 649, 684–85. On February 16, the original bill was debated by the House amid some confusion and failed to receive the two-thirds vote necessary to

suspend the rules in order to consider the bill. *Ibid.*, 1757–61. Presumably this is the action which Julia Grant considered a blow to her husband. But on March 3, the House passed the second bill, Arthur nominated Grant, and the Senate confirmed the nomination unanimously and with cheers. *Ibid.*, 2503, 2565–66. For the matter of staff officer Adam Badeau, see the Introduction.

10. Grant had no close friend named Hilton. On July 13, 1885, Governor David B. Hill of New York visited Grant. New York *Times*, July 14, 1885. It is not certain, however, that this is the person involved.

Index

daughter), 76, 85, 101, 103, 110, 131, 132, 134, 157-58, 161, 162, 170, 174, 180-81, 188, 192, 195, 198 n, 203, 208, 211, 216, 241, 242, 243, 244, 261, 262, 324

Grant, Frederick Dent (Julia's son), 18, 20, 24, 67, 70, 73, 74-75, 81, 85-86, 92, 97-98, 101, 110, 113, 119, 125-26, 127, 131, 132, 134, 135, 158, 170, 180, 181, 186, 192, 197, 243, 254, 262, 263, 269, 270, 274, 279, 282, 288, 289, 293, 296, 297, 301, 305, 306, 312, 318, 319, 324, 331, 332 n

Grant, Hannah Simpson (Grant's mother), 57, 64 n

Grant, Ida (Mrs. Frederick D.), 175, 181, 188, 192, 195, 270, 312, 318

Grant, Jesse Root (Grant's father), 3, 57, 76, 80, 82, 88 n, 98, 101

Grant, Jesse Root, Jr., (Julia's son), 19, 44, 85-86, 97-98, 101, 103, 105, 107, 109, 110, 124, 126, 132, 133-35, 155, 158, 161-62, 164, 170, 174, 178, 179, 201, 203, 207, 209, 211, 213, 218, 220, 221, 227, 228-29, 237, 239, 240, 324

Grant, Julia (Julia's granddaughter), 181, 196, 289

Grant, Julia Boggs Dent; ancestry of, 40-41, 62 n, 63 n; Arabia visited by, 263; army wife, life as, 58-62, 65-75; Austria visited by, 254-55; Belgium visited by, 208-10, 214; Burma visited by, 277-80; childhood of, 2, 33-37; children of, 67, 71, 76, 85-86; China visited by, 284-92; Civil War activities of, 89-114, 119-42, 146-54; Cochin China visited by, 283-84; courtship of, 48-52, 54-55; Cuba visited by, 313-14; Denmark visited by, 246-47; education of, 37-39, 45; Egypt visited by, 220-24, 227-32, 263; England visited by, 202-8, 214, 216; farmer's wife, life as, 75-80; Finland visited by, 250, 251; France visited by, 216-18, 243-44, 255, 260-62; Gibraltar visited by, 258-59; Greece visited by, 239-40; Germany visited by, 210-11; honeymoon of, 56-58; India visited by, 264-75; Italy visited by, 214, 218-19, 240-43, 263; Japan visited by, 292-97, 299-306; legend of, 1; Malaya visited by, 280-81, 283; Malta visited by, 219-20; marriage of, 2, 17-18, 55-56; *Memoirs*

of, 14, 18-26; Mexico visited by, 314-17; Netherlands visited by, 244-45; Norway visited by, 248-49; Palestine visited by, 232-36; parents of, 33, 40-42, 46, 51, 52, 58, 60, 76, 80, 81, 83, 84, 91, 113, 176, 181-82; Poland visited by, 254; Portugal visited by, 256-57; Russia visited by, 251-54; Scotland visited by, 214-16; Siam visited by, 281-83; sight deficiency of, 24, 126-27; slavery issue and, 2, 34-35; Southern tour of, 312-19; Spain visited by, 255-56, 257-58; Sweden visited by, 247-48, 249; Switzerland visited by, 211-14, 255; Syria visited by, 236-37; Turkey visited by, 237-39; Western tour of, 307-12; White House years of, 172-97; world tour of, 5-6, 201-24, 227-50, 251-75, 277-97, 299-319

Grant, Mary Frances (Grant's sister), 57, 250 n

Grant, Orvil Lynch (Grant's brother), 57

Grant, Samuel Simpson (Grant's brother), 76, 92, 115 n

Grant, Solomon K., 56, 64 n

Grant, Ulysses S.; bankruptcy of, 161, 327-28; burial of, 18; businessman in St. Louis and Galena, 80-87; children of, 67, 71, 76, 85-86; courtship of, 48-52, 54-55; 63 n; Civil War generalship of, 89-114, 119-42, 146-54; death of, 17, 331; drinking, 3-5, 22, 96, 114, 118 n, 143 n-44 n, 171-72; farming in Missouri, 75-80; financial problems of, 72-73, 83, 327-28; honeymoon of, 56-58; illnesses of, 80, 162, 327, 328-31; injuries suffered by, 100, 121; Lee's surrender to, 151-52; Lincoln's assassination and, 156-57; marriage of, 2, 17-18, 55-56; *Memoirs* of, 17, 19, 20-21, 22, 23, 98, 160, 329, 330-31; Mexican War experience, 2, 20, 52, 54, 315-16; military promotions, 91, 127-28; myth of, 3; ovations accorded to, 163, 197, 201, 247, 307, 313, 318, 327; Paducah proclamation of, 102; parents of, 57; partnership with Ward, 322-23, 327-28; postwar activities of, 160-66, 169-70; presidency of, 172-97; Republican Convention and election of 1880 and, 152, 321-22; resignation from the army, 75; secretary of war ad interim, 165-66, 169, 197 n, 198 n; Western campaign of, 92–114, 143 *n*; world tour of, 5–6, 201–24, 227–50, 251–75, 277–97, 299–319

Grant, Ulysses S., Jr. (Julia's son), 71, 73–74, 75, 81, 85, 95, 110, 119, 131, 132, 134, 135, 158, 168 *n*, 170, 187, 190, 191, 192, 193, 245, 307, 322–23, 324

Grant, Ulysses S., 3rd (Julia's grandson), 24, 26, 101

Grant, Virginia Paine (Jennie) (Grant's sister), 57, 73, 84, 167 *n*, 183

Grant family genealogy, 29

Grantown, Scotland, 214

Grant's Tomb, New York City, 73

Granville, Lord, 203

Grayson, John B., 69

Greece, 239–40

Greeley, Horace, 180, 198 *n*

Greene, Francis V., 237, 239

Grenada, Mississippi, 109

Grier, Robert C., 180

Hadden, William A., 224

Hague, The, Netherlands, 244

Hakone, Japan, 303

Halleck, Henry W., 95, 96, 115 *n*, 116 *n*, 128, 167 *n*

Hamburg, Germany, 246

Hamilton, Charles S., 331

Hancock, Winfield S., 101

Hanover, Germany, 245

Harlan, James, 149, 167 *n*

Harlan, Mary, 149

Harney, William S., 87, 88 *n*

Harris, Josephine, 48

Harrisburg, Pennsylvania, 197, 312

Harrison, Benjamin, 9, 174

Havana, Cuba, 313

Hawkins, Albert, 174

Hayes, Lucy Ware Webb, 9, 195–96

Hayes, Rutherford B., 9, 195–96, 200 *n*, 298 *n*

Hazlitt, Robert, 49, 63 *n*

Heidelberg, Germany, 211, 225 *n*

Heliopolis, Egypt, 231

Helsingfors (Helsinki), Finland, 250, 251

Hempstead, Stephen, Sr., 43, 63 *n*

Henderson, John B., 170

Hendley, Dr. Thomas H., 269

Henry von Phul, SS, 112, 113

Hess and Company, 317

Hewit, Dr. Henry S., 121

Hewitt, James, 56, 64 *n*

Hewitt, Richard M., 138–39, 144 *n*

Hill, Charles E., 288

Hiller, Mr., 111

Hillyer, William S. and Anna Rankin, 93, 94, 96, 105, 107, 110, 115 *n*–16 *n*, 130

Hiogo, Japan, 295

Hitt, Robert R., 257

Holcombe, Mr. and Mrs. Chester, 285, 286, 287, 288, 289

Holly Springs, Mississippi, 83, 105, 107, 108, 110, 117 *n*

Hong Kong, 284, 285

Hood, John B., 326

Hoskins, Charles, 48, 63 *n*

Howard, Bushrod B. and Helen, 90, 114 *n*

Howard, Douglas A., 90

Howard, Thomas B., 90

Howe, Timothy O., 194

Hoyt, John W., 320 *n*

Hughes, Thomas, 205

Humbert, King of Italy, 241

Hunt, Lewis C., 72

Hurlbut, Mary Emma, 120, 121

Hurlbut, Stephen A., 104, 116 *n*

Impeachment trial, 170

India, 264–75, 276 *n*

Indiana, SS, 201

Indianapolis, Indiana, 123, 312

Indian Ocean, 264

Ingalls, Rufus, 135, 136–37, 331

Interlaken, Switzerland, 211

Inveraray Castle, Scotland, 215

Inverness, Scotland, 214

Ireland, 261

Irrawaddy, SS, 283

Ischl, Austria, 254

Ismailia, Egypt, 232

Ismail Pasha, Khedive of Egypt, 221, 222, 223, 224, 226 *n*, 228, 230, 231–32

Italy, 115 *n*, 214, 218–19, 240–43, 263

Ito, Captain, 294

Itō Hirobumi, 301

Iwakura (Tomomi), 305

Jackson, Andrew, 9, 113

Jackson, Claiborne, 87, 88 *n*

Jackson, Tennessee, 104–5

Jacksonville, Florida, 313

Jaffa, Palestine, 232–33, 236

Jaipur (Jeypore), India, 269–70
Japan, 292–97, 299–306, 319 n–20 n
Jefferson Barracks, Missouri, 34, 47, 49, 51
Jerusalem, Palestine, 233, 234–36, 319
Jessup, Alfred D., 216
Jewell, Marshall, 187, 190, 199 n
Jews, 107, 117 n
Johnson, Andrew, 143 n, 156, 159, 164–66, 168 n, 169–70, 171, 197 n
Johnson, Mrs. Andrew, 164
Johnson, Claudia Alta Taylor, 9–10, 13–14
Johnson, Mortimer L., 305
Johnston, Joseph E., 136, 159, 325, 326, 332 n
Johore, Malaya, 281
Jones, Henrietta, 311
Jones, J. Russell, 199 n
Jones, John P., 312
Jubbulpore (Icbulpur), India, 267, 276 n

Kanagawa, Japan, 302
Kane, Thomas L., 251
Karnak, Egypt, 228, 229
Kasson, John A., 254
Kassr-el-Noussa Palace, Cairo, 221, 230
Kawamura, Sumiyoshi, 305
Kearny, Mrs. Stephen, 132
Keating, Dr. John, 262, 271, 286
Keneh, Egypt, 227
Kenney, Constance, 241
Kensington Palace, London, 205
Kercheval, Benjamin B., 66, 87 n
Key West, Florida, 313
Kirby, Colonel, 70
Kittoe, Dr. Edward D., 95, 115 n
Knight's Ferry, California, 88 n
Knoxville, Tennessee, 125
Kountz, William J., 95–96
Kung, Prince, 289, 301, 319 n

Lagow, Clark B., 117 n
La Grange, Tennessee, 105, 109, 117 n
Lake Maggiore, 214
Lake Tahoe, 311
Lansingburg, New York, 328
Lawrence, Alexander J., 268
Leamington, England, 216
Lee, Richard Bland, Jr., 48, 63 n
Lee, Robert E., 149, 152
Lee, Admiral and Mrs. Samuel P., 177
Leicester, England, 202

Leishman, Mr., 277
Leo XIII, Pope, 240
Leopold, King of Belgium, 209, 210
Leopold, Prince, 208
Le Roy, William E., 236
Lesseps, Count Ferdinand de, 231, 261
Lexington, Kentucky, 125
Li, Madame, 290–91
Li Hung-chang, Viceroy, 287, 291–92, 301, 319 n
Lincoln, Abraham, 83, 111, 114, 118 n, 128, 129–30, 137–38, 141–42, 143 n, 144 n, 145 n, 146, 147, 149, 150, 151, 154–55, 156–57, 167 n
Lincoln, Charles P., 284
Lincoln, Mary Todd, 1, 12–13, 21, 129, 130, 141–42, 145 n, 146–47, 149–50, 154, 155, 157, 166 n, 167 n, 260
Lincoln, Robert, 142, 149, 154, 157
Lindell, Peter, 42, 63 n
Lisbon, Portugal, 256–57
Little, Mr. and Mrs. R. W., 285, 286
Little Rock, Arkansas, 319
Liverpool, England, 202
Livingston, John W., 151
Logan, John A., 101, 321
Logan, Mrs. John A., 23
London, England, 203–8, 214, 216
Long, Ella, 38
Long, John F., 38, 62 n
Long Branch, New Jersey, 177–78, 189, 323, 328
Longstreet, James, 48, 63 n, 64 n, 125, 141, 144 n–45 n
Loochoo Islands, 301–2, 319 n
Loring, William W., 221, 225 n–26 n
Lorne, Marquis of, 205, 215
Louis, King of Portugal, 256, 257
Louise, Princess, 205, 215
Louisville, Kentucky, 56, 63 n, 101, 123, 124, 126, 312
Lowell, James Russell, 255
Lowell, Massachusetts, 238
Lucerne, Switzerland, 211
Lucknow, India, 272–73
Lum, Mr. and Mrs. William, 120, 122, 143 n
Lumbard Brothers, 115 n
Luxor, Egypt, 227, 228

Macao, China, 285
Mackay, John W., 311
Mackay, Mrs. John W., 261

Saalburg, Germany, 210
Sackets Harbor, New York. *See* Madison Barracks
Sacramento, California, 310–11
Saigō Tsugumichī, 301, 304
Saigon, Indochina, 284
St. Augustine, Florida, 313
St. Charles College, Missouri, 43–44, 46
St. Louis, Missouri, 33, 34, 41, 42, 47, 60, 62 n, 63 n, 65, 66–67, 69, 73, 76, 80, 83, 88 n, 113, 114, 115 n, 121, 126, 130, 131, 182, 186–87, 197, 199 n, 325
St. Petersburg, Russia, 251–53, 275 n
Salomon, Charles E., 88 n
Salt Lake City, Utah, 184, 185
Salvago, Consular Agent, 220
Salzburg, Austria, 254–55
Sami Bey, 222
San Antonio, Texas, 317–18
Sanford, Henry S., 209, 210
San Francisco, California, 72, 73, 307–9, 311
Sanjō Sanetomi, Prince, 304
San Stefano, Treaty of (1878), 237, 246, 250 n
Santiago, Cuba, 313
Sartoris, Mrs. Algernon. *See* Grant, Ellen (Nellie)
Sartoris, Algernon, Jr. (Julia's grandson), 196, 261
Savannah, Georgia, 313
Schenck, Robert C., 180–81
Schumaker, John G., 255, 276 n
Schuyler, Eugene, 237
Scotland, 214–16
Scott, Colonel, 67
Scott, Mr., 204
Seafield, Lord, 215
Seville, Spain, 257–58
Sèvres, France, 217–18
Seward, William H., 150, 166 n, 167 n, 169
Shanghai, China, 286
Sharon, William, 308
Sharp, Dr. Alexander, 91, 115 n, 186, 199 n
Shaw, John M., 4
Sheffield, England, 216
Sheridan, Philip H., 101, 148, 292, 312, 317, 318, 319, 320 n, 331
Sherman, William T., 98, 101, 109, 128–29, 135–36, 144 n, 159, 167 n, 169, 170,

172, 173, 180, 181, 197 n, 202, 225 n, 243, 254, 331
Shiguoka, Japan, 296
Shiloh, battle of, 98, 99–100, 116 n
Shurlds, Jane, 55, 64 n
Siam, 281–83
Sibley, Ebenezer S., 65
Sickels, David B., 281
Simla, SS, 277
Simons, James, 115 n
Simplon Pass, Switzerland, 213
Simpson, C. L., 292
Simpson, Sarah Hare, 57, 64 n
Sinclair, Sir John George Tollemache, 214
Singapore, Straits Settlements, 280–81, 283
Siut (Assiut), Egypt, 222–23, 229
Slaves, 34–37, 39–40, 41, 42–43, 49–50, 73–74, 76, 77–78, 80–81, 82–83, 88 n, 91, 101, 105, 111, 126, 311
Smith, John Brady, 48, 63 n
Smith, Julia, 48
Smith, Sidney, 48, 56, 63 n, 64 n
Smith, William Farrar, 124–25, 127, 143 n–44 n
Smith, William Sooy, 125
Smith, William W., 182
Smyrna, Syria, 236
Southampton, England, 216
Spain, 255–56, 257–60
Splügen Pass, Switzerland, 214
Stahel, Julius, 295
Stanbery, Henry, 169
Stanford, Mrs. Leland, 23, 24
Stanton, Edwin L., 139, 140, 144 n, 154
Stanton, Edwin M., 123, 130, 139, 140, 152, 154, 159, 164–66, 167 n, 168 n, 170, 179–80, 198 n
Stanton, Mrs. Edwin M., 139, 140, 154, 179
Steedman, Charles, 223
Steele, John B., 134
Stephens, Alexander H., 137
Stevens, Thomas H., 73, 88 n
Stewart, Alexander T., 183, 184, 274
Stockholm, Sweden, 249
Stockton, California, 309
Stone, Charles P., 221, 225 n–26 n, 229, 230, 263
Stoneman, George, 136
Story, William W., 241
Stoughton, Edwin W., 251, 253, 254

[344]